Mind Matters i

CW01460421

FSC®
www.fsc.org

MIX
Paper from
responsible sources
FSC® C014540

SECOND LANGUAGE ACQUISITION
Series Editors: Professor David Singleton, *University of Pannonia, Hungary and Fellow Emeritus, Trinity College, Dublin, Ireland* and Associate Professor Simone E. Pfenninger, *University of Salzburg, Austria*

This series brings together titles dealing with a variety of aspects of language acquisition and processing in situations where a language or languages other than the native language is involved. Second language is thus interpreted in its broadest possible sense. The volumes included in the series all offer in their different ways, on the one hand, exposition and discussion of empirical findings and, on the other, some degree of theoretical reflection. In this latter connection, no particular theoretical stance is privileged in the series; nor is any relevant perspective – sociolinguistic, psycholinguistic, neurolinguistic, etc. – deemed out of place. The intended readership of the series includes final-year undergraduates working on second language acquisition projects, postgraduate students involved in second language acquisition research, and researchers, teachers and policy makers in general whose interests include a second language acquisition component.

All books in this series are externally peer reviewed.

Full details of all the books in this series and of all our other publications can be found on http://www.multilingual-matters.com, or by writing to Multilingual Matters, St Nicholas House, 31–34 High Street, Bristol BS1 2AW, UK.

SECOND LANGUAGE ACQUISITION: 126

Mind Matters in SLA

Edited by

Clare Wright, Thorsten Piske and Martha Young-Scholten

MULTILINGUAL MATTERS
Bristol • Blue Ridge Summit

To the memory of Anne Vainikka,
for her contribution to child language acquisition,
second language acquisition and Finnish syntax

DOI https://doi.org/10.21832/WRIGHT1619
Library of Congress Cataloging in Publication Data
A catalog record for this book is available from the Library of Congress.
Names: Wright, Clare – editor. | Piske, Thorsten, editor. |
   Young-Scholten, Martha, editor.
Title: Mind Matters in SLA/Edited by Clare Wright, Thorsten Piske and
   Martha Young-Scholten.
Description: Bristol; Blue Ridge Summit: Multilingual Matters, 2018. |
   Series: Second Language Acquisition: 126 | Includes bibliographical
   references and index.
Identifiers: LCCN 2018020641| ISBN 9781788921619 (hbk : alk. paper) |
   ISBN 9781788921602 (pbk : alk. paper) | ISBN 9781788921640 (kindle)
Subjects: LCSH: Second language acquisition. | Psycholinguistics.
Classification: LCC P118.2 .M565 2018 | DDC 401/.93—dc23 LC record available at
   https://lccn.loc.gov/2018020641

British Library Cataloguing in Publication Data
A catalogue entry for this book is available from the British Library.

ISBN-13: 978-1-78892-161-9 (hbk)
ISBN-13: 978-1-78892-160-2 (pbk)

Multilingual Matters
UK: St Nicholas House, 31–34 High Street, Bristol BS1 2AW, UK.
USA: NBN, Blue Ridge Summit, PA, USA.

Website: www.multilingual-matters.com
Twitter: Multi_Ling_Mat
Facebook: https://www.facebook.com/multilingualmatters
Blog: www.channelviewpublications.wordpress.com

The policy of Multilingual Matters/Channel View Publications is to use papers that are
natural, renewable and recyclable products, made from wood grown in sustainable forests.
In the manufacturing process of our books, and to further support our policy, preference
is given to printers that have FSC and PEFC Chain of Custody certification. The FSC and/
or PEFC logos will appear on those books where full certification has been granted to the
printer concerned.

Typeset by Nova Techset Private Limited, Bengaluru and Chennai, India.
Printed and bound in the UK by Short Run Press Ltd.
Printed and bound in the US by Thomson-Shore, Inc.

Contents

	Acknowledgements	vii
	Contributors	ix
1	Introduction *Clare Wright, Martha Young-Scholten and Thorsten Piske*	1

Part 1: Language and Mind

2	What is Grammar? A Universal Grammar Approach *Andrew Caink*	11
3	Syntax and Acquisition: The Emergentist Story *William O'Grady*	35
4	Poverty of the Stimulus and Language Acquisition: From Ancient Philosophy to Neuroscience *Kook-Hee Gil, Heather Marsden and George Tsoulas*	52
5	Language Evolution and the Nature of the Human Faculty for Language *Andrew Feeney*	72

Part 2: Properties of Interlanguage Grammars

6	The Mystery of the Missing Inflections *Walid Kahoul, Anne Vainikka and Martha Young-Scholten*	93
7	The Second Language Lexicon *Vivienne Rogers, David Playfoot and James Milton*	117
8	Foreign Accent in a Second Language: Individual Differences in Perception *Joan C. Mora and Elena Safronova*	137
9	A Case of Extreme Phonetic Attrition in the German Rhotic *Esther de Leeuw, Aurela Tusha, Hui Zhao, Kyle Helke and Alice Greenfield*	162

Part 3: Transitions in Acquisition

10 Using Psycholinguistic Techniques in a Second Language
    Teaching Setting   185
    Theodoros Marinis and Ian Cunnings

11 Research in Memory and Processing in Second Language
    Acquisition   203
    Clare Wright

12 Processability Theory: Architecture and Application   220
    Jörg-U. Keßler, Anke Lenzing and Anja Plesser

    Glossary   249
    References   264
    Index   291

Acknowledgements

Our thanks to the following reviewers and editorial assistants:

Hadeel Awad, Newcastle University
Paul Booth, Kingston University
Qi Chen, Newcastle University
Wilson Cheong, Institute for Tourism Studies, Macao, China
I-Chin Chiang, National Chengchi University, Taiwan
Nancy Faux, Virginia Commonwealth University, USA
Andrea Hunt, Friedrich-Alexander-University Erlangen-Nuremberg, Germany
Colleen Ijiun, Georgia State University, USA
Matthias Jilka, University of Augsburg, Germany
Nel de Jong, VU University Amsterdam, Netherlands
Hadiseh Yadollahi Jouybari, Friedrich-Alexander-University Erlangen-Nuremberg, Germany
Merel Keijzer, Utrecht University, Netherlands
Mei Lin, Newcastle University
Geoff Poole, Newcastle University
Andreas Rohde, University of Cologne, Germany
Michelle Sheehan, University of Cambridge
Marcin Sosinski, University of Granada, Spain
Maggie Tallerman, Newcastle University
Richard Towell, University of Salford
Melinda Whong, University of Leeds

And especially to Ellen Harris for her wonderful cover illustration.

Contributors

Andrew Caink is Principal Lecturer at the University of Westminster. He was educated at local comprehensive schools and the universities of Oxford, Bristol and Durham, where he studied, respectively, English literature, education and linguistics. He taught at the universities of Durham, Wolverhampton and Lapland, before joining the University of Westminster to run the BA English language & linguistics and BA English literature & language programmes. Andrew teaches introductory grammar, pragmatics and syntax at the undergraduate level and literary pragmatics at the Master's level. His linguistic research has focused initially on the syntax of South Slavic languages and in recent years on literary pragmatics.

Ian Cunnings is a Lecturer in psycholinguistics in the School of Psychology and Clinical Language Sciences at the University of Reading. Before coming to Reading, he completed his PhD at the University of Essex and was a British Academy Postdoctoral Fellow at the University of Edinburgh. Ian's research interests are in psycholinguistics, in particular language comprehension in different populations of speakers. Much of his recent research has investigated the working memory mechanisms that support language comprehension in native and non-native language users.

Andrew Feeney is a Senior Lecturer in linguistics at Northumbria University. After completing his first degree in humanities (English and European literature) in 1986, Andrew embarked on a lengthy journey teaching English language in Spain, Colombia and the Middle East. Since returning to Britain and the northeast of England in 2000, he has worked at Northumbria University. Andrew's current research interests include language evolution and the nature of language, and he was awarded his PhD from Newcastle University in 2014.

Kook-Hee Gil is a Senior Lecturer in applied linguistics at the University of Sheffield. After her postgraduate degrees at the University of Edinburgh, she worked at the University of York before coming to Sheffield. Her main research interests range from formal syntax and semantics to second language acquisition, and also connecting these areas with their implications for language teaching and learning. Her recent research centred around second language knowledge of polarity items and *wh*-indeterminates and how formal linguistic features are acquired in first and second language knowledge.

Alice Greenfield is a student of speech and language therapy at City, University of London, having completed an MA in linguistics at Queen Mary University of London in 2012. Her research interests include gender, dysfluency and autistic spectrum disorder.

Kyle Helke currently teaches secondary level history at Ross School in East Hampton, New York. He completed his MA in linguistics at Queen Mary University of London in 2012 after completing a thesis on locative morphology in San Juan Tewa. Kyle's research interests include morphosemantics, bilingualism and pragmatics.

Walid Kahoul is an Assistant Lecturer in applied linguistics and TESOL at Northumbria University. He graduated in English literature and linguistics from Damascus University and, after a Master's from Essex University, completed a PhD in second language acquisition at Newcastle University. Walid's research interests include the acquisition of inflectional morphology by second language learners.

Jörg-U. Keßler is Professor of applied linguistics in the English Department at Ludwigsburg University of Education, Germany. His research encompasses (instructed) SLA, applications of Processability Theory to the language classroom, bilingual education (immersion & CLIL), early start programmes and EFL. Together with Manfred Pienemann and Bruno Di Biase, Jörg edits the book series on Processability Approaches to Language Acquisition, Research and Teaching (PALART) at John Benjamins.

Esther de Leeuw is Senior Lecturer in linguistics at Queen Mary University of London and Director of the Queen Mary Phonetics Laboratory. Her research focuses on phonetics, phonology, multilingualism in all of its forms and executive control in bilinguals. Esther teaches undergraduate and postgraduate modules related to the above, and the research presented in this publication arose in part with the collaboration of outstanding MA students in the module Sociophonetics in 2012.

Anke Lenzing is Assistant Professor of English linguistics and psycholinguistics at Paderborn University, Germany. Her second language acquisition research engages with early second language (L2) acquisition and the L2 initial state, L2 transfer, semantic aspects in L2 comprehension and the interface between L2 comprehension and L2 production.

Theodoros Marinis is Professor of multilingualism at the Linguistics Department at the University of Konstanz, and at the School of Psychology & Clinical Language Sciences at the University of Reading. He completed his PhD on first language acquisition at the University of Potsdam and before coming to Reading he worked at the University of Essex and at University College London. Theodoros' research interests include first and second language acquisition and processing in typically and atypically developing children and adults. He has published extensively on how sequential bilingual children and children with specific language impairment process sentences in real time.

Heather Marsden is Senior Lecturer in linguistics at the University of York. Her research investigates multilingual language acquisition from the perspective of generative linguistic theory. She uses psycholinguistic methods to investigate questions about the nature of non-native language knowledge and development, particularly in the areas of syntax and semantics. Heather is also interested in research that integrates language acquisition theory and language teaching practice.

James Milton is Professor of applied linguistics at Swansea University. A long-term interest in measuring lexical breadth and establishing normative data for learning and progress has led to extensive publications, including *Modelling and Assessing Vocabulary Knowledge* (with Michael Daller and Jeanine Treffers-Daller, Cambridge University Press, 2007), *Measuring Second Language Vocabulary Acquisition* (Multilingual Matters, 2009) and *Dimensions of Vocabulary Knowledge* (with Tess Fitzpatrick, Palgrave, 2014).

Joan C. Mora is Associate Professor in the Department of Modern Languages and Literatures and English Studies at the University of Barcelona (UB), Spain. He currently coordinates the PhD programme in applied linguistics at UB and the Barcelona L2 Speech Research Group. His research examines the role of input and aptitude in second language phonological acquisition and the effects of phonetic training, learning context and cognitive individual differences in the development of second language pronunciation and oral fluency in instructed SLA.

William O'Grady is Professor of linguistics at the University of Hawai'i at Manoa. After postgraduate studies at Harvard and Chicago, he worked at the University of Calgary before joining the faculty at Hawai'i. His research focuses on syntactic theory, language acquisition, Korean and heritage languages. William has published extensively on these areas, and particularly on emergentism – the idea that processing pressures shape both properties of grammatical systems and the manner in which those properties emerge in the course of development.

Thorsten Piske is Professor of second/foreign language learning and teaching at the Friedrich-Alexander-University of Erlangen-Nuremberg, Germany. His research focuses on first and second language acquisition and on bilingual education. He has conducted projects examining the production and perception of first and second language speech sounds as well as projects examining the effectiveness of different types of bilingual programmes in kindergartens and schools. His joint work with James E. Flege on factors affecting degree of foreign accent in a second language has received particular attention in the field of speech sciences. Thorsten's more recent publications reflect his strong interest in the implications of first and second language research for language classrooms.

David Playfoot is Lecturer in psychology at Swansea University. His research considers the processes involved in reading aloud and word recognition, which is informed by studying native speakers, second language speakers and individuals with acquired language impairments. David's interest in word association as a method for studying lexical structure and vocabulary began when working with Tess Fitzpatrick as a post-doctoral researcher, and he has published several papers in this area.

Anja Plesser is currently working as Head of the Language Department of the Community College in Soest, Germany. In her SLA research she takes a processing perspective focusing on the interface between writing and speaking, the role and shape of memory and developmental plateaus. Anja worked as a researcher and lecturer with Professor Manfred Pienemann at Paderborn University, Germany.

Vivienne Rogers is Senior Lecturer at Swansea University. She gained her MA in linguistics at Durham, and her PhD in the second language of French at Newcastle University. Her research interests mainly lie in the second language acquisition of syntax and its relationship to the acquisition of vocabulary, but she has a parallel interest in language learning aptitude and working memory.

Elena Safronova holds an MA and a PhD in applied linguistics from the University of Barcelona, Spain. Her current research investigates the contribution of phonological memory, acoustic memory and attention control to second language speech perception. Among Elena's other research interests are second language phonological acquisition, multilingualism, psycholinguistics and individual differences in second language speech learning.

George Tsoulas is Senior Lecturer in linguistics at the University of York. After an undergraduate degree in in linguistics and literature in Strasbourg, he studied for a PhD at the University of Paris VIII. His research to date has focused on formal syntax, the syntax-semantics and syntax-pragmatics interface, and more specifically on issues of quantification, questions, tense and modality, DO structure, number and the count/mass distinction, topic/focus articulation, particles, the nature of pronominal reference and the relation between language and music.

Aurela Tusha currently works at the University of London, helping with their Global MBA programme. She completed her MA in linguistics at Queen Mary University of London, undertaking original research into phonological native-language attrition. Her research interests pertain to language acquisition and more specifically changes to the phonological structure of one's native language in instances where a second language was acquired in adulthood.

Anne Vainikka was an adjunct faculty member at the University of Delaware where she taught language acquisition and psycholinguistics. She and Martha Young-Scholten began in the 1990s to collaborate on investigations of the acquisition of German morphosyntax. Her University of Massachusetts PhD focused on the formal analysis of Finnish syntax, to which she devoted much of her time.

Clare Wright is a Lecturer in linguistics and language teaching at the University of Leeds. After graduating from Cambridge University, she taught English for academic purposes for nearly 20 years, and then gained her MA and PhD in second language acquisition at Newcastle University. Clare's research investigates the interfaces between linguistic, cognitive and pedagogic factors in second language acquisition, with particular focus on teaching and learning Chinese as a second language.

Martha Young-Scholten is Professor of second language acquisition at Newcastle University. She studied primary education and German as an undergraduate and obtained her MA and PhD in linguistics on the second language acquisition of German at the University of Washington in Seattle. Martha is the author of numerous publications on the second language acquisition of German and of English morphosyntax, and on the reading development of migrant adults with little or no home language literacy.

Hui Zhao is a Research Associate in the Department of Modern Languages and Cultures at the University of Nottingham after recently finishing her PhD at Queen Mary University of London. Her research interests include bilingualism, language variation, speech perception and language attitudes, especially in the context of China and Chinese languages.

1 Introduction

Clare Wright, Martha Young-Scholten and
Thorsten Piske

The editors of this volume, *Mind Matters in SLA*, offer this as a companion volume to *Input Matters in SLA* (2009, Multilingual Matters); we examine key issues in theories of what language is and what happens in the mind during second language (L2) learning, in order to address the question: 'Why don't learners learn what teachers teach?' (Allwright, 1984: 3). As all teachers will know, this classic question remains an ongoing puzzle across any paradigm of L2 development. It remains a mystery why some language rules – such as the 3rd person singular -*s* in English – are easy for the teacher to present but difficult for learners to master, even after hours of discussion and drilling. It also puzzles learners and teachers alike why different tasks and types of language use cause difficulties and others do not. For example, complex grammar or vocabulary can be quickly memorized, accurately judged in a comprehension task and used when retelling a story. But when a learner tries to produce similar grammar and vocabulary in unplanned speech such as during an interaction task, this can result in hesitation or lack of fluency. Why should that be? Do learners have two types of language memory store to draw on? Some theories of language hold that we do indeed have two types of systems – implicit versus explicit (N. Ellis, 1994; Ellis *et al.*, 2009; Han & Finneran, 2014; Krashen, 1985a; Schwartz, 1993). What then is the best way of teaching or helping students learn? Teachers, schools and even government education policies may have to choose whether to prioritize direct explicit instruction with plenty of form-based error correction, or communicative, implicit exposure, leaving the learner to 'pick the language up' (see, for example, Bleyhl, 2009). Or can teaching more usefully combine a mix of form-focused instruction with a more communicative approach – and if so, how might this be most effective (Ranta & Lyster, 2017)?[1]

To address these issues, it is crucial to know what the deeper nature of language is like, and what learners do while they are in the process of acquiring it. That is, we need to understand the properties of the systems which not only children but also L2 learners of all ages unconsciously create during language acquisition. What would also be most helpful to know is how learners make transitions from one system or stage to the next, and how teachers can support classroom learners in making these transitions (see, for example, Pienemann's Teachability Hypothesis in Pienemann, 1984, 1989). Understanding these transitions was laid down as a challenge for second language acquisition (SLA) researchers over two decades ago by Gregg (1996) – i.e. to arrive at a theory to bring together what learners' language systems are like (the properties of these systems) and how learners develop those systems over time (transitions). Equipped with knowledge about properties and transitions, teachers will find it easier to identify the sources of learner errors and to determine what learners have already learned and what they have not learned yet, and what they can do in order to help their learners learn. However, SLA researchers may not yet typically provide a successful common manual or guidance to help teachers understand these issues (Piske & Young-Scholten, 2009; Whong, 2011) Some theories of SLA tend to focus more on how language systems are represented in the mind, separately from other cognitive functions. Other theories focus on how language processing and development over time depend on a range of cognitive functions which are not specific to language, including memory.

This volume covers both areas of theoretical approaches. But, as this volume will illustrate, our work to understand why learners do not always learn what teachers teach is not yet done. When researchers focus on different aspects of language, gaps can be left in our understanding of what externally and internally drives learners to change their linguistic system during acquisition, that is, in how learners make transitions. This is not wonderful news for teachers, but it is the current state of the wider fields of child and second language acquisition. It is therefore no surprise that this gap between research and teaching, coupled with a diversity of different theoretical approaches, results in a lot of ongoing debate. Implicit in the debate are the issues of how to consider what actually is being learned, what is stored in memory and what is retrieved by the learner in the moment of comprehending or producing language.

Input Matters in SLA, our earlier volume, presented views from a range of international researchers on how they think input functions in the SLA of the sound system and of grammar. *Mind Matters in SLA* broadens these ideas out within an unusually deep historical context for modern theories and debates over language acquisition, representation and transitions. We highlight just how long some of these questions have taxed scholars – we specifically include a chapter on language evolution, and other chapters make reference to the centuries of thinking about language, dating back to antiquity. The book thus combines wide-ranging chapters, by both established scholars and rising star researchers, to create a well-rounded resource which we hope will inspire the reader to think in new and exciting ways about second language teaching and learning.

In presenting research on what happens in the mind of the language learner in an accessible way, the book will be useful not only to teachers but also to students planning to teach language, who are on upper-level undergraduate and MA-level courses, doing degrees in TESOL/TEFL, modern foreign languages/heritage language teaching, applied linguistics or first and second language acquisition, anywhere in the world. It is also of interest to general readers without a specialist linguistic background who are keen to know, in a globalized world, the cognitive basis on which multilingual speakers come to be proficient (or not!) in using all their languages. We intend this volume to fill the gap between journals which require the reader to have considerable specialist knowledge, and textbooks with broad overviews of current theories and findings which are typically not written by the researchers themselves. Such textbooks thus often do not provide all the details readers need to really understand cutting-edge research, nor how to think about ways to apply it to their teaching. The gap is currently particularly wide when it comes to research based on formal linguistics. For this reason, our volume starts with a primer on syntax which, if the reader is unfamiliar with the relevant notions, can be used as a basis for understanding the next three chapters on language acquisition (including two competing theoretical frameworks) and on language evolution.

The first part of the book focuses on issues that are pertinent to our current understanding of language in general, and to first and second language acquisition specifically. There is much that is under ongoing debate. We therefore include discussions of why human language (in particular syntax) is special from a generative – Chomskyan – perspective versus why it is argued by others instead to be part of general cognition. The chapters include cross-linguistic examples which introduce the reader to comparisons of how languages differ and are similar syntactically and, as noted above, we include a chapter on a topic which is rare in books on SLA: language evolution. We do so to give the reader the chance to explore various lines of current, cutting-edge thinking about what makes the human faculty for language special. The second part includes work on issues currently debated in SLA, on morphosyntax, the lexicon, production and phonology/phonetics. The third part, focusing on research relating to explaining how L2 learners make transitions from one stage of development to the next, covers state-of-the-art psycholinguistic research relating to how L2 acquisition occurs in real time and includes discussion of models of L2 learning both in and out of the classroom.

Given the book's overarching focus on grammar and the mind, two baseline chapters for readers to start with are Caink's introduction to syntax in Part 1 and Marinis and Cunnings' chapter on psycholinguistic research techniques in Part 3. Readers unfamiliar with syntax or cognitive approaches to SLA are taken in stages through key issues, terminology and challenges, so by the end of these two chapters they will feel confident in tackling the more specialized research in the subsequent chapters in the book. The rest of the chapters can be read in any order, as key ideas raised in each chapter are, where relevant, cross-referenced throughout the volume. Each chapter's discussion of theories, frameworks, hypotheses and empirical data represents the specific questions and methodologies relevant to their field. Some of these may be more familiar to readers than others. The chapters take a range of perspectives and are written at increasing levels of advanced ideas and expression, to guide the less experienced reader into the complex debates and issues being presented. Within each of our three parts, some chapters, or later parts of chapters, are thus more challenging while others are deliberately set to be easy to follow, particularly by readers using English as a second language. A glossary is also provided to clarify key terms used throughout the volume which may be unfamiliar.

Part 1: Language and Mind

The first part provides the foundation for understanding syntax and relates to ideas that reappear in many chapters throughout the book. Andrew Caink's introduction to syntax outlines why syntax is special and illustrates this with lively examples for the non-specialist. He explores in an engaging and approachable way why language acquisition research in general, and SLA research in particular, is crucially dependent on one's understanding of syntactic structures and linguistic features from a generative, Chomskyan perspective which assumes an innate language faculty. For those with no background in syntax, this chapter is specifically aimed to provide a route to understanding the accounts of the acquisition of syntax elsewhere in this volume.

However, the generative perspective is not the only important framework for understanding syntax. The theory has been criticized for neglecting to cover cognitive constraints on how the mind processes language. William O'Grady, long a proponent of emergentism, argues against the generative approach and claims that language, its processing and its acquisition are inextricably linked. O'Grady draws on his previous and new work to outline emergentist perspectives on why syntax exhibits the particular properties that it does, and on how those properties are acquired by both children and second language learners.

The next chapter, by Kook-Hee Gil, Heather Marsden and George Tsoulas, then places Caink's syntax chapter within the wider context of the human language faculty, and the idea of 'Poverty of the Stimulus' (POS). POS is a cornerstone of generative linguistics and is based on the notion of an innate faculty of language (Universal Grammar), discussed in Caink's chapter, and argued in Gil *et al*.'s chapter as the bridge between the natural but impoverished input children and second language learners receive, and their eventual syntactic competence. This chapter exposes the reader to a more sophisticated level of argumentation, looking into the development of the POS argument itself, and its main empirical motivations to support its relevance for both first and second language acquisition.

Part 1 finishes with an unusual chapter in collections on SLA – Andrew Feeney's overview of the origins and nature of the unique human language faculty, and how far language evolution can be understood in terms of the mind. Feeney makes the point that much in the field of language evolution studies is 'either not fully understood or hotly disputed', thereby emphasizing the topic as both needing further investigation and being a good example for the reader of how critical academic debates in linguistics are currently constructed and presented (as with the previous chapter). Some of the terminology will likely be very unfamiliar to the reader, but Feeney's explanations, alongside the glossary, will allow the reader to gain new insights from this emerging field of study, and to stimulate wider consideration of what it means to be human acquiring both a first and a second language.

Part 2: Properties of Interlanguage Grammars

Moving to the more empirical second part of the book, the chapters here refer in more detail to the contributing authors' research as they address the key domains of syntax, the lexicon, phonetics/phonology and language production in English and other languages. The chapters refer to theories and frameworks within SLA to enable the reader to grasp the key questions and issues that are currently relevant, and then concentrate on illustrating these with the results of authors' recent studies. The reading level is set to draw the reader into the technical aspects of empirical SLA research with increasing understanding as this part of the book progresses: the final two chapters are thus at a more advanced specialist level, but are still designed to give the inexperienced reader an insight into the important questions addressed by the studies.

Walid Kahoul, Anne Vainikka and Martha Young-Scholten consider competing hypotheses on why morphosyntactic difficulties persist for older L2 learners, and consider how the L1s of the learners in their study may affect their progress. In this case they investigate 3rd person singular -s and past tense marking in English by Arabic and Chinese learners. They present unusual multiparadigm research evidence involving not only learners' production, but also their perception and their online processing as documented through the tracking of learners' eye movements. The three authors find that apparent similarities in learners' accuracy using just a single paradigm can mask subtle differences in underlying processing.

Vivienne Rogers, David Playfoot and James Milton share insights into their recent research on the L2 lexicon. They start by observing that previous lack of interest in the lexicon has changed, in that the lexicon has now 'clearly found a permanent place in … second language acquisition'. The authors note that the connection between lexis – words – and syntax remains underexplored, and aim to address this gap in the chapter, with a novel approach using French acquisition data to test whether lexical knowledge drives acquisition of syntax or vice versa.

Next, Joan C. Mora and Elena Safranova consider phonological and processing issues in SLA, in this case in terms of speech production, perception and fluency as components of oral proficiency. The development of L2 learners' oral proficiency fundamentally depends both on their pronunciation skills, including knowledge of phonetic forms and correct production, and on utterance fluency, in terms of learners' general smoothness in oral communication. The authors present details from their recent research to back up their claims, supporting the reader through technicalities of their approach with clear explanations. They underscore the benefit of taking a holistic approach to the development of L2 oral proficiency, where pronunciation skills and spoken fluency are not treated as separate components, but rather as related or complementary aspects of the cognitive processes underlying L2 speech production and perception.

To end this part, in the chapter by Esther de Leeuw, Aurela Tusha, Hui Zhao, Kyle Helke and Alice Greenfield, also in relation to phonetics and phonology, the reader is invited to consider language development in reverse – when an L2 becomes the dominant language, as when a migrant resides in a new country, and whether and how their L1 may fundamentally change, i.e. undergo attrition. Given the growing rise in migrant populations, the question of what happens to both the speaker's L1 and L2 when they immigrate is increasingly relevant to many. Here, after a broad discussion of key issues, the authors take a fresh approach by focusing not on groups, as is usual, but on individuals who go against the group trend. Highlighting the value of individual case study research in SLA, the authors promote this for building up understanding of how languages are represented in the mind, as they reveal 'what is *actually possible*, not just what *usually* happens'.

Part 3: Transitions in Acquisition

Moving on to the final part, this focuses on cognitive issues in learnability and teachability, discussing frameworks, methods and pedagogical practices to demonstrate the role of memory and processing constraints in an individual's transition through stages of development of internalized rules in a second language, and how far such rules represent unconsciously acquired, or implicit, knowledge, or more conscious forms of knowledge, often through explicitly taught instruction. In the initial chapter in this part, Theodoros Marinis and Ian Cunnings' discussion of teaching-friendly psycholinguistic approaches is the second baseline chapter of this volume. They review four research-based techniques focusing on syntax, together with ideas about how these techniques can be implemented by teachers and others to assess learners' internalized language abilities. We hope this chapter will bring fresh inspiration for teachers who want to know why their learners vary so much, and provide ideas about how to use psycholinguistic insights to target their teaching more effectively.

Clare Wright's chapter weaves together many of the cognitive ideas raised in other chapters to discuss current accounts of what memory is, both long-term memory and short-term or working memory, and how memory underpins language development over time. Wright, taking the reader forward into more detailed approaches to cognitive models and terminology, argues that many of the apparent distinctions and contrasts researchers make between different types of memory or knowledge (such as explicit versus implicit) may in fact be somewhat unhelpful in understanding the reality of how learners manage to develop linguistic knowledge for use in comprehension and production, promoting instead a 'coalition' view of learning, where memory systems co-exist in supporting the learning process. The chapter then finishes with a brief examination of results from two studies of acquisition of L2 morphosyntax (question formation), which used a combination of different methodologies to illustrate how different language tasks (offline versus online, written versus spoken) can reveal valuable insights into potential interactions between working and long-term memory, and language acquisition.

The final chapter of the book is by Jörg-U. Keßler, Anke Lenzing and Anja Plesser, describing a theory of L2 acquisition that, like O'Grady's emergentism, directly ties cognition to the language learning process – Manfred Pienemann's Processability Theory (PT). PT uses Lexical Functional Grammar to account for similarities across learners with different L1s in the stages of acquisition of specific morphosyntactic structures. After discussing the theory and providing empirical evidence, the authors finish with a useful section on applying PT to the classroom, introducing the notion of tracking a 'developmental hierarchy with regard to learner output' using simple classroom tasks. This will be useful for teachers tired of wielding a red pen over their learners' work, in favour of knowing when more targeted correction could actually make a real difference. This chapter thus serves as a reminder to readers to refer back to all the chapters in this volume in order to draw out the pedagogic value of thinking about the links between the mind and grammar in its broadest sense of internalized rules, and presented from a range of theoretical perspectives.

The three editors of this volume, all one-time language teachers and now academics, have long considered it essential for researchers and teachers to find ways of considering together the broad questions in SLA of what language is and how it changes over time and is processed in real time, in comprehension and production, across all its different stages of development – and relating pedagogy to SLA – in order to consider how teachers can effectively support students in learning an L2. However, we also have to acknowledge that for language teachers it is often difficult to get to the point of considering the implications of SLA research for teaching practice because of the very abstract nature and narrow focus of many theoretical models. Teachers, however, have to teach a 'language as a whole' and will therefore mainly benefit from models and studies attempting to explain how the many different aspects of language acquisition interconnect, and what they can do in order to support, for example, grammar learning without ignoring the development of phonological, lexical and communicative skills. We hope that this volume, taken as a whole, is written in an adequately accessible way to enable readers in making connections both between the many different aspects of language acquisition and between the findings of SLA research and language teaching.

Note

(1) According to Cameron (2001: 101) the results of research conducted by cognitive psychologists, for example, suggest that '[I]t seems increasingly likely that paying attention to grammatical features of language is not something that happens automatically in communicating, and that therefore some artificial methods of pushing attention are needed, i.e. teaching!'.

Part 1

Language and Mind

2 What is Grammar? A Universal Grammar Approach

Andrew Caink

Introduction: Things that We Know about Language #1

Everyone is interested in language. Language is about expressing oneself and being creative, and the idea of 'grammar' seems to be the opposite of this. There are formal ways of speaking and writing, and there are grammar rules for doing so, but when we speak with each other or write anything other than an academic essay, it's all about communicating, and 'grammar' isn't needed. You learn how to speak from your parents by imitating them when you're a child. When your baby brother says, 'We goed to the shops', or when he points at the wheel of his toy car and says 'ball', you correct him so that he gets it right. He can do it because he's got the time, he's a baby with nothing else to do, and he is motivated because he wants to be like you. Human language is like any communication system; your society uses it and you pick it up. This is obvious.

Well, actually, no. Most of the above is incorrect or over-simplistic – except that everyone is interested in language and everyone is creative with language. And grammar in this prescriptive sense of formal rules is not what we think it is. If you've never read a linguistics book before, this chapter will provide a useful introduction to what linguists think language is, focusing on grammar in particular, and one theory – Universal Grammar – that has been central to linguistic thinking for much of the last 60 years. We'll take you step by step to build up an understanding of language structure, with increasingly expert technical terminology, by asking questions about how language is acquired, how it is represented in the mind, and why grammar (or the more accurate linguistic term, syntax) is the foundation of language acquisition whether you speak one, two or many languages.

Who Needs Grammar?

Have a look at this sentence.

Example 1

The bibbles gabbed the mab loomishly florb the brakash.

It's nonsense, isn't it? Now answer these questions:

Example 2

What did the bibbles do?
How did they do it?
Where did they do it?

I doubt that you had any difficulty, but if you are disorientated by this nonsense, here are some possible answers:

Example 3

What did the bibbles do?
They gabbed the mab.

How did they do it?
Loomishly.

Where?
Not below or beside the brakash, but florb the brakash.

The sentence in Example 1 contains only made-up words, except for 'the'. How can you know anything about it? The simple response is that there is such a thing as grammar. Grammar involves words being put into certain orders and also in certain forms, e.g. involving **suffixes**. You know *bibble* is a **noun** because of the plural suffix -*s*, you know gab is a **verb** because of the past tense suffix -*ed* and you know that *loomish* is an **adjective** because of -*ish*, and with -*ly* it becomes an adverb. So you could produce a new sentence such as 'That bibble is loomish' or 'Florb the brakash is where I last saw the bibbles gabbing'.

If you are able to read this chapter, you already know the system of English in your mind/brain. If you're lucky and were brought up speaking more than one language, your mind/brain knows about the word orders and the suffixes and prefixes of words in other languages, too. That's grammar.

When non-linguists talk about 'grammar', they are usually referring to the 'correct way to speak or write'. In other words, they're talking about a particular sort of **register** (such as formal versus informal). However, what 'grammar' means when you're studying language as a system is the way in which words are put together (this is called **syntax**) and the prefixes and suffixes of words you use (these vary according to their function and are examples of **inflectional** and **derivational morphology**).

It is also not correct that grammar does not matter. Consider these two different, grammatical word orders: *The policeman with the marijuana saw me* and *The policeman saw me with the marijuana*. If you had to go to court, these word order differences could be crucial. And most speakers would know there were problems with saying *Called me tomorrow* instead of *Call me tomorrow!*

You also implicitly know when things are ungrammatical, even if you struggle to say why that is so. For example, if you have acquired the English language as a child, you know that all of these word orders are not right, even though in some cases you can still figure out what is meant:

Example 4

   *I looked up it on Wikipedia.
   *It's a wooden old lovely box.
   *I and Richard taught the class together.

(Linguists put an asterisk at the start of a sentence to indicate when it is ungrammatical.)

But you might be thinking: *These are just rules about word order, there is no explicit grammar involved; there are just agreed ways you say things, and you pick these up naturally because you constantly hear examples of them.*

In fact learning grammar implicitly is not like learning the rules for driving or other knowledge gained by practising. Linguists who look at the nature of grammar and how children acquire the grammar of a particular language have long claimed that it is not much like learning anything else that humans learn, at least in terms of experience (see Chapter 4 by Gil *et al.* in this volume). For a start, rules for driving are not very complex, and there are not that many things to learn. And figuring out how to use all the features on your new phone might take you a while, but there are still only a certain number of things to learn.

With learning language it is different because the number of possible sentences is infinite. This means that you cannot have heard someone say every possible sentence, never mind being able to memorize all of them. Example 1 illustrated this with made-up words, but we can also illustrate it with real words. For example, you have never heard this sentence before, but you know what it means and you know that it is grammatical: *Despite taking her umbrella, our hamster found that the rain made her eyeliner run*. What you need to know in order to understand that sentence, and in order to produce an equally novel response, is considerable. (You might respond: 'What? Well, our hamster Sally always wears waterproof eyeliner. She bought it at Boots.') An animal such as a hamster doesn't wear eyeliner, carry an umbrella or shop at Boots. But that's not the point here; you can understand the sentence: you know who took the umbrella (our hamster), what did the running (the eyeliner), that both hamsters are female and that one of them shops at Boots for her cosmetics. The fact that understanding the sentence is easy for you does not mean that it is not also very complex.

But let us return to our point about the sentences in Example 4. Even if it were possible to hear all the sentences needed for communication in a given language (just as it is possible to learn all the rules for driving), it would not help you in knowing that certain sentences are not possible. Every speaker of English agrees that these sentences are not possible; they are ungrammatical. This is because, just as there is an infinite number of grammatical sentences, there is an infinite number of ungrammatical sentences. How does a speaker know which is which?

What We Know and How We Know It and How We Know We Know It

We know a lot about language from children's acquisition. Children do not always get things right and, when that happens, a child's attempts can reveal how their young mind/brain imposes rules on the language input they're getting. For example, when they say something like 'We goed to the shops', this is not an imitation; it's not a mistake that any of the adults around the child will have made. The only way the child can have produced this is by subconsciously figuring out the grammar rule (attaching the suffix -ed) for regular past tense formation, and then over-applying it for verbs which have irregular past tense forms. Children get little or no explicit 'teaching', and while they may be corrected and even coached by adults in the case of their overgeneralized past tense -ed forms, research shows that they stubbornly stick to their overgeneralizations until these are gradually replaced by the grammatical irregular forms. And children acquiring English overuse -ed with irregular verbs at a certain point in their development regardless of their intelligence, or memory, or how good they are at using the language.

Grammar is not just about simple word orders and involves highly complex knowledge, as we will see throughout the rest of this chapter.

Let us look at some examples from questions starting with words such as *who, what, where, when, why* and *how*. The knowledge you have in your mind/brain about the use of these **wh-words** tells you, without even needing to think about it, that the first of each of these pairs of sentences is OK, but the second in each pair is ungrammatical:

Example 5

(a) (If Sue studied linguistics and *biology*)
    What did that student study linguistics with?
    *What did that student study linguistics and?
(b) You didn't know if who had been appointed?
    *Who didn't you know if had been appointed?
(c) You believe the claim that the teacher made about what?
    *What do you believe the claim that the teacher made about?

It is possible that you might have heard someone say one of the ungrammatical examples and then heard a teacher correct that person. It is also possible that you were formally taught that the asterisked sentences in Example 5 are ungrammatical. The likelihood of either is slim, though. Imagine what lessons would be like: 'Today, we're going to memorize another 10 sentences that you cannot say in English.'

There is a very important point here about ungrammatical sentences and why they are significant. Some linguists claim that there are better ways of accounting for language and its acquisition than we argue for in this chapter. However, they typically miss the fact that we do not have to just explain how we end up saying what we say. We also have to explain why we cannot say all the things we *cannot* say. In other words, the ungrammatical examples we have discussed so far are just as important in figuring out the underlying linguistic system as the grammatical utterances.

If grammar were simply about communicating, then many of these ungrammatical sentences could be OK, because you can figure out what was meant. But the point here is that the grammatical system of a language, within the perspective of this chapter, is independent of word meaning. That is why the nonsense sentence in Example 1 is grammatical, even though most of the words do not exist in English.

We have established that you know things about English grammar that no-one can ever have taught you. But there is more to grammar than just the string of words that you speak and write. The sentence in Example 1 is not simply a string of words. Hearing it or reading it gives you that impression, but there is structure hidden behind the words. Your mind/brain processes this structure every time you speak, write or read a sentence or listen to someone else speaking. And just to be clear – linguists interested in acquisition talk about how grammar is represented in both the mind *and* the brain, because while the brain is clearly responsible for language, we currently know far more about how language is represented in the abstract entity we call the mind.

Another example relates to the ambiguity of some sentences. Consider *The president discussed having coffee with his intern*. If you think about it, you can see that the sentence has at least two possible meanings. It can mean that the president had a discussion with someone else (e.g. a journalist) about having coffee with his intern, or it could mean that he chatted to his intern about having coffee.

To see this, consider your (up to now implicit) sense of the words grouping together in different ways:

Example 6

(a) The president discussed ⟨having coffee with his intern⟩.
(b) The president discussed ⟨having coffee⟩ with his intern.

You can also see the hidden structure with a word like *himself* in Example 7 which refers back to a person earlier in the sentence:

Example 7

(a) The ₍ᵢ₎prime minister admires ₍ᵢ₎himself.
(b) A ₍ᵢ₎friend of the ₍ⱼ₎prime minister admires ₍ᵢ/*ⱼ₎himself.

In examples like 7a and 7b, linguists use subscript letters to show what can and cannot grammatically be linked in terms of the meaning (formally, what is 'licit'). So in Example 7a *himself* refers back to *The prime minister*. But in Example 7b *himself* cannot refer to the prime minister; it can only refer to the friend, hence (i) is licit but (j) is not, as shown by the tiny asterisk in front of (j).

Why is that? If it was just a string of words, there is no obvious reason why *himself* can refer back to the **noun phrase** 'the prime minister' which precedes the verb *admires* in Example 7a but not in Example 7b. Notice that this is not just a preference either; you cannot 'force' *himself* to refer to 'The prime minister' in Example 7b by giving it emphasis.

The reason is the hidden structure of the sentence, involving a linguistic phenomenon known as Binding (Chomsky, 1980a) which explains how nouns, personal pronouns and reflexives refer to each other in various sentence types (see Fromkin *et al.*, 2013: Chapters 3 and 4 for an introduction to syntax and meaning; Radford, 2016: Chapter 3 will take things further).

So although grammar is independent of the meaning of individual words, grammar certainly has an influence on what the sentence as a whole means (or can mean). We saw an example of this when we looked at word order (*The policeman with the marijuana saw me* versus *The policeman saw me with the marijuana*). You can even see it a bit with the nonsense sentence in Example 1: although the words have no meaning in English, you will have had a sense of a possible meaning from your knowledge of what is known as functional morphology. For example, in addition to your knowledge of word order (so a word like *the* often precedes a noun), you also know that the derivational suffix -*ish* turns a noun (*loom*) into an adjective, and the suffix -*ly* makes it an adverb.

So far, we have said that our knowledge of the grammar of our native language does not come to us through explicit teaching. This statement is not completely correct. People indeed impose social conventions to mould or shape grammar; this is called **prescriptive grammar** – someone prescribes rules about what you *should* say or write, like a doctor prescribing medicine. Prescriptive grammar has rules like telling you to always avoid 'splitting the infinitive' (you may notice that I split the infinitive there with *always*, because it comes between the *to* and the verb *avoid*; we routinely do this and it sounds fine!). Prescriptive grammar also tells you that you should never end a sentence with a **preposition**, although linguists wonder what prescriptive grammarians are talking about (oops, that sentence ended with a preposition). Not paying attention to prescriptive grammar rules is more typical of spoken English than formal writing. It is, then, a question of register, and written registers tend to reflect the standards of traditional grammarians, and sometimes expect the use of earlier forms of the language.

Prescriptive grammar is no more about grammar – as linguists understand it – than the dress code at your favourite club. When we talk about grammar in this chapter and in the rest of this book, we are not talking about manners and social convention. When we talk about grammar rules, these are more like **algorithms**; that is, they are procedures we follow, in the way that your computer follows instructions when you switch it on.

Similarly, we are not talking about rules that can improve the effectiveness of your speech or writing. There are lots of rules that it is advisable to follow if you want to write a great essay or report, or if you want to persuade a potential customer to buy your new product. But those 'rules' are to do with *using* the language; they are to do with how well you *perform*. It is important, but it has nothing to do with our focus here on the underlying knowledge that you have of your own native language.

The grammar rules that linguists are interested in are the ones that are part of the fantastically complex system that is one's native language, the language (or languages) acquired as a child. Despite its complexity, even five-year-olds already have a solid knowledge about their native grammar, even if they are not sure why something is ungrammatical or how to explain it. We have that knowledge even if we are not great poets or brilliant at selling used cars.

We have been making a distinction here between the implicit, unconscious knowledge that you have of your language on the one hand and the way in which you make conscious choices when you use the language on the other. Linguists refer to the internalized system as an Internal Language (or **I-language**) to distinguish it from the External Language produced in speech, with all its glitches, mistakes, half-finished sentences and accompanying gestures. (Some linguists are interested in how the two systems interact – as you can see in later chapters in this volume, such as Chapters 10 and 11 by Marinis & Cunnings and Wright, respectively). You will also hear linguists refer to the I-language as a speaker's linguistic **competence**. In either case, we are talking about knowledge of the language system that is largely, if not almost completely, unconscious knowledge. It is knowledge that is entirely independent of how well you manage to put it to use in speaking or writing, and it is knowledge that was learned long before you could do most things that adults do.

That, of course, raises the question of how you managed to get this I-language. How does a child go from gurgling incomprehension to having a very sophisticated knowledge of the language system in a matter of a few years? We will come back to that question, but first let us talk about what it is that babies have to learn, in a little more detail.

Underlying structure

Although we speak and write in phrases and sentences that have one word following another in a linear string, the grammatical system actually relies on a hidden or 'underlying' structure that is not in fact linear. We saw this above where we considered the ambiguity of exactly who the president was having a discussion with in Example 6.

A sentence is not a string of words but rather a collection of groups of words that fit together (**constituents**) in a complex structure in an abstract hierarchy behind any sentence you utter or write. To illustrate this, consider this sentence:

Example 8

Can you believe everything **politicians** tell you?

We could retain exactly the same grammar in this sentence while adding additional information about the kind of politicians we are referring to:

Example 9

(a) Can you believe everything **old politicians** tell you?
(b) Can you believe everything **those old politicians** tell you?
(c) Can you believe everything **those old politicians from the country** tell you?

We could go on for ever adding more information about the politicians. In fact, being able to do so is an important fact about grammar: all grammatical systems in human languages spoken around the world can generate sentences that are infinitely long.

What use is that? Not much, as our mind/brain would soon cease to handle the flood of information. But this is one of the curiosities of human language: we use it for communication, but there are structural things which are possible within that system that are completely useless for communication. This suggests that the system itself is not purely for, or about, communication (see Feeney's Chapter 5 on language evolution). Notice that adding those words in Example 9 does not change the overall sentence: its basic meaning is exactly the same; we are just able to throw in more information about the particular sort of politicians we are talking about.

We could put the same words into completely different positions in other sentences:

Example 10

(a) It's those old politicians from the country that are often right.
(b) Whenever you meet one of those old politicians from the country, you always know you're in for a dull time.

So we know this is not something special about the position of these words in Example 9.

The most important word in the group is *politicians*. We could leave out the other words in the group without any problem, but if we leave out the most important word, *politicians*, then the sentence becomes nonsense:

Example 11

(a) Can you believe everything ~~politicians~~ tell you?
(b) Can you believe everything old ~~politicians~~ tell you?
(c) Can you believe everything those old ~~politicians~~ tell you?
(d) Can you believe everything those old ~~politicians~~ from the country tell you?

So, the essential word in this group is the noun *politicians*. Here the noun is referred to as the 'head' of this group of words because it is the one that the whole group is about. We then call the whole group of words (all six words in Example 9c) a Noun Phrase or NP.

The important point here is that the head word in this constituent is the noun, and that noun may have words and phrases on either side (as in Example 9c) that provide more information about that head noun, qualifying (modifying) it in some way. English is a left-headed language, i.e. the head is at the left of the group; other languages use different word order, e.g. the head is at the right of the group, so they are right-headed languages (such as Japanese).

Turning to pronouns, we find more evidence for the grammatical system using the abstract notion of a constituent. We can replace the nouns 'students' and 'everything' in Example 12a with pronouns, as in Example 12b:

Example 12

(a) Students know everything.
(b) They know it.

But is this the rule, that a pronoun replaces a noun? Or is the word 'pronoun' actually a misnomer, i.e. it does not represent just a noun? If we hypothesize that pronouns replace nouns, we can test this hypothesis by examining some more data. Consider the sentences in Example 13:

Example 13

(a) Students of history are often the best students.
(b) The assistant in the shop couldn't tell whether the new garments were correctly priced.
(c) Please extinguish your cigarettes.
(d) The weather in Italy is better than the constant rain here.

But there is a problem if we simply replace the nouns with pronouns:

Example 14

(a) *<u>They</u> of history are often the best <u>they</u>.
(b) *The he in the shop couldn't tell whether the new they were correctly priced.
(c) *Please extinguish your them.
(d) *The it in Italy is generally better than the constant it here.

Even assuming that you know what the pronouns are referring to from the context, these sentences are still ungrammatical. Clearly a pronoun does not simply replace a noun. It replaces the whole NP (the head noun and its modifiers). The point is that there must be such a thing as an NP in the grammatical system if there are words that replace such words as a group of words, i.e. there must be constituents. However, no-one teaches children exactly what pronouns can replace. If you were doubtful of the existence of an NP, it turns out that your internal knowledge already contained the notion of an NP.

For further evidence of constituents, let us have a look at the morpheme that expresses the idea of possession in English. When we are speaking, we add the /s/ sound to a noun and place the word in front of the noun that is possessed. When we are writing, we put an apostrophe between the noun and the letter *s*, for example, *The Queen's corgis*. Keep in mind that the apostrophe is simply an aspect of spelling or orthographic convention, a way of visually representing what we say.

Possessive -*s* attaches to the noun that possesses the following noun. Is this a sufficient account? Let us treat this as a hypothesis and test it on some more data. Let us say you want to make it clear which queen you are talking about. How would you represent the idea of these small dogs belonging to *The Queen of England*? You would say (and write): *The Queen of England's corgis*. Notice the apostrophe *-s* now follows *England*, not *Queen*, despite the fact that the corgis are not possessed by *England*, but by the Queen.

Some more examples:

Example 15

(a) I just found **that boy that I met last week**'s mobile phone.
(b) **The celebrity in the paper**'s wife is consulting a lawyer.

It sounds clumsy the more words involved, but you know intuitively that adding the *'s* after the NP is grammatical. It is what you say in conversation. In contrast, look how weird it sounds if you put the *'s* on the noun that really 'possesses' the second noun:

Example 16

(a) *I just found that boy's that I met last week mobile phone.
(b) *The celebrity's in the paper wife is consulting a lawyer.

Again, these are completely ungrammatical. So the rule is that the apostrophe *'s* doesn't attach to the noun that is doing the possessing; it attaches to the NP that has that noun as its head. Once again, it turns out that you've been using NPs all along – you just did not realize it. Unlike driving a car, though, you were not ever taught how to do it.

Inside a constituent

What things can we find in the NP and in what order? There might be only the head, as in Example 17a below, or there might be additional modifiers, as in the example we've just seen, set out here in Example 17b:

Example 17

(a)

head noun

Freedom

(b)

determiner	*head noun*	*preposition + noun phrase*
the	celebrity	in the paper

Articles like *the* and *a* are called **determiners**, and appear in the same slot as the **demonstrative determiner** *that* or *those* (in Example 18). And, of course, there can be another slot for the adjectives:

Example 18

determiner	*adjectives*	*head noun*	*preposition + NP*
those	new	garments	in the shop window

As noted above, an NP therefore consists of the main noun, called the head, and any modifiers, because they are modifying the noun. There are other phrases that can post-modify the head noun, for example, **relative clauses**:

Example 19

determiner	adjective	head noun	relative clause
the	hilarious	clown	that you met last week

Or we can have **a non-finite** verb post-modifying the noun:

Example 20

determiner	adjective	head noun	non-finite verb
the	best	person	to ask

And instead of determiners, we could have a possessive pronoun, or the noun and possessive -*s*. This slot is a 'specifier' slot, as the word in this slot specifies whether something is definite or who possesses it:

Example 21

specifier	adjectives	head noun	non-finite verb
your	best	person	to ask
John's	favourite	game	to play

These NPs can be used in various ways in sentences; or, to put it another way, they can play many different roles in the sentence:

Example 22

(a) The celebrity in the newspaper has had his hair done again.
(b) You know, I reckon I just saw the celebrity in the newspaper.
(c) The hilarious clown that you met last week just left a message.
(d) While I was talking to the hilarious clown that you met last week, I missed the bus.
(e) Your best person to ask is your mum.
(f) I've always thought that your best person to ask would be a taxi driver.

Moreover, every time you have a noun in a sentence, at an abstract level there must be an NP, even if there is only a noun on its own in the NP, as in Example 17a.

Other constituents

NPs are not the only constituents in a grammar. Adjectives and adverbs are also heads of their own phrases. Consider one of the examples above: *your best person to ask*. One of the pre-modifiers is the adjective *best*. Notice that we could qualify, or modify, the adjective with an adverb like *very*:

Example 23

I've always thought that your ⟨very best⟩ person to ask would be a taxi driver.

The word *very* modifies the adjective *best*, not any of the other words in the sentence. So in its underlying structure, it is part of the constituent headed by the adjective *best*, and it specifies the intensity of the description of *person*. Just as with the NP, it is the word category of the head that gives the constituent its name, in this case **Adjective Phrase**, or AP. We might have a post-modifier of the adjective too, just like we did in an NP. That will be part of the AP too:

Example 24

specifier	head adjective	preposition + NP
extremely	proud	of his dog
unusually	fond	of his newts
	tired	of life

Notice that the adjective *fond*, unlike *proud* and *tired*, requires the phrase beginning with *of* to follow it. You can't just say **he's very fond*. Remember that your linguistic competence knows what you cannot say just as much as what you can say. So if we put these APs into full sentences, we could have:

Example 25

My boyfriend is ⟨extremely proud of his dog⟩.
A man who is ⟨unusually fond of his newts⟩ is ⟨tired of life⟩.

Verbs and prepositions involve phrases too: **Verb Phrase** (VP) and **Preposition Phrase** (PP), as in Example 26:

Example 26

(a) Your boyfriend just ⟨cruelly kicked the dog⟩.
(b) Your keys are ⟨right on the table⟩.

The VP in Example 26a includes the direct object *the dog* and any **adverbs** modifying the verb, like *cruelly*. The PP in Example 26b is headed by the preposition *on* and is pre-modified by *right*, intensifying the specificity, and post-modified by the NP *the table*, telling us the object it is on.

Recall that the adjective *fond* in Example 24 requires a PP to follow it. Similarly, verbs and prepositions often require certain obligatory constituents to follow them. For example, what traditional grammar calls transitive verbs need an NP to follow (traditionally called the 'direct object'), as in Example 26a. Hence, if you left the NP *the dog* out of the VP in Example 26a, it would not be grammatical (**Your boyfriend just kicked*). In the same way, if you left the NP *the table* out of the PP in Example 26b, it would also be ungrammatical in the sense intended (**Your keys are right on*).

So to summarize, a **clause** (to use the term that linguists use; see Example 33) consists not just of a string of words in a linear order. Rather, a sentence is a group of constituents. Sometimes constituents might comprise a clause and have only one item in each phrase, the head:

Example 27

Students snore.

This clause consists of an NP followed by a VP, both of which have only a head inside them:

Example 28

NP[Students] VP[snore]

And sometimes the constituents have many more words:

Example 29

NP[Students with small noses] VP[snore]

Notice also that there are constituents inside constituents. For example, *with small noses* consists of a preposition *with* followed by the NP *small noses*. It is a PP inside the NP. But using many boxes gets too clumsy to read, so, as in linguistics textbooks, we will use brackets:

Example 30

NP[Students PP[with NP[small noses]]] VP[snore]

In fact, inside the NP, the adjective *small* modifies *noses*. The adjective *small* is an AP inside the NP inside the PP inside the NP:

Example 31

NP[Students PP[with NP[AP[**small**] noses]]] VP[snore]

We could put more words in any of the phrases. For example, we could modify the adjective *small* with *very*:

Example 32

NP[Students PP[with NP[AP[**very small**] noses]]] VP[snore]

We know the *very* is inside the AP because it modifies the adjective *small*; it is not modifying the noun in this clause because we do not mean *very noses*.

Using brackets can get confusing. Linguists also use tree diagrams to represent the constituents nested inside each other, as in Example 33. It is the same information as in Example 31, just in a clearer format:

Example 33

```
                        clause
              ┌───────────┴───────────┐
             NP                        VP
      ┌───────┴───────┐                │
      N               PP               V
      │         ┌──────┴──────┐        │
   Students     P            NP      snore
                │         ┌────┴────┐
              with       AP         N
                         │          │
                         A        noses
                         │
                       small
```

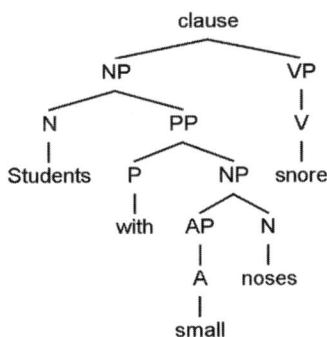

Linguists talk about the parts of the tree as if it is a matrilineal (female-line) family tree. So, for example, we say that P and NP are 'sisters', because they appear on the same level beneath PP, just as two sisters are in the same generation under their mother. Remember, this is an abstract model that attempts to capture the things we have observed about language, just as diagrams of molecules are abstract models to depict what is going on at the molecular level.

The hidden or underlying structure of phrases

Many grammar rules only apply to whole constituents. For example, you can give a PP prominence by moving it to the front of the sentence:

Example 34

PP[On the table] I put it, just now!
PP[Out of the window] she flew.

We've seen that all four phrases (NPs, APs, PPs and VPs) have elements that can precede and follow the head. Some verbs, some prepositions, and one adjective (*fond*) require specific kinds of phrases to follow them. Such obligatory phrases are called complements and, in a way, they are part of the meaning of the head. For example, in the sentence *My boyfriend kicked the dog*, you cannot have just some kicking going on; *kick* – in traditional grammar terms – is a transitive verb and so there needs to be something that is being kicked.

Notice that all complements in English follow the head in a phrase, as in Example 35.

Example 35

[The neglect [of his children]]

Here, the head is *neglect*, a noun, so we know that Example 35 is an NP; the complement is the PP *of his children* and the specifier of the NP is *the*.

But note also that languages across the world vary as to whether complements follow or precede the head. In Japanese, for example, complements precede the head. In Example 36, the direct object *inuo* 'dog' precedes the verb *ketta* 'kicked':

Example 36

Watashi-no	*kareshi-ga*	*inu-o*	*ket-ta*	(Japanese)
My-poss	boyfriend-top	dog-obj	kicked-past	

'My boyfriend kicked the dog.'

We have seen that there can be elements inside a phrase on either side of the head. However, these elements themselves are structured. The complement and the head combine first [head + complement], and then that constituent combines with the specifier to create the whole phrase. It is clearer to show this combination with an intermediate level or constituent in the tree structure we showed earlier:

Example 37

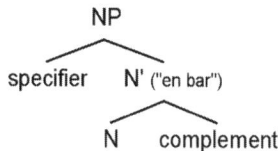

This is because there are times when it is clear that the grammatical system makes use of the head + complement constituent, so we need a way of referring to it. Above, you can see this intermediate constituent is called N'. (It used to be N with a bar above it, which was easy to draw, but in the early days of word processing it was difficult to typeset; now the name, shown in brackets in Example 37, has remained.)

We saw above that pronouns stand in for whole NPs, and not simply nouns. The word *one* is a **pro-form** whose function is like that of pronouns. However, it stands in for an N' rather than an NP. Consider this sentence:

Example 38

That phone with the touch screen is superior to your phone with the coffee-making app.

There are two NPs that we are interested in here, bracketed in Example 39a, and we know that we can replace both of them with pronouns as in Example 39b:

Example 39

(a) [That phone with the touch screen] is superior to [your phone with the coffee-making app]
(b) [It] is superior to [yours]

But, instead of replacing the whole phrase with a pronoun, we could also replace the N' with the word *one*, leaving the specifier intact:

Example 40

[That one] is superior to [your one]

What does the first *one* mean here? It means 'phone with the touch screen' – in other words, the N'. If it didn't mean that, we would not know which phone is being referred to. As for the second *one*, it is referring to the N' *phone with the coffee-making app*. (Note that this also now explains the grammatical version of the example above in 14a, which would be *The ones of history are the best ones* … awkward, but grammatical!)

Notice that pro-forms such as pronouns or the word *one* do not substitute for strings of words that are not constituents. So, for example, we know that in Example 39a the string of words *phone with the touch screen* is an N' constituent, and that the string of words *with the touch screen* is a PP modifying the noun *phone*, but the string *phone with the* is not a constituent; in the tree diagram, those three words would not appear under a single node in the tree, any more than *phone with* can. As a result, *one* cannot substitute for just those words:

Example 41

(a) *That one touch screen is superior to your one.
(b) *That one the touch screen is superior to your one.

If words were not grouped in such ways, and if there was no such thing as the underlying constituent N', then it would be impossible for your mind/brain to know what the function of *one* is, what it can and cannot stand in for. It would also be impossible for a child's mind/brain to figure this out.

Various ideas have been discussed in linguistics research on these structures, but AP, PP and VP are all seen as having an intermediate level too:

Example 42

(a) Your phone is $_{AP}$[remarkably $_{A'}$[**poor** at getting a connection]].
(b) Your phone is $_{PP}$[right $_{P'}$[**on** the table]].
(c) You can $_{VP}$[$_{V'}$[**eat** your breakfast]].

The head of each of the phrases in question is in bold. In each case you can see that within each phrase, there is an intermediate constituent consisting of the head and the complement. Each of the specifiers in Example 42 combines with the intermediate constituent to form the phrase.[1]

Here it helps to think of algebra. To capture patterns in numbers, it makes more sense to use letters instead of specific numbers. An equation is a kind of shorthand, capturing the pattern in the numbers. If we want to capture patterns in language about constituents, such as the fact that they have the same internal structure regardless of the type of phrase, we can replace the specific categories of noun or preposition with the letter X:

Example 43

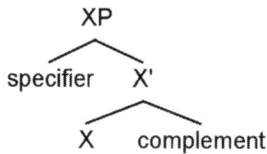

What we're doing is generalizing these patterns, noting that any phrase, whether the head is N, A, V or P, may consist of a specifier combined with an X' and, in turn, X' consists of the head of the phrase with a complement. It is called an XP because the head is an X. So if X represented 'mickey mouse', then XP would be a 'mickey mouse phrase'. The point about this 'X-bar structure' shown in Example 43 is that it is claimed to be true of any constituent, regardless of what the head is.

As research in linguistics has developed, linguists have found that not just the major lexical categories, N, A, V and P, are heads of constituents like Example 43, but other elements in the clause head a phrase such as Example 43 too. Eventually, some linguists argued that determiners were also heads and not specifiers. If Determiner (D) is a head, then it must be the head of a DP, requiring an NP as its complement.

Linguists also worked out that the inflectional morpheme on a verb (*I walked; he walks*) is a head and they called it I, after Inflection. This head requires a VP complement. The Inflectional Phrase (IP) has the subject of the clause in its specifier position. Auxiliaries such as *have* and forms of *be* and modal auxiliaries such as *must* are the head of I.

Subordinating conjunctions such as *that* (called a **Complementizer**) were also shown to be heads. C is the head of CP, a Complementizer Phrase, which requires an IP as its complement. Each phrase may have the same structure as Example 43, although some structures may be simpler (for example, we know that not all heads need a complement, such as the **intransitive** verb *snore* in Example 28).

So, in the sentence *I thought that John must want some chocolate*, the **embedded clause** is a complement to the verb *thought* and the structure is as shown in Example 44:

Example 44

   I thought …

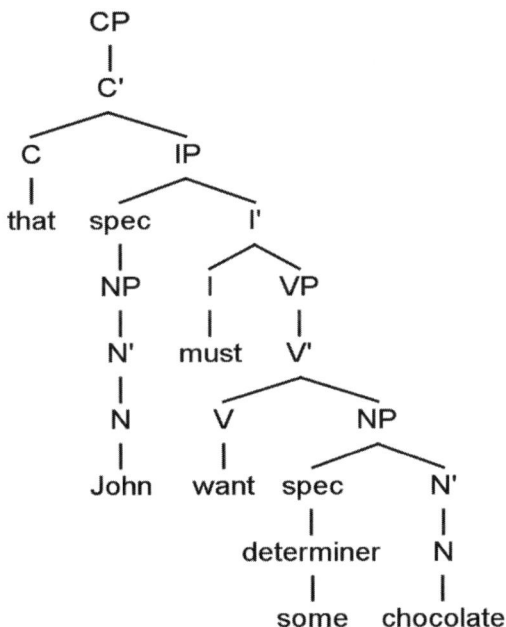

It is not possible for a toddler to know all of that from the outset, but she arrives at this knowledge remarkably fast. This occurs through a combination of hearing language spoken in the environment, and her mind/brain listening out for what in the speech stream is needed to construct a structure like Example 44. Babies seem to be born equipped to listen for X′ structure.

How to learn something too complex to learn

One of the obvious things about human language is the way that constituents get moved around. For example:

Example 45

(a) John kissed the dog.
(b) The dog was kissed ___ by John.
(c) The dog John kissed ___, not the cat!
(d) Which dog did John kiss ___ ?

How might we model a system that could account for these four clauses? We could just establish that the verb *kiss* requires a complement such as *the dog* and then list all the places that it can appear in the clause, immediately following the verb in Example 45a, appearing at the front of the clause in Example 45b, c, d. When you look at all the places where it might appear, and think of all the verbs that require complements, that is a clumsy model because it just lists all the possibilities. It is certainly difficult to see how a child could learn such a list.

Alternatively, we could first establish that the young language user knows that the verb *kiss* is one of the verbs that requires an NP complement, like *the dog*. Then we could capture some form of what we call movement rules in the grammar that would mean the similarities in the clauses in Example 45 just follow from the fact that the complement can be moved.

Why is this easier to acquire than memorizing a list? Instead of needing a ludicrously long list of 'facts', if the child already 'knows' the structure of language and that there are movement rules, the child then just has to learn words (we know children learn words quickly, and at a phenomenal rate), and some key facts about the language (such as whether the complements follow the head or precede it). Structure and the idea of movement are already built into the system.

This is what is meant by language being innate. It does not mean that a baby is born talking a language. It means that the baby has a predisposition to absorb the language spoken around her, and to use that information to establish the particular characteristics for that particular language. The movement rules, along with the X-bar structure in Example 43, are part of that innate predisposition.

Chomsky (1980b) has suggested that the predisposition for language is like the baby's visual system: the propensity for binocular vision (using your two eyes to focus on things) is part of the baby's mind/brain, but it does not develop properly unless the baby has things to look at and gradually to focus on. Hence a baby does not really seem to be looking at you when it is first born, but within a few months the baby is clearly focusing on your face and gurgling away happily. Chomsky's claim is that the mind/brain is also genetically programmed for language, just as genes equip the body to develop binocular vision. For vision, it is the combination of that genetic readiness on the one hand, and exposure to relevant stimuli in the environment (things to look at) on the other, that enable the baby's binocular visual system to develop. There may be an important timespan or critical period for such biological stimulus (which many researchers believe also applies to some degree to language – see, for example, Harley & Wang, 1997; Singleton & Ryan, 2004). If a baby were prevented from seeing things during the critical period for developing binocular vision, that poor baby would never do so (Pinker, 1997: 237–241). This argument for language acquisition maintains that, without exposure to language before the assumed critical period, language acquisition would be impaired or impossible.

The predisposition to learn language is part of human nature, but the human language we use all day only develops from a combination of language that the child hears (or sees if she is deaf) and the biological predisposition for language. Given that all children must have this predisposition, because all children learn whatever language they get exposed to, the ability to speak and understand a language must be universal, part of the make-up of the human mind/brain. Hence the term Universal Grammar. This is a kind of abstract grammar that linguists propose underlies all human languages (but not computer languages like Basic or Fortran, or animal communication systems). By studying human languages, looking at what their possibilities are, what they have in common and what is not possible in any language, we can gradually build up an understanding of what Universal Grammar is, and hence what that special innate predisposition in the human mind/brain is like. But some people reject the idea of a Universal Grammar (for a wider view on this debate, see, for example, Ambridge & Lieven, 2011).

Some might think that a Universal Grammar denies individuality, as though having no innate, genetic predispositions in some way gives a person more character. This is a peculiar notion. Are you any less an individual because your genes triggered binocular vision? Or because your genes made you grow 10 fingers (instead of however many you would like to have)?

Some may think that a Universal Grammar is too mechanistic a way of describing the wonderful variety of language and meaning on our planet. Of course languages differ in many ways. But a grammar whose structure enables an infinite number of sentences in a given language is highly creative, and every human language can do so. Furthermore, it is through the language system that you can be creative: you can coin new words because the system is there to fit them into. And if you are feeling poetic, you can break the rules to draw attention to your language, but only because the rules are already there.

Others may be bothered by such a mathematical way of treating language, because language seems to be squishy and indeterminate. That is how language might appear, but then lots of things in the natural world appear many and various, but through careful scientific inquiry we can begin to understand how they work. If you spend any time examining language, you will observe the regularities we have seen in this chapter and many more. Regularities and patterns are the stuff of rational enquiry.

Finally, there are those who may dislike the idea of a Universal Grammar because it seems so unlikely that all humans would have a similar mind/brain when it comes to language. But consider the alternative: the human mind/brain has no apparent structure when the child is born; everything is somehow programmed in those early years. It is very hard to see then why it is that all normally functioning humans in a given speech community would end up with the same general linguistic competence, regardless of their levels of intelligence, interest, culture, education or feelings. It is not about incentive either: children do not vary in how much they want to acquire language. They vary only in when they choose to use it and how well they use it.

We already know that there are many things about us that are genetically determined: your sex, the fact that your nose is like your mother's but your knees are like your father's. We are fascinated by our genetic make-up but that does not deny that our environment is not extremely influential as well. The wrong kind of nutrition, a lack of sunlight or even just a lack of exercise will each affect our biology as we grow up, of course. It is not a simple-minded choice between nature and nurture, but a highly complex interplay, and different theories take different positions with respect to that interplay (see O'Grady's Chapter 3 in this volume – and Ambridge & Lieven's 2011 book on different theoretical approaches to child language acquisition).

The term 'language acquisition device' (LAD) has been used to refer to the innate predisposition for language. This term has probably misled some people to picture it as a box inside the head. Instead of being concentrated in a box-like manner, what we refer to as the human language faculty is physically realized in one's brain in more diffuse ways that neurolinguistics is only slowly coming to understand.

Studying language may suggest it is a distinct, discrete, separate component or faculty in the mind (although see O'Grady, Chapter 3 in this volume, for an alternative view). Language has different ways of working compared to other things the mind/brain does. For example, the rules of the language faculty do not use counting: there are no rules in any language where you move the third element in a string of words to create a question, or emphasize something by topicalizing the fifth word. Instead, language involves constituency and hierarchical structure, as we have seen above. The idea that different aspects of the mind/brain are distinct from other aspects is called **modularity**. The **language faculty** is a distinct module in the mind and brain. This is why peculiar things can happen when things go wrong; after an accident involving the brain, for example, someone may lose an aspect of their language, such as speech, even though they can still engage in many other cognitive activities.

Things that We Know about Language #2

As we saw at the start of this chapter, everyone is interested in language. Now we know some new, more refined ideas and evidence about language. Language is indeed all about expressing ourselves, it is about creativity, and we are able to express ourselves and be creative because of the grammar rules: if we coin new words, we use the grammar to make it possible. If we bend the word order, we do so knowing that it will create an effect because it is not the 'normal' word order. There are different registers, and they all have grammars. They are, in effect, all just slightly different languages. We use the language system to communicate, but there are aspects of the grammatical system that are not of much use for communication.

A child acquires language by having a predisposition in the mind/brain that picks up the language being used in the environment, and finds enough information to establish the 'settings' in the particular language being spoken. The examples of language that the child hears are not enough for the child to figure out the grammatical system; this is only possible through a combination of the child's innate propensity for language and the language she hears spoken or signed in the environment. Furthermore, you can often witness a child's mind/brain figuring out the grammar rules when she makes mistakes that she would not have heard from the adults ('We goed to the shops', etc.).

As for adults, everyone knows they are often poor at acquiring a new language, although many can do it well enough to get by. The question is: Why is it so easy for toddlers and so hard for adults? Adults can study for degrees, learn to work complex machinery and gabble away in their mother language all day long without even thinking about it, but here they cannot do something a toddler can do. Is it because they no longer have access to the kind of special predisposition that the toddler has (Universal Grammar)? Or do they only have *some* access to Universal Grammar? Or are they in fact doing something completely different, learning a new language like they learn to drive a car or to work a machine, while handling all the other complex cognitive tasks of adult life? These are open questions.

Whether analysing human languages to figure out the nature of the native speaker's underlying linguistic competence, or studying children's emerging competence, or tackling the problem of what adults do when they try to learn a language, these are exciting areas of exploration. Unlike many areas of research that require years of training before you get to the chalk face, in linguistics you can very quickly get to where the new discoveries are taking place. The more we discover, the more we are learning about the human mind/brain, and therefore the more we are learning about human nature – ultimately what it is to be human. Everyone's interested in language.

Further reading

Fromkin, Rodman and Hyams' *An Introduction to Language* (2013) gives a cheerful and thorough overview of different aspects of linguistics, including language acquisition. It's worth flicking through just for the cartoons. For general Chomskyan background, Chomsky's own *Language and Problems of Knowledge* (1987) does not assume any prior linguistic knowledge. For a more critical perspective, if a more challenging level of reading, Ben Ambridge and Elena Lieven's *Child Language Acquisition* (2011) sets out generative ideas in contrast to other linguistic approaches. For some more introductory background to syntax across languages, Maggie Tallerman's *Understanding Syntax* (2014) is ideal. If you want more specific help with minimalist theory, Andrew Radford's *Analysing English Sentences* (2016) takes you through things effectively. On creativity in language use, Chapter 2 of Geoffrey Leech's *A Linguistic Guide to English Poetry* (1969) is still good, but to get the crosslinguistic perspective on how verbal art around the world exploits linguistic form, Nigel Fabb's *Language and Literature* (1997) is a fascinating starting point. And for second language acquisition, the current volume will do nicely.

Note

(1)   The specifier position of the VP in Example 42c came to be seen as the place where the subject NP (*you* in Example 42c) starts out; see also syntactic movement in the next section, p. 30.

3 Syntax and Acquisition: The Emergentist Story

William O'Grady

Introduction

From the early 1960s, research on language has often focused on two related questions, one involving syntax and the other language acquisition:

(i) The syntax question: How are sentences built and interpreted?
(ii) The acquisition question: How do children learn how sentences are built and interpreted?

Over the years, two very different sorts of answers have been put forward – one committed to the idea that there are inborn grammatical principles (Universal Grammar, UG) and the other wed to the idea that the properties of language reflect the synergistic effect of non-grammatical factors such as processing, working memory and pragmatics. The latter approach is an example of 'emergentism', a style of explanation that seeks to understand complex phenomena by studying the interaction of simpler and more basic factors and forces.

A good deal of this chapter is devoted to sketching an emergentist approach to language and its acquisition. I will begin by discussing constraints on the interpretation of pronouns, first from the perspective of UG and then from the perspective of emergentism, drawing on the much more detailed proposals made in O'Grady (2005, 2015a, 2015b). The next two sections offer an account of how the capacity to interpret pronouns emerges in the course of first and second language acquisition. The chapter ends with a brief set of concluding remarks.

Universal Grammar

An underlying theme of work on UG is that our understanding and use of language is made possible by abstract grammatical principles that are inborn rather than learned.[1] The classic UG analysis of pronoun interpretation is a case in point.

Principle A

A defining feature of reflexive pronouns (*himself, herself, themselves*) is that there are sharp restrictions on who they can refer to. For example, *himself* can refer to *Richard* (its **antecedent**) in Example 1a, but not in Example 1b.

Example 1

(a) **Richard** distrusts **himself.**
(b) *****Richard** thinks [Mary distrusts **himself**].

The classic UG constraint on the interpretation of reflexive pronouns is Principle A, which can be paraphrased as follows, in the spirit of Chomsky (1981).[2]

Example 2: Principle A

A reflexive pronoun must have a higher antecedent in the same clause.

The reflexive pronoun in Example 1a is fine, since its antecedent, *Richard*, is both higher (closer to the top of the tree) and in the same clause.

Example 3

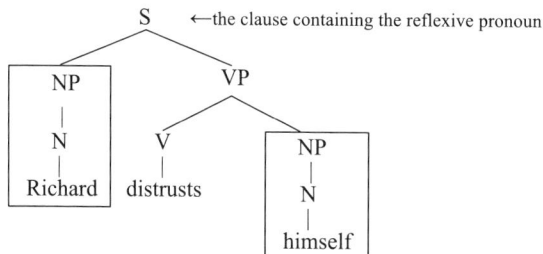

In contrast, the intended antecedent in Example 1b lies outside the clause containing *himself*. As a result, the sentence violates Principle A, and is ungrammatical.

Example 4

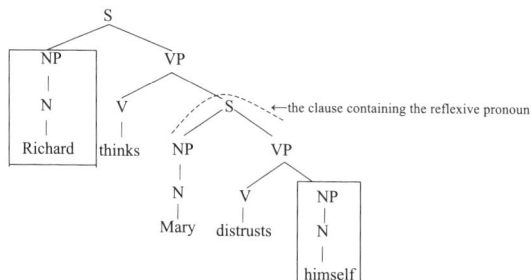

Principle B

Unlike reflexive pronouns, plain pronouns (*he, him, she, her, they, them*) are able to have an antecedent almost anywhere – as long as it is not a higher NP in the same clause.

Example 5: Principle B

A plain pronoun must not have a higher antecedent in the same clause.

The effect of Principle B can be seen in how listeners interpret sentences such as Example 6.

Example 6

Richard thinks [Carl distrusts **him**].

Here, *him* can refer to Richard, or to someone not mentioned in the sentence (perhaps the speaker was talking about his neighbor, Morley). But it cannot have *Carl* as its antecedent, since that NP is both higher than the pronoun and in the same clause.

Example 7

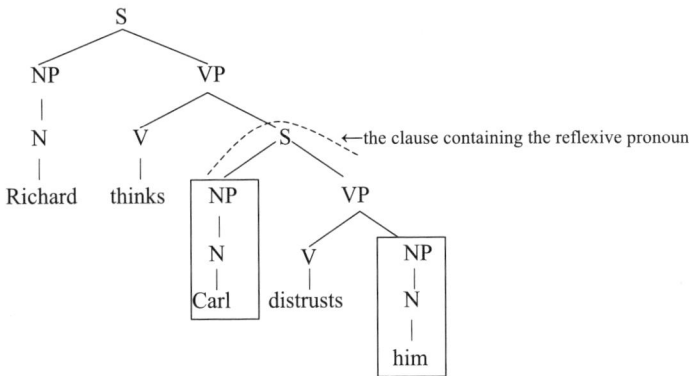

The UG picture

In sum, on the UG account, pronoun interpretation is constrained by abstract principles that operate on tree structures. The constraints have no counterpart in other areas of cognition (there is no equivalent of Principle A in logic, in vision or in chess), and the tree structures are not directly manifested in experience – children hear only strings of words.

How then can Principles A and B be learned? The most common answer is that they cannot: they and other principles of UG must be inborn (innate).

… Universal Grammar [is] an innate form of knowledge specific to language. (Yang, 2004: 451)

Where does linguistic knowledge come from? … this knowledge is inborn. (Guasti, 2002: 17)

… children are born with a set of universal linguistic principles … many aspects of adult grammar are innate. (Crain *et al.*, 2006: 31)

We can now see the outlines of the UG-based answers to the two research questions stated at the outset, at least insofar as pronoun interpretation is concerned.

(i)   The syntax question: How are sentences built and interpreted?
      Answer: Principles of UG determine how the system works. Reflexive pronouns take the antecedent that they do because of Principle A; plain pronouns are interpreted the way they are because of Principle B; and so on.
(ii) The acquisition question: How do children learn how sentences are built and interpreted?
      Answer: The necessary principles are inborn, and do not have to be learned.

These ideas contrast with those offered by the emergentist perspective on language, to which we turn next.

An Emergentist Approach to Syntax

On the emergentist view of syntax, sentences do not have syntactic structures, and they do not obey abstract grammatical principles. Rather, the properties of syntactic phenomena are treated as a side-effect of other things, especially processing.

Processing and syntax

Everyone agrees that processing takes place at many different levels as we produce and comprehend sentences. In the course of a conversation, for instance, it is necessary to simultaneously process information pertaining not only to sounds, morphemes and words, but also to what we know about the listener, the surroundings, the topic of conversation, and so on. For the sake of convenience, let us assume that at least two types of processing occur as we use language.

(i)   Sentence-level processing focuses on the form and composition of the utterance, including its words, their inflectional marking, their order, and so on.
(ii) Pragmatic processing focuses on the situation and context in which a particular sentence is spoken or heard.

My goal will be to show that the interaction of these two types of processing can explain why pronouns are interpreted in the way they are, as well as how learners figure this out in the course of acquiring a first or second language.

An important part of interpreting a sentence, whether it contains a pronoun or not, involves building an argument structure for the verb, as illustrated below.

Example 8

Richard introduced Charlotte.

   <r c>

In this particular example, the verb has two 'arguments' – the agent Richard (represented by the symbol r) and the patient or undergoer Charlotte (c). There is of course much more to meaning than this,[3] but everyone agrees that there cannot be *less*.

Now let us consider a sentence such as *Richard introduced himself*, in which the verb's second argument is a pronoun.

Example 9

Richard introduced *himself*.

   <r x>

In such cases, the processor has an extra job to do: it must find a referent for the pronoun, which is represented in the argument grid as the variable x, to indicate the need for further interpretation. How might this further interpretation take place?

Everyone agrees that sentences are built and understood incrementally, one word at a time and as quickly as possible. In listening to a sentence such as *Charlotte introduced herself*, we think of who Charlotte is as soon as we hear her name, we identify her as the introducer as soon as we hear the verb, and we begin to look for an antecedent immediately upon realizing that the verb's second argument is a pronoun. The precise manner in which that search is conducted reveals a lot about how language works and how it is acquired.

A processing approach to pronoun interpretation

In the processing-based theory that I propose (O'Grady, 2015a), the interpretation of pronouns is shaped by two competing forces, each motivated by limitations on working memory.

(i) a drive to resolve referential dependencies as quickly as possible;
(ii) a sensitivity to an item's prominence (**salience**) in memory.

As we will see next, the interpretation of reflexive pronouns is largely shaped by the first force, while plain pronouns are interpreted under the influence of the second factor.

The processor and working memory

The term **sentence-level processor** provides a convenient way to refer to those parts of the brain whose activation is relevant to the determination of sentence-level form-meaning relationships. It doesn't imply that there is a single mechanism in a particular part of the brain that does this work.

The term **working memory** simply refers to the brain's ability to maintain the neural activation needed to hold information and carry out operations on that information in the course of processing (e.g. MacDonald & Christiansen, 2002). This doesn't mean that that there is (or isn't) a separate working memory for language, or that the information and operations supported by working memory are located in any single part of the brain.

Reflexive pronouns

Let us begin with Example 9 above, with the verb's second argument expressed as a reflexive pronoun and the first argument serving as its antecedent – the prototypical reflexive pronoun construction in English (Jespersen, 1933: 111). One scenario for the interpretation of this pattern by the sentence-level processor plays out as follows.

Example 10
Richard introduced **himself**.

(a) The noun *Richard* is assigned an interpretation.
Richard
   r

(b) The verb is encountered, and Richard is identified as its first argument (agent).
Richard *introduced*
        $<r\_>$

(c) The reflexive pronoun is encountered and identified as the verb's second argument. (As before, the symbol x indicates that the referent of the pronoun is yet to be determined.)
Richard introduced *himself*.
        $<r\ x>$

(d) The pronoun's antecedent is identified as *Richard*, which is already in the verb's argument grid.

Richard introduced *himself.*

       $<r\ x>$

          ↳ *r*

As illustrated in the final step, *Richard* offers an immediate opportunity to interpret the pronoun, so the processor selects it as antecedent. Anything else would unnecessarily increase the burden on working memory.

This approach also gives the right result in the case of a more complex sentence such as Example 11, in which the reflexive pronoun must find its antecedent in the inner clause – *himself* can refer to Richard, but not to Harry.

Example 11

Harry said [***Richard*** *overestimates* ***himself***].

On the processing account, this interpretation arises because only *Richard* is available at the point at which *himself* is encountered and added to the argument grid of the verb *overestimate.*

Example 12

(a) The reflexive pronoun is encountered and added to the verb's argument grid:

Harry said [Richard overestimates **himself**].

      . . . $<r\ x>$

(b) The reflexive pronoun is interpreted within the same argument grid:

Harry said [Richard overestimates himself].

      . . . $<r\ x>$

                ↳ *r*

As a first approximation, then, we can say that the interpretation of reflexive pronouns arises as a side-effect of the way in which the sentence-level processor goes about doing its job. Because of the need to complete its work as expeditiously as possible, the processor ends up selecting an antecedent for reflexive pronouns from within the same argument grid, creating the processing operation, or 'routine', summarized below.

Example 13: Interpretive routine for reflexive pronouns

Find an antecedent immediately in the same argument grid.

$<a\ x>$

   ↳ *a*

Closeness in the argument grid is what counts

The search for an antecedent takes place inside argument grids, not in the sentence per se. That is why the antecedent for a reflexive pronoun is not always the closest NP in the string of words making up a sentence. The following example illustrates this point:

Who does Harry think criticized **himself**?

Here the closest potential antecedent for *himself* is *Harry*, but of course the actual antecedent is *who*. This follows from the processing approach. As the sentence is processed in the usual incremental way, the *wh*-word is interpreted as the first argument of the verb *criticize* – just before the reflexive pronoun is encountered. This leaves just one opportunity to interpret the pronoun within the argument grid of *criticize* – use the *wh*-word (represented here by the symbol *w*) that is already there.

Who does Harry think [*criticized himself$_x$*]?

$$\ldots \quad <w\ x>$$
$$\llcorner w$$

Plain pronouns

But what about plain pronouns such as *him* and *her*? Why do they reject a nearby antecedent, unlike reflexive pronouns?

Example 14

*Richard overestimates **him**.

The interpretation of plain pronouns requires pragmatic processing, which focuses on the situation and context in which a sentence is used. Let us therefore assume that when the sentence-level processor encounters a plain pronoun, it passes responsibility for interpreting it to the pragmatic processing system, as depicted below.

Example 15: Interpretive routine for plain pronouns

Pass responsibility for finding an antecedent to the pragmatic system ($\mathcal{P}$).

$$<a\ x>$$
$$\searrow \mathcal{P}$$

The pragmatic system cares about ease of processing too, of course, and it looks for ways to find an antecedent with the least possible effort. One way that it does this is to select a referent that is contextually salient (e.g. Foraker & McElree, 2007; Song & Fisher, 2007: 1961), presumably because such referents are easier to retrieve from memory.

Why then can the pragmatic system not select *Richard* as antecedent for *him* in Example 14, especially if Richard is the most prominent person in the situation? The reason is simple: as noted by various scholars (e.g. Levinson, 1987: 410; Reinhart, 1983: 166), the interpretation with *Richard* as antecedent is the meaning that speakers express via a reflexive pronoun (as in *Richard overestimates himself*). All other things being equal, reflexive pronouns are 'cheaper' than plain pronouns, because their interpretation is determined by the sentence-level processor, which does its job immediately, inside the argument grid containing the pronoun (see, for example, Reinhart, 2006: 181ff; Reuland, 2011: 127). So, if a reflexive pronoun **can** be used, it **must** be used. If a plain pronoun is selected, it is because the speaker intends to express an interpretation other than the one that a reflexive pronoun would give. Hence *him* in Example 14 cannot have the interpretation that *himself* would have: it cannot refer to Richard.

Reflexive pronouns that behave like plain pronouns

The sentence-level and pragmatic processing systems offer complementary approaches to pronoun interpretation – the first committed to immediate action within the argument grid and the second focusing on salience in a potentially much larger domain. Thus, in the examples we have seen so far, the sentence-level processor is called upon for the interpretation of reflexive pronouns, while responsibility for plain pronouns falls to pragmatic processing.

Interestingly, English has a class of patterns in which there is no antecedent for the reflexive pronoun in the same argument grid. The second sentence in Example 16 illustrates such a situation.

Example 16

Richard told Mary that he was very happy. A picture of **himself** was about to appear in the newspaper.

At the point at which the sentence-level processor comes upon the reflexive pronoun and identifies it as an argument of *picture*,[4] there is no immediately available opportunity to interpret it within the same argument grid.

Example 17

a picture of **himself**
   <x>
   ↳?

The sentence-level processor therefore transfers responsibility for interpreting the reflexive pronoun to the pragmatic system, which then selects the contextually salient subject of the preceding sentence as antecedent.

Example 18

Richard told Mary that he was very happy. A picture of **himself** ...

$$<x>$$
$$\searrow \mathcal{P} \Rightarrow \text{Richard}$$

Crucially, though, this transfer of responsibility takes place only as a last resort. If there is an opportunity to find an antecedent for a reflexive pronoun in the same argument grid, the sentence-level processor does so. Thus, upon encountering the reflexive pronoun in Example 19, the processor must take advantage of the opportunity to link it to *Bob*, which is present in the same argument grid.

Example 19

Richard said something disturbing. Apparently, **Bob** sees **himself** as the new boss.
$$<b\ x>$$
$$\downarrow b$$

In sum, the basic system for interpreting reflexive pronouns in English can be summarized by the following protocol:

Example 20: Protocol for reflexive pronoun interpretation in English

- Interpret the reflexive pronoun immediately, within the same argument grid. (e.g. Example 19)
- If this is impossible, pass responsibility for interpreting the reflexive pronoun to the pragmatic system. (e.g. Example 18)

As we will see next, the interplay between the two types of processing is also the key to understanding how the capacity for pronoun interpretation emerges in the course of first and second language acquisition.

First Language Acquisition

An intriguing feature of the processing account of reflexive pronouns is that it leaves very little for children to learn, other than the form of the pronoun itself (e.g. *himself*, not *hisself*) and the fact that it requires an antecedent. Beyond that, we need only assume that a child's brain seeks to process linguistic input in a way that minimizes the burden on working memory, just as an adult brain does. This guarantees a preference for the selection of an antecedent from within the same argument grid – the right result.

The developmental facts provide independent support for this idea. As established in a variety of comprehension studies (see Guasti, 2002: 285 for a review), children typically interpret reflexive pronouns correctly from the earliest point at which they can be tested – even three-year-olds

Figure 3.1 Sample picture based on Chien and Wexler (1990)

can be right 95% of the time or more. Thus they correctly answer 'yes' in response to the query in Example 21.

Example 21

> This is Mama Bear; this is Goldilocks.
> Is Mama Bear touching herself?

This is exactly what we would expect if the interpretation of reflexive pronouns reflects a 'least-effort' response that involves immediately selecting an antecedent from within the same argument grid.

Interestingly, children fare considerably less well when the question contains a plain pronoun (*Is Mama Bear touching her?*). As first noted by Chien and Wexler (1990) and subsequently confirmed by Conroy *et al.* (2009), some preschool children respond in the affirmative, treating *her* as if it meant *herself*. (Errors of this type often fall into the 15–30% range.)

Why might children be tempted to interpret plain pronouns as reflexive pronouns, but not vice versa? Perhaps because, all other things being equal, the routine for interpreting reflexive pronouns incurs less processing cost. One piece of evidence for this idea comes from Love *et al.* (2009), who report that children aged five to 13 years improve dramatically on their interpretation of plain pronouns when test sentences are presented more slowly (at the rate of 3.19 syllables per second rather than 5 syllables per second). This is just what we would expect if errors in the interpretation of plain pronouns reflect an increased stress on processing resources. Lessening the processing demands (by giving children more time to carry out the necessary interpretive procedures) leads to improved performance.

A study by Clackson *et al.* (2011) provides further insights into the processing side of pronoun interpretation by monitoring eye movements as children and adults looked at a picture that was accompanied by a pair of sentences, similar to those in Example 22. Note that the argument grid for *buy* contains three arguments – the agent *Mr Jones* (*j*), the patient *popcorn* (*p*) and the pronominal benefactive (*for him*).

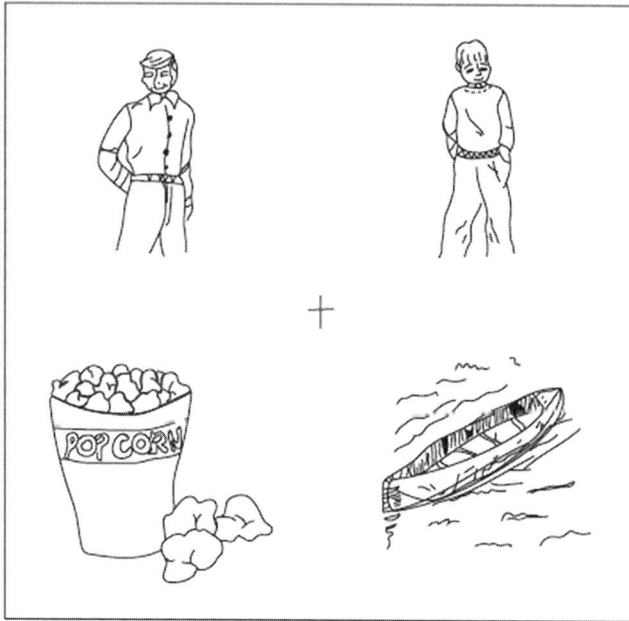

Figure 3.2 Sample picture from Clackson *et al.* (2011: 143). The man in the upper left is Mr Jones; the boy in the upper right is Peter

Example 22

> *Peter* was waiting outside the corner shop.
> He watched as *Mr Jones* bought popcorn for **him**.
> <j p for x>

Forty children aged six to nine years participated in the study, along with 40 adults (mean age 21;3). Eye fixation patterns revealed that children (and to a lesser extent) adults showed signs of considering Mr Jones as a possible antecedent for the pronoun, suggesting that exposure to a plain pronoun activates both processing systems, especially in young learners.[5] In other words, even as the pragmatic system (correctly) focuses on the salient sentential topic Peter, the sentence-level processor tries to select an antecedent (Mr Jones) from within the same argument grid as the pronoun. Ultimately, the choice of antecedent depends on which routine wins out over the other. At least in young children, the processing advantages associated with the sentence-level routine appear to encourage its overuse, yielding interpretive errors on plain pronouns.

These facts open the door to a new understanding of development. As suggested by O'Grady (2013b, 2015a), what we think of as language acquisition is really processing amelioration – the gradual strengthening of the routines appropriate for particular patterns (e.g. the sentence-level routine for reflexive pronouns, and the pragmatic routine for plain pronouns). Even when initial interpretive preferences are shaped by processing-related factors, use of a routine becomes surer and more automatic with experience: the sentence-level routine solidifies its pre-eminence over the pragmatic routine for the interpretation of reflexive pronouns, and the reverse happens in the case of plain pronouns. As a result, processing becomes faster and more accurate – the goal of linguistic development.

Second Language Acquisition

Many of the most revealing phenomena in the study of second language acquisition (SLA) arise in cases where the first language differs in some significant way from the second language. The interpretation of reflexive pronouns offers an example of just such a difference.

As we have seen, for example, the reflexive pronoun in an English sentence such as Example 23 must refer to Richard.

Example 23
Harry said [**Richard** overestimates **himself**].

Interestingly, though, things work differently in languages such as Japanese, Korean and Chinese, in which the equivalent sentence is ambiguous – the reflexive pronoun can refer to either Richard or Harry. (I use *self* to stand for the reflexive pronouns *zibun*, *caki* and *ziji* in Japanese, Korean and Chinese, respectively.)

Example 24
Harry said [**Richard** overestimates **self**].

In fact, as noted by Kang (1988), there are even examples in Japanese, Korean and Chinese where a reflexive pronoun looks past a possible antecedent in its clause to a referent outside the sentence.

Example 25
Tom went to the police station. It was because the chief had summoned **self**.

The existence of these interpretive options suggests an intriguing possibility: languages like Japanese, Korean and Chinese allow their reflexive pronouns to be interpreted by **either** the sentence-level processor **or** the pragmatic system. Unlike English, they are not compelled to select an antecedent from within the same argument grid, just because one is available there (as discussed above).

Example 26: Protocol for reflexive pronoun interpretation in Japanese, Korean and Chinese

- Interpret the reflexive pronoun immediately, within the same argument grid.
  or
- Pass responsibility for interpreting the reflexive pronoun to the pragmatic system.

Example 27: Protocol for reflexive pronoun interpretation in English

- Interpret the reflexive pronoun immediately, within the same argument grid.
- If this is impossible, pass responsibility for interpreting the reflexive pronoun to the pragmatic system.

Thus, in a pattern such as Example 24 in Japanese, Korean or Chinese, repeated here as Example 28, the sentence-level processor can give an interpretation in which the reflexive pronoun refers to Richard, and the pragmatic system can yield an interpretation in which it refers to Harry.

Example 28

Harry said **Richard** overestimates **self.**

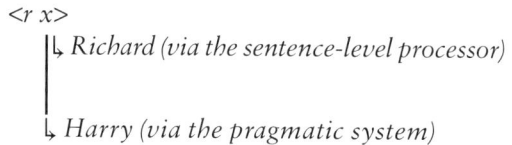

<r x>

↳ *Richard (via the sentence-level processor)*

↳ *Harry (via the pragmatic system)*

The idea that the sentence-level processor and the pragmatic system can each yield an acceptable interpretation for reflexive pronouns in some languages fits well with the idea that two different systems are involved in pronoun interpretation, one focused on immediate opportunities within the argument grid and the other on salience within a potentially much larger domain. Whereas the former system dominates the interpretation of reflexive pronouns in English, both systems are active in languages like Japanese, Korean and Chinese, as evidenced by the ambiguity illustrated in Example 28.

Turning now to SLA, what happens when, say, a Japanese speaking learner of English tries to interpret sentences such as Example 23, repeated here as Example 29?

Example 29

Harry said [Richard overestimates himself].

The answer, documented by Hirakawa (1990) and Thomas (1991) among others, is that Japanese second language learners often choose the pragmatically prominent but distant antecedent *Harry* as antecedent in such cases. Similar observations have been made for speakers of other languages that allow pragmatically interpreted reflexives, including Cantonese (Jiang, 2009) and Turkish (Demirci, 2000).

A second line of research, initiated by Felser *et al.* (2009), focuses on the course of processing in more advanced learners, who have already attained a high level of success in interpreting reflexive pronouns. Working with 22 adult native speakers of Japanese (with grammar scores on the Oxford Proficiency Test ranging from 'mid-intermediate' to 'very advanced'), Felser *et al.* report two key findings.

First, as a group, the L2 learners were as accurate in interpreting reflexive pronouns in a written questionnaire as a group of 21 English native speakers (96.1% versus 96.3%). This suggests that it is possible to suppress the Japanese protocol for processing reflexive pronouns, given sufficient experience and/or instruction.

Secondly, when reading sentences like those in Example 30, the Japanese speaking L2 learners slowed down at the reflexive pronoun in the second pattern, in which both names (*John* and *Richard*) match the gender of the reflexive pronoun. No such difference is seen in native speakers of English.

Example 30

(a) Jane said [Richard had cut himself with a very sharp knife].
(b) John said [Richard had cut himself with a very sharp knife].

The L2 learners appear to have been affected by the presence of the salient gender-matching NP *John* in the first clause of Example 30b – to the point where they temporarily considered it as a possible antecedent for the reflexive pronoun. This is exactly what one would expect if the sentence-level processor enjoys primacy (hence the consistent selection of the correct antecedent in comprehension tasks), but is not yet strong enough to pre-empt temporary activation of the pragmatic system (hence the slowdown).

In sum, native-like proficiency arguably involves more than just being able to produce and interpret sentences correctly. There is also the question of whether success is achieved via processing **routines** that are comparable in strength and efficiency to those employed by native speakers. As things now stand, there is some reason to think that even advanced second language learners fall short in this regard: in contrast to native speakers of English, their sentence-level routine apparently lacks the strength to suppress the pragmatic routine when a reflexive pronoun is encountered.[6] Instead both are activated, initiating a competition which is ultimately won by the sentence-level routine, but presumably at the cost of reduced efficiency.

Developmental profile for Japanese speaking learners of English

Beginning The processing protocol for reflexive pronouns that is transferred from Japanese offers two ways to interpret reflexive pronouns – one via the sentence-level processor and one via the pragmatic system. This incorrectly yields ambiguity in English sentences such as *Richard thinks Jerry overestimates himself.*

More advanced The balance tips in favor of the sentence-level processor, bringing an end to interpretive errors, but the pragmatic system continues to show significant activation in response to reflexive pronouns.

Conclusion: The Emergentist Story

Returning now to the two questions posed at the outset, we can summarize the emergentist approach to syntax and acquisition as follows.

(i) The syntax question: How are sentences built and interpreted?
Answer: Processing pressures shape the manner in which sentences are formed and comprehended. Reflexive pronouns are interpreted in the way they are because the sentence-level processor minimizes the burden on working memory by selecting an antecedent from within the same argument grid. The interpretation of plain pronouns is shaped by the pragmatic system's preference for antecedents that are contextually salient and hence easily accessible.

(ii) The acquisition question: How do children learn how sentences are built and interpreted?
Answer: The same processing pressures that govern the interpretation of pronouns in adults are present in children, directing them to particular interpretive choices. As the correctness of these choices is confirmed through ongoing experience with the language, the corresponding processing routine is strengthened and eventually entrenched.

By focusing on the role of processing pressures in shaping both language and learning, the emergentist program departs quite radically from the classic UG view. Indeed, if the ideas proposed here are on the right track, there are no inborn grammatical principles, traditional syntactic structure does not exist, and language acquisition consists of the formation of processing routines. These are jarring conclusions, of course, and they deserve to be treated with some skepticism. But they at least offer the opportunity to consider in a fresh light the nature of the human language faculty, opening the door for possible new insights regardless of what the final picture may turn out to be.

Notes

(1) Recent work has led to a reconceptualization of UG (e.g. Chomsky, 2005, 2011, 2013); see O'Grady (2012) for commentary. However, for the purposes of this chapter, I will focus on the classic UG system.

(2) The actual formulation of Principle A is considerably more technical ('A reflexive pronoun must be bound in its governing category'), but the simplified version will suffice for our purposes.

(3) For example, there is the fact that Charlotte is female and Richard male, that each is human, that the described event took place in the past, and so on.

(4) Note that nouns, like verbs, can have arguments and argument grids if they have the type of meaning that can be 'filled out' by some other element. In Example 17 *of himself* fills out the meaning of *picture* by specifying the person that the picture depicts.

(5) Clackson *et al.*'s results show a similar competition when a reflexive pronoun is heard, with the pragmatic system raising the possibility of a distant antecedent even as the sentence-level processor insists on an antecedent from within the same grid as the pronoun. Here, though, virtually no actual interpretive errors were observed, even in young children, suggesting a clear advantage for the sentence-level routine, presumably because of its very low cost.

(6) This seems to be true even for L2 learners whose native language is more similar to English than Japanese is. Felser and Cunnings (2012) report that native speakers of German, with reflexive pronouns very similar to those of English, also manifest over-activation of the pragmatic routine. This does not lead to actual errors, but does suggest that the sentence-level routine is not strong enough to fully suppress the pragmatic routine when a reflexive pronoun is encountered. See O'Grady (2013a) for some discussion.

4 Poverty of the Stimulus and Language Acquisition: From Ancient Philosophy to Neuroscience

Kook-Hee Gil, Heather Marsden and George Tsoulas

Introduction

Humans know a lot of things. Some of that knowledge is what we call *propositional* (**declarative**), meaning knowledge of facts such as 'H_2O boils at 100°C'. Other knowledge is **procedural**, which refers to knowledge of *how* to do something – to fix a leaking radiator, for example – which does not involve the knowledge of any specific proposition, but of a procedure by which to achieve something. From a different point of view, some of our knowledge is considered the result of explicit instruction or study. This is the case for our knowledge of history. But there is also knowledge that derives only from reason and does not derive from experience. While one needs instruction to know that 'Rome is in Italy', once you know that you also know that 'Rome is *not* in Mexico', without instruction. It is that last type of knowledge that falls generally within what Charles Darwin refers to in *The Descent of Man* (1871) as *instincts*, highlighting language as a prime example:

> [Language] certainly is not a true instinct, for every language has to be learnt. It differs, however, widely from all ordinary arts, for man has an instinctive tendency to speak, as we see in the babble of young children, whilst no child has an instinctive tendency to brew, bake, or write. (Darwin, 1871: 55)

Humans possess knowledge far more intricate and far more extensive than their interaction with the environment would allow. This is the 'Poverty of the Stimulus problem': the 'stimulus' (i.e. interaction with – or input from – the environment) does not provide enough evidence from which to deduce all of the knowledge of language or otherwise that a human eventually comes to have. The question of how Poverty of the Stimulus is overcome has occupied thinkers since antiquity, and various solutions have been put forward. In linguistic theory, Poverty of the Stimulus has been the central motivation for the proposal that language development must be shaped by innate linguistic knowledge. The aim of this chapter is, first, to explain the role played by the concept of Poverty of the Stimulus in theoretical linguistics, and then to illustrate how this concept has shaped research in first language (L1) acquisition, and therefore also why it is argued to be central in key theories of second language (L2) acquisition. We begin by briefly presenting the history of Poverty of the Stimulus in the broad context of **epistemology**, including knowledge of language. The next two sections then illustrate experimental studies in L1 and L2 acquisition, respectively, which are designed to investigate Poverty of the Stimulus phenomena and whose findings support the proposal that innate linguistic knowledge must account for language learners overcoming Poverty of the Stimulus problems.

From Geometry to Language: Illustrating Poverty of the Stimulus

Slave boys, music and virtue

The concept of the Poverty of the Stimulus goes back to the ancient Greek philosophers. In Plato's *Meno* (see Cooper, 1997), Socrates demonstrates how untutored individuals (using an uneducated slave boy as an example) can display complex geometrical knowledge, namely how to double the size of a square. All it takes for the demonstration is a few simple geometrical figures drawn in the sand and some skilful questioning by Socrates to bring out the knowledge that clearly exists *inside* the slave boy. How did he come to possess this knowledge without any explicit instruction in geometry? Plato's simple solution is to suggest that there is knowledge which has its origins within the individual human being, as part of human nature, and which does not derive in any meaningful way from experience. Crucially, Plato shows that this knowledge must be brought out through appropriate means, and that if it is left dormant it might not be expressed at all. Plato extended these ideas to other areas; in *Phaedrus* and *Republic* he extended it to the origins of aesthetic pleasure and moral virtue. Plato's philosophy underpins the assumption that the knowledge that humans display is far superior to what they can possibly have experienced, and therefore must be attributed to the human mind as an innate characteristic.

The issue of how humans know more than they experience has remained a subject of lively debate. Recent advances allow us to pose the question in areas beyond those where the issues were originally discussed. Music is such an example. Music seems to be a universal aspect of human behaviour and its connections to language are also very well established. The idea that language and music share syntactic resources is put forward by, among others, Patel (2008), Tsoulas (2010) and Katz and Pesetsky (2011), and is known as the '**identity thesis**' between language and music. It is based on evidence that humans seem to respond to elements of musical structure (rhythm, tonal structure, pitch) in the same instinctive and systematic way that they do to language. To understand all this in more detail, let us now turn to language.

Language

The claim about the role of innate knowledge has long been applied to language through the nativist or generative paradigm put forward principally by Noam Chomsky (e.g. 1959, 1965, 1975, 1986, 1995). The nativist account has argued that Plato's Problem, or Poverty of the Stimulus, exists in human knowledge of language. The Chomskyan proposal for language acquisition is as follows. Humans have a faculty of language, genetically determined, which allows them to acquire the natural language of the community they are growing up in, once they have contact with sufficient environmental stimulation, that is, linguistic input. Children typically acquire language remarkably effortlessly, relative to other types of knowledge development.

We can then ask: is the *stimulus* received in the form of linguistic input sufficient to determine the final form and content of the grammar acquired? The answer to this question is, in simple terms, *no*. The grammar children acquire has intricate properties for which they have not received enough explicit evidence (as we will illustrate below). Children are therefore capable of selecting the appropriate grammar for the language they are acquiring on the basis of incomplete evidence. How can children do that, if not helped by some kind of innate linguistic knowledge? Without such innate knowledge, Poverty of the Stimulus in the domain of language could not be overcome. This is, in informal terms, the argument for an innate linguistic system, based on Poverty of the Stimulus. This innate knowledge is often referred to as a 'language faculty' or '**language acquisition device**'. '**Universal Grammar**' (UG) is proposed as a component of the language faculty, offering a set of universal linguistic principles which constrain the development of grammar during language acquisition.

Other arguments, counter to this innatist proposal, suggest that (i) there is enough systematic information in the input and (ii) the child is endowed with learning mechanisms powerful enough to induce the complete grammar from the available input, rather than to deduce some of its aspects through innately given knowledge. For such a view, see the **emergentist** account presented in Chapter 3 of this volume.

Let us be clear: the debate is not about whether there is innate knowledge or not. The issues concern the nature of the innate knowledge – whether the innate knowledge is 'domain-general', meaning it applies to any area of cognitive development, or 'domain-specific', i.e. linguistic only. The domain-general view comes from **empiricist theory**, which holds that all knowledge arises primarily through experience. The domain-specific view comes from rationalist, or **nativist**, theory and, as the term 'nativist' suggests, holds that certain knowledge is hard wired from birth. Note here that the nativist view does not for a moment deny the existence of learning mechanisms, the statistical nature of learning or the fact that language acquisition is input/data driven (as some criticisms of the nativist approach have accused). The claim is that, in order to overcome Poverty of the Stimulus in language, there must, in addition, be innate knowledge that is specific to language.

Poverty of the Stimulus in language: An illustration

The basic logic of the Poverty of the Stimulus argument is simple. Let us assume that during language acquisition the child unconsciously makes hypotheses about his/her language based on the linguistic input. If the child appears to have selected the correct hypothesis (H) to analyze that input, *and also* she has no evidence either that confirms that H is indeed the correct hypothesis or that disconfirms any competing hypotheses, then it follows that the child must have prior, innate knowledge of H. Probably the best-known illustration of the argument involves the case of *yes/no* question formation in English, which involves **inversion** of the auxiliary verb and the subject, as in Example 1 (here and elsewhere, the blank line indicates the site where the auxiliary originates in a declarative sentence):

Example 1

(a) Has Millie _____ fed the cat?
(b) Are the children _____ sitting in the living room?

On the basis of sentences such as Example 1, the child may come up with many different hypotheses regarding the correct way to form *yes/no* questions, including the following, which is arguably the simplest:

Example 2
Move the first auxiliary to the front.

This hypothesis fails, however, as soon as we try to form a question in a sentence with a subject that includes a relative clause with an auxiliary:

Example 3

　　*Has the girl who _____ fed the cat is happy?

The ungrammatical question in Example 3 would be the result of fronting the first auxiliary according to the hypothesis in Example 2 to form a question from the following sentence:

Example 4

　　The girl who has fed the cat is happy.

Of course, the correct analysis for *yes/no* question formation relies on knowledge of linguistic structure, since questions are formed by fronting the auxiliary (or modal or copula) that follows the main clause subject NP of the sentence that is the basis of the interrogative (the main clause subject NP being *the girl who has fed the cat* in the case of Example 4). (See Chapter 1 for a full discussion of what we mean by linguistic structure and by level of embedding.) In other words, the correct hypothesis is **structure dependent** (where 'structure' refers to linguistic structure), unlike Example 2 which is dependent on linear order and not linguistic structure. In fact, children do not seem to entertain hypotheses like Example 2 (as we show below, discussing an important study by Crain & Nakayama, 1987). Since the input that children encounter does not come with labels about which part is a subject, or about the fact that the level of embedding of a clause affects linguistic operations, or even that these properties of language matter, the question arises as to what inhibits young children learning English from trying out Example 2. The nativist answer is that innate linguistic knowledge, and specifically knowledge of the structure dependence of language, rules out the child's trialling of a structure-independent hypothesis like Example 2. If children are born with the knowledge that linguistic operations are dependent upon linguistic structure (e.g. subject; main clause versus embedded clause, etc.), although the input itself does not come with any instruction about how to go about analyzing it, then the Poverty of the Stimulus in this case is overcome. Structure dependence is thus hypothesized to be a principle of UG.

The argument from the Poverty of the Stimulus that children's linguistic development is guided by an innate language faculty has motivated a considerable programme of research on L1 acquisition. This, in turn, has provided a rigorous foundation for investigation of L2 acquisition theories which suppose that all language acquisition, whether first or second, is constrained by the same innate faculty. The following two sections summarize experimental studies on syntax and semantics, whose findings show that in both L1 and L2 acquisition learners abide by structure-dependent rules and make constrained hypotheses about language.

Poverty of the Stimulus in First Language Acquisition

Children's knowledge of subject-auxiliary inversion: Crain and Nakayama (1987)

Crain and Nakayama aimed to test the proposal outlined above that children only make structure-dependent hypotheses about question formation, and do not try out hypotheses based on linear order. They set out the two hypotheses that a child might make: a structure-independent hypothesis (Example 5), which hinges on the linear order of elements in a sentence; and a structure-dependent hypothesis (Example 6), which could only operate if linguistic structure (i.e. in this case, the concepts of 'main clause' and 'subject') is innate.

Example 5 Hypothesis 1

In *yes/no* questions, the leftmost verbal element of a declarative (*is, can*, etc.) has been moved to the front of the sentence. (Crain & Nakayama, 1987: 525)

Example 6 Hypothesis 2

In *yes/no* questions, the auxiliary verb in the main clause of a declarative is inverted with the subject noun phrase. (Crain & Nakayama, 1987: 526)

To find out which hypothesis children apply, they conducted an experiment in which *yes/no* questions based on biclausal declarative sentences such as Example 7 were elicited from 30 children aged 3;2–5;11 (mean age 4;7).

Example 7

The dog that is sleeping is on the blue bench.

If children use a structure-independent hypothesis, then they will form ungrammatical questions in which the embedded clause auxiliary (i.e. the leftmost verbal element) is moved to the front, as in Example 8, whereas a structure-dependent hypothesis will result in the grammatical form in Example 9:

Example 8

*Is the dog that _____ sleeping is on the blue bench?

Example 9

Is the dog that is sleeping _____ on the blue bench?

To elicit the questions, an experimenter showed the child a picture to give the context (e.g. for Example 7, a picture showing two dogs, one asleep on a blue bench and the other standing up). Then the experimenter prompted the child to ask a question about the picture to a Jabba the Hutt toy figure, manipulated by a second experimenter, using the prompt *Ask Jabba if …* followed by the target declarative sentence (e.g. Example 7). The child then made the question, Jabba answered, and if the child judged that Jabba's answer was right, the child got to reward him by feeding him. Note that it is the child's question formation and not the child's judgement of Jabba's answer that is of interest to the researchers. However, including judgement of the answer and then some kind of reward for the puppet turned the experiment into a game for the children, and thus made it more likely that they would remain interested.

Analysis of the results yielded 60% grammatical question formation and 40% ungrammatical. However, among the ungrammatical answers, none was of the form given in Example 8. Instead, the ungrammatical questions were of two main types: either they involved an extra auxiliary, so that the question started with an auxiliary but then still retained both the embedded and the main clause auxiliaries (Example 10); or they involved a restart containing a pronoun (Example 11):

Example 10

   *Is the dog that is sleeping is on the blue bench?

Example 11

   *Is the dog that is sleeping, is he on the blue bench?

These results are compatible with Hypothesis 2, the structure-dependent hypothesis. However, Crain and Nakayama went on to conduct a follow-up experiment designed to test whether the 'extra-auxiliary' questions such as Example 10 could, after all, be evidence in support of Hypothesis 1. Specifically, if the auxiliary at the front of such questions were found to be a copy of the embedded auxiliary, this would support Hypothesis 1, since it would suggest that children were using some kind of linear, structure-independent rule whereby the first verbal element plays a role in question formation. The second experiment thus used biclausal utterances in which the embedded verb differed from the main clause verb, as in Example 12.

Example 12

   The boy who can see Mickey Mouse is happy.

The participants in the second experiment were 10 of the children who had made 'extra auxiliary' errors in Experiment 1. It was predicted that, if they were using a structure-independent, linear strategy to create the extra auxiliary questions, then they would produce ungrammatical questions such as Example 13, in which the modal *can* occurs twice:

Example 13
> *Can the boy who can see Mickey Mouse is happy?

The results of the second experiment showed a high rate of errors in the children's production, with only seven 'correct' responses (e.g. *Is the boy who can see Mickey Mouse happy?*) out of the 34 elicited. Errors included restarts and idiosyncratic errors (e.g. *The boy should be sleeping is snoring?*), as well as six utterances that were ambiguous with regard to whether the child's question could have been formed via Hypothesis 1 or by another strategy. However, it is significant that there were no instances of questions like Example 13. Thus, overall, the findings did not provide evidence that children's hypotheses about question formation are based on a linear strategy involving moving the first verbal element to the front. Rather, they suggest that acquisition of subject-auxiliary inversion is constrained by structure dependence.

Infants' knowledge of syntax and semantics: Lidz *et al.* (2003)

Lidz *et al.* (2003) also investigated knowledge of structure dependence in children, using a different phenomenon. Their experimental study investigated infants (aged 16–18 months) rather than children of age three or above and, additionally, they used corpus data to ascertain that the input children encounter could not be the sole source of their eventual knowledge. The phenomenon investigated is interpretation of the **anaphoric** pronoun *one*, as in Example 14 (Lidz *et al.*, 2003: B67):

Example 14
> I'll play with this red ball and you can play with that one.

Linguists agree, as discussed in Chapter 1, that in adult grammar a full NP containing a determiner, adjective and noun has the hierarchical structure illustrated in Example 15a below, and not the flat structure of Example 15b (Baker, 1978):

Example 15
> (a) Hierarchical structure   (b) Flat structure

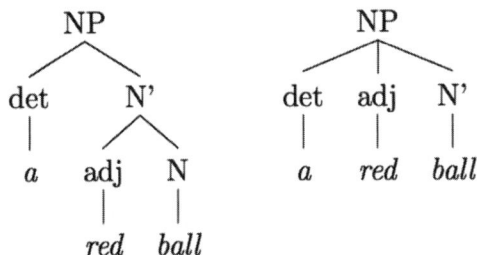

The anaphor *one* can replace a nominal element, which can be a full NP or a subconstituent of that NP. The nominal constituents of NP in Example 15a include the N' *red ball* and the N *ball*:

Example 16

(a) Did you see a red ball?
(b) Yes, I saw that one. (*one* = red ball)
(c) No, I saw a green one. (*one* = ball)

However, in the flat structure in Example 15b, *red ball* cannot be isolated as a constituent in its own right, therefore *red ball* could not be replaced by *one* (i.e. the answer shown in Example 16b would not be possible). Lidz *et al.* (2003) investigated what infants understand *one* to refer to, in order to find out whether the internal structure of NP in child grammar is adult-like (Example 15a) or whether children entertain other hypotheses including the non-hierarchical representations like Example 15b or that *one* is anaphoric only to N.

One possibility is that children could start out allowing any structure, and that eventual rejection of a flat structure – if that is what the child hypothesizes – could be driven by input that provided evidence that the flat structure is incorrect. The question here is whether it is reasonable to assume that such input both exists and is frequent enough for the child to notice it and therefore revise her initial hypothesis of a flat structure, given that the correct adult grammar is the one with hierarchical structure. Suppose, for example, that a child's initial hypotheses are that *one* is anaphoric just to N, within a flat structure (and therefore not anaphoric to N'). What sort of evidence should the input provide in order to lead the child to revise these hypotheses? Take a sentence like Example 17. Assume further that Example 17 is uttered in a context where Max has a blue ball:

Example 17

Chris has a red ball but Max doesn't have one. (Lidz *et al.*, 2003: B67)

In this context, what *one* is meant to refer to is a 'red ball'. This type of sentence, assuming it was frequent enough, would be sufficient to lead the child to revise the hypothesis that *one* is anaphoric to N alone since this would lead to the interpretation that Max has no ball at all, contrary to what is known from the context. But even though the child is led to reject the hypothesis that *one* is anaphoric only to ball, even these sentences are not sufficient evidence in order to reject the flat structure hypothesis since the child might simply assume that *one* is anaphoric to the whole NP. This is easy in the case at hand since we have the indefinite article *a*; given the semantic vacuousness of the indefinite article *a*, anaphora to N' and anaphora to NP cannot be disambiguated by the context as is the case with anaphora to the N alone. Lidz *et al.* (2003) conducted a corpus analysis of parental speech directed at two children in the CHILDES database of child language. Among 54,800 parental utterances, they identified 792 sentences that contain *one* used anaphorically. Among these, only two cases (0.2% of the anaphoric cases) belong to a context where *one* refers unambiguously to the element of the category N' (as in Example 17). What this means is that the evidence that would lead the child to revise a potential initial hypothesis of a flat structure is vanishingly rare. Given that children unfailingly converge on the correct adult grammar which contains the hierarchical structure, it follows that the most reasonable conclusion from the above discussion is that the child never actually entertains either the hypothesis of a flat structure or the hypothesis that *one* is anaphoric only to N. The corpus study confirms that acquisition of NPs, and the concomitant adult-like use of *one*, is a clear Poverty of the Stimulus problem. The correct grammar cannot be achieved by the child without prior knowledge of linguistic structure.

The next step in Lidz *et al.*'s (2003) study was an experimental investigation of knowledge of anaphoric use of *one* in 18-month-old children, using a **preferential looking task**. Notice that the children at this age are likely to still be at the two-word stage of language development: they may not yet be producing sentences. Twenty-four infants participated in the experiment. The procedure began with a familiarization phase where the children were shown a single object (e.g. a yellow bottle) three times in either the left or the right side of a television monitor, accompanied by a recorded voice naming the object. After this familiarization phase, a test phase followed, in which infants experienced either the control condition or the anaphoric condition. In the anaphoric condition, each infant was shown two objects of a category used in the familiarization phase (e.g. bottles), one on each side of the monitor. One was the same colour as the familiarization object (e.g. a yellow bottle) and the other was a different colour (e.g. a blue bottle). The difference between the two conditions was the linguistic stimulus, and the infants were observed to see which object they looked at in response to the linguistic stimulus. The infants in the control condition heard a neutral phrase such as '*Now look. What do you see now?*', which does not trigger any preference towards either of the objects. Thus the prediction for the control group was that they would prefer to look at the novel image (the blue bottle). In the anaphoric group, on the other hand, the infants heard a phrase containing anaphoric *one*, such as '*Now look, do you see another one?*'. Given such a linguistic stimulus, the infants' looking pattern should reveal what they perceive to be a potential referent of *one*, thus demonstrating what their structural representation of the NP is. The prediction is that if the infants assume the flat structure in which *one* would have to refer to the N category bottle, then both objects (the yellow bottle and the blue bottle) will be potential referents. In this case, the infants are predicted to behave in the same way as the control group and look at the novel object, the blue bottle. However, if the infants assume the nested structure, they are predicted to pick out the N' category (yellow bottle) as the potential referent of *one*, and thus look at the yellow bottle.

The results supported the predictions. The control group tended to devote more attention to the novel object (the blue bottle), compared to the familiar object (the yellow bottle). In the anaphoric group, however, this pattern was reversed, and infants showed a preference for looking at the familiar object (the yellow bottle). The results reveal that 18-month-old infants interpret *one* as anaphoric to the N' category and thus they represent the nested structure for NP (Example 15a). In other words, they have the relevant aspects of the adult grammar, that is, structure dependent representations, from the outset. Taken together with the finding from the corpus study that the input lacks sufficient evidence to ever motivate rejection of a flat structure should *one* be hypothesized, this study strongly suggests that infants' representation of the nested NP structure is not input driven, but rather is inherent in their linguistic knowledge.

Poverty of the Stimulus in semantics: Gualmini (2005)

Now we outline an investigation of the Poverty of the Stimulus in the domain of semantics. Specifically, the investigation focuses on **quantifying** words, which include the words *some, none* and *any*. Gualmini (2005) conducted a number of experimental investigations of children's knowledge of a property known as '**downward entailment**'. The findings reveal that children have knowledge of very subtle and complex semantic properties that pose severe Poverty of the Stimulus problems.

A linguistic expression has the property of downward entailment if it permits ('licenses') logical inferences from the main proposition to its subsets (hence 'downward'). To illustrate this, the quantified expression [*none of the* N] in the two sentences in Example 18 is a downward-entailing expression. If Example 18a is true, then the listener can infer (⇒) that the subset claim in Example 18b is also true.

Example 18

(a) None of the students has written a paper yet.
(b) ⇒ None of the students has written a good paper yet.

This contrasts with other kinds of NP expressions shown in Examples 19 and 20, in which neither the referential NP *John* nor **the existentially quantified** NP *some of the students* allows a similar inference (⇏). Therefore these are not downward-entailing expressions.

Example 19

John has written a paper.
⇏ John has written a good paper.

Example 20

> Some of the students have written a paper.
> ⇏ Some of the students have written a good paper.

Another important rule about downward-entailing expressions such as *none of the* N is that they can be used in negatively linked expressions (so-called **polarity**-sensitive items, such as *any*), whereas non-downward-entailing expressions like *some* cannot (as in Example 21). They can also yield a conjunctive (*and*) interpretation of the disjunctive connector *or* Example 22a. This is in direct contrast to non-downward-entailing expressions, where the opposite situation occurs: *or* can only receive a disjunctive interpretation (Example 22b).

Example 21

(a) None of the students saw anyone.
(b) *John saw anyone/*Some of the students saw anyone.

Example 22

(a) None of the students ate the cake or drank the coffee.
> ⇒ None of the students ate the cake AND none of the students drank the coffee.
> ⇏ None of the students ate the cake OR none of the students drank the coffee.
(b) John (Some of the students) ate the cake or drank the coffee.
> ⇒ John (Some of the students) ate the cake OR John (some of the students) drank the coffee.
> ⇏ John (Some of the students) ate the cake AND John (some of the students) drank the coffee.

Gualmini identifies acquisition of the complex set of distributional and interpretive effects of downward-entailing expressions as a Poverty of the Stimulus problem. Ultimate L1 knowledge of all of the relevant facts, such as those presented in Examples 18–22, is underdetermined by the evidence that children encounter in the input. For example, it is difficult to see how induction from the input alone could lead to a grammar that allows a conjunctive interpretation of *or* in Example 22a but not in Example 22b. Gualmini argues that, if children show adult-like knowledge of the facts of downward-entailing expressions, this supports the argument for UG (see Gualmini, 2005 and references therein, for theoretical linguistic accounts of the data presented here, and proposals about how exactly UG may guide the acquisition of downward entailment).

Gualmini investigated children's knowledge of downward entailment by means of a number of **truth-value judgement tasks**. We summarize just one here, whose focus is the interpretation of *or* as a conjunctive in the scope of the *none of the* N, as in Example 23:

Example 23

None of the pirates found the jewel or the necklace.

Thirty children aged 3;10–5;10 (mean age, 4;07) took part in the study. In order to find out about their interpretation of sentences like Example 23, a story context was presented, and then a puppet commented on the story, and included the target sentence for judgement in his commentary. Thus, for Example 23, the story involved an Indian and some pirates. The Indian hides three knives, a jewel and a gold necklace in barrels in his camp, to try to safeguard them from a band of pirates. Three pirates then enter the camp and search for treasure. Each pirate finds a knife, and they are about to leave the camp when one of them decides to have one more look, and at that point finds the jewel. The puppet then comments:

Example 24

This was a story about an Indian and some pirates, and I know what happened. Every pirate found a knife, but **none of the pirates found the jewel or the necklace.**

The child indicates his or her judgement by giving the puppet a reward if the puppet's statement is correct or a 'punishment' if the statement is false. The target statement in Example 24 is false, under an adult interpretation (i.e. none of the pirates found both the jewel AND the necklace). Thus, if the downward-entailing property of *none of the* N is part of child grammar, then children should reject the puppet's utterance. This is indeed what Gualmini (2005) found. The task included four exemplars of target utterances like Example 23, as well as **filler** test items. The children's mean rate of adult-like rejection of the target sentences was 87.5%. Gualmini argues that this provides evidence for UG constraint of children's acquisition of downward entailment. The rationale for the argument is that, if children had to acquire such subtle phenomena through trial and error, with no internal constraint on the range of possible hypotheses, it would not be expected that by age four children already demonstrate almost adult-like knowledge of downward entailment.

The studies outlined in this section are only a small part of the now large database of evidence from experimental studies that children's linguistic development is constrained by innate linguistic principles (e.g. Crain & Thornton, 1998; Crain *et al.*, 2000; de Villiers & Roeper, 2011; Eisenbeiss, 2009; Musolino *et al.*, 2000; Thornton & Wexler, 1999; Wexler, 1990; Yang, 2002, 2004). In the next section, we turn to the question of whether the same innate principles apply in L2 acquisition.

Poverty of the Stimulus in Second Language Acquisition

Poverty of the Stimulus also arises in L2 acquisition (Schwartz & Sprouse, 2000; White, 1989, 2003). However, in L2 acquisition, identifying a Poverty of the Stimulus problem is more complex than in L1 acquisition. This is because L2 learners already possess linguistic knowledge in the form of their L1. It is well documented that the L1 grammar influences L2 development, although the precise nature of L1 influence is a topic of ongoing debate and research (e.g. Ionin & Montrul, 2010; Marsden, 2009; Odlin, 1989; Schwartz & Sprouse, 1994, 1996; Slabakova, 2000; Tsimpli & Dimitrakopoulou, 2007; Yu & Odlin, 2015, among many others; see also Kahoul *et al.* in this volume). This means that that a Poverty of the Stimulus problem for L1 learners of a particular language X cannot be considered to be a Poverty of the Stimulus problem for L2 learners of X when the L1 and the L2 both share the same grammatical phenomenon. In this scenario, the learners may already 'know' the target grammar via transfer from their L1. An additional factor that differentiates L2 acquisition from L1 acquisition concerns the input: L2 learners in a classroom setting are likely to encounter explicit instruction about many properties of the target language. A phenomenon that is explicitly taught in the classroom cannot also be categorized as a Poverty of the Stimulus problem. Thus, in L2 acquisition, learners face a Poverty of the Stimulus problem only when the target grammatical property is underdetermined by the input – including classroom instruction – and also does not form part of the L1 grammar. Fortunately for the researcher, there are enough such cases to allow exploration of the Poverty of the Stimulus in L2 acquisition.

Investigation of whether the Poverty of the Stimulus can be overcome in L2 acquisition forms an important body of L2 acquisition research. This is because it has a bearing on a key question in the field: is L2 knowledge – particularly that of adults – epistemologically the same as L1 knowledge? One influential view, the **Fundamental Difference Hypothesis** (Bley-Vroman, 1989, 1990, 2009) proposes that, for post-puberty learners, L2 knowledge is not of the same type as L1 knowledge. According to this view, whereas L1 grammar grows out of innate linguistic knowledge prior to a **critical period**, usually around puberty, L2 grammar when learned after childhood is no different from other learned skills such as how to play chess. If this view is correct, then it would be expected that older learners cannot overcome Poverty of the Stimulus in L2 acquisition, since they presumably would not be able to make use of the innate linguistic mechanisms proposed to account for L1 acquisition. On the other hand, if L2 learners can acquire subtle linguistic phenomena in the target language for which there is no direct evidence in the input or from their L1, this would be evidence that L2 acquisition is constrained by Universal Grammar in the same way as L1 acquisition.

A number of L2 acquisition studies provide such evidence. While many of these focus on Poverty of the Stimulus problems in the L2 acquisition of languages other than English (e.g. Dekydtspotter *et al.*, 2001; Kanno, 1997, 1998; Marsden, 2008, 2009), we outline two Poverty of the Stimulus studies on L2 English about similar phenomena discussed above for L1 children. The first, Yusa *et al.* (2011), relates to the topic of structure dependence, discussed above. The second, by Gil and Marsden (2010), is about acquisition of constraints on the distribution of the polarity item *any*.

Structure dependence in second language acquisition: Yusa *et al.* (2011)

Yusa *et al.* (2011) investigated whether Japanese speakers studying English obey structure dependence when acquiring literary-style fronting of negative adverbs such as *never*. This type of fronting, shown in Example 25a, triggers inversion of the auxiliary *will* with the subject *I*, while Example 25b is the standard version of the same sentence in which no auxiliary movement occurs. Example 25c shows that, without subject-auxiliary inversion, the sentence starting with *Never* is ungrammatical. Example 25d shows that fronting of other adverbs, such as *often*, does not trigger subject-auxiliary inversion.

Example 25

(a) *Never* will I _____ eat sushi.
(b) I will *never* eat sushi.
(c) **Never* I will eat sushi.
(d) **Often* will I _____ eat sushi. (But, *Often, I will eat sushi.*)

As with acquisition of subject-auxiliary inversion in L1 English, acquisition of '**negative inversion**' appears superficially as if it could involve structure-independent rules along the lines of 'place *never* at the front, followed by the leftmost verbal element'. However, in more complex multi-clause sentences, such a rule does not work, as shown in Example 26.

Example 26

(a) [Those students who will fail a test] are *never* hardworking in class.
(b) **Never* will [those students who _____ fail a test] are hardworking in class.
(c) *Never* are [those students who will fail a test] _____ hardworking in class.

If the above structure-independent rule is applied to Example 26a, the result is the ungrammatical sentence in Example 26b. The leftmost verbal element is the auxiliary *will* inside the relative clause, but to create a grammatical negative inversion structure it is the main clause auxiliary that must move to the front after *never*, as shown in Example 26c. Thus, just like question formation, acquisition of negative inversion involves concepts of linguistic structure, namely subject and clause level.

Yusa *et al.* (2011) argue that negative inversion is underdetermined by the input for Japanese learners of English. There is no comparable structure in Japanese, so negative inversion could not transfer directly from the L1. Moreover, the construction is infrequent in the input, due to it being a literary form, so it is unlikely that learners could acquire it through general exposure to English. Nor is it covered in English language textbooks (Yusa *et al.*, 2011: 2718). Yusa *et al.* (2011) hypothesized that, if the UG principle of structure dependence is available in adult L2 acquisition, then Japanese-speaking learners of English will be able to acquire the facts shown in Example 26 (i.e. that Example 26c is grammatical but Example 26b is not), even if they do not encounter direct evidence of negative inversion in complex sentences in the input.

They tested this hypothesis by conducting a study with two groups of 20 adult Japanese students enrolled at a university in Japan. All participants had begun learning English at around age 12 after the critical period. One of the two groups (the 'Instructed Group') was given instruction on negative inversion in simple monoclausal sentences, but crucially the instruction did not cover negative inversion in multi-clause complex sentences containing relative clauses. The instruction took place over eight one-hour training sessions during a one-month period. The role of instruction was to make sure the learners were exposed to this construction, given its rarity. The training sessions ran alongside the group's regular English classes. The second group (the 'Non-instructed Group') also followed regular English classes, but did not receive any training on negative inversion. Prior to the start of instruction, both groups participated in a pre-test to investigate their existing knowledge (if any) of negative inversion in monoclausal and complex sentences. The same test was taken again as a post-test, following the instruction period.

The test itself involved **grammaticality judgements**, which the participants made while undergoing **functional magnetic resonance imaging (fMRI)** scans. Thus, both intuitional data and neurolinguistic data were obtained. The sentences for judgement included both simple (monoclausal) and complex negative inversion sentences, with grammatical and ungrammatical tokens of each (i.e. sentences along the lines of those shown in Examples 25 and 26). In addition, grammatical and ungrammatical control sentences were included, which contained *never* in a non-fronted position.

The key finding from the grammaticality judgement task was that, for the Instructed Group, there was a statistically significant drop in the error rates on the negative inversion sentences – in both grammatical and ungrammatical – between the pre-test and the post-test.

Most interestingly, this drop occurred on the complex sentences, about which the group had received no instruction, as well as on the simple sentences. By contrast, the Non-instructed Group showed no significant difference between the pre-test and the post-test on any of the negative inversion sentence types. Taken together, the findings suggest that, after exposure to the negative inversion through monoclausal sentences, the Instructed Group's L2 development was guided by innate knowledge of structure dependence which could be applied even to complex structures they had not encountered in the instruction.

The key finding from the neuroimaging data was evidence, found in the Instructed Group but not the Non-instructed Group, of significant activation in an area of the brain known as the left inferior frontal gyrus, for the complex negative inversion sentences at the post-test compared with the pre-test. Other studies (see Yusa *et al.*, 2011) provide evidence that this area of the brain is implicated in the acquisition of syntactic rules in L1 development, as well as in L2 development including for older learners. This finding thus suggests that the underlying syntactic knowledge of the L2 learners in Yusa *et al.*'s study had undergone change following their instruction on negative inversion on simple sentences, and that L2 syntactic knowledge is epistemologically the same as L1 syntactic knowledge.

In terms of L2 Poverty of the Stimulus, the two sets of findings together suggest that learners were able to go beyond the input they received (i.e. the instruction about negative inversion in simple sentences), extrapolating this to complex sentences, without entertaining structure-independent hypotheses. In other words, the findings suggest that the UG principle of structure dependence continues to apply in adult L2 acquisition. If structure dependence were not available in L2 acquisition, then the learners would not have been able to differentiate between grammatical negative inversion in complex sentences (Example 26c), in which the main clause auxiliary was inverted with the subject, and ungrammatical sentences (Example 26b), in which the first auxiliary in the sentence was moved to follow the fronted adverb *never*.

Properties of quantifiers in second language acquisition: Gil and Marsden (2010)

In Gil and Marsden (2010), Korean learners' knowledge of the English polarity item *any* is investigated. As mentioned in page 62, *any* in English can only occur in certain semantic environments. Gil and Marsden follow Giannakidou (1998) and assume that *any* can occur in contexts that are 'non-veridical', meaning contexts that do not correspond to actual events. Thus *any* is grammatical in environments such as interrogatives and conditionals (Example 27), but *any* is ungrammatical in veridical contexts (which *do* correspond to actual events), including progressives and episodics (Example 28) (Gil & Marsden, 2010: 41).

Example 27

(a) Is *anyone* playing the piano?   (Interrogative)
(b) If *anyone* crosses the finish line, raise the flag.   (Conditional)

Example 28

(a) *Anyone is playing the piano.   (Progressive)
(b) *Anyone went to the party.   (Episodic)

For Korean-speaking learners of English, acquiring the *ungrammati-cality* of *any* in sentences such as Example 28 meets the set of criteria that identify an L2 Poverty of the Stimulus problem. First, learners' naturalistic exposure to English will not include examples that illustrate where *any* is ungrammatical. Additional sources of linguistic evidence in L2 acquisition include the learners' L1, as well as classroom instruction. However, for Korean learners, their L1 equivalents of *any* – known as *wh*-indefinites – are not subject to such distributional restrictions that apply in English. *Wh*-indefinites in Korean share the same morphophonological forms with *wh*-question words but, in addition to their *wh*-word function, they are also interpreted as indefinites, e.g. *nwu(kwu)* ('who/someone/anyone'), *mwues* ('what/something/anything'). Korean *wh*-indefinites can occur both in non-veridical contexts, as in Examples 29a and 29b, and in veridical contexts (Example 29c):

Example 29

(a) *Nwu*-ka   cha-lul   masiko   iss-nayo?   (Interrogative)
      who-NOM   tea-ACC   drink   prog-Q
      'Is anyone drinking tea?'

(b) *Nwu*-ka   sen-ul   nemu-myen,   kispal-ul   tul-era.   (Conditional)
      who-NOM   line-ACC   cross-COND   flag-ACC   raise-IMP
      'If anyone crosses the line, raise the flag.'

(c) *Nwu*-ka   piano-lul   yencwu   hako-issta.   (Progressive)
      who-NOM   piano-ACC   play   do-PROG
      'Someone (*anyone) is playing the piano.'

Consequently, the ungrammaticality of English *any* in Example 28 cannot be inferred from L1 Korean. That is, if Korean learners transferred the distributional property of *wh*-indefinites to *any*, this would result in a wrong assumption that *any* in Example 28 is grammatical just as the *wh*-indefinite is in Example 29c in Korean. Finally, classroom instruction could be another potential source of evidence for L2 learners about the restrictions on the use of *any*. However, although English language textbooks often include information about the distributional patterns of *any*, this is limited to presentation of some of the most frequent *grammatical* contexts for *any*, namely negation and interrogatives. Crucially, they do not provide instruction about the contexts (such as progressives) where *any* **cannot** occur. This means that, if learners unconsciously make the wrong assumption that *any* behaves like Korean *wh*-indefinites, textbooks do not provide information that might change that assumption. To sum up, Korean learners face an L2 Poverty of the Stimulus problem in acquiring the distributional restrictions on *any* since direct evidence about this distribution is not found in the L2 input, via the L1 or from classroom instruction.

Gil and Marsden (2010) tested Korean learners of English using a grammaticality judgement task that included three sentence types: progressive, conditional and interrogative; we focus here just on the data relating to the Poverty of the Stimulus. The participants were 22 Korean learners at upper-intermediate English proficiency level: all were resident in the UK at the time of testing and all had been exposed to English after the end of the critical period. The key finding in group terms was that, while Korean learners correctly accepted the grammatical instances of *any* in interrogatives and conditionals, they also wrongly accepted ungrammatical instances of *any* in progressives, at a rate of >84%. These results immediately suggest L1 influence. Korean learners allowed *any* in all of the three environments investigated, just as if *any* had the properties of a Korean *wh*-indefinite. The group result thus suggests that the learners did not overcome Poverty of the Stimulus.

However, a participant-by-participant analysis revealed that there were two individual learners who were target-like in that they consistently rejected the ungrammatical instances of *any* in progressives, while accepting *any* in interrogatives and conditionals. These individuals thus displayed unambiguous knowledge of the distributional restriction on *any*, despite Poverty of the Stimulus. Strikingly, the biographical data on these two learners showed that, of all the participants in the study, they had had longest residence in the UK. While the group average duration of residence was three years, the residence lengths of these two individuals were 10 years and six years. These two learners, then, had been exposed to more (naturalistic) input, in comparison with the other learners in the study. In short, the individual analysis suggests that acquisition of the distributional properties of *any* is possible despite Poverty of the Stimulus, albeit only with exposure to rich and prolonged L2 input. A crucial point to note is that even rich and prolonged L2 input does not provide direct evidence of the contexts in which *any* is ungrammatical. Therefore, the ungrammaticality of *any* in progressives cannot be induced from the input. In fact, acquisition of the distribution of *any* is a Poverty of the Stimulus problem for children acquiring English as their L1, as well as in L2 English by Korean speaking learners. Gil and Marsden (2010) assume that whatever innate linguistic knowledge must necessarily facilitate acquisition of this phenomenon in L1 English is also available to facilitate acquisition in L2 English – once sufficient relevant data from the input has been processed. The richer and more prolonged exposure experienced by the two learners who rejected *any* in progressives had presumably furnished enough of the relevant stimulus for the target-like knowledge to emerge, mediated by UG. The two studies outlined in this section thus illustrate how the concept of Poverty of the Stimulus has informed experimental investigation of L2 acquisition, and the findings provide evidence that L2 knowledge is epistemologically the same as L1 knowledge.

Conclusion

The notion that developmental outcomes are underdetermined by experience is virtually uncontroversial in the whole field of human biology. In the field of the study of the development of language, taking this statement seriously has given rise to an extremely productive research programme which has led to some of the most important discoveries regarding the nature and acquisition of language, opening up the possibility of detailed empirical investigation of the language-specific, innately specified part of the human cognitive architecture. We have given in this chapter an overview of some recent work covering Poverty of the Stimulus effects in the acquisition of both a first and a second language, by adults. But the idea discussed here, that the input received by the young language learner is significantly less than is required for her to attain the adult grammar, has come frequently under fire in various forms. In the main, the Poverty of the Stimulus detractors claim that the input is amply sufficient and can lead to the adult grammar only with help from general learning mechanisms, that there are statistical algorithms which could learn specific constructions from some input or, finally, that the argument itself is not well formulated or unclear. However, the debate that can be achieved at present is limited since there is no sufficiently explicit theory with significant empirical coverage and which uses only independently required domain-general mechanisms that we can set against the theory that we have presented here. This state of affairs makes the interpretation of results from statistical studies very difficult as there is no general framework where they can be neatly incorporated. We refer the reader to Gil, Marsden and Tsoulas (in preparation) for further elaboration on these points.

5 Language Evolution and the Nature of the Human Faculty for Language

Andrew Feeney

Introduction

It has often been claimed that the human faculty for language (FL) is the only unique ability that distinguishes *Homo sapiens* from all other species. Indeed the origin of human language has been the object of fascination throughout history. In the 7th century BCE, the Egyptian King Psamtik I was reported to have isolated two children at birth to discover which language they would spontaneously produce and which, it was concluded, was therefore the 'natural' language of humankind (it was claimed that the first sounds they produced resembled the word 'bread' in Phrygian, a now extinct language that was spoken in parts of modern-day Turkey). Along with several other similar 'experiments' there is a tradition of meditation and speculation on the origins of language, from Plato's 4th century BCE *Cratylus* dialogue, which discusses how words arose and the extent to which they have natural or purely arbitrary relationships to their real world referents, continuing into ensuing centuries to far less esteemed and wilder speculations, such as claims that language originated out of early hominims' cries of pain, grunts from heavy lifting or their imitations of sounds in the environment (for brief overviews see, for example, Fromkin *et al.*, 2013; McMahon & McMahon, 2012). It was, in fact, in response to the plethora of such speculations that the Linguistic Society of Paris included Article 2 in its statutes in 1866, which stipulated that 'La Société n'admet aucune communication concernant, soit l'origine du langage, soit la création d'une langue universelle' (*The Society does not accept articles on either the origin of language or on the creation of a universal language*).

For much of the 20th century, a time when linguistics was anxious to strengthen its reputation as a 'scientific' discipline, discussion of the origins of language were infrequent and it was not until the 1970s that the topic began to be rehabilitated (e.g. Bickerton, 1981; Lieberman, 1975).

Then, seminal papers such as Pinker and Bloom's (1990) argument that the evolution of the human FL can be explained by gradual **Darwinian** natural selection (see discussion below) sparked a renewed, vigorous interest in language evolution which has resulted in a vast output of research in recent years. However, despite (or possibly because of) such an intensity of investigation, there remains much that is either not fully understood or is hotly disputed. Reviewing the evolutionary linguistics field in 2007, Bickerton concludes that there are only four things that researchers generally agree on: first, language emerged somewhere between 3.5 million years ago (mya) and 50 thousand years ago (kya); secondly, the earliest form of language was a much simpler '**protolanguage**' than the complex systems of today (although there is much disagreement concerning its nature); thirdly, there was some **selective pressure** that enabled language to spread – probably social intelligence of some form; and finally there is some relationship between the evolution of language and of cognition more generally. As broad as these tenets are, there is not even acceptance by all researchers of these – Bickerton himself, for example, is adamant that social intelligence was not the adaptive factor in language evolution.

The reasons why there is so much disagreement in the field are not difficult to fathom since they arise from the cross-disciplinary nature of the investigation as well as from the paucity of palaeontological evidence and the total absence of any linguistic evidence per se from the periods at the heart of the question. Spoken language leaves no fossil trace, and the earliest known writing systems at approximately 6000 years old are far too recent to shed light on the origins of language. Furthermore, even the scant fossil record of our ancestors that we do have contains no direct fossils of the vital organs involved in speech and language: the brain, the respiratory organs (although see MacLarnon, 2012, for some evidence of fossilization in relation to breathing control) and the vocal apparatus. In addition to this, the study of language evolution involves contributions from disciplines as diverse as evolutionary biology, palaeontology and its subgroup palaeobiology, anthropology, physiology, neuroscience, genetics, primatology and computer science, as well as linguistics. There are disagreements in each of these fields, and breakthroughs and discoveries in any one discipline can have a significant knock-on effect in the study of language evolution (for an extensive overview see papers in Tallerman & Gibson, 2012).

In this chapter we will begin by looking at some of the evidence from a number of these contributory disciplines and how they add to an understanding of hominin evolution. We will then review current theories of language evolution against the criteria of the most plausible explanation or 'abduction' that can be made about the nature of the FL which is commensurate with the scarce evolutionary data available. This will involve a consideration of three possible explanations of language evolution as outlined in Table 5.1. The first two, based on innate theories of the FL, often

Table 5.1 Possible accounts of language evolution

	Gradual	Sudden
Module of the mind	A	B
Sociocultural system	C	

referred to as '**nativist**', are: (A) a module of the mind/brain for language evolved in a Darwinian-like manner, through natural selection; (B) a module of the mind/brain for language emerged suddenly (in evolutionary terms). A range of non-nativist hypotheses are included in the third option (C) that language itself evolved as a **domain-general**, sociocultural system, possibly adapting to the learning biases of the hominin brain (as assumed in Chapter 2 in this volume). A fourth option that language appeared suddenly with no **domain-specific** modification to the brain is ruled out as beyond the limits of plausibility. As we shall see, there are also problems with each of the first three scenarios. However, because there is little doubt that the human FL is special, researchers will continue to search for clues to how language evolved.

The Evolution of Modern Humans

The nature of evolution

Before we consider the evolution of the FL, let us look briefly at what we know about how evolution is currently thought to take place, in order to understand its relevance to human language. Evolution requires imperfect heredity, i.e. offspring which are not exact genetic copies of a parent. This is what leads to variation in a species and to evolution. This variation enables members of a species to compete for resources; when they succeed, this results in the opportunity to replicate themselves with this new genetic variation. This is what is known as the process of natural selection; it ensures that those organisms which are more finely adapted to their given environment are more likely to reproduce, further spreading the modified gene or **allele**, which conferred the advantage of that adaptation, to spread through that group of the species. On the basis that major changes would be harmful (an often-used analogy is making large, random changes to a car engine) or even lethal to the organism, evolution is presumed to be gradual and incremental (for a comprehensive discussion, see Ridley, 2004). However, while no-one doubts the role of evolution by incremental, advantageous changes in natural selection, it is by no means the whole picture. A number of mechanisms, complementary to natural selection, are generally recognized by researchers. These include random genetic drift, where alleles that offer no competitive advantage are still likely to be distributed among the population. Similarly, a neutral or negative trait could survive if it is correlated with a positive one. Thus features that emerged under one **adaptive pressure** that may eventually bestow an advantage could be taken on (exapted) for another purpose. Alternatively, traits that were never functional themselves but rather the side-effects of ones that were could become utilized. A classic example of **exaptation** are bird feathers. Feathers existed on flightless dinosaurs so it is unlikely that they first evolved to enable flight. Rather, they probably evolved out of reptile scales as a means of retaining warmth and only later did they become exapted for flight (Arthur, 2011). So it is possible to consider that, as humans evolved, language evolution could have similarly emerged through genes conferring an initial positive advantage, or become exapted over time. To consider this further we must now turn to look at human evolution as a species.

The origin of the genus *Homo*

When it comes to the evolution of language, one source of evidence lies in the analysis of how modern *homo sapiens* emerged from our **hominin** ancestors and our closest living relatives in the animal kingdom, *Pan troglodytes* (common chimpanzees) and *Pan paniscus* (pygmy chimpanzees, or bonobos). The formation of new species is not a straightforward concept, and the explanation of speciation depends to some extent on the theoretical perspective adopted (Gould & Eldredge, 1993). In general terms, the hominin line split from our last common ancestor (LCA) with the other **hominids** somewhat more than 7 mya. As the first hominins ventured onto the savannah of East Africa, the evolution of body morphology resulted in the emergence of bipedal (upright) walking. The consequences also include changes to the thorax and oral tract that were almost certainly taken on or exapted as a feature which turned out to be beneficial to vocalization. For the duration of the early hominin genera *Ardipithecus* and *Australopithecus* during the subsequent 4 million years or so, no evidence points to a change in brain size or to any cultural behaviour to distinguish early hominins from the LCA (Reader, 2011; Stringer, 2011). Brain growth is first evident in the emergence of the genus *Homo* approximately 2.5 mya with the main spurt of this initial brain growth taking place around 2 mya, so that by 1.5 mya, when *Homo erectus* had evolved, the hominin brain had doubled in size from 400 to 800 cc. The fossil record indicates that this first phase of rapid hominin brain growth was accompanied by the initial signs of complex cultural behaviour, including sophisticated tool use and possible use of fire, beyond that demonstrated by chimpanzees. We also find evidence of the first migration out of Africa, with *erectus* fossils found in China and Indonesia. There is only a small degree of brain growth over the next million years, until the final jump begins more than 500 kya with the emergence of *Homo heidelbergensis* and, shortly after this, the first recorded use of pigments and ritual burial (Wynn, 2012). The result, at least by 200 kya, was larger hominin brains, of around 1350 cc, and the appearance of anatomically modern *Homo sapiens* (Stringer, 2011). Thus evidence of larger brain size and cultural group behaviour indicating the likelihood of language is clearly established by 200 kya. Some time after this, these hominins undertook the last migration out of Africa – presumably with a fully developed FL.

Brain size matters. Jerison (1974) noted that all vertebrates have approximately the same proportional body to brain size except for birds and mammals whose brains are considerably larger than those of other classes. Among the mammals, chimpanzees stand out by virtue of having slightly larger than expected brains, but the human brain is proportionally, on average, a massive three times that of other mammals and 2.3 times that of chimpanzees. However, this increase in brain size is not uniform across the structure of the brain. In mammals as a whole, there is greater mass in the neocortex as opposed to primary sensory and motor areas, while uniquely in humans the prefrontal cortex is twice the area that even such a large neocortex would predict. Duncan *et al.* (2000) have reported that the prefrontal cortex is most highly activated in complex cognitive tasks such as problem solving and rule processing. It seems highly likely that these structural changes played a major role in the evolution of language.

The role of genes

Although humans share over 99% of their genes with chimpanzees, we cannot overlook the way in which genes are variably expressed as well as other developmental factors. Significant variations within the human genome are also potentially useful sources of information in understanding language evolution. For example, for the vast majority of right-handed people, language processing is lateralized in the left hemisphere of the brain; that is, the brain is asymmetric. The development of greater hemispherical asymmetry in the hominin brain, a consequence of which is handedness, is much less apparent in chimpanzees (Hopkins & Cantelupo, 2003). Asymmetrical brains are more susceptible to the consequences of trauma, so this genetic change must therefore have bestowed some evolutionary advantage to compensate for this. One reason why asymmetry may have evolved in hominins is brain size, creating a potential connection problem (Allen, 2009) whereby a larger brain needs a greater number of (longer) neural connections which may reduce efficiency. In an asymmetric brain, neurons are concentrated in functional areas; by locating areas with interrelated functions adjacent to each other, the connection problem is greatly reduced. Location of specific cognitive functions in one or the other hemisphere of the brain would have allowed for greater specialization, for example, in Broca's area for the speech production aspects of language with which it is associated. Crow (2002) identifies one particular gene (ProtocadherinXY) for cerebral asymmetry and argues that the significant mutation in the hominin line occurred at the same time as the first spurt of brain growth, and that there was already evidence of significant asymmetry in *Homo erectus* ancestors.

Numerous other genetic differences with chimps have been proposed as contributing to our unique cognitive abilities including language (e.g. Endicott *et al.*, 2010; Glazko *et al.*, 2005; Hughes *et al.*, 2010). The most widely discussed is FOXP2. The gene was first reported in 1990 where a single nucleotide change in the gene sequence was responsible for a condition in some members of the 'KE' family in London (Hurst *et al.*, 1990). The features of the condition include a speech defect known as 'orofacial dyspraxia' resulting in problems of motor control and language comprehension, although non-verbal IQ is normal (Vargha-Khadem *et al.*, 1995). FOXP2 is generally a very stable gene; for example, there have been no changes between chimps and rodents since their LCA some 90 mya. However, two changes have arisen in the hominin line in only the last 7+ million years. In humans the FOXP2 gene is involved in regulating over 100 other genes – a function lacking in its ancestral form – and Diller and Cann (2012) have suggested that the significant mutations occurred between 1.8 and 1.9 mya, shortly after the species *Homo* emerged. FOXP2 undoubtedly plays a significant role in human linguistic abilities, but attempts to characterize this or any other single gene as the 'language gene' are hugely wide of the mark.

Theories of Language Evolution

Brain size, genes and functional neural specialization clearly play a role in language evolution, but how far do they account for the role of an innate language faculty (LF), capable of complex hierarchical language? Chomsky is well-known for his comment that to reject the assumption that language is innate is 'to say that there is no difference between my granddaughter, a rock and a rabbit' (Chomsky, 2000: 50). This comment may be provocative and attract accusations of flippancy, but is nevertheless essentially true. Even our closest relatives in the animal kingdom, although undoubtedly able to communicate, do not have a complex language system in their natural environment and are unable to acquire it in artificial settings (see discussion below). Other non-nativist accounts such as O'Grady (2006, see also Chapter 3 in this volume), may be making the same point as Chomsky, although in more measured language, when noting 'there is general agreement that the acquisition of language is innately guided – this much has been widely acknowledged even by those opposed to the idea of an innate Universal Grammar' (O'Grady, 2008b: 620). The question that remains is exactly what is innate: in other words, what is the nature of the FL, particularly if it is a separate module or not (Fodor, 1983; see chapters in this volume, especially comparing Caink (Chapter 2) and Gil *et al.* (Chapter 4) versus O'Grady (Chapter 3)).

The reasons for language evolution

The mainstream tradition within discussion of language evolution has assumed a Darwinian-based account, or natural selection. In order to posit such an account of language evolution we need to consider what the **selective advantage** of language is. In other words, what is the 'purpose' of language (or at least what was the initial function)? Numerous hypotheses have been proposed including hunting (and in particular, scavenging), toolmaking, sexual selection, childcare and teaching (see Számadó & Szathmáry, 2012, for an overview of a number of competing theories of reasons for language evolution).

One proposal that has received a lot of attention is that language emerged as a method of maintaining social relations in large social groups. Biologist Robin Dunbar (1996, 2012) points out that the dominant mode of sustaining social bonds in non-human primate groups is through mutual manual grooming, but this would limit a group to around 50 in size – the norm among primates. However, the emergence and evolution of language as a social replacement for manual grooming would have enabled early hominins to interact with more than one other member of the group at a time, and also to simultaneously engage in other useful survival activities. As a consequence, Dunbar argues, hominin groups could expand, terminating at around 150 group members at the time of *Homo heidelbergensis*.

Other theorists are sceptical of these speculations as the initial adaptive pressure which drove the evolution of language, and prefer the intuitively obvious explanation that language evolved to enable instrumental and social communication for a range of purposes.

Gradualist Nativism

Linguists Steven Pinker and Ray Jackendoff (2005: 218) emphasize that 'the design of language – a mapping between meaning and sound – is precisely what one would expect in a system that evolved for the communication of propositions'. The selective advantage that this communication system bestows is uncontroversial: the communication of propositions facilitates the transmission of complex cultural constructions in a species that cooperated beyond its immediate family, e.g. in groups larger than 50. Vitally, this would have enabled a speaker to pass on information regarding various advantageous survival processes – for example, how to fish or avoid danger. Language from this perspective is a complex adaptive system, constituting a specified module of the mind comparable to other biological systems (such as the human visual system, e.g. Pinker & Bloom, 1990) that can only be explained in terms of gradual adaptation and natural selection.

In any proposal for a gradualist account of language evolution, there is still a need to explain how non-combinatory units such as individual signs or sounds used to communicate about specific items of reference, as used by chimps in the wild, were replaced by units that could be combined in linear strings and later hierarchical structures – in other words, the evolution of a protolanguage.

Protolanguage

Communication among animals may include rule-governed vocalizations (such as birdsong; see Slater, 2012) and a clearly attested range of meaningful, if rudimentary, signs and sounds for communication. So the unique feature of human language is hierarchical, **recursive** syntax (Tallerman, 2012a). Syntax is understood to be a **compositional** system by which complex, hierarchical structures are composed from items in the lexicon (mainly 'words' but also smaller units or morphemes, and larger compounds and formulaic chunks including idioms – see Caink in this volume). One of the major focuses in language evolution, for both nativist gradualists and non-nativists, is how to account for the development of syntax through simpler, non-hierarchical protolanguage.

A number of writers (e.g. Wray, 1998) have argued that early protolanguage was holistic, consisting of fully propositional, **non-compositional** units or calls. Over time these calls were 'fractionated' until arbitrary patterns became established as compositional units. Wray (1998: 55) gives the hypothetical examples of 'mebita' and 'kamebi' which may correspond to 'give her the food' and 'give her the stone', respectively. The starting point would be a purely coincidental occurrence of the sounds 'me' and the meaning 'give her' in both, but on this basis the two occurrences would become associated as sound-meaning pairings. Tallerman (2007, 2012b) identifies several flaws in this proposal, including the fact that the trained bonobo Kanzi (see below) appeared to use discrete units such as these, which corresponded to verbs and nouns. On the basis of arguments presented by Tallerman I think it is safer to assume that human protolanguage was a compositional system.

The earliest protolanguage would be at least as complex as symbolic (i.e. non-natural) communication systems that bonobos and other chimpanzees have been shown to be able to acquire. Some early studies claimed that chimpanzees could have considerable success in learning communication systems (e.g. Gardner & Gardner, 1985; Rumbaugh et al., 1975). These claims were challenged by Terrace et al. (1979), who argued that displays of animal communication could be explained as conditioned behavioural responses, as in the 'Clever Hans' effect where the horse that appeared to be counting was in fact reacting to changes in its trainer's body language. However, subsequent work by Savage-Rumbaugh and others with the bonobo Kanzi (see Savage-Rumbaugh & Lewin, 1994) seems to put beyond doubt the ability of some chimpanzees to acquire and use a fairly large set of symbols (in Kanzi's case around 250) and display significant comprehension when these symbols are used by the researcher. The authors claim that Kanzi's ability is comparable to, and in some respects better than that of a two-year-old child's early speech.

In addition to hierarchical structure, a universal feature of syntax is the use of function words as opposed to purely content words. The study of how function words evolve from content words in specific human languages is known as grammaticalization (e.g. Heine & Narrog, 2010). This is a gradual, diachronic process in which a lexical item undergoes various changes that result in a new form for signalling linguistic relations such as tense, aspect, and so on. This idea has been applied to language evolution as an explanation of how a simple protolanguage of purely content words could have gradually given rise to a complex syntax (Heine & Kuteva, 2007). The basis of grammaticalization is that a sociolinguistic choice by a group of language users extends the context in which a particular content word is used. This is followed by 'desemanticization' whereby aspects of the meaning of the word that do not fit the new context are 'semantically bleached' or disappear. Then the word loses its inflectional and derivational morphology (for example, being able to take a plural -s or nominal suffix like -ness) and ultimately its syntactic autonomy (this is known as decategorization). Finally, there is the process of 'phonetic erosion' whereby single sounds or even complete syllables may be lost or simplified.

An example is the English indefinite article 'a/an' as grammaticalization of the numeral 'one'. There has been semantic bleaching of its numeral meaning, decategorization such that 'a/an' no longer functions as a pronoun without a head noun (there is one / *there is a / there is a book). Phonetic erosion means the vowel is reduced to the most neutral vowel sound, schwa [ə], in rapid speech.

Problems with a gradualist nativism

However, there are a number of difficulties with a gradual, nativist account of language evolution. First, there is the question of what period of time would be necessary for the evolution of a highly intricate module of the mind necessary for language. Other complex biological systems, including the visual system, are known to have evolved over several hundred million years, yet the most optimistic timespan for the emergence of a language module is something in the region of 7.5 million years, and agreed by most to be far less (Bickerton, 2007). And the actual evidence of evolutionary change is remarkably small, as Fodor points out:

> our brains are, by any gross measure, very like those of apes. So it looks as though relatively small alterations of brain structure must have produced very large behavioural discontinuities in the transition from the

ancestral apes to us. If that's right, then you don't have to assume that cognitive complexity is shaped by the gradual action of Darwinian selection. (Fodor, 1998: 4)

Christiansen and Chater (2008) and Chater *et al.* (2009) emphasize that not only is the time factor anomalous, but something which changes as rapidly as we know languages do does not provide the necessary form of an environment for the co-evolution of a biological genetic faculty or module (FL). They argue that evolution requires a relatively stable environment, and languages change just too fast for adaptive biological advantages to be selected for. Christiansen and Chater may be confusing individual languages with the faculty for language; however, even if such evolutionary development had occurred in the short period of time thought to be available, it is surprising that evolution of the FL ceased at the time of the last migration from Africa. The common response to this charge is that the amount of time that has passed since the African exodus is not sufficient for evolutionary change to be observable, but this simply brings the argument back to the lack of time for language to have emerged in the first place.

A final objection to a gradualist account that explains the adaptive advantage in terms of communication is that, unlike the visual system, which brings immediate benefits to its beholder wherever she is (given the necessary presence only of light), language (*if* the adaptive pressure was its utility in communication) requires an interlocutor. Pinker and Bloom argue that arbitrary features of language that have no clear functional advantage evolved because they 'defined parts of a standardized communicative code in the brains of some critical mass of speakers' (Pinker & Bloom, 1990: 718). Thus, they argue, an arbitrary linguistic constraint such as the binding condition which stipulates how pronouns and anaphors occur in relation to their referents (Chomsky, 1981; and see O'Grady, Chapter 3 in this volume) is an accident of evolution and there could easily have evolved alternative constraints that would regulate co-referential items (rather as SCART or HDMI are alternative forms of interconnection between input and output information technology devices). But Pinker and Bloom offer no explanation as to how any such arbitrary feature could enter the minds of a 'critical mass', i.e. a large enough section of the population for the feature to spread. Indeed, there is no explanation of how such arbitrary features could spread at all: there is no value in a SCART output when the input to the next device in the chain is HDMI. Any single mutation in the evolution of the FL is going to be internal to one individual and thus of no communicative advantage. A unique feature would in fact bring no discernible advantage until it had spread throughout the community of speakers, but a Darwinian explanation stipulates that it would not spread unless it already bestowed an advantage.

Sudden Nativism

If we reject a gradual adaptationist theory of the evolution of a nativist FL, then an alternative account of the evolution of an innate FL requires a sudden jump (saltation). In a saltationist account, language is seen as the result of an abrupt change resulting from a mutation in an organism which then has significant consequences for a population. As a general rule in evolutionary theory, such explanations are excluded when an alternative adaptationist narrative can account for the same phenomena, and both nativist and non-nativist gradualists argue that the abstract and highly intricate nature of language excludes saltationist descriptions. Pinker likens them to 'the proverbial hurricane that blows through a junkyard and assembles a Boeing 747' (Pinker, 1994: 361). However, biologist Richard Dawkins (1986) contrasts the implausibility of an accidental 747 with a significant leap resulting from a single change to an existing organism, and extends the aeronautical analogy in terms of the creation of the Stretched DC-8 as a modification of the standard DC-8: it is in this latter sense that one can talk of saltationist origins of language. Linguist Norbert Hornstein defends this approach to language origins in terms of random mutation, arguing that such a position 'is not outlandish if what we are talking about is the emergence of one new circuit rather than a highly structured internally modular FL' (Hornstein, 2009: 10, footnote 19).

In two seminal papers, Hauser, Chomsky and Fitch (2002) and Fitch, Hauser and Chomsky (2005) argue that it is the mistake of 'treating "language" as a monolithic whole … [which] confuses discussion of its evolution and blocks the consideration of useful sources of comparative data' (Fitch *et al.*, 2005: 181). Language, they argue, needs to be considered in terms of a general system (Faculty of Language: Broad) which includes two components: first, the sensory-motor system where sound or phonetic form is interpretable, and secondly the conceptual-intentional system where meaning as logical form is interpretable. Added to this is a narrow syntactic **computational** module (Faculty of Language: Narrow). The authors, in both these papers and elsewhere (e.g. Chomsky, 2002), stress that they do not consider language to be 'for' communication and that it is in fact poorly equipped for the job (for example, in terms of the amount of redundancy, ambiguity and the like inherent in language). Fitch *et al.* (2005) argue that communication is only one use of language (uses also include private thoughts, problem solving and other functions); as we have seen, current utility is no indication of 'why' a trait initially emerges.

Language needs to be subject to the standard process of establishing 'purpose' in evolutionary study, which is by way of the comparative method. This involves studying a genetic feature which occurs as a homologue, a gene similar in structure and evolutionary origin to one in another species; by studying the different uses to which the homologue is put today we try to understand why it first emerged and how it subsequently developed. Fitch *et al.* argue that by studying the peripheral aspects across the broad faculty of language we can try and logically establish what is or is not part of the evolutionary story of human language. For example, Fitch (e.g. 2010) claims to have demonstrated that the lowering of the larynx is not uniquely human and is therefore not part of a gradual adaptation for speech. Temporary larynx lowering is not uncommon among mammals, and there appear to be two species of deer with a permanently lowered larynx. Fitch draws the conclusion that in the human species 'once the larynx attained a permanently lowered position, for whatever reason, the new vocal anatomy could be "exapted" for its phonetic utility' (Fitch, 2002: 37). In other words, the larynx permanently lowered for some adaptive pressure and was then available for utilization in speech once the remaining aspects of the broad language faculty were in place. The general conclusion that Hauser *et al.* (2002) draw is that all the apparatus of the broad language faculty have homologous or analogous counterparts in the animal world. The sole exception is the narrow syntactic language faculty. This narrow FL is understood to be the module that employs recursive syntax to merge objects which have phonetic and semantic properties (i.e. lexical items), and is thus a uniquely human procedure for mapping sound to meaning. Hauser *et al.* claim that recursive syntax is uniquely human, emerging as a saltation or Great Leap; therefore seeking a more gradual original purpose of language through homologue comparison is futile. Chomsky (2006) has since reaffirmed that this is his position, commenting that:

> there is no empirical or serious conceptual argument [for positing a gradual evolution of language] ... a more parsimonious speculation is ... that the Great Leap was effectively instantaneous, in a single individual, who was instantly endowed with intellectual capacities far superior to those of others, transmitted to offspring and coming to predominate. (Chomsky, 2006: 184)

'Perfection' in language

Chomsky frequently expresses the belief that the evolutionary leap that resulted in language (i.e. the narrow syntactic module) produced a 'perfect' system. This raises two questions: (i) perfect for what purpose? and (ii) how should perfection be evaluated? With regard to the former of these queries, it is quite apparent that Chomsky takes the function of language to be simply the mapping of sound to meaning as a perfectly efficient mechanism.

It is the second question – how should perfection be evaluated – that proves to be more problematic. Kinsella (2009) devotes considerable time to arguing that evolution does not favour 'perfect' solutions, preferring the back-up resources made available by redundancy and constantly being burdened with the vestiges of previous adaptations. However, as Chomsky has made it clear that he does not favour an adaptationist evolutionary account of language, then such criticism is immaterial. For Chomsky, perfection lies rather in the internal structure and the degree of optimality with which the narrow syntactic faculty is able to interact with other necessary systems. Just as the liver is 'beautifully designed for interaction with the circulatory system and the kidneys and so on' (Chomsky, 2002: 107), the narrow faculty is designed for interfacing with other systems of the broad language faculty (the sensory-motor and conceptual-intentional systems). Within the latest form of Chomsky's models of grammar, known as the Minimalist Program, such matters are elevated to play a central role whereby the aim of a theory of language is to go 'beyond explanatory adequacy' (Chomsky, 2004) and to understand *why* features of Universal Grammar are like they are. Chomsky (2005) has argued that the linguistic system that an individual ultimately acquires is the result of three factors. The first two factors are the result of genetics (Universal Grammar) and experience (the language a child is exposed to). The third factor is understood to be non-linguistic and non-cognitive, but rather part of the biological or even physical/atomic make-up of the world which constitutes a 'perfect' system. Thus if any syntactic operation 'follows from some principle of efficient computation … it's because that's the way the world works' (Chomsky & McGilvray, 2012: 61). A snowflake takes the form it does because it is determined by the laws of physics, and the same is said to apply to Universal Grammar.

Using snowflakes and the law of physics as an appropriate analogy to an internal, hardwired language faculty is not obvious. Certainly not everyone is convinced by this. Seuren (2004: 134), for example, dismisses discussion of perfection in Chomsky's Minimalist Program as 'nothing but the vague idea that it is difficult to imagine that things could be different'. Similarly, Kinsella discusses the notion of 'perfection' in nature at length and concludes, on the basis of Minimalist Program architecture, that 'The minimalist is not justified in claiming simplicity and economy for the human language faculty' (Kinsella, 2009: 183).

If not perfection as such, at least the idea of maximal optimality is critical for a saltationist explanation, as such an account depends on the degree of mutational change, regardless of the magnitude of the consequence of that change. Any claimed genetic modification must be sufficiently minor to be plausible – along the lines of a stretched fuselage from existing structure rather than the assembly of a fully operational aircraft from random components. Fitch, Hauser and Chomsky may argue that their proposals regarding the evolution of language do not depend on the explanation of the nature of language inherent in the Minimalist Program, but this simply will not do. Unless FLN is reducible to absolute minimal operations, e.g. recursive syntax alone, then their explanation of the origin of FL falls at the first fence, and it is precisely this reduction that the Minimalist Program seeks to portray. As Kinsella (2009: 66) points out, 'the choice appears to be this: show that minimalism is correct, and rule out the gradual adaptationist evolutionary account, or show that gradual adaptationism is correct, and rule out the MP'. In other words, the theory of the FL inherent in the Minimalist Program is incompatible with Darwinian gradualism. The Minimalist Program requires a sudden nativist explanation of the emergence of language, and a sudden nativism requires a theory of language at least very similar to the Minimalist Program.

Problems with sudden nativism

Substantial problems arise when, on evolutionary grounds, the syntactic component is reduced to recursive, unbounded merging of lexical items (e.g. Hauser *et al.*, 2002). **Merge** was understood as being feature driven, whereby lexical items were specified with a number of features (e.g. a noun had the feature 'nominal') that determined which items could and could not be merged together. So, for example, a determiner and a noun could merge to form a noun phrase (the + book = NP) and the noun phrase in turn could merge with a preposition to form a prepositional phrase (on + the book = PP). The multitude of features and operations that licensed Merge (see Hornstein *et al.*, 2005) ensured that non-grammatical derivations were avoided – so called 'crash-proof' grammars (Boeckx, 2010; Putnam, 2010). However, in recent years, Chomsky has proposed a Strong Minimalist Thesis (e.g. 2004, 2007), which takes 'unbounded' merge as the sole operation in the syntactic component. In essence, all of the lexical items to be merged are pre-specified in a 'lexical array' (although there is no real attempt to explain how this is done) and all possible combinations of binary merge are permitted. Deviant derivations are then filtered out at the sensory-motor and conceptual-intentional interfaces. In this model there is only a single syntactic feature, an edge feature which shows mergeability.

The problem for minimalists is that both models bring unwanted consequences. The crash-proof approach requires enormous complexity in the lexicon and numerous feature-driven operations that are entirely unminimalist in character. They are also highly implausible on evolutionary grounds. On the other hand, the 'unbounded merge' approach reduces the syntactic component to a trivial operation. The generation of all possible derivations from a single lexical array, all but one of which is then eliminated on legibility grounds, is inefficient; 10 lexical items could be merged in 3.6 million different ways (Putnam & Stroik, 2010). It also strips the model of any pretence at explaining psychologically real processes. The development of the Minimalist Program in the direction of 'unbounded merge' does seem to vindicate Seuren's fierce criticism of the model as 'a "random-generator" view of language' (Seuren, 2004: 3).

Domain-general Accounts

Alternative approaches treat language as **non-domain specific** and thus consider it as part of the general cognitive machinery (along the lines of O'Grady, Chapter 3 in this volume). From the most radical non-nativist perspective, the question of language evolution excludes the evolution of any specific mental capacities solely for language processing; instead all cognitive machinery is understood to have evolved independently under adaptive pressures other than for language. It is common in such explanations of FL and evolution to treat language as simply another aspect of culture. But the problem with this is that language and culture are just too different: three-year-old linguistic geniuses are generally incompetent in other components of culture. Furthermore, the question of how infants are able to acquire language on the basis of insufficient and degenerate input indicate that language is something special (see Gil *et al.*, Chapter 4 in this volume, on Poverty of the Stimulus). Even Sapir, whose entire career was devoted to emphasizing the cultural nature of language, was forced to admit (ironically in language that is culturally unacceptable today) that 'when it comes to linguistic form, Plato walks with the Macedonian swineherd, Confucius with the head-hunting savage of Assam' (Sapir, 1921: 234).

Another radical non-nativist argument is founded on the undeniable point that languages must be learnable; otherwise they would die out. The claim is then made that languages have actually evolved in order to be easily acquirable. Thus children's first intuitions about language are likely to be the correct ones because languages have adapted to the way the human brain works. Christiansen and Chater (2008: 507) echo this view that language is shaped by the brain in order be learnable and processable: 'languages have adapted to conform to the most popular guess'. Although Christiansen and Chater admonish other writers for what they claim is circularity of argument, it is a charge to which they themselves are clearly susceptible. Language, they maintain, is learnable because it conforms to learning biases therefore it must have evolved to be so, although they do not specify the process by which this could have occurred (for discussion, see Számadó & Szathmáry, 2012). Evidence in support of this position is often drawn from formal, or computer-based, modelling (for a brief review, see Smith, 2012). However, while these simulations are becoming increasingly sophisticated, and provide valuable insights into the nature of iterative learning, so far they have only had a peripheral impact on the study of language evolution. Bickerton's (2007: 522) comment that the approach is 'a classic case of looking for your car-keys where the street lamps are' remains pertinent.

A theory based on learnability begs the question: for whom is language easy to learn? Not for a chimpanzee clearly, nor perhaps for most adult second language learners. Indeed, there is no evidence that language has adapted to hominin learning biases other than the fact that it is acquired by all children. Furthermore, as Dessalles (2008) points out, in every language there is a massive lexicon, ambiguity and redundancy. In short, there is a range of features that militate against the argument of evolution of language solely for learnability. In addition, we might expect a far smaller degree of linguistic variation and change if ease of learning were the single, specific, non-physiological constraining factor (even if there are additional, presumably universal cognitive constraints such as limits to short-term memory). We might ask, therefore, why language has not evolved into a single optimal 'learnable' form. The most convincing reason is that such an explanation would fall into the error of confusing two things (Tallerman *et al.*, 2009) – confusing language evolution (the initial emergence of language) with cyclic diachronic change (the patterns of historical change that all languages undergo).

One reason why learnability is posited as the main source of evolutionary pressure rather than other functional factors, such as communicative expressiveness, arises from attempts to account for the logical problem of language acquisition in non-nativist theory (see also Gil *et al.*, Chapter 4 in this volume). Christiansen and Chater emphasize the role of frequency patterns in language acquisition and claim that '[language] "universals" are ... akin to statistical trends tied to patterns of language use' (Christiansen & Chater, 2008: 500). Fodor criticizes this approach in cognitive science for its reliance on the tradition of empiricism and associationism, rejecting the claim that:

> The human mind is a blank slate at birth. Experience writes on the slate, and association extracts and extrapolates whatever trends there are in the record that experience leaves. The structure of the mind is thus an image, made *a posteriori*, of the statistical regularities in the world in which it finds itself. (Fodor, 1998: 11)

Passingham similarly rejects a purely domain-general account of language and agrees that 'it is implausible that there were no modifications in the microstructure in the evolution of the human brain' for language (Passingham, 2008: 120). In other words, some degree of cognitive **nativism** is needed to explain how language can be acquired.

Evolution of Cognitive Abilities

Most accounts of language evolution agree that there are a number of specific cognitive abilities that are prerequisites for language. Research into chimpanzee cognitive behaviour has contributed valuable, if sometimes controversial and uncertain, findings into the nature and evolutionary timescale of these abilities (e.g. Gardner & Gardner, 1985; Savage-Rumbaugh & Lewin, 1994; Terrace *et al.*, 1979; Tomasello & Call, 1997). It is clear from such studies that chimpanzees have a rich conceptual system, the ability to learn from humans a limited number of symbols for these concepts, and the basic perceptual sensory-motor system necessary to discriminate among these symbols. It is highly likely that these attributes were also shared by our LCA and thus the earliest hominins. However, evidence for cognitive abilities beyond these is much less conclusive.

There certainly exists a 'mental gap' between humans and chimpanzees, and this is often described as 'intentionality', 'theory of mind' (Baron-Cohen, 1995) or 'mentalizing' (Frith & Frith, 2006). It has been argued that chimpanzees are unable to follow eye gaze (Povinelli & Eddy, 1996), nor do they display the joint attention infant children readily do with their caregivers (Carpenter et al., 1998). And unlike infants, chimpanzees display at best very poor ability at imitation for a parallel objective (Call et al., 2005) or pattern finding (Burling, 2005). And finally, it does appear to be the case that chimpanzees appreciate members of their own species as intentional beings with their own needs and desires; however, there is little or no evidence that chimpanzees have appreciation of other individuals with independent belief systems, and chimpanzees routinely fail 'false belief' tasks such as the one discussed below (Call & Tomasello, 1999; Tomasello, 2008). These properties are fundamental to language in which 'communication depends upon the ability of human beings to attribute sophisticated mental states to others' (Sperber & Origgi, 2004: 2). Decoding is only part of the process of language use and recognizing the speaker's intentions is fundamental.

The characteristics of theory of mind may be largely absent in human neonates but quickly emerge in infants. Almost immediately following birth, the human baby processes faces (Goren et al., 1975) and by the early stages of the second year demonstrates coordinated joint attention with caregivers based on gaze and pointing (Scaife & Bruner, 1975). Young children are typically engaged in secondary representations, that is, suspending beliefs about reality, through pretend play by the end of the second year (Leslie, 1988). Fully operational second-order intentionality, the ability to know that another individual's belief may differ from one's own, is not usually evident until the fourth year. This is often assumed to be demonstrated through the successful completion of false belief tests such as the 'Sally-Ann task', where a subject watches two dolls in the same room, one of whom, Sally, hides an object and then leaves the set. While she is away the other doll, Ann, removes the object and hides it in another place. If the participant can correctly identify the previous hiding place as the spot where Sally will look for her object, then she has passed the task (Baron-Cohen et al., 1985). While Haeckel's dictum that 'ontogeny replicates phylogeny' (the belief that evolutionary development of a species is represented in the stages of development from embryo to adult in an individual) is no longer taken as proof that any trait appeared at a certain stage in evolutionary history, because it does emerge in humans and not in chimpanzees, it is still reasonable to conclude that these properties evolved early in hominin evolution during the first period of brain growth, bestowing on their possessors the advantage of cooperating with other members of the group on the basis of joint intentions. Such advantages enabled sufficient cooperation for the first hominin colonization of the world outside Africa, and possibly the first use of arbitrary symbols for communication.

A non-nativist, cognitive account

One common misconception made by non-specialists (and some specialists) is that language evolved from the **call systems** of other primates (see, for example, Johansson, 2005). It is one of the more certain claims for the origins of language that this is not the case. No animal call system displays basic **semantic compositionality**, let alone the complex hierarchical syntax of language. Even primate vocalizations are very largely instinctive and involuntary, i.e. not under cortical control (Corballis, 2012). Tomasello (2008) argues instead that great ape gestures, learnt in infancy and used flexibly, are the first indications of intentional communication. It has been further argued (e.g. Arbib, 2006; Corballis, 2009) that language is essentially a gestural system that may have evolved from neural connections between two areas of the brain in primates. It has long been known that one part of the brain, Broca's area, which partially overlaps with Brodmann's area 44 (Arbib & Bonaiuto, 2008; Rizzolatti *et al.*, 1996), plays a crucial role in the production of language in humans. In macaque monkeys, the performance of grasping and also the mere observance of a similar grasping action results in the firing of 'mirror neurons' in the homologue macaque area to Brodmann's area 44 (Arbib & Bonaiuto, 2008; Rizzolatti *et al.*, 1996). Recently it has been shown that stimulation of this area elicits both hand and orofacial movements in the monkeys (Petrides *et al.*, 2005), suggesting a relation between the two forms of action. Corballis (2009) proposes that humans evolved capacities for complex intentional imitation from such simple gestural imitations as can be observed in chimpanzees and other primates. In the absence of a ready-made system of conventionalized vocal symbols, it seems likely that gestures, especially as they are effective for iconic representation, would be appropriated for early protolanguage. Even today, speech is heavily accompanied by hand gestures (McNeill, 1992), and early protolanguage may well have been multimodal. The reluctance among many language evolutionists to accept this may be attributed to the traditional conception of language as 'sound with a meaning' and the emphasis of the primacy of sound systems in acquiring language, despite considerable uncontroversial evidence now that human signed languages only differ from spoken languages in their modality.

According to Tomasello (2008), communication among primates is limited to requesting or demanding actions from others. It is only the result of the greater cognitive abilities discussed above that equipped hominins with the capacity for recursive mind reading which enabled them to engage in joint cooperation. The earliest communication based on shared intentionality may have involved gestures and pantomiming which became correlated with arbitrary meaningless vocalizations. Tomasello (2008) argues that these vocalizations 'piggybacked' on the indexical and iconic gestures and eventually came to replace them as the end result of a process of the 'drift to the arbitrary'. Greater cooperation led hominins to forms of communication beyond that of requests, including informing and sharing attitudes and emotion. As these last two involve displacement and finely nuanced meaning, they drove the evolution of complex syntax and the development of modern language.

Conclusion

There is little doubt that the human FL requires the development of a number of cognitive abilities lacking in all non-human primates. If these abilities were not present in our LCA, then this means they must have evolved in the last 7+ million years and were most likely related to the substantial increase in brain size (along with some brain reorganization) in hominins. Whether there is a specific module that is hard wired and unique to language remains unresolved, although there are problems from the evolutionary perspective for gradualist and sudden explanations of the presence of such a module. Similarly there are problems with a non-native functionalist approach which presupposes that learnability must have shaped language evolution.

At the moment a reasonable picture is that the appearance of more sophisticated tools, the use of fire and the first migration from Africa by 1.5 mya suggests a cognitive breakthrough that may well have been accompanied with the earliest forms of protolanguage, taking forward the kind of gestural encoding needed for communicative effectiveness.

Further cognitive developments, of the type discussed above, in the period 500–200 kya, were accompanied by physiological changes that resulted in anatomically modern humans, presumably with a fully developed faculty for complex structured language, which was exported out of Africa some time in the last 100 thousand years and which does not appear to have evolved further since then. Time lines, however, are constantly being revised along with data from disciplines other than linguistics, and the picture will change as our understanding increases. This is what makes language evolution such an exciting field to be involved in.

Part 2

Properties of Interlanguage Grammars

6 The Mystery of the Missing Inflections

Walid Kahoul, Anne Vainikka and Martha Young-Scholten

Introduction

Second language acquisition researchers and teachers have long suspected that even though learners with plenty of target language exposure vary in their production of inflectional morphemes such as regular past tense and 3rd person singular -*s* (the only agreement suffix in English), they do know these forms. Researchers ask why learners don't invariably produce these forms if they know them. But do they really know them? To answer these questions, we need to ask what it means to 'know' (have acquired) an inflectional morpheme. Under current thinking, a learner's knowledge of morphological forms marking tense and agreement is connected to the abstract syntactic features they represent. As noted in other chapters in this volume (e.g. Chapter 2 by Caink and Chapter 4 by Gil *et al.*), in generative, Chomskyan, linguistics human languages share a common core of syntactic principles, and differences among languages revolve around language-specific mental lexicons. The lexicon of a language contains the semantic, phonological, morphological and syntactic properties of lexical categories such as verbs, nouns, adjectives and prepositions and **functional categories** such as negation, tense, aspect and agreement.

Under more recent ideas about syntax known as Minimalism (Chomsky, 1993, 1995, 1998, 2001), the lexicon contains functional morphemes with their **formal features** such as [+/− past] which determine a language's specific syntactic structure or its projections. Lexical projections include VP whose head is a V (verb) and whose arguments (e.g. a direct object) either precede or follow the head (Farsi and Japanese versus Arabic, Chinese or English). Under **X'-Theory** (Jackendoff, 1977), every head (X) in a sentence projects a phrase (XP) in a hierarchical or tree structure as illustrated in Example 1 below, in an English example. In the VP, the lowest projection, relations between the verb's arguments – e.g. subject and object – are established. The higher verbal projections in the tree are functional: AspP (aspect phrase), TP (tense phrase) and AgrP (agreement phrase).[1] DP (determiner phrase) is a nominal projection which in English includes functional morphemes such as articles. For further details on syntactic structure, see Caink's Chapter 2 at the start of this volume.

Example 1

AgrP
- DP
  - The man
- Agr'
  - Agr
    - +3sg
    - was
  - TP
    - Spec
    - T'
      - T
        - +past
      - AspP
        - Spec
        - Asp'
          - Asp
            - +progr
          - VP
            - Spec
            - V'
              - V
                - reading
              - DP
                - the newspaper

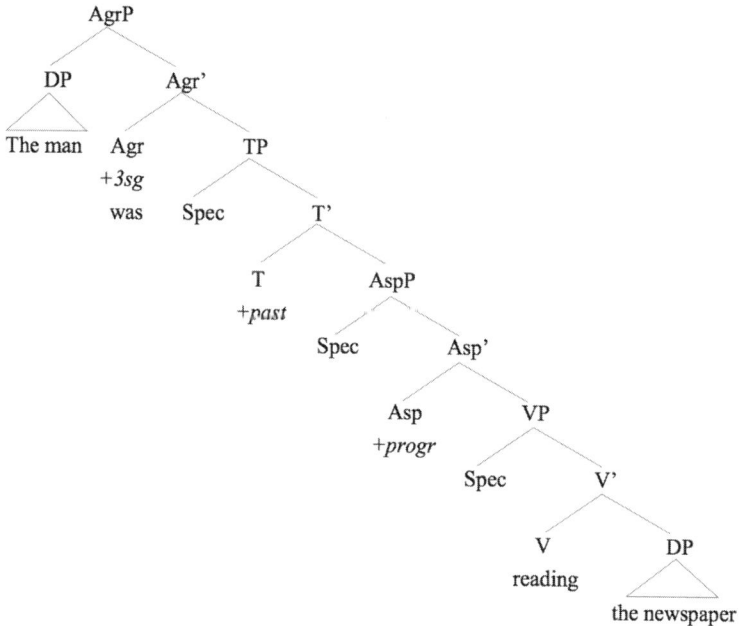

Morphosyntax refers to the position of constituents in a sentence (i.e. word order) in relation to functional morphology in a sentence. Acquisition is a process of receiving input about the nature and type of features in that language. When second language (L2) learners inconsistently produce *-ed* or *-s*, researchers ask whether their **interlanguage** contains AgrP or a TP, taking one of two positions: (1) the learner's interlanguage contains these projections, but the learner does not always produce the morphemes due to the pressure of producing something during a conversation or for phonological reasons, i.e. the learner's first language (L1) disallows the consonant clusters which result from suffixation of *-ed* or *-s* to a word-final consonant as in 'grabbed' or 'drinks'; (2) the learner's interlanguage has no AgrP or TP. This chapter argues for view (2) on the basis of evidence from a set of different experiments, which we briefly discuss, to explore whether learners have acquired the relevant syntax. We start with what we know about L1 acquisition given the commonalities we assume between L1 and L2 acquisition.

What is Missing in the Morphosyntax of Children?

Children's first multi-word utterances reveal their early grasp of VP word order. At age one year and 10 months (1;10), little German learner

Meike produced the complement before non-finite *gehen* 'go' as in Example 2, i.e. a head-final German VP. But this is not adult German: the verb follows the subject and precedes the preposition phrase: *Ich gehe nach Hause* 'I go home' or *Ich will nach Hause gehen* 'I want to go home' (Mills, 1985). Adam at age 2;3 placed the complement 'doggie' after 'give', as in Example 3, in keeping with the head-initial English VP (Brown, 1973).

Example 2

> Hause gehen
> home go-INF

Example 3

> Give doggie.

Children's utterances lack certain elements: in both examples the subject is missing, and in the German one, the verb is non-finite (in English lack of agreement is more difficult to ascertain).[2] Where an auxiliary verb is required, it is clearer that L1 English children omit functional elements, e.g. in typical *wh*-questions at an early stage (Klima & Bellugi, 1966):

Example 4

(a) Where go?
(b) What doing?

Children learning other European languages show similar omissions.[3] Similar examples from children at the early stages show omission of functional elements required in adult speech including bound morphemes and free morphemes such as auxiliary and modal verbs.[4] Early views were that this initial system involved roles such as Agent and Patient and that children moved in a discontinuous way from a semantic system to a syntactic one. Alternatively, children's earliest system could be syntactic, constrained by Universal Grammar (UG; Chomsky, 1981) whose syntactic principles require finite clauses to have subjects and inflected verbs (the specifier of AgrP assigns nominative case to a subject). Innately driven language acquisition has long been supported by studies revealing strikingly uniform developmental patterns across children. These include Brown's (1973) longitudinal study of three children learning English and de Villiers and de Villiers' (1973) cross-sectional replication with 21 children. It has been noted that the likelihood of these common patterns being due to chance is practically zero (Laurence & Margolis, 2001; see also Stromswold, 2000).

Under UG-driven acquisition, adult languages share functional categories, and principles relate to a common syntactic structure for all languages (apart from variation expressed as parameters, e.g. for word order). Even though children's tense and agreement suffixes may be missing from their utterances, their syntax nonetheless contains TP and AgrP (this view is known as Strong Continuity; see Boser *et al.*, 1992; Hyams, 1992, 2007; Lust, 2006; Poeppel & Wexler, 1993; Wexler, 2004). But if children's syntax contains TP and AgrP, why do they omit similar suffixes as well as subjects? Researchers have proposed that the child truncates their underlying syntax in a way not possible for adults. Children do so until the principle of 'categorical uniformity' matures around age three years.[5]

Maturation of categorical uniformity would be an ideal solution if older, already mature L2 learners did not produce similar utterances. But they do, as we will see below. An alternative Weak Continuity view holds that UG provides the tools for the child to select the specific subset for their language from a universal set of functional categories. Vainikka and Young-Scholten (2007) discuss an analysis by Culicover and Jackendoff (2005) of the historical development of ideas in generative syntax and how these ideas should but only sometimes do relate to children's language acquisition.

In his seminal contributions to children's acquisition of English, Radford (1988, 1990, 1995) proposed that children's early system is syntactic, but it lacks functional projections. Examples 2, 3 and 4 and footnote 4 all involve a **minimal tree** – just a VP without AgrP or TP. Radford also took a maturation approach whereby all functional categories mature together (see Clahsen, 1991; Clahsen & Penke, 1992; Clahsen *et al.*, 1994, for similar ideas for German). A more refined, non-maturationist approach involves the child building syntactic structure, one functional projection at a time. Vainikka (1993/1994) considered data from children from CHILDES.[6] One child, Nina, at age 1;11–2;0 produced utterances with incorrect *my*-subjects along with non-finite verbs, as in Example 5a, and produced nearly no modals, no auxiliary verbs, past or agreement suffixes, embedded clauses or inverted questions. The absence of all of these indicates a VP-only grammar. At 2;1 Nina produced numerous nominative *I*-subjects along with previously omitted verbal morphology as in Example 5b. A window on Nina's immature morphosyntax is provided by *my*-subjects in *wh*-constructions as in Example 5c which suggest no functional projections above AgrP for production of adult-like questions requiring the higher projection CP (complementizer phrase) for question formation, relative clauses and embedded clauses. The subject in *wh*-constructions remains in VP, but cannot get nominative case for 'I'.

Example 5

(a) My make a house.   [Nina 2;0]
(b) I don't break 'em   [Nina 2;1]
(c) Look what my got.   [Nina 2;3]

A later longitudinal study by Ingham (1998) suggests that between 2;6 and 2;9 children acquiring English acquire TP following the tree in Example 1, building syntactic structure from the bottom up, from the VP. There was not yet evidence for an AgrP: the child's utterances did not show contrasts for case (on pronouns) or for agreement.

What is Missing in the Morphosyntax of Second Language Learners?

Researchers also disagree about whether L2 learners at early stages have a full syntactic tree or a minimal VP tree. For those who assume UG-driven acquisition across the lifespan, the L2 learner also brings their knowledge of their L1 to the task of L2 acquisition. There is a long tradition – dating at least back to Lado's (1957) Contrastive Analysis Hypothesis (CAH) – of considering how the L1 shapes L2 acquisition. In the 1970s the CAH was rejected on various conceptual and empirical grounds, including evidence from studies of L2 English revealing a common acquisition order. That is, not only child, but also adult L2 learners regardless of their L1, displayed in cross-sectional studies common accuracy orders in production of inflectional morphology, and common stages in acquisition of questions and negation. L2 learners' early production showed omission of functional morphemes and their systematic emergence (Bailey et al., 1974; Dulay & Burt, 1974). Despite rejection of L1 influence, researchers continued to investigate how the L1 influences L2 acquisition, because (1) omission of functional elements persists and (2) its rate varies across L1 groups. This has meant an ongoing search for the source of missing inflections: for L2 English see White (2003), and Haznedar (2001) for L1 Turkish; see Ionin and Wexler (2002) for L1 Russian and Lardiere (1998, 2007) for L1 Chinese; see Prévost and White (2000a, 2000b) for various L1 learners of L2 French or L2 German; see Vainikka and Young-Scholten (2011) on various L1 learners of L2 German. To account for missing inflections, there are three general approaches: Strong Continuity, Weak Continuity and processing.

Full competence

Full Competence is the Strong Continuity approach in L2 acquisition, expressed by Schwartz and Sprouse's (1994, 1996) Full Transfer/Full Access Hypothesis. It assumes that the L2 learner's initial state of knowledge includes their L1 syntax, in addition to UG. The solution to the mystery of missing inflections is the Missing Surface Inflection Hypothesis (MSIH): learners' interlanguage grammar is a full syntactic tree, but inflectional morphology has to be learned and the phonology involved also has to be mastered. Others argue that learners cannot acquire the relevant syntax if tense and agreement are not part of their L1 syntax; their interlanguage syntax is 'defective'.

The Missing Surface Inflection Hypothesis (MSIH)

One piece of evidence supporting the MSIH (Epstein *et al.*, 1998; Haznedar & Schwartz, 1997; Lardiere, 1998) is L2 learners' production of pronominal subjects in correct, nominative case, regardless of whether learners produce non-finite or finite verb forms in the same utterance. This indicates that learners have an AgrP (and a TP) since AgrP is syntactically required for prominal subjects to get nominate case. Why then should learners sometimes omit the inflection involved in AgrP if they have acquired the syntax? To explain why learners variably produce the relevant suffix, those who support MSIH apply **Distributed Morphology** (Halle & Marantz, 1993). The explanation is as follows: in attempting to produce morphology, the speaker has several possibilities. Let us consider the agreement paradigm in a richly inflected language such as Spanish with its separate suffixes on the verb which mark 1st, 2nd and 3rd person in both singular and plural. When the language learner has to match a suffix to the right person and the right number, there is competition, and what we refer to as the least specified suffix will win. This could be a form without a suffix at all. Distributed Morphology accounts for what researchers often observe during acquisition: the learner makes systematic errors of omission of inflection, e.g. the learner uses non-finite or stem forms as in Examples 2 and 3 above rather than using the wrong inflection (e.g. a 2nd person suffix for 3rd person) (so-called errors of commission). This variable production of inflection by the learner is the result of problems with sufficiently rapid processing (there isn't enough time for the learner to retrieve the correct suffix). This seems to be a problem for older L2 learners (i.e. adults). O'Grady (2006) and his Chapter 3 in this volume describe a similar approach, although he takes a general cognition rather than a UG approach.

Variable production of inflection could be due to the influence of the learner's L1 phonology. Goad *et al.* (2003), in their Prosodic Transfer Hypothesis, considered data showing that the L2 English production of speakers of Chinese, which allows no consonant clusters at the beginnings or ends of words, depended on mode of production. The speaker in Lardiere's (2003, 2007) study produced past tense 78% of the time in written production, but only 35% of the time in oral production. That this is a phonological problem is shown in her more successful oral production of irregular forms without clusters such as 'saw', and in omission of consonants in words with single morphemes with final consonant clusters such as 'strict'. According to O'Grady (2006), inflection marking is carried out by the learner's general cognitive processor and it works linearly, in the order that clauses are produced or processed.

Defective syntax

Other accounts for variable production of inflection are the Failed Functional Features Hypothesis (Hawkins & Chan, 1997) and its successors, the Local Impairment Hypothesis (Beck, 1998), the Representational Deficit Hypothesis (Hawkins, 2003) and the Interpretability Hypothesis (Tsimpli & Dimitrakopoulou, 2007). We refer to these as defective syntax hypotheses and all of them hold that older L2 learners can only acquire those features present in their L1; access to Universal Grammar is partial. Hawkins and Liszka (2003) found lower production of English past -ed by speakers of [−tense] Chinese (63%) than by speakers of [+tense] Japanese (92%). But this raises the question of how Chinese speakers come to mark tense at all? It is possible that we observe the marking of tense because the evidence of variable production of past tense comes from instructed learners, and their tense marking may be a result of what they have learned in the classroom rather than what they have acquired (Krashen, 1985b; Schwartz, 1993). It is also feasible that Chinese learners are using a verbal feature in their L1, namely their aspect feature, as tense in English, a view expressed in Lardiere's (2008) Feature Reassembly Hypothesis. Under this hypothesis, learners recruit their L1 features and, if required, assemble them differently for the language they are in the process of acquiring.

Weak continuity in second language acquisition

Another approach to missing morphology is a Weak Continuity approach under which the learner starts with a syntactic structure which lacks functional projections, i.e. a VP projection, the base of the tree shown in Example 1 above. As input is received, the learner then develops functional projections in succession. Vainikka and Young-Scholten's (2011) Organic Grammar holds that learners start with a minimal tree and then build functional structure. The theory dates back to Vainikka and Young-Scholten's (1994) **Minimal Trees Hypothesis** in which they argued on the basis of data from uninstructed adult immigrants in Germany that the learner's 'initial state' when they start acquiring an L2 is a bare VP. This VP is initially transferred from their L1; that is, it has the word order of the VP in their native language. Under the MSIH, the assumption is that utterances with non-finite verb forms involve full syntax, so subjects are marked with nominative case by AgrP. We find the same L2 early multiword utterances which, however, lack subjects as we find in L1 acquisition. (L2 beginners also produce the same sort of single-word and verb-less utterances children learning their L1 produce; see Myles, 2005.) An example in the L2 acquisition of English comes from Yamada-Yamamoto (1993) of her Japanese speaking son's earliest stages of acquisition. He starts with his Japanese object-verb VP word order and then he shifts to the correct English verb-object word order. These sub-stages are labelled VPi and VPii since the only change in the learner's syntax is the word order of the VP. There is also evidence from L2 learners of English who start with head-final/object-verb VP Turkish (Haznedar,

1997) and Farsi (Mobaraki *et al.*, 2008). These utterances are similar to the examples from children learning English as their L1: there is no evidence for any functional syntax.

Example 6

(a) VPi: Japanese object-verb (OV) order
   bread eat
   bananas eating

(b) VPii: English verb-object (VO) order
   eating banana
   wash your hand

After the learners' initial reliance on their L1, they begin to acquire the inflectional morphology and syntax of the target language; in other words, they begin to add functional projections to their interlanguage English. The order in which they do so is common for learners of a given target language regardless of the learners' L1s, their age, the context of their exposure or their educational background (Hawkins, 2001). As with children learning their L1, internal linguistic mechanisms drive acquisition as the learner (subconsciously) responds to the input around him or her. Under the theory of Organic Grammar, the learner's consistent (but not necessarily always accurate) production of inflectional morphology represents the associated syntax. That is, the learner's consistent production of past-tense *-ed* indicates that the learner's interlanguage has a TP and the learner's consistent production of 3rd person singular *-s* indicates an AgrP in his/her interlanguage system. The criteria for the acquisition of subject-verb agreement in English use of *-s* to consistently distinguish it in function from other morphemes is its use with more than one stem and in more than one linguistic context and its use in contexts which require it. Several correct uses of a form by a learner do not indicate its acquisition; these could be use of unanalyzed forms by L2 learners, for example Myles (2004) in her study of older children learning French in the classroom and Wagner-Gough (1978) in her longitudinal study of a young immigrant boy learning English. Depending on the language, there may also be syntactic indicators for learners' acquisition of AgrP, e.g. nominative case marking for pronomination subjects.

The steps in the acquisition of English morphosyntax are shown in Example 7. Under Organic Grammar, each syntactic projection in the tree in Example 1 above is recognized as a stage of syntactic development, and these stages move from the bottom of the tree upwards. The first step for the learner is identifying in the input the head of a projection. With continued input, the learner's innate capacity for language, in the form of Universal Grammar, then provides the syntactic structure. We assume – along with many other adult L2 acquisition researchers – access to

Universal Grammar across the lifespan. For Organic Grammar this means that, apart from initial L1 influence for VP word order, the same stages are predicted for children and adults, for both L1 and L2 acquisition (for more evidence on the adult L2 acquisition of English, see Young-Scholten & Ijuin, 2006).

Example 7 Stages in the acquisition of English under Organic Grammar

> *VP-stage*: verb and its arguments (bare verb, or a single form of verb occurs – e.g. *is* or *are* for *be*); first L1 word order, followed by L2 word order.
>
> *AspP-stage*: the *-ing* suffix on the verb, contrasting with a bare form (no auxiliary yet); non-nominative subjects as well as optional nominative subjects might occur up to the AgrP stage.
>
> *PerfP-stage*: participle form of the verb (*-en*; without auxiliary) – possible aspectual contrast with *-ing*.
>
> *NegP-stage*: sentential *not* follows subject DP (or, *don't* overgeneralized to all tenses and persons).
>
> *TP-stage*: past tense *-ed* acquired on regular verbs (also, auxiliaries are expected to emerge – beyond *don't* – but not always correctly marked for person agreement yet);
>
> *AgrP-stage*: person agreement (in particular, 3rd person singular *-s*) acquired; person forms of *be* acquired (*am, is, are; was, were*); null subjects no longer possible; non-nominative subject pronouns no longer possible;
>
> *CP-stage*: embedded clauses with an overt complementizer and full structure within the embedded clause; object *wh*-questions with full structure.

Psycholinguistics and second language processing

In the quest to solve the mystery of missing inflections, researchers usually collect oral and sometimes written production data from L2 learners. Data might have been spontaneously produced during conversation with the interviewer or during a range of specific tasks with learners' production recorded and then transcribed. The problem with such data is that they probably do not reveal the full extent of learners' underlying syntactic competence. Researchers have therefore increasingly turned to psycholinguistic, experimental techniques which examine online processing during listening or reading (Clahsen, 2007; Clahsen *et al.*, 2010). There is now a range of options which measure responses not only to syntactic stimuli but to a range of other linguistic stimuli (see chapters by Marinis & Cunnings and by Wright in this volume). When it comes to past tense and subject-verb agreement, processing studies confirm L2 adults' difficulties. Studies by Chen *et al.* (2007), McDonald (2000, 2006), McDonald and Roussel (2010) and Sato and Felser (2008) used different techniques and showed interesting yet sometimes contradictory results for adult L2 learners from a variety of L1 backgrounds. In general, these processing studies confirm what the oral and written production studies show. However, the focus of these studies has not been on identifying the source of learners' variable production of forms. One way to make progress in solving the mystery is to collect not only production data but also perception and processing data from the same group of adult L2 learners.

Solving the Mystery: Methodology

The data presented here are from Kahoul's (2014) PhD for which L1 speakers of Arabic and Chinese at varying levels in their L2 English were compared. The two languages differ in important ways. Arabic marks both subject-verb agreement and past tense while Chinese marks neither. Under the Full Transfer/Full Access hypothesis, Arabic learners are predicted to transfer TP and AgrP to their L2 English. If there is variable production of past tense or agreement suffixes, this will be a case of Missing Surface Inflection rather than an absence of TP or AgrP. When it comes to Chinese learners, they cannot rely on their native language except perhaps for reassembling their Chinese aspect feature as tense (see above). This is because Chinese lacks TP and AgrP. Their continued access (= Full Access) to Universal Grammar will help them acquire these features. Thus Full Tranfer/Full Access predicts that Arabic learners will exhibit a different as well as a more rapid acquisition trajectory than the Chinese learners of English. L1-based variation will also be due to what researchers refer to as Prosodic Transfer: like English, Arabic allows clusters of consonants at the ends of words but Chinese does not. This is important because, in attaching to stems, tense suffixes and agreement suffixes which are single consonants often attach to stems with one or more consonants, as in 'She talked loudly on the bus' [lkt] and 'He bends during yoga' [ndz].

Like Full Transfer/Full Access, Organic Grammar predicts that Arabic and Chinese learners will acquire TP and AgrP but that they will follow the same route of acquisition. Thus while Full Transfer/Full Access predicts superiority for Arabic learners from the early stages onwards because L1 gives them TP and AgrP, Organic Grammar predicts parity for Arabic and Chinese. Under Organic Grammar, acquisition of TP and AgrP in an L2 is based solely on the ability to acquire new syntactic structure from scratch. This is known as X'-Theory and is part of Universal Grammar. Learners do so in response to the English input to arrive at the tree in Example 1. Finally, deficit hypotheses, where adult L2 learners are no longer able to access Universal Grammar and cannot therefore acquire new features such as tense and agreement, predict that Chinese learners will perform badly from the start and at all further levels of proficiency, and much worse than Arabic learners.

Kahoul (2014) recruited 34 speakers of Arabic (12 Syrian, eight Libyan, five Iraqi, four Egyptian, three Jordanian and two Saudi) and 37 speakers of Chinese who were improving their English in the UK. He then placed them at three different levels of English proficiency in a cross-sectional study meant to mimic actual development over time. At the time Kahoul collected data, they had resided in the UK from two months to eight years and had started learning English in school in their home countries after the age of seven. Thus they were all instructed learners who had then received at least some if not considerable amounts of input in the target language country. In a cross-sectional study, the researchers need to make sure they use as robust as possible an objective test of placing learners at distinct proficiency levels, if the researchers intend to show how actual acquisition over time occurs. Researchers rely on various oral and written tests such as the Oxford Quick Placement Test used to place students on English-as-a-second-language programs. However, Kahoul adopted the more rigorous test developed by Unsworth (2005, 2008) as a three-step assessment resulting in an Age-Sensitive Composite Proficiency Score. Table 6.1 below shows Kahoul's placement of the 71 learners at what is standard in research: three proficiency levels, Low (beginner) Mid (intermediate) and High (advanced).

Kahoul posed two research questions: (1) Is learners' oral production of tense and agreement consistent? (2) Do learners' data from perception and processing tasks reveal the same patterns as the oral production data? The tasks Kahoul gave his participants were elicited imitation and picture-choice tasks which were supplemented with a measurement of reaction time and eye tracking.

Reaction Time measures the individual's speed in responding to test stimuli which indicates processing load. Mastery of a linguistic feature – a feature that comes to be represented in the learner's mind – results in rapid, automatic performance while non-mastery involves slow responses. The researcher's decision as to whether reaction times are rapid or slow is not absolute. Rather, times are relative and based on native speakers' performance on the same task. The tracking of an individual's eye movements in response to various stimuli also reveals information about what the viewer's mind represents. This is based on the observation that when we

Table 6.1 Proficiency groups

	Arabic speakers	Chinese speakers
Low	11	13
Mid	14	13
High	9	11

are presented with visual stimuli we move our eyes to focus attention on what interests us or what is relevant. In addition to reaction times, eye movements provide the researcher with insights into underlying cognitive processes (Hayhoe & Ballard, 2005; Liversedge & Findlay, 2000). The researcher can track participants' saccades (eye movement from one fixation or gaze to another) in response to visual stimuli which are presented with auditory stimuli to provide information about real-time language processing with regard to a range of specific linguistic features (Tanenhaus & Trueswell, 2006). For example, Arnold *et al.* (2000) looked at how gender information inherent in English pronouns influenced moment-by-moment interpretation. Participants saw pictures containing choices between characters and heard pronouns referring to just one of them. Results showed that participants looked at the target character in the picture within 200 milliseconds after they heard the pronoun and their eyes fixated longer on the target character than on the incorrect one, the so-called competitor. In the present study, Kahoul undertook these two eye movement measures: first look and length of look.

Kahoul tested oral production with an elicited imitation task where participants heard 50 recorded sentences (mean: 12 syllables in length) and had to repeat them. To avoid rote imitation and to check participants' comprehension of the sentence, the participant then saw three pictures and had to choose the correct picture before repeating the sentence (see Erlam, 2006, 2009; also Marinis & Cunnings, Chapter 10 in this volume for more on the elicited imitation technique). The following is an example of a sentence imitation + picture item:

Example 8

Yesterday, John ate his breakfast before he went out.

Results

We address each research question: (1) Is learners' oral production of tense and agreement consistent? (2) Do data from perception and processing tasks reveal the same patterns as the oral production data? In the process of addressing these questions, we also consider the three hypotheses discussed above, Organic Grammar, Full Transfer/Full Access and deficit hypotheses.

Oral production

Table 6.2 shows the results for correct past tense production and Table 6.3 shows the results for subject-verb agreement. For past tense, comparisons between the same-proficiency different-L1 groups showed no significant language-based differences between the two groups at the two lower levels but there was a significant language-based difference between the two High groups (Arabic High versus Chinese High).

For subject-verb agreement, for 3rd person singular -s, the Low and Mid groups did not differ significantly based on their native language, but at the highest level of proficiency the Arabic learners of English were significantly better at producing agreement marking than their Chinese counterparts.

These oral production task results support Organic Grammar for the Low and Mid learners: at the lower levels of proficiency, learners have not acquired TP and AgrP. The Full Transfer/Full Access hypothesis is rejected as it predicts differences at the early stages under the assumption that only Arabic speakers can transfer their TP and AgrP. A comparison of percentages of correct suppliance of tense and of agreement forms by learners at the Mid level points to the acquisition of TP preceding the acquisition of AgrP, as predicted by OG, as per the tree in Example 1 and the steps in Example 7. There is an obvious native language effect at the highest proficiency levels: Chinese speakers lag behind their Arabic counterparts. There could be phonological reasons for this; recall that Chinese does not allow word-final consonant clusters. The Prosodic Transfer Hypothesis was mentioned above in connection with the MSIH and Full

Table 6.2 Correct production of past tense by Arabic and Chinese learners

Arabic speakers				Chinese speakers			
	Score	%	SD		Score	%	SD
Low (n = 11)	177/317	55.83	24	Low (n = 13)	193/411	46.95	16
Mid (n = 14)	276/416	66.34	21	Mid (n = 13)	202/399	50.62	22
High (n = 9)	275/297	92.59	5	High (n = 11)	269/362	74.30	13

Table 6.3 Correct production of verbal agreement by Arabic and Chinese learners of English

Arabic speakers				Chinese speakers			
	Score	%	SD		Score	%	SD
Low (n = 11)	140/298	46.97	27	Low (n = 13)	192/354	54.23	11
Mid (n = 14)	170/342	49.70	20	Mid (n = 13)	168/352	47.72	23
High (n = 9)	226/260	86.92	8	High (n = 11)	217/298	72.81	12

Transfer/Full Access, but it is also compatible with Organic Grammar. Chinese learners' oral production of forms ending with consonant clusters is predicted to be worse than Arabic speakers' oral production of these, and forms without consonant clusters are predicted to be more successfully produced by learners. Kahoul's analysis of the elicited imitation data thus looked at the production of suffixes by **allomorph** and by regular and irregular verbs (shown in Table 6.4).

No significant phonological effects were observed in the results of the Chinese speakers, but the Arabic speakers displayed some phonological effects in their production of regular past tense: allomorph type was significant for the consonant + *t* allomorph, significantly lower than for consonant + *d* allomorph at the Low and Mid levels, and the consonant + *t* allomorph was significantly lower than the CVV-*d* allomorph at the Mid level. There were no significant differences for any other combinations. Production of consonant cluster versus non-cluster forms showed no significance at the Low or High levels, but did at the Mid level. A comparison between participants' production rates of past on regular and irregular verbs also revealed no significant differences at any of the three levels for the Arabic speakers. However, the Chinese speakers showed significantly higher target-like production of irregular verbs than regular verbs at Low and Mid levels, but not at the High level. If native language phonological constraints act on production of clusters in verbs with regular -*ed*, rates for irregular verbs should have been higher. Therefore, the advantage of Arabic learners over their Chinese counterparts is only for High-level learners where the Chinese High-level learners' production of regular versus irregular morphology no longer differs statistically.

For 3rd person singular -*s* agreement, rates of production for Arabic proficiency groups with allomorph type as a factor showed no significant

Table 6.4 Correct production of regular versus irregular past tense verb morphology suffixes

	Regular			Irregular		
	Score	%	SD	Score	%	SD
Arabic						
Low (*n* = 11)	111/202	54.95	27	66/115	57.39	23
Mid (*n* = 14)	183/278	65.82	24	93/138	67.39	17
High (*n* = 9)	193/211	91.46	7	82/86	95.34	6
Chinese						
Low (*n* = 13)	118/275	42.90	19	75/136	55.14	15
Mid (*n* = 13)	119/262	45.41	26	83/137	60.58	16
High (*n* = 11)	177/248	71.37	16	92/114	80.70	9

differences at any level. For the Chinese learners at the High level, one of the allomorphs, a short vowel followed by -z, showed significantly better production than the CVV-z allomorph.

Perception

To compare participants' oral production data with perception and processing data relating to tense and agreement, a computerized picture-choice task presented individual learners with arrays of three pictures related to various times of day (for tense) and various numbers of people (for agreement). There was a target picture (= the correct choice), competitor picture (= a possible but wrong choice) and a foil (a completely unrelated picture to make sure the participants were following instructions). Participants listened to sentences matching the target, and for each sentence they had to indicate which picture matched. A distractor item or trial which was not included in the data analysis first introduced the context of time; the participant's response to the nine o'clock picture indicated the participant's understanding of the tense context.

Example 9

(a) Distractor trial
    It's ten o'clock right now. Listen and choose:
    'He was climbing something one hour ago.'

(b) Experimental trial
    'He climbed up the mountain.'

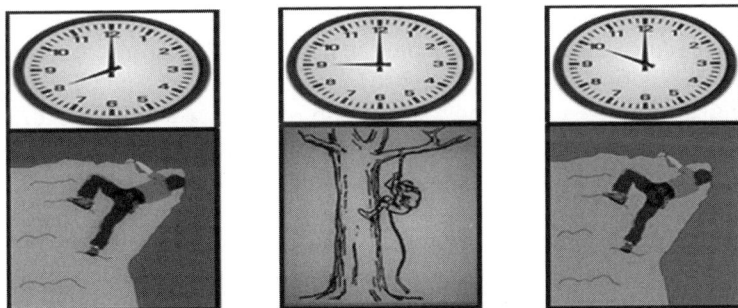

Establishment of the time as 10 o'clock and perception of the past tense inflection on the verb 'climb' in Example 9b was expected to prompt participants to choose the eight o'clock picture.

Subject-verb agreement was tested with one oral stimulus, two stimuli depicting the same action (dancing in the example below) and one foil picture (playing football in the example below). To prevent the participants from using the subject as a clue, the subject of each sentence was not provided but rather masked with silence.

Example 10

'Every party [...] dances happily'

Perception of the *-s* agreement inflection on 'dances' was expected to prompt participants to choose the target picture, the single character who dances at every party. The task consisted of 88 items or trials with 10 training trials, 27 experimental trials, 39 distractors and 12 experimental-like fillers. A high number of distractors and fillers is necessary in such tests to prevent participants from figuring out what is being tested and monitoring their performance.[7] The sentences in the experimental trials contained verbs inflected for either agreement or past tense. The task contained 15 items inflected for past and 12 items inflected for agreement. As in the production task, allomorphs of these suffixes were also manipulated to see whether the phonological form of the suffix had an influence. Unlike the production task, a control group of 10 similarly aged native English speakers was included to confirm test validity and to compare the L2 learner groups' behavior with that of native speakers. The results show that all three Chinese groups and the Low and Mid Arabic groups had problems perceiving past tense, and all apart from the Arabic High group were significantly different from the native speaker group.

Perception rates for past tense for separate Arabic and Chinese speaking groups by proficiency sub-group showed a significant difference among the Arabic Low and Mid versus the Arabic High group (see Table 6.5). Perception of agreement was similar: there was a significant difference among the two lowest Arabic groups and the highest group, and this group (unlike all other groups) also did not significantly differ from the group of native speakers. For the Chinese groups, no such effects were found in the perception of past or agreement (see Table 6.6).

Table 6.5 Successful perception of past tense by Arabic and Chinese learners

Arabic				Chinese				Native		
	Score	%	SD		Score	%	SD	Score	%	SD
Low (*n* = 9)	77/135	57.03	19	Low (*n* = 11)	102/161	63.35	20	139/150	92.66	10
Mid (*n* = 13)	133/195	68.20	26	Mid (*n* = 13)	107/180	59.44	24			
High (*n* = 9)	117/135	86.66	10	High (*n* = 10)	104/150	69.33	26			

Table 6.6 Successful agreement perception by Arabic, Chinese and native speakers

Arabic				Chinese				Native		
	Score	%	SD		Score	%	SD	Score	%	SD
Low (n = 9)	80/108	74.07	16	Low (n = 11)	104/130	80	10	117/120	97.5	4
Mid (n = 13)	112/156	71.79	18	Mid (n = 13)	118/156	75.64	15			
High (n = 9)	100/108	92.59	9	High (n = 10)	94/120	78.33	18			

Native language prosodic constraints might also be acting on perception. As noted above, the perception results were also examined by suffix allomorph, cluster versus non-cluster and regular versus irregular. These variants revealed no significant differences for the Arabic speakers; that is, phonology had no influence. For the Chinese there were significant differences, but only for Low level, where perception of a long vowel preceding the consonant -d marking past tense was significantly worse than that of a short vowel CV-d, and for Mid level, perception of a consonant followed by the consonant -t was significantly better than for the other allomorphs.

In the perception of 3rd person singular -s there were no significant differences for Arabic learners at any level. The Chinese results also showed no significant differences for cluster versus non-cluster at any level, and no significant differences for Mid- and High-level learners with respect to allomorphs. However, for Low-level Chinese learners, the consonant -z following a long vowel was significantly better than other allomorphs and the consonant -z following a short vowel was significantly worse in perception than the C-z allomorph.

Processing: Reaction times

The picture-choice task also measured learners' reaction times for further insights into their underlying linguistic competence. Only the reaction times on the experimental trials which were answered correctly are of interest and are therefore presented here. Similar to the results discussed thus far, this measure did not show any differences between the two native language groups by proficiency level. For each group, results demonstrate learner improvement on past tense with rising proficiency, but not to native speaker level. For the Arabic learners, there were no significant differences between Low- and Mid-level and Mid- and High-level groups, but there were significant differences between Low- and High-level groups. Chinese results showed a significant difference among proficiency where Low- and Mid-level learners performed similarly as did Mid- and High-level learners, and High-level learners performed significantly better than Low-level learners. For agreement, development of English as measured by faster reaction times by proficiency level revealed significant differences between all proficiency groups and the native speakers, and no significant difference between the Low- and Mid-level groups, but reaction times showed that the High-level groups performed significantly better than the Low-level groups.

Processing: Eye tracking

This measure provided the most interesting data in the entire study in terms of native language and proficiency effects. Length of eye-look and first look to target measure were applied to the perception data described above. Length of eye-look, as shown in milliseconds (ms) in the figures below, shows to what extent learners prefer the target picture over the competitor (eye-looks to the foil are unrelated to tense or agreement). First look is a measure of how rapidly learners spot the target picture after hearing the sentence, as shown in Figure 6.1.

For past tense, the Low-level Arabic and Chinese speakers looked for equal lengths of time at target and competitor, and Mid- and High-level Arabic speakers – but not Chinese speakers – spent a longer time looking at targets. They patterned with native English speakers who looked significantly longer at targets than competitors.

The Arabic and Chinese Low-level groups initiated looks to both target and competitor pictures in the same manner, with no apparent preference for either, as shown in Figure 6.2.

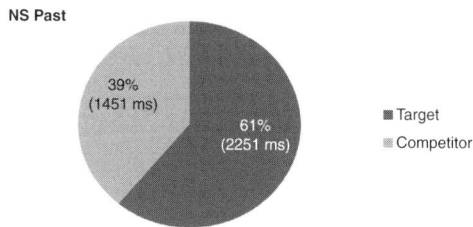

NS Past

39%
(1451 ms)

61%
(2251 ms)

■ Target
▨ Competitor

Figure 6.1 Eye-looks in past tense items by native English speakers

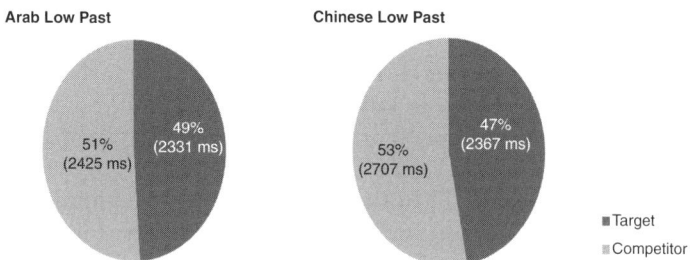

Arab Low Past

51%
(2425 ms)

49%
(2331 ms)

Chinese Low Past

53%
(2707 ms)

47%
(2367 ms)

■ Target
▨ Competitor

Figure 6.2 Eye-looks in past tense items by Low-level non-native groups

Arab Mid Past

42%
(1898 ms)

58%
(2605 ms)

Chinese Mid Past

47%
(2268 ms)

53%
(2565 ms)

■ Target
■ Competitor

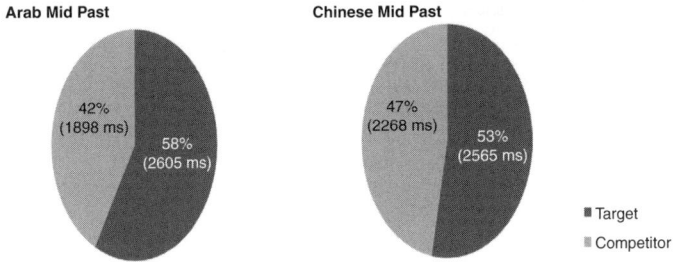

Figure 6.3 Eye-looks in past tense items by Mid-level non-native groups

Mid-level Arabic learners looked significantly more at targets than competitors while there were no significant differences for Chinese learners: they looked at target and competitor pictures in the same manner; see Figure 6.3.

Figure 6.4 shows that Arabic and Chinese High-level learners patterned differently and statistical tests show that, while the Arabic group looked at targets significantly more than at competitor pictures, the Chinese group did not.

While past tense showed no preference for either native language group at the lowest proficiency level, and at the two higher levels only for the Arabic group, the eye tracking of subject-verb agreement showed significant preference for the target picture by all groups. For the native English speakers and for all three proficiency levels and for each language group, eye-looks at target pictures were significantly more frequent than at competitor pictures.

In the measurement of first look, i.e. how quickly a participant looks at the target picture immediately after presentation of the stimulus (as shown in Figures 6.4 to 6.8), Arabic speakers' sensitivity in past tense trials, as shown by speed, increases with proficiency: there were no significant differences between the Low- and Mid-level groups but the High-level group differed significantly from the Low- and Mid-level groups. The Chinese speakers' speed for first look increases significantly from Low to Mid levels, but then decreases for the High-level learners. Results for native language

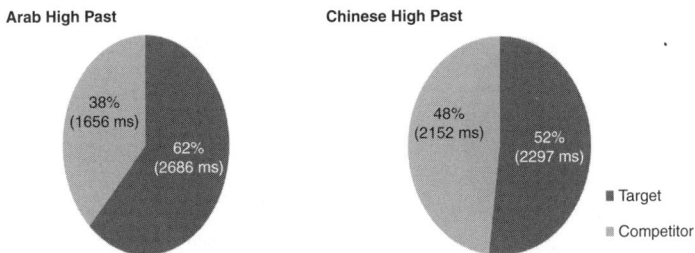

Arab High Past

38%
(1656 ms)

62%
(2686 ms)

Chinese High Past

48%
(2152 ms)

52%
(2297 ms)

■ Target
■ Competitor

Figure 6.4 Eye-looks in past tense items by High-level non-native groups

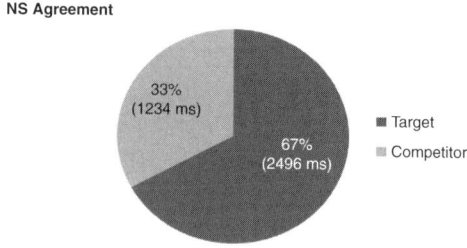

Figure 6.5 Eye-looks for agreement by native English speakers

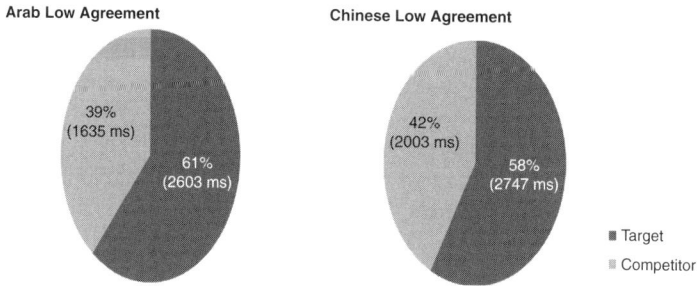

Figure 6.6 Eye-looks in agreement items by Low-level non-native groups

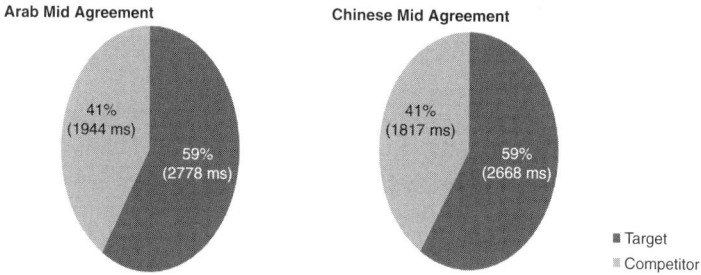

Figure 6.7 Eye-looks in agreement items by Mid-level non-native groups

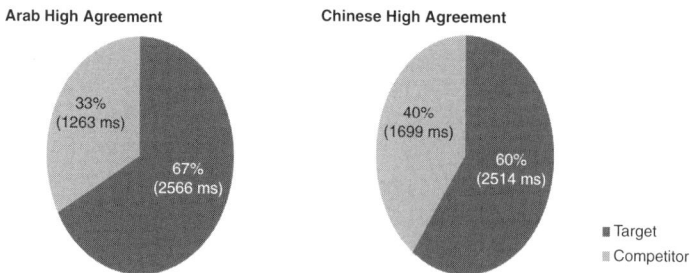

Figure 6.8 Eye-looks in agreement items by High-level non-native groups

showed significant differences between the Arabic and Chinese groups at Low level and High level but not at Mid level. Results for the native English speakers versus non-native speakers showed no difference between the native speakers and the Arabic High-level group but significant differences between the native speaker group and the other non-native groups.

Arabic and Chinese learners' speed with respect to agreement increased with rising proficiency; however, at the highest proficiency level Chinese learners' sensitivity then decreased. Similar proficiency groups in each language were not significantly different at either the Low level or Mid level, but at High level Arabic learners' sensitivity to agreement was significantly higher than that of their Chinese counterparts, and the Arabic High-level learners and native speakers hardly differed with their scores approaching significance.

Discussion

Considering the clues to solving the mystery

What do these results tell us about missing inflections? By all measures discussed above, Low- and Mid-level learners from two very different native language backgrounds followed a similar route in acquisition of TP and AgrP, as predicted by Organic Grammar. No significant differences were found between the two groups at these proficiency levels, neither in production nor in the various measures of perception and processing. A significant difference emerged at the highest level of acquisition, however. The Low-level Arabic and Chinese speakers produced agreement and tense morphology variably, they experienced perceptual limitations, they exhibited slower reaction times and slower first looks and they showed no gaze preference for the target pictures during eye tracking. At the Mid level, they all improved and the same patterns were observed.

With increasing overall proficiency, the Arabic and Chinese speakers began to differ: at High level, Chinese speakers continued their variable oral production while Arabic speakers became consistent. All speakers' perception showed improvements at the highest level. No differences were found for reaction times, but for eye movement, patterns for past tense for Arabic speakers showed a significant preference for the target and significantly faster first looks not only for past tense but also for agreement. Table 6.7 shows the group mean results underlying the results of the tests for statistical significance referred to above, namely the percentages for accuracy for production and perception, correct eye-looks at target and the milliseconds in reacting to the picture stimulus and in looking first at the correct target picture.

Solving the mystery?

Variable production of 3rd person singular -s and past tense morphology by the Chinese learners at the Low, Mid and High proficiency levels

Table 6.7 Development of tense phrase (TP) and agreement phrase (AgrP) (group means)

		Arabic Low	Arabic Mid	Arabic High	Chinese Low	Chinese Mid	Chinese High	Natives
Production (%)	Past	56%	66%	93%	47%	51%	74%	–
	Agr	47%	50%	87%	54%	48%	73%	–
Perception (%)	Past	57%	68%	87%	63%	59%	69%	93%
	Agr	74%	72%	93%	80%	76%	78%	97%
Reaction time (ms)	Past	2668	2153	1503	2729	2640	1854	1017
	Agr	2485	2300	1379	2468	1867	1541	857
Looks at target (%)	Past	49%	58%	62%	47%	53%	52%	61%
	Agr	61%	59%	67%	58%	59%	60%	67%
First look at target (ms)	Past	1246	940	773	1654	1126	1425	695
	Agr	1109	933	741	1195	878	1046	589

and by Arabic learners at Low and Mid levels, coupled with perceptual limitations of the same morphological items, indicates that the source of learners' problems is representational, i.e. due to learners' morphosyntax lacking a TP or an AgrP. Learners' development with rising proficiency, particularly for Arabic speaking learners in their oral production and perception of morphology, indicates a gradual building of syntactic representations. That is, the Low- and Mid-level Arabic speakers and all levels of Chinese speakers gradually acquire TP and AgrP. The Arabic speakers show no initial or intermediate advantage over the Chinese speakers but pull ahead at High level. This difference cannot be traced to phonology in any obvious way. The data presented here thus do not provide support for the MSIH. The comprehension and processing experiments would have revealed competence in these suffixes, contrary to what was found: production, comprehension, reaction time and eye tracking provide consistent results at the various proficiency levels. Deficit approaches, and Full Transfer/Full Access (whereby all functional projections are present in the L2 learner's internal grammar throughout acquisition) are thus not supported by these data. Full Transfer is not supported: Arabic learners were expected to but did not produce, perceive and process 3rd person singular and past tense morphology better than their Chinese counterparts from early on. They only did so at High level. The data from the Low- and Mid-level Arabic and Chinese learners of English support Organic Grammar in that absence of TP and/or AgrP explains these patterns whereas the High-level Arabic learners' patterns point to their acquisition of TP and AgrP.

No hypothesis discussed thus far predicted what we found for the High-level learners. There are two possibilities here: (1) Hawkins' (2001) Modulated Structure Building, according to which learners build structure and when functional projections are acquired during development, the learner's native language can provide assistance in acquiring a new projection; or (2) the High-level Chinese speakers, in fact, are high intermediates, and there are speakers at a more advanced level who acquire TP and AgrP. In Hawkins' version of structure building, it is not clear exactly what the predictions would be for Chinese learners of English, since the Arabic and Chinese learners pattern the same at lower levels.

For Chinese High-level learners, it is possible that there is a stage at which TP and/or AgrP is being acquired, although later than the Arabic learners: the U-shaped learning curve shown in the 'Sensitivity to Past' graph in Figure 6.9 for the picture choice task results mirrors the tense/agreement of children's L1 acquisition of French reported in Davidson and Legendre (2003). They argue that TP is acquired first, then once agreement shows up there is competition for space (no AgrP yet) and performance on tense declines before TP and AgrP are then both projected.

The production results indicate that, for the Arabic learners, TP is acquired before AgrP; for Chinese learners, AgrP is not acquired until TP is. However, the perception and processing results do not seem to support this. One possible reason for this discrepancy is the role of the perceptual salience of the sibilant fricatives [s] and [z] in facilitating processing of 3rd person singular agreement as in the four allomorphs in 'sits', 'loves', 'crushes' and 'knows'. Therefore, (i) the oral production data present evidence for the acquisition of TP before AgrP, but (ii) the perception and processing data cannot be considered evidence against the acquisition of TP before AgrP because the perceptual salience of the agreement suffix allomorphs makes the comparison unreliable. We also have to take into consideration that all of the learners in this study were instructed prior to moving to the UK, and instruction in agreement and past tense is inevitable.

Our results do not warrant the conclusion that adult L2 learners have only partial access to Universal Grammar, i.e. they do not support the deficit hypotheses discussed above. At the early stages of development, both language groups pattern extremely similarly. Under Organic Grammar, with direct access to Universal Grammar, this is predicted.

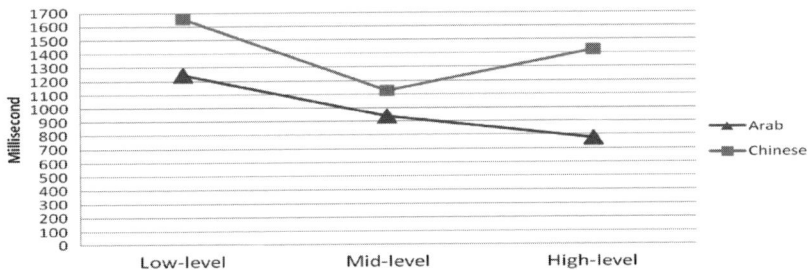

Figure 6.9 Learners' perceptual sensitivity to past tense (picture choice task)

Why exactly Chinese speakers' development initially proceeds like Arabic speakers' development but then stalls remains another mystery to be solved. We suggest this might be investigated by looking closely at the minor phonological differences detected in the oral production and perception tasks. These might reflect learners' phonological problems in processing the target language input as they search for information in the input to trigger their acquisition of TP and AgrP in English (for elaboration on this idea, see Vainikka & Young-Scholten, 1998). In this sense, too, L2 learners are detectives in solving their own mystery of missing inflections.

Notes

(1) Much recent Minimalist theorizing (e.g. Chomsky, 2008) excludes AgrP for theory-internal reasons, but we continue to assume AgrP.
(2) An anonymous reviewer points out that utterances such as Examples 2 and 3 might reflect fuller adult sentences the child hears, e.g. 'Do you want to give doggie a bone?' without missing inflection.
(3) Referred to as Root Infinitives (Rizzi, 1993/1994), Optional Infinitives (Wexler, 1994) and Root Defaults (Paradis & Crago, 2000).
(4) Further examples of non-adult syntax (from Castro & Gavruseva, 2003; Gagarina & Gülzow, 2008; Hyams, 2007) include:
   (i)   *Papa schoenen wassen.*   [Dutch]
          Daddy shoes wash-INF
   (ii) *Michel dormer.*   [French]
          Michel sleep-INF
   (iii) *Jag ocksa hoppa där a där.*   [Swedish]
          I also hop-INF there and there
   (iv) *Lomat koleso.*   [Russian]
          break-INF wheel-ACC
   (v)   *Mi hacer otra.*   [Spanish]
          me make-INF another
(5) This is Rizzi's (1993/1994) Truncation Hypothesis and Wexler's (1994) Optional Infinitive Stage; see also Wexler *et al.* (1998).
(6) The Child Language Data Exchange System (MacWhinney (2000) https://childes.talkbank.org/-) is an open-source databank of orthographically transcribed, coded speech samples from children acquiring a range of languages. Anyone can query it for counts or co-occurrences for syntax, morphology and lexis.
(7) Six were similar to the past tense trials and six were similar to the verbal agreement trials. These were experimental-like in that they used the same auditory stimuli of the experimental trials but with bare verbs. The rationale for this was to detect whether participants considered all verbs presented inflected and gave responses based on this, which would be a deceptive indicator of their perception. The inclusion of these items meant that they did not so do, i.e. this strategy was successful.

7 The Second Language Lexicon

Vivienne Rogers, David Playfoot and
James Milton

Introduction

A feature of the literature on learning and teaching second/foreign languages over the last 20 years has been the burgeoning interest in vocabulary, i.e. the mental lexicon. Publications such as Lewis's (1993) *The Lexical Approach* and Nation's (1990) *Teaching and Learning Vocabulary* mark a change in the prominence given to this aspect of language. Earlier approaches to language learning and description had downplayed the significance of vocabulary, particularly within formal approaches to language acquisition. Wolter (2013) observes that nowadays the lexicon has clearly found a permanent place in research on applied linguistics and second language acquisition (SLA), although the connection between lexis and grammar (or syntax) remains underexplored. We thus explore this claim in more detail in this chapter.

Two features unite the current wide range of issues addressed in the literature on the learning and teaching of the lexicon. One is the attempt to reassert the centrality of the development of a lexicon of an appropriate size and quality in the teaching and learning of foreign languages. For example, among 10 key issues in SLA identified by Schmitt (2010), the importance of the lexicon, of vocabulary learning, is listed first. The second is that the lexicon cannot be fully understood in isolation but rather is inextricably linked to other domains of language, such as syntax. Wolter (2013) further suggests that when the description of a language is approached from a lexical perspective, the division between lexis and syntax breaks down.

Research into the lexicon can be categorized into three broad strands (Schmitt & McCarthy, 1997). The first strand concentrates on the lexicon, or what exactly words are (lexico-semantics). The second strand focuses on how elements of the lexicon are stored and accessed at a psychological level. The third strand incorporates research on the teaching, learning and assessment/measurement of the lexicon. This chapter begins with an overview of the current state of research on the second language

(L2) lexicon, and will concentrate only on the first two strands in Schmitt and McCarthy's (1997) classification; see Milton (2009) for an overview of assessing L2 vocabulary acquisition. However, these two strands overlap and research in one will both draw from and have implications for the other. Research into lexical storage, for example, will need a description of what the units are, single words or otherwise, that are being stored. The second part of the chapter reports on two different areas of current research on the mental lexicon. The first examines word associations and what these can tell us about the lexicon in first (L1) and second language acquisition. The second area considers the relationship between the acquisition of vocabulary items/words and syntax.

Description of the Lexicon

The creation of good, workable and useful definitions and descriptions of the words or units that make up the mental lexicon has been the goal of the study of lexico-semantics over many years. However, the units or components that form the lexicon must be interpreted with a degree of elasticity (Milton & Fitzpatrick, 2013). A lexicon that is large and sophisticated enough for efficient L1 or L2 communication is likely to include knowledge not just of words, however defined, but also of units smaller than words, i.e. the word parts known as morphemes, and word combinations or collocations (see Barfield, 2013, on collocations). In his classic work, Palmer (1921) pointed out that in English lexical components include knowledge that suffixes such as -*er* and -*ist* can change a verb into a noun that marks who is doing what (the agent), so a *baker* is someone who *bakes* and *cyclist* is someone who *cycles*. This knowledge is also likely to include common phrases (or **formulaic chunks**) such as *of course* and *in spite of* which function like single words, despite the fact they are made up of several words (see Wray, 2009, for an overview of formulaic language). The list of possible components in the lexicon has grown since the time of Palmer. Nation (2001) provides one of the most comprehensive and well-used lists for these, shown in Table 7.1. In this list, words and word knowledge includes an understanding of the grammatical functions and structures of words, word referents, word associations and collocations, and the limitations and constraints which users place on words.

One of the challenges for vocabulary research is how to investigate the different elements of knowledge represented in Table 7.1. Knowledge of the form and its meaning is commonly termed vocabulary *breadth*. This can be distinguished from the use or how these words divide or combine with other words, called vocabulary *depth* (as in Daller *et al*., 2007). Both of these terms can be separated from considerations of the ease and speed with which a speaker can call words to mind and use them, called *vocabulary fluency* (Daller *et al*., 2007). These three areas develop the productive-receptive vocabulary knowledge dichotomy into a three-dimensional model of the lexicon. Meara (1996) suggests that fluency and depth may be combined as a single dimension: vocabulary *organization*. This is based on the ease and speed with which a speaker can access a word for use which may depend on the degree to which items are linked to other items through collocation, structure, association and the other features of depth in the speaker's lexicon.

Researchers' confusion over what the term *word* might include has largely been overcome, as shown in Table 7.1. This makes it clear for modern vocabulary teaching that simple word lists or single-word L1-L2 translations will not suffice in developing the kind of breadth and depth of lexical knowledge that speakers need. But how are words learned? Modern studies of the lexicon no longer treat every inflected and derived form of a base word as a separate learning task. The different inflections of a word, e.g. *run, running, ran* are termed '**lemmas**'. Together with their different derivations (e.g. *run, runner*), words are grouped into *word families* (Nation, 2001). This is a result of an understanding of the way words and their sub-parts, morphemes, are stored and retrieved and will be examined in the next section.

Table 7.1 What is involved in knowing a word?

Form	Spoken	R	What does the word sound like?
		P	How is the word pronounced?
	Written	R	What does the word look like?
		P	How is the word written and spelled?
	Word parts	R	What parts are recognizable in this word?
		P	What word parts are needed to express the meaning?
Meaning	Form and meaning	R	What meaning does this word form signal?
		P	What word form can be used to express this meaning?
	Concepts and referents	R	What is included in the concept?
		P	What items can the concept refer to?
	Associations	R	What other words does this word make us think of?
		P	What other words could we use instead of this one?
Use	Grammatical functions	R	In what patterns does the word occur?
		P	In what patterns must we use this word?
	Collocations	R	What words or types of words occur with this one?
		P	What words or types of words must we use with this one?
	Constraints on use	R	Where, when and how often would we expect to meet this word?
		P	Where, when and how often can we use this word?

Notes: R = receptive; P = productive.
Source: From Nation (2001: 27).

Storage, Access and Processing

There is growing evidence that L1 learners store a base form of a word (the lemma) associated with a semantic concept in their mental lexicons. Pienemann (1998), for example, places an understanding of the lemma at the heart of all language learning (see also Kessler *et al.*, this volume).

Once a speaker retrieves a word or lemma from memory for use, it can undergo inflection by regular rules. So, if an L2 English learner wants to talk about a prime minister governing, in grammatical terms of when this happened, then only *govern* is retrieved from the lexicon; this can be changed to *govern-ed* for past actions, or to *govern-s* for present. Researchers also hold that, at least in English, derivational morphological variations of such base forms which both change the part of speech and change the meaning, for example the two morphemes in *govern-or*, are each stored and processed separately. They are, in effect, different entries in the mental lexicon. In L1 acquisition the development of this kind of lexical knowledge proceeds well into adolescence when the already large lexicon further expands (Aitchison, 2003). Adult foreign language learners appear to transfer word family insight very rapidly into their L2; even if they do not get these forms right all the time, they do attempt early on to process language in this way (Schmitt & Meara, 1997).

Vermeer (2001) articulates current thinking in this area in observing that the lemma, both in its base form and with its most frequent and regularly inflected forms, is the most appropriate unit reflecting learners' use and understanding of vocabulary (see also Gardner, 2007, for a review of research in this area). Most measures of vocabulary size among L2 learners, therefore, will use a lemma as the basis for their estimations. Thus, *govern*, and its **inflectional** morphology, e.g. *governed, governs* and *governing*, would be counted as a single word, but the **derivation** *governor* as a different word. What emerges from tests using this method of word count are reliable, believable and useful measurements of vocabulary knowledge.

There is also considerable evidence that the mental lexicon is not ordered alphabetically like a print dictionary, which is commonly (but not helpfully) used as an analogy. Instead it is a network of interconnected words (Collins & Loftus, 1975; Collins & Quillian, 1969; Fodor, 1983; Steyvers & Tenenbaum, 2005; Wilks & Meara, 2002). In such models, the lexicon contains a node for each lemma in the individual's vocabulary, and there are links from each node to any number of other nodes (Figure 7.1). The presentation of a particular lemma prompts the language user to access its representation in the lexicon, and all the attached nodes are made slightly easier to access (*primed*) in case they are needed. To give a non-linguistic example, consider a scrum in rugby union. The scrum half waits at the back of the scrum ready to receive the ball. Either side of the player are a string of team mates. When the scrum half picks up the ball at the base of the scrum (i.e. the player accesses it), the nearest couple of players to the player's

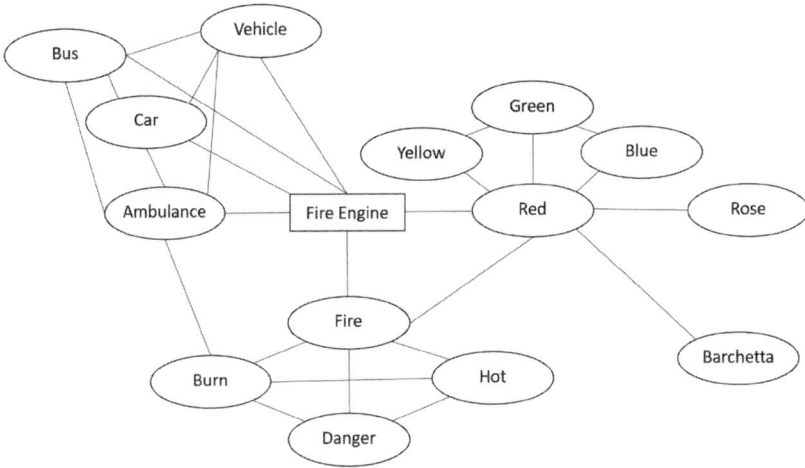

Figure 7.1 An example of a semantic network structure

Notes: The rectangle indicates the activated concept. Ovals contain related concepts. Lines connecting concepts vary in length depending on the strength of the relationship, with longer lines indicating weaker links.

left and right are ready to take the pass (they are primed). If the scrum half makes a pass to the player on their left, then the players on the right are less likely to be needed immediately. In contrast, the players further along the chain towards the left touchline are making themselves ready in case the ball comes to them. In lexical network theory, this is referred to as **spreading activation** – accessing one word makes other words more or less ready to be accessed on the basis of their proximity in the network. This is illustrated in Figure 7.1, where each circle represents a node in the network. Lines between nodes indicate potential intra-lexical links.

The first step for the language user in processing the meaning of a word is to access it in the lexicon. Simply put, when somebody encounters a written letter string or a series of speech sounds they must determine whether it is a word that they know. A word in the lexicon can be accessed from either its written form (orthography) or its spoken form (phonology). Although the precise mechanisms for recognizing written and spoken words are slightly different, the basic principles are the same. Essentially, the task begins with activating all possible matches in the lexicon and discarding any words that become unviable as the language user extracts more information from the input,[1] until only one word remains. If the process of elimination does not result in *any* words remaining, then the input or stimulus is either a nonword or, at least, a word that the language user has not yet learned.

By way of an example, consider the word *take* in written form. According to the Interactive Activation and Competition Model (McClelland & Rumelhart, 1981; Rumelhart & McClelland, 1982), the language user's recognition of a written word is achieved by simple processing *units* at three levels. The lowest level is concerned with the visual features of the stimulus. At the feature level the system identifies basic information about the shape of the letters on the page – the presence or absence of vertical lines, horizontal lines, diagonals and curves. This information is passed on to the second level of processing in which units correspond to individual letters. Any letter that matches the features is turned on (activated). In our example, the combination of a vertical line and a horizontal line activates the letter 'T' but inhibits activation of letters such as 'C' because the features do not match the input. The activation of the letter 'T' is fed into the third and final level of the system in which each unit represents a whole word. Again, any word which begins with a 'T' is activated and all others are inhibited. So, the initial letter of the stimulus activates *take* but also *task* and *time*. Processing proceeds to the next letter in the stimulus, in this case 'A', and the analysis of the visual features begins again. The identification of the letter 'A' is compatible with both *take* and *task* but does not match *time*, so this is inhibited. The identification of the next letter in the stimulus 'K' makes *take* a likely candidate, but *task* is no longer compatible so it is discarded. McClelland and Elman (1986) proposed a model of spoken word recognition called TRACE, derived from the above model, which suggests a similar method for how the language user determines whether phonological input matches an entry in the lexicon.

Word recognition processes are commonly examined using a 'lexical decision task'. Participants are presented with a series of letter strings (or a spoken input) and asked to determine whether the stimulus is a word or not, indicating their choice as quickly as possible by pressing one of two buttons. Experiments using this type of task have identified a number of factors which affect the language user's ease of word recognition. Words are recognized more quickly if they are frequently encountered in daily life, if they were learned early in life or if they are *imageable*, i.e. they easily evoke a mental image (Balota *et al.*, 2004; Hino & Lupker, 2000; Morrison & Ellis, 2000). Researchers theorize that these effects are due to the role that words learned early or frequently accessed have in the structure of the semantic network presented in Figure 7.1. Readers interested in this are directed to Steyvers and Tenenbaum (2005) for a full discussion of how this might work.

Of further interest is that researchers who propose models of the structure of the language system propose that all of these lexicons map onto a single semantic system; that is to say, separate written and spoken lexical entries are connected to a common representation of meaning. In the context of this volume, this notion is important because the majority of the available empirical evidence suggests that first and second languages share one lexical and semantic system. Specifically, *common-store* models say that words in the language user's L1 and L2 are stored together and directly connected (Paivio *et al.*, 1988). Support for this idea comes from **semantic priming** studies. In such studies words are presented as targets in a lexical decision task but, just before the target appears to the participant, another word (the prime) with a similar meaning is presented too quickly to be consciously noticed. The presentation of the prime accesses the word's node in the semantic network. Through spreading activation, the node for the word that is presented as a target is already prepared for access, and hence the participant is able more quickly to decide which word they have heard. The classic study with native speakers is by Meyer and Schvaneveldt (1971), in which the researchers determined that recognition of *doctor* was quicker following the presentation of *nurse* than it was following *bread*. In studies using bilingual participants, researchers have shown that semantic priming effects can be elicited even if the prime and the target are presented in the speaker's two different languages (for a review, see Altarriba & Mathis, 1997).

When a new word is learned it must be integrated into the semantic system. This means a node is added to the semantic network, and this node must be connected or associated to at least one other node. In the framework of common-store/single-lexicon models, whether the new word is in a bilingual speaker's L1 or L2 is unimportant – it is the same network that grows, potentially in the same way, in either language. The word association technique has been popular in both psychological and applied linguistics research for more than a hundred years. It is a task which is specifically geared towards accessing the connections between words in the lexicon and is particularly useful in evaluating the depth and breadth of L2 vocabulary knowledge. The following section investigates the relevance of word association techniques to vocabulary acquisition. We discuss the influence that vocabulary depth (as previously discussed) may have on the organization of the lexicon, and determine whether different patterns of lexical access are likely for L2 learners with large versus small vocabulary scores. Therefore, we will first briefly assess the structure of the lexicon and examine how the researcher can gather important information about learners' lexical networks using a word association task. The potential influence of vocabulary acquisition, both on the lexicon and on word association responses, will be discussed. An overview of the word association research regarding vocabulary development for native speakers and L2 acquisition will be provided, and new native speaker acquisition data will be presented which further highlights the importance of aspects of vocabulary knowledge in lexical retrieval.

The word association task

Although there are a number of variations on the word association theme, this discussion will focus on the *discrete free association* task. Discrete association requires participants to respond with the first word that comes to mind when they are presented with a stimulus or cue word, and it requires them to provide only *one* response. Free association refers to the participant being free to respond with any word they think of, and that they do not have to respond with a specific member of a particular semantic category (e.g. an animal) or word class (e.g. a verb). As mentioned above, the strength of the links between one word and the next in the lexicon determines how easy it is for a language user to retrieve that association. Researchers therefore assume that the participant's response to a cue word (e.g. *black*) is the word that has the strongest link in their lexicon (e.g. *white*).

By collecting word association responses to the same words from a large number of people, researchers can build a picture of what constitutes a 'normal' response to a given cue (a cue-response pair). Lists of responses like this are published as word association norms, and there are a large number of commonly cited norm lists available (Kent & Rosanoff, 1910; Kiss *et al.*, 1973; Moss & Older, 1996; Nelson *et al.*, 1998; Palermo & Jenkins, 1964; Postman & Keppel, 1970). These lists detail responses to word association cues in order of their popularity among a given participant sample, typically native language speakers. By relating the word association responses of one participant to the norms list of responses from a relevant sample, researchers can get an indication of how typical the individual is of the group.

Another way researchers quantify word association responses is to attribute each cue-response pair to an underlying type of link. That is to say, the connection that is made between *cat* and *dog* could be described as being 'semantic', as they have features in common (pets, four legs, with hair, etc.). In other examples, the link between cue and target could be due to their co-occurrence in sentences or compound-nouns (*fence* and *post* is an example of a collocation or position link as in fence-post). Also common are associations based on the phonological form of the cue word such as *bake* and *lake*. This gives the researcher useful information about the way in which a language user's lexicon is structured, and the process by which an association is made. According to Collins and Loftus (1975), the probability of a particular response being generated in relation to a cue word depends on two aspects of the lexical network. The first is the number of links which emanate from the cue word's node. Each link which stems from the cue word is activated to some degree when the cue word is presented. Nodes with a large number of links have to share out that activation between a greater number of connected nodes, so each individual connection is activated less than for nodes with only a few connections. The second factor in the probability of the language user activating a particular associate for a cue is the strength of the connection between the nodes for cue and response. Researchers argue that any given link between two words increases in strength every time the link is activated (see de Groot, 1989, for a discussion of this issue), and stronger links are easier to activate. The word association task is designed to examine these intra-lexical links between nodes.

Of course, size and content of the lexicon varies considerably across individuals and across the lifespan. People continue to encounter and learn new words well into advanced age (Kemper & Sumner, 2001; Verhaegen, 2003). This is true for native language as well as second language speakers. The mechanisms by which a language user integrates new words into the lexicon are not fully understood, but a number of models have been proposed (Monaghan & Ellis, 2010; Steyvers & Tenenbaum, 2005). In each case, the acquisition of new words affects, and is affected by, the words which are already present in the lexicon. In Steyvers and Tenenbaum's (2005) model the new words are related to existing words in a way that results in a word learned earlier having a greater number of connections stemming from it. Monaghan and Ellis (2010) describe a model which becomes increasingly less efficient in creating and integrating new nodes, such that there is an advantage for earlier learned words – except in cases where late-acquired words can be mapped onto existing representations. Whatever the exact mechanisms are, however, the changes to the structure of the lexicon are liable to have an effect on word association particularly in relation to age of acquisition (Brysbaert et al., 2000; Playfoot & Izura, 2013); that is, words learned early in life elicit associations more quickly, and with less variability, than words learned later. Researchers assume that the lexicon is efficient, and unlike other aspects of language the brain does not ever lose the 'plasticity' to add new words. Inefficiency is connected to a word increasing vocabulary size by 1, and the number of links between nodes by not less than 1. Within the framework that Collins and Loftus (1975) discuss, this could result in an increased variability in the language user's response during word association as a consequence of increasing the number of intra-lexical links. It could equally, according to Steyvers and Tenenbaum (2005), result in a consolidation and strengthening of the links that already exist in the lexicon, and thus increase the likelihood of one particular response.

It is no surprise, therefore, that the word association task has long enjoyed popularity in studies which assessed vocabulary development in L1 (e.g. Entwisle et al., 1964; Ervin, 1961) or L2 (Meara, 2009) or in studies relating to language attrition due to old age, dementia and clinical disorder (e.g. Burke & Peters, 1986; Gollan et al., 2006; Hirsh & Tree, 2001), given its advantages for illuminating the structure of the lexicon, and providing evidence as to how words are organized as vocabulary develops.

A full review of the literature concerning word associations in SLA is beyond the remit of this chapter. Those interested in a greater depth are encouraged to read the work by Meara (2009). However, a brief glance at this body of research shows that findings are equivocal. A large number of studies suggest that learners of English provide highly variable (although not necessarily non-systematic) word association responses. Even less consistent are the findings relating to the category of link between cue and response. In the vast majority of studies, L2 learners give a greater number of surface-level, form-based (look-alike or sound-alike) responses than native speakers (e.g. Meara, 1983); increased proficiency seems to reduce the number of form-based responses that researchers record. It is unclear whether this reduction in form-based responses mirrors a 'syntagmatic-paradigmatic' shift (Entwisle *et al.*, 1964) found in L1 language acquisition. Entwisle *et al.* (1964) reported that as children become more adept in their native language they begin to make fewer associations based on the position of words in sentences (syntagmatic responses like '*go-home*') and instead start to favour associates based on meaning (paradigmatic responses such as *go-went*). In relation to L2 acquisition, paradigmatic responses have been shown to be more common in proficient learners (Piper & Leicester, 1980; Söderman, 1993; Zareva, 2007), but this is not always the case (see, for example, Nissen & Henriksen, 2006).

Although the L2 research suggests a link between learners' vocabulary and word association behaviour, there are issues with using L2 learners in this type of study. The main issue is that learning a language does not only entail acquiring additional vocabulary, but also acquiring syntax, phonology, pragmatics and the various sociolinguistic factors that govern the way in which the language is spoken. Increases in vocabulary size do not occur in a vacuum. As will be discussed later in this chapter, there may be a link between increases in vocabulary knowledge and the acquisition of syntax structures. Thus differences between low-proficiency learners and high-proficiency learners may stem from any facet of language learning, some of which may be tied to vocabulary, others of which will be vocabulary independent. This poses a problem in the interpretation of L2 word association data.

It is for this reason that we illustrate the discussion above with data from an empirical study on lexical retrieval using native English speakers. The participants were therefore all assumed to have similar knowledge of their native language, in order to allow for a clearer assessment of the main issue – the influence of vocabulary knowledge on lexical retrieval. The results can be applied to L2 research because it has been demonstrated that there is a correlation between the word association responses of participants performing the task in their L1 and in their L2 (Fitzpatrick, 2009).

Methodology

Forty participants were selected from a much larger cohort, part of a genetic heritability study at Queensland Institute of Medical Research (QIMR). All participants were aged 16, and native speakers of Australian

English. There were 25 male and 15 female participants for this study. As part of the larger data collection, all participants took the Wechsler Adult Intelligence Scale (WAIS) to test for individual cognitive differences. The participants described here were the 20 highest and lowest scorers from the QIMR cohort on the Vocabulary sub-test of the WAIS. There was a significant difference between vocabulary scores of the high and low vocabulary group [$t(1) = 19.895$, $p < 0.001$].

The cues selected for this study were chosen from the first 2000–3000 most frequent words (mostly nouns) identified in the British National Corpus. These are frequent enough to be known to the majority of the participants, but not so frequent that they will produce only a few different responses. The 100 cues were presented 50 to a page in two equal columns. Next to each cue was a space for the participant to write their response. Participants were instructed to write down the first word that they thought of when reading each cue, and told that there were no right or wrong answers. Participants were allowed up to 10 minutes to complete the task. All participants finished the task before the time limit.

Results

Word association responses were assessed in relation to the category of association between cue and response, and were scored for *stereotypy* and *idiosyncrasy*. A stereotypy point was scored for every cue for which the participant's response matched the most popular answer on the norms list (available in Fitzpatrick *et al.*, 2013). Idiosyncrasy points were accumulated by giving an association to a cue that was not represented on the norms list at all. Responses were classified under the broad headings of *semantic, positional, form-based* and *semantic & positional*. When cue and response were synonyms (*delay-impede*), hyponyms (*bean-vegetable*) or co-hyponyms (*bean-pea*), responses were classified as semantic. Positional links (collocations) were instances in which the cue and response commonly occur together in sentences or short phrases, but do not share aspects of meaning or form (e.g. *spark* and *plug*). A response was categorized as form-based when cue and response were similar in orthography, phonology or both (*fence-hence*), or when morphologically related (*plug-unplug*). The semantic and positional links were classified as such because both types of link existed between cue and target (e.g. *knife* and *fork*) and it was not possible to objectively determine which was the more important (if either). (Thus for each participant there were seven scores available – six word association measures and their Vocabulary score from the WAIS.) (See Fitzpatrick *et al.*, 2013, for a full description of the procedure for treating and scoring the data.) Table 7.2 presents the mean score and standard deviation of scores for the high and low vocabulary groups.

Table 7.2 Descriptive statistics for word association variables split by vocabulary score

	Low vocabulary scorers		High vocabulary scorers	
	Mean	SD	Mean	SD
Overall vocabulary score	10.4	1.5	31.4	4.5
Stereotypy	22.3	7.6	21.8	6.7
Idiosyncrasy	33.0	12.4	29.9	10.2
Semantic links	76.4	5.1	73.9	6.6
Positional links	13.9	6.1	**20.9**	6.1
Form-based links	**4.4**	3.5	1.9	2.1
Semantic and positional links	1.1	0.2	0.9	0.9

The table shows large differences between the high and low vocabulary scorers in some aspects of word association, but small differences in others. Notably, on average the low vocabulary scorers made a significantly greater number of form-based links than high vocabulary scorers ($t(1) = 2.817, p < 0.01$). Participants with high vocabulary scores were significantly more likely to respond with a positional (collocational) associate for the cue word ($t(1) = 3.627, p < 0.01$). No other comparisons reached statistical significance (all $p > 0.1$).

Discussion

The data described here indicate a difference in the word association response styles of native English speakers relative to their vocabulary. This clearly relates to the research on L2 word association behaviour, regarding one of the most common and consistent findings that learners offer a greater number of form-based responses than native speakers (e.g. Meara, 1983). A larger number of form-based links was also observed in low vocabulary scorers in the present study. However, it is still unclear from this cross-sectional study design whether this form-based ordering of the lexicon is a feature of small vocabularies or a temporary solution to the problem of integrating words in a developing network. What is clear is that the current study implicates vocabulary size as a determinant of word association behaviour even without the confounding factor of having to learn L2 syntax concurrently. We now turn to the unanswered question of whether there is a link between vocabulary development and the acquisition of syntactic features. More specifically, is there a critical mass of vocabulary that one has to have acquired before certain aspects of syntax can be acquired?

Vocabulary and Syntax: An Experimental Investigation

In this section we consider links between the acquisition of vocabulary items and syntactic features in L2 within a generative framework to explore the interconnectedness that some have argued for (Wolter, 2013). We first outline a study by David *et al.* (2009), before presenting a reanalysis of data from Rogers (2009) to address the co-development of syntactic features and lexical development.

The role of the lexicon in generative linguistics has undergone considerable revision since the early instantiations of Universal Grammar (Chomsky, 1965, 1986). The advent of the **Minimalist Program** (Chomsky, 1995) introduced a model which assumes only a few key rules or computations as the mechanisms for creating syntax. In this model the lexicon has taken on a much more central and significant role. Linguists have always held that the lexicon has at least some information about features of words (see Table 7.1 above), such as word class or lexical features. However, under Minimalism, specific syntactic features are now also located in the lexicon; syntactic computations are mainly limited to the checking of these features (see, for example, Caink, this volume, for more on this), such as checking features on the subject (singular/plural, 3rd person, etc.) with agreement and person features on the verb, to result in grammatical subject-verb agreement as in *he goes*. This has resulted in a need for linguists to examine the structure of the mental lexicon in much greater detail. However, how generative linguists view the lexicon and how vocabulary researchers view the lexicon differs (see Pustejovsky *et al.*, 2013, for a state-of-the-art discussion of Generative Lexicon Theory). Emonds (2001), developing work from Ouhalla (1991), reconceptualized the lexicon in UG terms as the '**syntacticon**', thus maintaining the lexicon for conceptual ideas.

> [T]here should in principle be a distinction between two notions of the lexicon, a grammatical lexicon which contains functional categories and which belongs to the domain of UG, [and] a mental lexicon which contains substantives and which exists independently of UG, that is an autonomous module of the mind/brain. (Ouhalla, 1991: 7–10)

This view maintains a division between the lexicon or, in Emonds' terminology, *the dictionary*, where the words with semantic meaning are stored, i.e. nouns, verbs, adjectives and some prepositions, and those items associated with syntax or derivations. The former is open for new items or words to be added; however, the latter category is a closed class containing a small number of grammatical features. For example, many languages such as French have a syntactic feature on nouns relating to gender. There is nothing about the noun itself that determines if it is 'masculine' or 'feminine', but when a noun is used, the correct determiner form must be used. So the determiner and noun must agree in gender features and if an adjective is present then it also must agree (e.g. *the white house* in French is $La_{(fem)}$ $maison_{(fem)}$

blanche(fem) and not *la*(fem) *maison*(fem) *blanc*(masc)). Syntactic features also include abstract features that are not seen in the surface morphology. For example, in English there is an abstract, syntactic feature on lexical or main verbs (i.e. not auxiliaries or modals) that disallows them from appearing before negation (*She wants not to go to the cinema). Instead English requires *do*-support for subject-verb agreement (*She does not want to go to the cinema*). This is known as the '**uninterpretable** tense feature' and we will return to it when considering the reanalysis of Rogers' (2009) data.

A full discussion of the nature of the syntacticon is outside the scope of this chapter; see Emonds (2001). However, Emonds argues that the task for a child learning their first language is to acquire the combination of these syntactic features in the syntacticon specific to their L1. By extension, the same applies to the L2 learner. Emonds' syntacticon simplifies and limits the learning task to the acquisition of syntactic features. How do learners acquire features? One suggestion is that there is a link between the acquisition of the syntactic features in the syntacticon and the acquisition of vocabulary items in the lexicon/dictionary. This suggestion has been investigated by two recent studies of English speakers learning French in the classroom. David *et al.* (2009) looked at acquisition of verbs (VP), Tense and Agreement (TP), gender (DP) and interrogatives (CP) as well as productive vocabulary knowledge. The second study reanalyzed data from Rogers (2009), which focused on several syntactic measures of Tense (TP) and a receptive vocabulary task (see Caink in this volume for an introduction to the syntactic terminology used here).

Study 1

David *et al.* (2009) tested three groups of 20 English-speaking learners of French after one, three and five years of school-based instruction. The groups had received approximately 100 hours, 240 hours and 525 hours of instruction, respectively. They were tested using a battery of semi-elicited oral production tasks. In the first part of each task learners were shown stimulus photographs with people engaged in age-appropriate activities (routines of daily life, pets, holidays, etc.). In the second part of the task, researchers questioned learners on a similar range of topics. These tasks were analyzed in terms of the following aspects:

- **Mean Length of Utterance** (MLU) (as a general proficiency measure).
- Grammatical gender (as evidence for DP); French has masculine/feminine nouns with the determiner changing accordingly.
- The number of verbless utterances (as evidence for VP).
- Verb movement (as evidence for TP), through the use of subject clitic (or contracted) pronouns with finite verbs (e.g. *j'ai mange* – *I ate*).
- Embedded/relative clauses (as evidence for CP).
- Productive lexical diversity (measured using **Guiraud's index**).

These syntactic structures were chosen because they represent each element of the underlying sentence structure, as shown in Figure 7.2. For further details on the acquisition of syntactic features and underlying tree structure, see Cain (Chapter 2 in this volume). For an introduction to how L2 learners are argued to build up syntactic tree structures layer by layer, see Hawkins (2001) or Vainikka and Young-Scholten (2005) for a fuller account of structure-building approaches to L2 acquisition.

The results were analyzed in terms of Pearson correlations between the productive lexical diversity measure, Guiraud, and between each of the levels (projections CP, TP, VP and DP) of syntactic structure as represented in the tree diagram in Figure 7.2 as well as a general measure of production, namely MLU. The researchers found a significant positive correlation between MLU and **lexical density** ($r = 0.619$, $N = 60$, $p < 0.01$). More importantly, they found significant correlation between lexical diversity and (a) the projection of VP as measured through the number of verbless utterances ($r = -0.258$, $N = 60$, $p < 0.05$), and (b) the projection of CP through use of embedded clauses ($r = 0.633$, $N = 60$, $p < 0.001$). That is, the fewer the verbless clauses and the more complex the syntax, the greater the lexical density. However, they found no significant development between the groups in the acquisition of gender (DP). As the learners used very few different nouns, there was therefore no correlation with lexical density. There was also no correlation found between the use of subject **clitic pronouns** with finite verbs (TP) and vocabulary density.

The authors suggest that learners increase their syntactic complexity in relation to their vocabulary acquisition; however, the authors conclude that this does not extend to abstract syntactic features (i.e. DP and TP) despite the evidence for CP, which is syntactic. These abstract features are some of the same features as in Emonds' (2001) syntacticon. This suggests that the syntactic-only features in the syntacticon may not be related to the increasing development of the lexicon/dictionary.

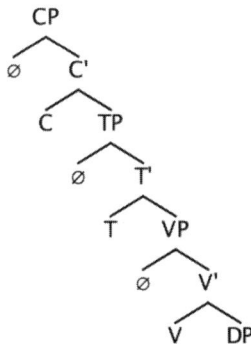

Figure 7.2 X-bar tree

However, there are some limitations of this study that may have impacted on the TP results, in addition to the limited number of nouns produced affecting the DP results, as mentioned above. The use of subject clitics with finite verbs by English learners of French is a theoretical argument for evidence of TP; these utterances could be accounted for under a VP-only projection as the L2 learners may have mis-analyzed the subject clitics in French to be similar to **weak pronouns** in English (Hawkins, 2001). Moreover, French lacks verbal morphology differences in oral language: the 1st, 2nd and 3rd person verb forms are pronounced similarly in regular verbs, so the use of a default form in this case (Prévost & White, 2000a), cannot be ruled out. Therefore, unambiguous evidence of the projection of TP (and DP) would be required in order to clarify whether syntactic-only features develop separately, and are not co-related to the development of the lexicon/dictionary.

Study 2

Rogers reanalyzed the results presented in 2009 for a fuller analysis of TP acquisition investigating the obligatory movement of the main verb in French from VP to TP, unlike in English (Pollock, 1989). This is seen in surface word order differences with negation and adverbs, in which the adverb or negator appears post-verbally in French but pre-verbally in English (see examples in Table 7.3). The task for the English-speaking learner of French is to acquire this movement to TP which involves acquiring the 'strong' abstract feature of Tense, located in the syntacticon, using Emonds' (2001) analysis.

Five groups of 15 instructed English learners of French and a group of 10 native French speaking controls were given the battery of tests outlined below. The learners were all English-native speakers who were learning French in an instructed environment (secondary school or university) in the northeast of England. Details of the groups are given in Table 7.4.

The learners were tested using a semi-elicited oral production task and a grammaticality judgement task to examine their production and acceptance of verb placement with negation and adverbs. The elicited production task contained 15 obligatory contexts for the production of either a negative or an adverb. The learners were shown a picture on a card and asked to say what the person was doing using either a negative (indicated

Table 7.3 Word order differences in French and English

French	English
Je regarde souvent la télé. (SVAO) *I watch often the TV	I often watch TV. (SAVO) *Je souvent regarde la télé
Je (ne) regarde pas la télé. (SVNegO) *I watch not the TV	I don't watch TV. (SNegVO) *Je (ne) pas regarde la télé

Table 7.4 Participant details from Rogers (2009)

Group	Age	Hours of instruction	Years learning French
Beginner	12–13	75–94.5	1
Low-intermediate	15–16	275–345	4
High-intermediate	17–18	521–708	6
Low-advanced	19–31	2nd year uni	8
High-advanced	21–24	4th year uni	10+ 6–9 months in a French speaking country

by a cross) or the word printed on the card. There were also five distractor items including neither a cross nor a word. The grammaticality judgement task contained 64 sentences equally divided between grammatical and ungrammatical sentences. There were 16 sentences testing negation and 24 testing adverb placement, although only eight of each will be directly relevant to this reanalysis. The remaining 24 sentences were distractors. For their judgements, learners used a 4-point Likert scale with an 'I don't know' option.

The learners were also tested on their receptive vocabulary knowledge using a paper-based version of X-lex (Meara & Milton, 2003). In this task the learners were asked to indicate if they knew a word or not from a list of 120 words. The test contains 100 real French words (20 from each of the top five frequency bands) and 20 false words. Participants are scored for each correct word ticked (50 points) and then 250 points are deducted for each false word ticked. This gives a total score of 5000, indicating a vocabulary of this size.

The group results are given in Table 7.5. Due to the low numbers in each group (15), the median score is given as well as the total number of target utterances (post-verbal adverb/negator) out of 225 (15 obligatory items for each of 15 participants) in the oral production task and the total correct acceptance of the target structure (eight grammatical items for negation, eight for adverbs) in the judgement task. An overall score combining the adverb and negation group totals results was calculated for both the oral production (out of 450) and the judgement task (out of 240). This is given as a percentage. For more detailed analysis of the results including an account for the low suppliance of adverbs, please see Rogers (2010).

The results clearly show that the learners increased in performance across the groups for all tasks and that they performed much better on the judgement task than the oral production task, as would be expected. There was also a steady increase in their receptive vocabulary (X-lex) scores. These trends are shown in the graphs in Figures 7.3 and 7.4. Pearson's correlations between the oral production and the grammaticality judgement results showed medium-strong positive correlations for both adverbs ($r = 0.482$, $p < 0.01$) and negation ($r = 0.785$, $p < 0.01$).

Table 7.5 Results from reanalysis of Rogers (2009)

Group	X-lex vocab	Oral production task			Grammaticality judgement		
		Negation	Adverbs	Overall	Negation	Adverbs	Overall
Beginner	300	0 0/225	0 4/225	1% 4/450	4 55/120	5 76/120	55% 131/240
Low-intermediate	600	1 44/225	1 18/225	14% 62/450	6 86/120	5 72/120	66% 158/240
High-intermediate	2100	14 179/225	2 48/225	50% 227/450	8 107/120	7 107/120	89% 214/240
Low-advanced	2800	15 214/225	1 45/225	58% 259/450	8 114/120	7 100/120	89% 214/240
High-advanced	3250	15 210/225	4 88/225	62% 278/450	7 110/120	0 112/120	93% 222/240
Controls	4800	15 150/150	10.5 101/150	84% 251/300	7 70/80	8 80/80	94% 150/160

Syntactic development

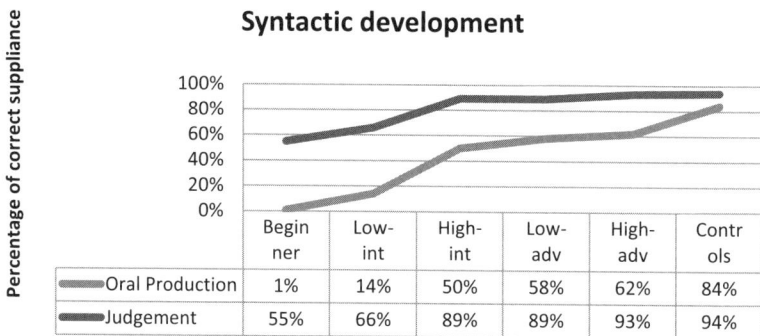

	Beginner	Low-int	High-int	Low-adv	High-adv	Controls
Oral Production	1%	14%	50%	58%	62%	84%
Judgement	55%	66%	89%	89%	93%	94%

Figure 7.3 Target-like structure in oral production & grammaticality judgement tasks

Receptive vocabulary scores

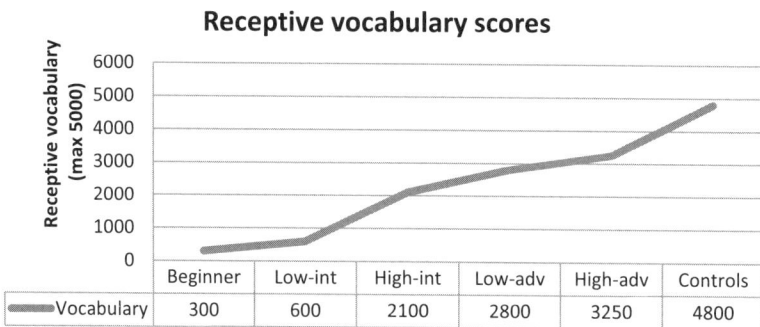

	Beginner	Low-int	High-int	Low-adv	High-adv	Controls
Vocabulary	300	600	2100	2800	3250	4800

Figure 7.4 Receptive vocabulary results (X-lex)

In order to determine if there is a link between the acquisition of abstract features in the syntacticon and the acquisition of vocabulary items in the lexicon/dictionary, Pearson's correlations were carried out. The first correlation test was carried out between the receptive vocabulary measure and the overall oral production results. The results showed a statistically significant correlation between oral production and receptive vocabulary size ($r(74) = 0.704$, $p < 0.01$). The results show that receptive vocabulary size accounted for 50% of the variance in oral production scores ($r^2 = 0.496$). A second Pearson's correlation was carried out between the receptive vocabulary size scores and the overall performance on the grammaticality judgement task. The results showed a statistically significant correlation between receptive vocabulary size and judgements on the grammaticality judgement task ($r(74) = 0.729$, $p < 0.01$). This shows that receptive vocabulary size accounts for over 53% of the variance in results ($r^2 = 0.531$). Finally, as the oral production score and judgement task results were strongly correlated (see previous), an overall syntactic measure was calculated by combining the oral production and grammaticality judgement overall measures. A final Pearson's correlation was carried out. The results showed a statistically significant positive correlation between the learners' receptive vocabulary score and their overall syntactic scores ($r(74) = 0.740$, $p < 0.01$), which accounted for 55% of the variance in the results ($r^2 = 0.548$).

The reanalysis of Rogers' (2009) data suggests that there is a strong link between the acquisition of syntactic features in the syntacticon, as measured through the acquisition of TP, and the receptive acquisition of vocabulary in the lexicon. However, there are limitations to this reanalysis. First, the syntactic measures are limited to TP. As a measure of TP, the test used here is much more comprehensive, and theory neutral, in comparison with David et al. (2009), but unlike David et al., this reanalysis only covers one aspect of syntax, namely TP. Moreover, on the vocabulary side, there is also only one measure of vocabulary, namely X-lex for receptive vocabulary. Future research in this area will need to investigate several areas of syntax, and consider both receptive and productive vocabulary measures. However, the results are striking in that vocabulary scores can account for over 50% of the variance in oral production and grammaticality judgements.

But does this correlational data imply causation? Does the lexicon drive acquisition of syntax, or does syntax drive the vocabulary learning? Towell (2003) has suggested that lexis might be a driving force for development in syntax, but this has mainly been considered in terms of the acquisition of lexical features rather than actual vocabulary items (see van de Craats, 2003). Can the acquisition of vocabulary items drive the acquisition of syntactic features? If so, what characteristics would the lexicon need to have in order to drive syntactic development? For example, would the lexicon need to consist of a critical mass of verbs before the abstract syntactic-only features associated with verbs are acquired? Is there a threshold? Alternatively, perhaps the number of verbs would not be the critical issue but rather the number of links between the items or nodes as per the discussion of word association data above? These questions remain to be addressed.

Conclusion

Vocabulary acquisition research is a dynamic, burgeoning, interdisciplinary field, which has developed from examining form-meaning mappings into the investigation of the complex mental networks of nodes that learners construct. We initially gave a broad overview of some of the key areas of investigation and challenges in the field. We argued that the 'word' may be better understood in terms of 'word families' and that determining if a person 'knows a word' is not as simple as it might first appear. We introduced the concepts of lexical depth and breadth and provided an overview of how lexical items are stored and retrieved. This overview allowed us to go into further depth in two areas of current investigation. First, we examined word association data in terms of the development of networks in L1 acquisition. We argued that young native speakers differed in the types of associations made in relation to their vocabulary size. This relates strongly to the L2 word association data examined in that section. The second empirical investigation considered L2 vocabulary size and abstract syntactic features. The reanalysis of Rogers (2009) presented here argues for a strong correlation between the receptive vocabulary and the acquisition of abstract syntactic features (e.g. TP as shown by verb movement). We suggest that vocabulary acquisition may be the driving force behind the acquisition of syntax. However, the nature of this driving force remains to be investigated. Which element of vocabulary acquisition is relevant remains an unanswered question. Is it the breadth of vocabulary knowledge? The depth? The links between words (word associations)? Perhaps it is a combination of all these elements. The interface between syntax and lexicon has not been extensively explored in this manner, and has the potential to unlock how L2 learners develop.

Note

(1) It is true that there are many factors which feed into the lexical search procedure, and that not all of these are characteristics of the stimulus itself. Top-down influences such as the proficiency of the listener, the context in which the message is being spoken, the relationship between the participants in the conversation or the language that is being spoken play a role in the process. Here, 'input' is being used as a proxy for 'information on which the lexical search is based', regardless of whether that comes directly from the stimulus or from other contextual cues.

8 Foreign Accent in a Second Language: Individual Differences in Perception

Joan C. Mora and Elena Safronova

Introduction

Variation across learners in their second language (L2) performance is inherent to the changing nature of learners' developing interlanguage systems regardless of which domain of language we consider. But there is also variation across domains of linguistic competence: development does not occur evenly and reach the same final point. While individual differences across learners play a role in all domains of language (Dörnyei, 2006; Gardner, 2007; Robinson, 2002; Segalowitz, 1997), inter-individual variation in ultimate attainment is especially true of L2 learners' pronunciation. Even when learners are relatively advanced in domains of language such as syntax and lexis, it is common to find great variation in degree of foreign accent. This suggests that L2 phonological competence develops independently of other domains of linguistic competence. Speech acquisition research has shown that L2 learners' performance in both perception and production is extremely variable. Do learners exist who may be endowed with a special talent for L2 pronunciation? Does individual variability in the efficient use of speech-processing skills provide more skilful individuals with an advantage in the acquisition of L2 phonology? Answers to these questions are pursued in this chapter.

It turns out that variability in foreign accent cannot be accounted for solely by age- or experience-related factors, i.e. the age at which learning started or whether the learning context was a classroom or the target language country (see Bohn & Munro, 2007, for a review). An early, pre-puberty start has been associated in numerous studies with more successful phonological learning, i.e. a lower degree of foreign accent (but cf. Moyer, 2014a). Moreover, language acquisition in **immersion settings** is believed to result in more successful phonological development than in the foreign language classroom. Yet there is still considerable inter-learner variability within each learning context. This raises a number of questions including how pronunciation in L2 is related to phonological representation in the learner's mind.

Let us consider the data in Figure 8.1, which come from two different groups of upper-intermediate to advanced level adult L1-Spanish learners of English. The figure illustrates variability by relating learners' perception (left panel) and production (right panel) of a difficult English vowel contrast (/iː/–/ɪ/) to their L2 vocabulary size, a good estimator of their overall L2 proficiency. The figure on the left shows the results of a categorization task where learners were presented with English minimal-pair words for identification in a study by Cerviño-Povedano and Mora (2015). As the learners heard words over headphones (e.g. *beat* or *bit*), they chose one of two responses on a computer screen (*beat* versus *bit*). Their vocabulary was measured by a vocabulary knowledge test (Meara & Miralpeix, 2007). Learners' perception accuracy scores were plotted as a function of their vocabulary size and suggest that learners with similar vocabulary sizes (e.g. about 7000 words) vary considerably in their L2 perceptual skills, ranging from 50% to 90% correct identification, despite the moderate significant correlation between the vocabulary and perception measures ($r = 0.495$, $p = 0.005$). L1-Spanish learners' ability to distinguish /iː/ from /ɪ/ in production may vary considerably irrespective of vocabulary size (data from Darcy *et al.*, 2014). The figure on the right plots the size of the qualitative difference between /iː/ and /ɪ/ in production as a distance measure in **Bark** (a psychoacoustic measure of acoustic vowel quality closely representing a listener's perception of vowel quality differences). The larger the Bark score, the more distinctly the two vowels were produced and the more distinctly the vowels would be perceived. Vocabulary size was not significantly related to vowel quality distances in production ($r = 0.295$, $p = 0.142$). In this study, learners with similar vocabulary sizes obtained very different vowel quality distance scores.

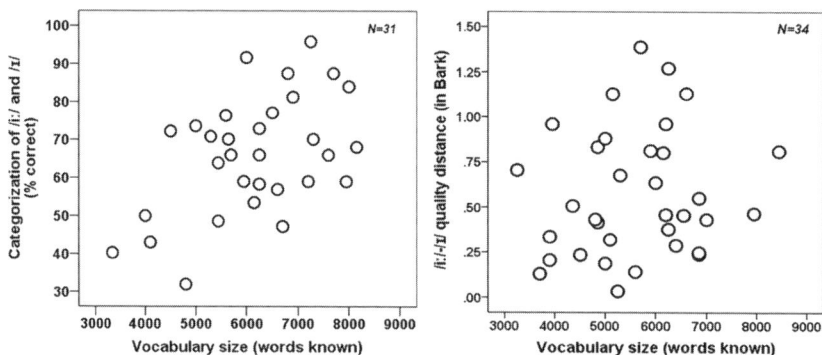

Figure 8.1 Scatterplots illustrating the relationship between vocabulary size and L1-Spanish learners' perception (left) and production (right) of English /iː/–/ɪ/

This is one example of many studies showing such variation, and it is therefore important to identify the sources of the kind of inter-learner variation shown in Figure 8.1. Here we can assess the role of input (amount and quality of L2 input received), age-related factors (e.g. onset of L2 learning) and learning context (classroom instruction versus naturalistic acquisition in the target language country) and how these three factors interact with learners' additional individual differences. These include motivation and learners' attitudes (Moyer, 1999, 2014b), **sound processing ability** (Golestani & Zatorre, 2009; Lengeris & Hazan, 2010) and cognitive skills such as **phonological memory** (Cerviño-Povedano & Mora, 2011; MacKay *et al.*, 2001), **attention control** (Darcy *et al.*, 2014; Safronova & Mora, 2013) and **inhibition** of unwanted knowledge (Darcy *et al.*, 2016; Lev-Ari & Peperkamp, 2013, 2014). Research investigating L2 phonological acquisition by post-puberty learners has revealed considerable inter-learner variability, not only when data is collected in naturalistic language learning settings, i.e. from immigrants (Bradlow *et al.*, 1999; MacKay *et al.*, 2001) but also in laboratory settings, where the effects of phonetic training range from complete lack of improvement to dramatic gains in perception and production (Aliaga-Garcia *et al.*, 2011; Kim & Hazan, 2010). This suggests that individual cognitive factors play an important role in L2 speech learning regardless of experience. Are there learners endowed with a special talent for L2 pronunciation? Does individual variability in the efficient use of speech-processing skills provide more skilful individuals with an advantage in the acquisition of L2 phonology?

This chapter addresses these questions through three L2 speech studies which examined the role of individual differences in cognitive ability (**phonological memory, acoustic memory** and **attention control**) in post-puberty learners' perception of L2 English sound contrasts primarily through formal classroom instruction. The studies also investigated the role of individual differences in listeners' perception of non-native speech produced by L2 learners. These are two different but closely related perspectives on the perception of L2 speech, that of the language learner acquiring an L2 phonology and that of the listener (the teacher/tester) assessing L2 learners' speech. In the first case we focus on the acquisition of L2 sounds (i.e. the segmental phonology) and assume, in line with current models of L2 speech acquisition (Best & Tyler, 2007; Flege, 1995; Kuhl *et al.*, 2008), that the development of L2 perception precedes accuracy in production. In the second case we focus on two perceptual dimensions of non-native speech, degree of foreign accent and oral **fluency**. Here we assume that teachers/testers undertake the task of assessing learners' L2 speech with some broad mental representation of what constitutes a weak/strong foreign accent or a fluent/dysfluent stretch of speech which is based on their previous experience with L2 learners' accented speech. Thus, experience-related factors such as type and amount of input matters in L2 phonological acquisition (see Piske & Young-Scholten, 2009, for a review) as much as it does in the perception of non-native speech (e.g. Derwing & Munro, 1997; Kennedy & Trofimovich, 2008). Individual differences in cognitive ability may affect speech processing similarly in L2 learners and raters of their speech. Superior processing abilities will enhance learners' formation of more accurate L2 sound representations, and will provide raters (teachers) with greater sensitivity in their judgement of others' L2 speech.

This chapter seeks to contribute to our present understanding of several of the cognitive and experience-related variables relating to individual differences to identify the source of inter-learner variation in degree of foreign accent. It aims to show that *mind matters* in L2 speech perception.

Individual Differences in Cognitive Ability and Second Language Speech Processing: Measures of Phonological Memory, Acoustic Memory and Attention Control

The role of individual differences in cognitive ability and speech perception has received relatively little attention in the L2 speech research literature. L2 speech research has focused primarily on the sort of investigation of age- and experience-related effects on L2 speech perception and production discussed above. Research has, however, identified factors independent of experience which have an impact on L2 phonological development and these include learners' motivation, learners' sound processing ability and other cognitive skills. For motivation, Moyer (1999), for example, found that a high level of professional motivation was related to a low degree of foreign accent in very advanced L2 learners working as foreign language instructors. With respect to processing, Lengeris and Hazan (2010) found that learners' skills in processing L1 vowels in noisy conditions and discriminating L1 vowel frequency correlated with their amount of improvement in L2 sound perception and production after they had received several phonetic training sessions. Studies investigating the role of individual differences in L2 speech processing and development also suggest the involvement of other cognitive skills such as attention (Darcy *et al.*, 2014; Safranova & Mora, 2013), **inhibitory control** (Darcy *et al.*, 2016; Lev-Ari & Peperkamp, 2013, 2014) and phonological short-term memory (Cerviño-Povedano & Mora, 2011; Mackay *et al.*, 2001). These may contribute in different ways to learners' L2 phonological acquisition, and in ways that at present are not fully understood. For example, the behavioural and electrophysiological evidence which shows a relation between phonological short-term memory and L2 pronunciation aptitude appears to hold for lower level L2 learners, but not for more advanced learners (Hu *et al.*, 2013; Reiterer *et al.*, 2011).

Establishing a causal relationship between learners' individual differences in cognitive ability and their L2 perceptual and productive phonetic skills is difficult. This is largely due to the complexity of the dynamic interaction between cognitive skills and L2 acquisition. Learners may need to make use of different cognitive resources and may need to use them to various extents at different stages in the acquisition process (Hu *et al.*, 2013) or under different learning conditions (French & O'Brien, 2008; O'Brien *et al.*, 2007; Skrzypek, 2009).

In the following three subsections we describe the cognitive skills we focus on in the present chapter, namely **phonological memory**, **acoustic memory** and **attention control**, and how these skills were measured in the studies reported in the section following on the Individual Differences Approach (see also Wright's Chapter 11 in this volume).

Phonological (short-term) memory (PM)

According to Baddeley's (2003) modular model of working memory, phonological short-term memory (also called the *phonological loop* and often referred to in the SLA literature as *phonological memory* or PM) is a limited-capacity memory store responsible for temporarily storing verbal-acoustic information, such as sequences of speech sounds, over a few seconds. This allows the encoding of phonological elements and their serial order and PM is therefore essential in the processing of speech. PM auditory traces decay rapidly (after a few seconds) as speech input continues to feed the listener's auditory system, but individuals can refresh the decaying auditory traces through sub-vocal rehearsal to keep information in memory for longer periods of time. This is similar to mentally repeating a telephone number after looking it up in the telephone directory in order not to forget it before dialling the number. When it comes to individual differences, individuals vary in how skilful they are at doing this. In the domain of language acquisition, research has shown that children and adults with poorer PM function are less successful in learning the sound structure of new words (Baddeley *et al.*, 1988; Gathercole & Baddeley, 1989; Papagno & Vallar, 1995; Service & Kohonen, 1995 – and see also Wright's chapter in this volume). Once a learner has established his or her native language phonological system, PM function is supported by both lexical and sub-lexical (syllabic-phonotactic) phonological long-term knowledge, so that frequent words and familiar sound sequences are more easily retained in PM than nonwords or unfamiliar sound sequences. This suggests that PM performance is to a large extent language specific (Thorn & Gathercole, 1999). Individuals' PM is therefore normally measured in the participants' native language, where it is most efficient and presumably unaffected by individual differences in linguistic knowledge (since all native speakers have comparable linguistic competence). A well-established task for measuring PM is to ask participants to repeat nonwords of increasing syllable length (Gathercole & Adams, 1994) or to ask them to repeat short nonwords presented in sequences of increasing length (Cheung, 1996). See also French and O'Brien (2008), and Papagano *et al.*

(1991) for details on testing design and methodology. Such nonword repetition tasks provide repetition accuracy measures which reflect speakers'
PM capacity.

In the studies included here, we used a different type of PM task developed by Cerviño-Povedano & Mora (2011), where PM was operationalized as participants' performance on a forced-choice serial nonword
recognition task. This task, unlike nonword repetition tasks, avoids articulatory constraints on performance (Isaacs & Trofimovich, 2011; O'Brien
et al., 2007; Snowling *et al.*, 1991) and minimizes lexical knowledge effects
(Gathercole *et al.*, 2001). Participants are presented with 24 trials for
same-different discrimination, each consisting of a pair of sequences of
language-appropriate CVC nonwords (in these studies, in Catalan). Half
the pairs (12) consist of two identical sequences of nonwords ('same
pairs'), and the other half (12) consist of two sequences of nonwords
which are identical except for a change in the serial position of one of the
nonwords in the second sequence ('different pairs'). The sequences differ
in item length (sequences of five, six and seven nonwords) with four of the
same and four different pairs of sequences at each item length. For example, on any given trial participants would hear a pair of sequences of nonwords and they would need to decide whether the two sequences were the
same (/for, ʎɛn, sid, dul, tɛdʒ, ʒɔl/–/for, ʎɛn, sid, dul, tɛdʒ, ʒɔl/), i.e. the
same items appeared in the same order, or *different* (/pɛɲ, bor, <u>dup, lap</u>,
meʃ, ʒit/–/pɛɲ, bor, <u>lap, dup</u>, meʃ, ʒit/), i.e. the same items appeared in a
different order. For full details see Cerviño-Povedano & Mora (2011).

This task provides a measure of participants' PM capacity by testing
their ability to retain sequences of L1 phonological units and thus taps into
the phonological sound processing required, for example, in the segmenta-
tion of strings of sounds into word-sized units in an L2. However, L2 learners also need to be able to discern acoustic differences between the incoming
L2 speech sounds and their perceptually closest match in the L1, if they are
to develop accurate L2 phonological categories for L2 sounds distinct from
those of the L1 (Flege, 1995) in the input to encode these.

Acoustic memory (AM)

Acoustic memory is defined as an auditory sensory memory store that
holds acoustic information before phonological encoding takes place for
further processing to make speech intelligible (Blesser, 1972; Crowder &
Morton, 1969; Scott *et al.*, 2000). AM therefore taps into more general
auditory processing skills than the speech-specific processing of sequences
of phonological elements making up word-like units. AM is involved,
together with PM, in the perception of cross-language acoustic differences
between L2 and L1 speech sounds, but AM may be more directly related
than PM to learners' perceptual sensitivity to L2-specific phonetic properties of speech sounds which allows them to identify and appropriately use

the linguistically relevant phonetic cues in the L2 phonology (i.e. L2 perceptual cue-weighting). In order to obtain a measure of AM independent from PM, stimuli need to be non-intelligible to prevent phonological encoding from taking place. Moreover, in order to be able to relate individual differences in AM to L2 perceptual cue-weighting, stimuli need to be acoustically as complex as real speech and to retain speech-like features such as differences in duration between segments, the formant structure determining the quality of vowels (spectral information) or the pitch movement patterns associated with certain meanings expressed through intonation.

We obtained such stimuli by spectrally rotating the Catalan CVC nonwords we used in the PM task. Spectral rotation is a speech manipulation technique that renders speech unintelligible while preserving its spectral and temporal variation, including pitch contours (Narain *et al.*, 2003; Scott *et al.*, 2000, 2006), by transforming high-frequency energy into low-frequency energy and vice versa. This is visible in the spectrogram of the Catalan CVC syllable /doʃ/ in Figure 8.2 by comparing the top spectrogram (normal) with the bottom one (rotated); the auditory consequence of this frequency rotation is some kind of 'alien speech' consisting of a sequence of segment-sized sound units that are not recognizable as any known speech sound.

We operationalized AM as participants' performance on a serial nonword recognition task consisting of spectrally rotated CVC nonwords made up of three-, four-, five- and six-item sequence pairs. The rotated CVC syllables in any given sequence were separated with 200 ms silence intervals. The instructions for participants and task procedures were the

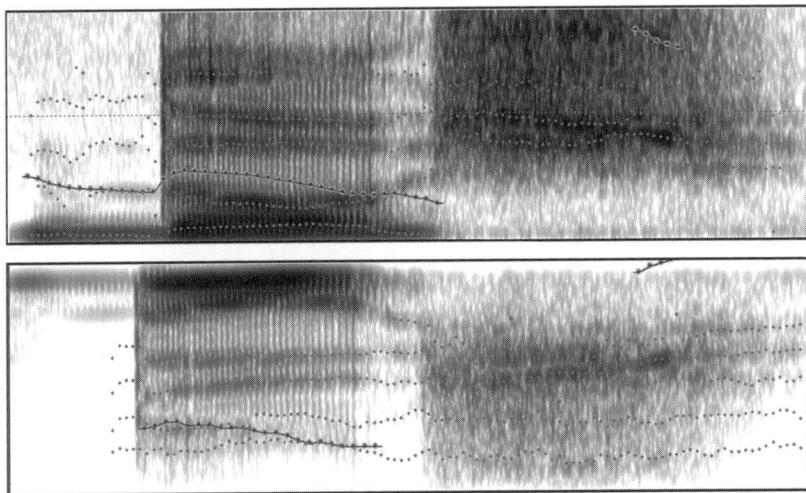

Figure 8.2 Spectrogram of the Catalan nonword [doʃ] (top) and its spectrally rotated version (bottom)

same as for the PM task. However, because stimuli were unintelligible, participants could not phonologically encode them and consequently participants could not sub-vocally rehearse the CVC sequences to refresh their auditory traces in memory. Thus, the sequences of rotated nonwords were perceived as sequences of sound units varying in speech-like dimensions such as duration, intensity, frequency structure and pitch. In order to perform the task, listeners had to keep in memory the changes in duration, intensity, frequency and pitch taking place across the rotated CVC syllables in the first nonword sequence of a trial, and then compare them to those occurring in the second sequence, and decide whether the two sequences in each trial (a sequence pair) were the same or different. As in the PM task, task difficulty increased as sequence item-length increased. An AM weighted score was computed by assigning three, four, five and six points to every correct response as a function of item length and then summing up all points up to a maximum total of 144 points.

Attention control (AC)

Speakers' use of spoken language in communicative interaction is a complex cognitive skill requiring expert control over the foregrounding and backgrounding of linguistic information which is necessary to guide the listener towards the decoding and interpretation of the intended message. Listeners, in turn, need to efficiently switch their focus of attention to whatever linguistic cues become relevant at a given moment during communicative interaction. Within this view of communication, language is conceived of as an attention-directing system and the skilful use of language as speakers/listeners exercise rapid and flexible control over those linguistic aspects that serve the purpose of directing attention (Segalowitz, 2010). Exercising control of attention in language use is thus understood as a person's ability to shift attention from one linguistic dimension to another to bring a given linguistic aspect under the focus of the attentional foreground.

Segalowitz and Frenkiel-Fishman (2005) operationalized AC in language by adapting Rogers and Monsell's (1995) task-switching paradigm. In Segalowitz and Frenkiel-Fishman's task, participants are required to switch attention between two linguistic dimensions in given stimulus sentences (e.g. Sentence A: past/present in time adverbials; and Sentence B: causal/non-causal relationship in conjunctions). The switching costs (difference between switches [A-B]/[B-A] and non-switches (repeat) [A-A]/[B-B] trials), and error rates, are used as a measure of AC. Switching cost was measured by **reaction time** (RT), that is, the time it takes (in milliseconds) for a participant to react to a stimulus. In order to investigate AC in speech perception we designed a speech-based adaptation of Segalowitz and Frenkiel-Fishman's (2005) task. In our novel version of the task, participants were required to shift focus of attention from one speech-based attention-directing function (segmental duration: long versus short) to another (voice quality: female versus male) in the perception of vowel sounds (Safronova & Mora, 2013). Both these speech dimensions are often exploited linguistically in a context-dependent manner, requiring language learners to make use of their attention-switching skills during conversation. For example, in English, duration can be used as a cue to voicing for stop and fricative consonants when devoiced in word-final position (the diphthong in *place* /pleɪs/ is much shorter than the one in *plays* /pleɪz/ because it precedes a voiceless /s/ rather than a voiced /z/), whereas duration differences between contrasting tense-lax vowel pairs (*beat* /biːt/ versus *bit* /bɪt/) are not essential to vowel quality distinctions. L2-English learners need to learn to rely on duration as a cue to voicing (/pleɪs/ versus /pleɪz/) and to ignore duration and rely on quality differences (/biːt/ versus/bɪt/) when distinguishing between vowels.

For full details of this task, see Safronova and Mora (2013). In brief, participants listened to sets of vowels which they had to categorize depending on duration or voice quality, i.e. *long* or *short*; *male* or *female* and combinations of these (*long male*; *short female*, etc.). Stimuli were presented in pairs which were either repeated (Duration/Duration) or switched (Duration/Voice Quality).

Simultaneous with the auditory presentation of a vowel sound, a visual cue (a speaker) appeared in one of the four cells shown in Figure 8.3. The position of the speaker, which changed predictably in a clockwise fashion (right > bottom > left > top), determined the alternating speech dimension under focus: duration in the top two cells, voice quality in the bottom two cells. Participants used designated keys to identify a vowel sound as *long/male* or *short/female*. RTs on switch trials are predicted to be longer than RTs on repeat trials, reflecting the processing

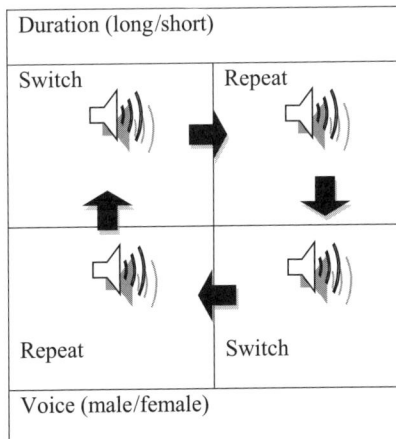

Figure 8.3 A speech-based version of the task-switching paradigm

cost to the participant of reallocating attention on a different dimension. Consequently, shorter switch costs are indicative of more efficient attention switching (Monsell, 2003; Prior & MacWhinney, 2010). Participants' ability to efficiently and flexibly shift focus of attention from one speech-based dimension to another was determined through measuring shift costs (RTs on switch trials minus RTs on repeat trials) and error rates (percentage of wrongly categorized stimuli).

In the next section we present the results of three studies exploring individual differences in the perception of L2 speech using the paradigms and tasks we have just outlined.

An Individual Differences Approach to Listeners' Perception of Second Language Sounds and Foreign Accent

Study 1 examines the role of cognitive skills in L2 learners' perception of an L2 vowel contrast. Study 2 explores the role of listeners' L1 and experience in the perception of foreign accent and fluency in L2 speech produced by L2 learners. Finally, Study 3 investigates the role of cognitive skills in listeners' sensitivity to perception of foreign accent differences in L2 speech.

Study 1: Individual differences in cognitive ability and the perception of second language vowels

This study examined the role of PM, AM and AC in the perception of a difficult L2 vowel contrast. The participants were 56 L1-Spanish English majors (mean age 20.5, range 18–39 years) at an upper-intermediate to advanced level of L2 proficiency, according to a vocabulary size test (X/Y_ Lex; Meara & Miralpeix, 2007). They had received EFL instruction at school (three to four hours weekly) since age 12 and none of them had spent periods of study abroad in an English-speaking environment longer than four weeks. They performed the PM, AM and AC tasks described above. They also performed a categorial AXB discrimination task (explained below) developed by Moya-Galé and Mora (2011) which served as a measure of L2 perceptual phonological competence. The stimuli in the discrimination task were English minimal pairs (e.g. *beat–bit*) contrasting the English high front vowels /iː/ and /ɪ/. This is a difficult contrast for Spanish learners of English because both vowels tend to be assimilated to Spanish /i/, the only vowel category occupying that portion of the vowel space in Spanish.

Methodology

In the discrimination task, participants had to decide whether in any given 'AXB' word triad the 'X' word was the same as the preceding 'A' word or the same as the following 'B' word. In each triad (e.g.

beat–beat–bit) every word was from a different speaker (e.g. AAB: A = male1, A = female3, B = male2), which forced listeners to ignore phonetic variability due to speaker characteristics and to instead attend to the spectral and temporal cues distinguishing the English tense /iː/ from its lax counterpart /ɪ/ and draw on their long-term memory representations for these sounds (Flege, 2003b). There were 10 minimal pairs contrasting /iː/–/ɪ/ in 10 contexts (/b_t/, /p_k/, /p_t/, /t_k/, /b_d/, /d_d/, /f_l/, /h_d/, /h_l/, /s_d/) produced by six native speakers of British English (three male, three female) who contributed 40 words each (6 × 40 = 240 words). Every minimal pair was presented in four orders (AAB, ABB, BAA, BAA) so that participants responded to 40 trials (10 minimal pairs × four orders).

In addition, another 40 trials were created by manipulating the duration in the vowels. This allowed us to obtain a measure of participants' over-reliance on temporal as opposed to spectral cues (Ylinen *et al.*, 2010), a well-attested trend in Spanish speakers' perception of English /iː/–/ɪ/ (Cebrian, 2006; Escudero & Boersma, 2004; Morrison, 2008, 2009).

The vowel duration manipulation consisted of *neutralizing* duration differences within each one of the 40 trials where tense vowels were shortened and lax vowels were lengthened to the mean duration of the three words within each trial (Moya-Galé & Mora, 2011). Thus, in the duration-neutralized trials, participants were forced to rely solely on spectral cues (vowel quality differences), whereas in natural trials they could use both spectral and temporal cues in discrimination. The more heavily participants relied on duration, the lower the discrimination score they were expected to obtain in the duration-neutralized trials. We also predicted that individuals with higher PM, AM and AC capacity would be more capable of avoiding over-reliance on duration in the duration-manipulated stimuli. The 80 trials (40 natural + 40 manipulated) were presented to participants in a fully randomized order.

Results

Learners' mean percent correct discrimination scores were virtually the same between the tense vowel /iː/ and the lax vowel /ɪ/. We therefore opted for averaging the discrimination scores between the two vowels in further analyses. Preliminary correlational analyses (Pearson-*r*) revealed that PM, AM and AC error rates (but not AC shift costs) were moderately correlated with one another. Learners with lower error rates in the AC task obtained significantly higher PM and AM scores, suggesting that both PM and AM were involved in learners' ability to correctly identify a vowel as being short/long or being produced by a male/female voice. PM and AM, as expected, were moderately related, suggesting that learners' ability to retain in memory acoustic changes along several speech dimensions supported their ability to retain phonological units and their serial order in short-term memory. However, only AM and AC error rate appeared to correlate with the discrimination of natural vowels and duration-manipulated vowels.

In order to further explore the role of cognitive skills in learners' perception of the /iː/–/ɪ/ vowel contrast, we conducted group analyses by assigning learners to Low and High PM, AM and AC groups through a series of **median** splits (see Table 8.1). Participants assigned to the High AC groups were those who obtained shorter shift cost RTs and lower error rates, as this indicates greater AC.

Overall the results revealed that learners whom we assigned to the High PM, AM and AC groups outperformed those whom we assigned to the Low PM, AM and AC groups in the AXB discrimination task (Figure 8.4). This appears to be a consistent trend across all cognitive tasks, suggesting that learners with better memory and attention skills are better able to develop more accurate phonetic categories for L2 sounds.

Discrimination scores were subjected to a series of ANOVAs with *stimulus type* (natural versus manipulated) as a within-subjects factor and ability group (Low versus High) as a between-subjects factor for our four cognitive measures (PM, AM, AC shift cost, AC error rate). These analyses showed a significant main effect at 0.001 of *stimulus type* in all cases, which indicates that learners found it harder to discriminate /iː/ from /ɪ/ in trials where duration differences between /iː/ and /ɪ/ had been neutralized than in trials where duration was available as a cue to this vowel quality distinction. This suggests that these L2 English learners relied on duration differences in the distinction of this vowel contrast. The main effect of *ability group* did not reach significance for PM, but closely approached significance for AC shift cost (at 0.059), and was significant for AM and AC error rate. None of the *stimulus type × ability group* interactions was significant.

These results suggest that learners' individual differences in AM and AC, but not PM, explain some of the observed inter-learner variation in L2 phonological competence we noted in the introduction to this chapter. However, it is possible that the discrimination task we used conditioned learners' listening behaviour, as the task required them to listen for differences/similarities between vowel sounds in word contexts.

Table 8.1 Group means with standard deviations (SD) and median scores of the Low and High PM, AM, and AC groups

	Low			High			Group
	N	Mean	*SD*	*N*	Mean	*SD*	Median
PM (% correct)	28	47.2	12.3	28	71.0	9.1	60.5
AM (% correct)	27	53.2	8.8	29	69.7	6.0	62.0
AC Shift cost (ms)	28	321.4	132.3	28	75.3	49.3	155.0
AC Error rate (% error)	25	11.4	1.7	31	2.1	1.6	4.0

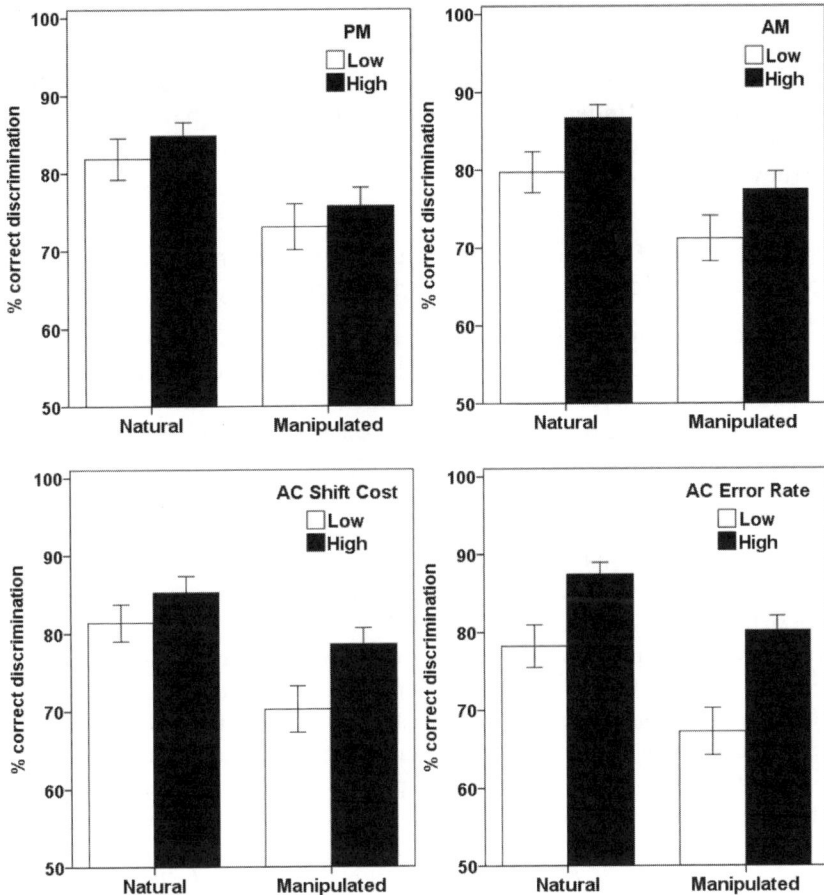

Figure 8.4 Mean percent correct discrimination as a function of Low- and High-ability groups in PM, AM and AC

Note: Error bars indicate ± 1 standard error.

This might have forced them to adopt a listening mode with a focus on acoustic detail, to which AM would make a greater contribution. PM might make more of a contribution in categorization tasks where listeners are required to hold a string of sounds in memory while the string is compared to its long-term memory representation. It is also possible that PM, as suggested in previous studies, makes more of a contribution in the initial stages of language acquisition and does not account for inter-learner differences at the more advanced levels of proficiency of the learners involved in this study (also see Hu *et al.*, 2013).

Taken together, the results suggest that individual differences in cognitive skills such as PM, AM and AC are related to L2 speech perception and may explain inter-subject variation in perceptual learning and phonological acquisition, eventually leading to inter-learner differences in

L2 pronunciation. In the following two studies we examine L2 speech from a listeners' perspective, reporting on data that illustrate the role of individual differences in the perception of non-native speech. The independent factors under investigation are listeners' L1 background and experience (Study 2) and individual differences in cognitive ability (Study 3).

Study 2: Role of listeners' first language and experience in perception of foreign accent and speaking fluency

Foreign accent studies often use trained and untrained listeners to judge L2 learners' foreign accent and **speaking fluency**. Even untrained listeners have been shown to be very skilled at detecting all kinds of non-native phonetic features in the incoming speech signal (Flege, 1984). This perceptual sensitivity allows listeners to identify various degrees of accent or fluency within a given set of non-native speech and sometimes a mixture of non-native and native samples (Derwing *et al.*, 2006; Piske *et al.*, 2001). Such perceptual judgements correspond closely to objective, instrumentally obtained measures of pronunciation accuracy or speaking fluency (Kormos & Dénes, 2004; Magen, 1998; Towell *et al.*, 1996), although recent research suggests a closer link between objective measures and perceptual judgements for fluency than for foreign accent (Pinget *et al.*, 2014). There is variation in the amount and range of non-native features listeners can detect, and it turns out that this is not exclusively attributable to properties of the speech signal. Listeners' perceptual sensitivity is affected by individual characteristics such as their L1 background and their familiarity with the type of non-native speech they are asked to rate (Derwing *et al.*, 2008; Kennedy & Trofimovich, 2008; Munro *et al.*, 2006). Munro *et al.* (2006), for example, found that listeners' extent of previous exposure to non-native speech positively influences **intelligibility** (i.e. the extent to which non-native speech is understood) but not necessarily their **comprehensibility** ratings (i.e. listeners' perception of difficulty in their understanding of non-native speakers rated on a Likert scale) or their **accentedness** ratings (i.e. listeners' perceived degree of foreign accent rated on a Likert scale).

There has been little research on speaking fluency taking into account the role of L1 background and experience in a formal language instruction context, where listeners were either language teachers or language learners, and so the study discussed here aimed to fill that gap. Sixty-nine listeners were required to assess speech samples produced by L1 bilingual Spanish/Catalan learners of English varying in proficiency level in the programme on which they were studying within an intermediate-advanced range. In addition, differences in processing difficulty between foreign accent and speaking fluency were explored through listeners' RTs in judging the speech samples.

Methodology

Speech samples from 35 EFL learners (mean age 20.3, range 18–25 years), recruited from the same student population as the learners in Study 1 and with the same kind of EFL experience, were obtained by means of a picture-elicited narrative task ('The Dog Story' from the Barcelona Age Factor Project, Muñoz, 2006). Each of the 35 participants performed the task individually and it was digitally recorded in a soundproof booth. The narratives were 80 seconds long (112 words) on average, but differed considerably from speaker to speaker (range 26–238 seconds, SD 41.5; range 31–288 words, SD 48.1), suggesting that the participants were not a homogeneous group as regards their oral narrative skills. Twenty-second excerpts from the beginning of each narrative were edited, normalized for peak intensity, and presented randomly to listeners in two separate rating tasks (one for fluency, one for foreign accent) for evaluation on 5-point scales. The speaking fluency scale endpoints were defined as 1 = Extremely fluent and 5 = Extremely dysfluent, and the foreign accent endpoints were 1 = No foreign accent and 5 = Very strong foreign accent. The 20-second excerpts were analyzed for pronunciation accuracy and temporal speaking fluency and the scores obtained were compared to listeners' perception of foreign accent and speaking fluency. Listeners' degree of experience with (and comprehensibility of) Spanish/Catalan-accented English was assessed by means of a questionnaire.

The following five listener groups (LGs; mean age 32.4, range 23–52) evaluated the speech samples for speaking fluency and foreign accent (Spain = Catalan-speaking region):

(1) LG1 ($n = 14$): L1-English teachers of English as a foreign language in Britain.
(2) LG2 ($n = 15$): L1-English learners of Spanish as a foreign language in Britain.
(3) LG3 ($n = 10$): L1-English teachers of English as a foreign language in Spain.
(4) LG4 ($n = 13$): L1-Spanish teachers of English as a foreign language in Spain.
(5) LG5 ($n = 17$): L1-Spanish learners of English as a foreign language in Spain.

Thus the LGs differed in L1 (Spanish/Catalan versus English) and amount and type of experience with Spanish/Catalan-accented English due to their teaching/learning context (Britain versus Spain). LG1 and LG2 (L1-English) were 'inexperienced' in that they were unfamiliar with Spanish/Catalan-accented English and were not normally exposed to it. LG3 was L1-English, the same as LG1 and LG3, but unlike them, those in this group received daily exposure to Spanish/Catalan-accented English. L1-English listeners were speakers of British English. LG4 and LG5 also received daily exposure to Spanish/Catalan-accented English, but were native speakers of Catalan and Spanish holding a degree in English. LG1, LG3 and LG4 were experienced EFL teachers, whereas LG2 and LG5 were FL learners. The rating data were collected in Salford (UK) (LG1, LG2) and Barcelona (Spain) (LG3, LG4, LG5). DmDx software (freely available language processing software, Forster & Forster, 2003) was used to run the experiment and record responses and RTs. Thirty-five speech samples were presented to listeners in two different sessions (1 = fluency, 2 = foreign accent) at least five days apart in order to avoid interference between perceptual dimensions on the listeners' judgements.

The speech samples were presented over headphones at a self-adjusted volume level. Instructions were pre-recorded and presented audio-visually on the computer. A few practice items were included to familiarize the participants with the rating task and the use of the fluency and foreign accent scales. Listeners pressed a number key 1-2-3-4-5 on the computer keyboard to rate the speech samples. They were instructed to make use of the whole scale and to rate every speech sample as accurately and as fast as possible.

Time- and syllable/word-based ratios were calculated for all measures to compensate for differences in amount of speech material produced by each participant. Fluency measures included speech rate (SR: syllable rate, i.e. syllables per minute including pause time), mean length of fluent run (MLoR: mean number of syllables/words between pauses longer than 300 ms), pause frequency ratio (PF: mean number of clause-internal pauses longer than 300 ms per minute) and dysfluency ratio (DysR: number of repetitions, restarts, self-corrections, hesitations and drawls per minute). A measure of accuracy (error rate, ER) was also calculated on the basis of grammatical and lexical errors. The foreign accent measure was based on the number of mispronunciations and phonemic substitutions per word (PhonErr).

Results

Inter-rater reliability (intra-class correlations) showed that raters within the five listener groups rated the 34 speech samples similarly (Cronbach's alpha ranged between 0.908 and 0.954). Pearson r correlations between the five LGs' mean fluency and foreign accent ratings were all significant ($p < 0.01$) and ranged from $r = 0.870$ to $r = 0.943$. These analyses suggested strong agreement *within* and *between* LGs. We first present the results of correlational analyses exploring the relationship between objective scores and listeners' judgements and examine the relationship between fluency and foreign accent judgements. We will then present the results of further statistical analysis, i.e. ANOVAs, conducted to explore the role of listeners' L1 and experience on the fluency and foreign accent ratings.

For all five LGs, most objective fluency scores correlated significantly with listeners' fluency ratings, and objective foreign accent scores (PhonErr:

Table 8.2 Pearson *r* correlations between fluency and foreign accent ratings and scores

	Fluency					Accuracy	Accentedness	
	Rating	SR	MLoR	PF	DysR	ER	Rating	PhonErr
LG1	3.21	−0.787**	−0.726**	0.488**	0.070	−0.438**	3.55	−0.617**
LG2	3.12	−0.720**	−0.671**	0.520**	0.166	−0.464**	3.40	−0.557**
LG3	3.07	−0.745**	−0.730**	0.586**	0.244	−0.454**	3.42	−0.562**
LG4	3.40	−0.732**	−0.654**	0.522**	0.212	−0.493**	3.56	−0.652**
LG5	3.43	−0.783**	−0.732**	0.574**	0.175	−0.499**	3.69	−0.678**

Note: ** = $p < 0.01$.

$M = 0.12$, $SD = 0.08$) correlated significantly with foreign accent ratings. This suggests that listeners were sensitive to the differences in fluency and foreign accent in the speech samples captured by the objective measures (Table 8.2). However, DysR did not significantly correlate with listeners' ratings and PF appeared to be more weakly related to fluency ratings than SR and MLoR, which appear to be more closely related to listeners' perception of fluency, in accordance with previous research (Kormos & Dénes, 2004; Towell *et al.*, 1996). Significant moderate negative correlations were found between fluency ratings and ER, suggesting that speech samples containing more errors were generally given lower fluency ratings.

Fluency and foreign accent ratings were strongly correlated, suggesting that speech samples perceived by the listeners as being less fluent were also perceived as having a stronger foreign accent (Table 8.3). However, significant correlations between PhonErr and, MLoR and PF indicate that the correlation between fluency and foreign accent ratings was not due to one dimension having had an effect on listeners' perception of the other, but to the fact that speech samples with a slower speech rate, shorter fluent runs and containing more pauses also happened to contain more phonological errors and were thus perceived as being more strongly accented.

Table 8.3 Mean fluency and foreign accent ratings (standard deviation in parentheses) by listener groups and Pearson *r* correlations

	Fluency	Foreign accent	Pearson's *r*
LG1	3.21 (0.79)	3.55 (0.67)	0.705**
LG2	3.12 (0.75)	3.40 (0.60)	0.843**
LG3	3.07 (0.79)	3.42 (0.67)	0.645**
LG4	3.40 (0.80)	3.56 (0.79)	0.758**
LG5	3.43 (0.76)	3.69 (0.77)	0.767**

Note: ** = $p < 0.01$.

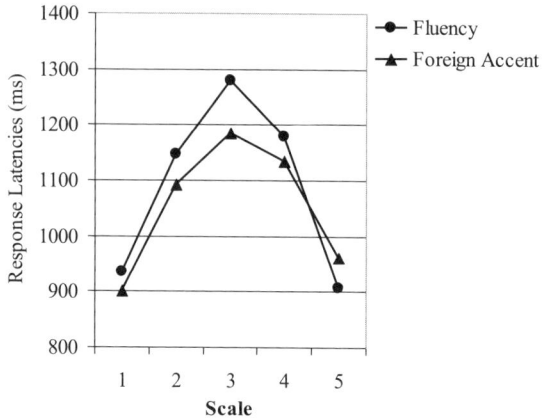

Figure 0.5 Mean RTs in foreign accent and fluency ratings on a 5-point scale

We next examined differences in processing speed (RTs) between fluency and foreign accent listener ratings. We interpret such differences as an index of processing difficulty, with longer RTs indicating greater difficulty in reaching a decision when judging a speech sample. These data revealed, as expected, that speech samples identified with any of the two ends of the scale (1 = Extremely fluent/no foreign accent; 5 = Extremely dysfluent/very strong foreign accent) were faster to rate than speech samples of intermediate fluency and foreign accent. Interestingly, listeners were slightly slower at rating the speech samples for fluency than at doing so for foreign accent, suggesting that they found fluency a slightly more difficult dimension to rate than foreign accent (Figure 8.5).

It is possible, however, that L1 or experience with Catalan/Spanish-accented English also led to differences in speed of rating the speech samples. This is indeed what the data show when listeners are grouped according to *L1* (Spanish [$n = 30$] = LG3 + LG4 versus English [$n = 39$] = LG1 + LG2 + LG3) and *experience* (with Catalan/Spanish accented English; experienced [$n = 40$] = LG3 + LG4 + LG5 versus inexperienced [$n = 29$] = LG1 + LG2). Note that, logically speaking, none of the L1-Spanish/Catalan groups was inexperienced with Spanish/Catalan-accented English. These listeners were much faster than English listeners at rating the Spanish/Catalan-accented speech samples for both fluency (1044 ms versus 1211 ms) and foreign accent (949 ms versus 1204 ms). However, whereas listeners with extensive exposure to Spanish/Catalan-accented English were much faster at rating the speech samples for foreign accent (1005 ms) than listeners without such experience (1214 ms), this was not the case for fluency (1157 ms versus 1112 ms) (Figure 8.6).

We further assessed these results by submitting listeners' RTs to an ANOVA with *L1* (Spanish versus English) and *experience* (experienced versus inexperienced) as between-subjects factors, and *speech dimension*

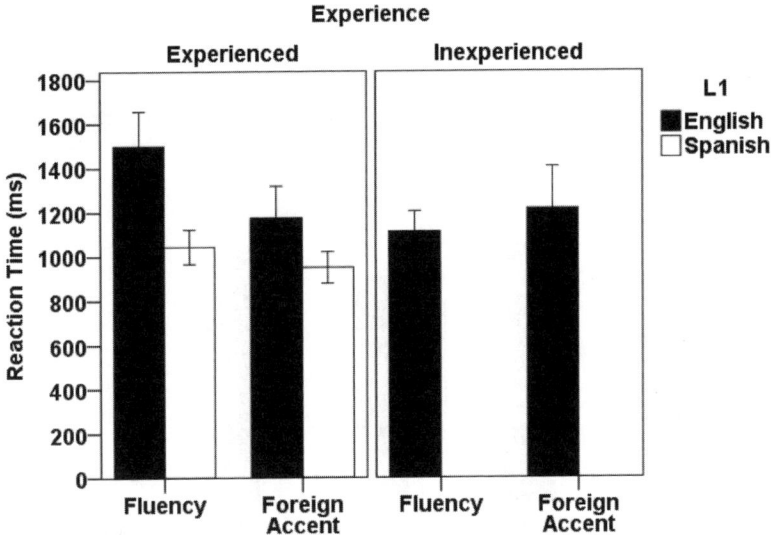

Figure 8.6 Mean RTs (ms) in fluency and foreign accent judgements as a function of listeners' *L1* and *experience*

Note: Error bars indicate ± 1 standard error.

(fluency versus foreign accent) as a within-subjects factor. These analyses yielded non-significant main effects of *speech dimension* and *experience* with none of the interactions reaching significance. The main effect of L1, however, closely approached significance at 0.065, suggesting that *L1* is potentially the factor affecting listeners' RTs the most.

We next assessed whether the fluency and foreign accent ratings themselves differed as a function of listeners' *L1* and *experience*. Spanish/Catalan listeners rated the speech samples slightly more harshly than English listeners did for both fluency (3.36 versus 3.10) and foreign accent (3.62 versus 3.42); that is, they perceived the speech samples to be less fluent and more strongly accented than the English listeners did. Listeners with extensive exposure to Spanish/Catalan-accented English perceived the speech samples to be more strongly accented (3.57 versus 3.42) and less fluent (3.28 versus 3.12) than less experienced listeners (Figure 8.7). Fluency and foreign accent ratings were submitted to an ANOVA with *L1* (Spanish/Catalan, English) and *experience* (experienced, inexperienced) as between-subjects factors and speech *dimension* (fluency, foreign accent) as a within-subjects factor. The results revealed a significant main effect of *dimension* and *L1* and a non-significant main effect of *experience*, with none of the interactions reaching significance. This suggests that speech samples were perceived to be more heavily accented than dysfluent, and that Spanish/Catalan listeners were more severe than English listeners in their judgements of L2 speech.

The results of the present study highlight the importance of listeners' L1, and familiarity with a specific type of accent, to a lesser extent, in the

Experience

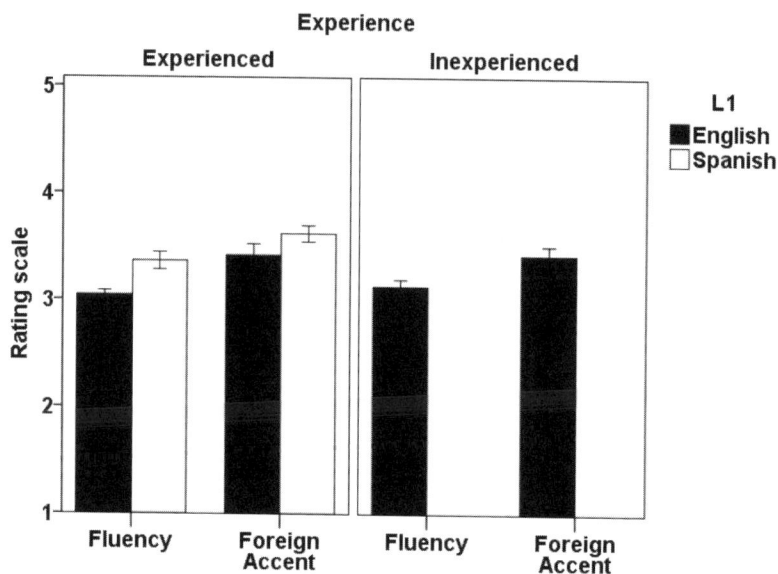

Figure 8.7 Mean fluency and foreign accent ratings as a function of listeners' *L1 and experience*

Notes: 1 = Extremely fluent/no foreign accent; 5 = Extremely dysfluent/very strong foreign accent. Error bars indicate ± 1 standard error.

perception of L2 speech, both as regards processing speed (RTs) and perceptual judgements (fluency and foreign accent ratings). Listeners detected a higher degree of foreign accent when their L1 matched that of the speech samples than when it did not. In the next section we further explore the role of listeners' characteristics in the perception of L2 speech by assessing the effects of cognitive factors on their ability to perceive differences in degree of foreign accent.

Study 3: The role of cognitive skills in the perception of foreign accent

This study adds to the findings from Study 2 in its investigation of the role of listeners' individual differences in cognitive ability (PM, AM and AC) in the perceptual judgement of foreign accent in L2 speech. Research investigating the effect of listeners' individual differences in cognitive skills on their rating of non-native speech is rare. To the best of our knowledge only one study has previously addressed this issue. Isaacs and Trofimovich (2011) examined the relationship between PM, attentional control and musical aptitude and listeners' judgements of non-native speech for foreign accent, comprehensibility and fluency. They found that music majors were significantly more severe than non-music majors in their foreign accent ratings, but neither PM nor AC appeared to affect listeners' judgements of non-native speech. The aim of our study, however, was not to assess how listeners would vary in their overall foreign accent *ratings*, but to investigate to what extent listeners varied in their ability to *detect differences* in the degree of foreign accent in the speech samples, and whether such differences were related to inter-listener differences in PM, AM and AC. We predicted that listeners who were better able to keep sound sequences and their acoustic information in short-term memory (PM and AM) and were better able to focus their attention on non-native acoustic features of speech sounds (AC) would also be better able to perceive differences in degree of foreign accent in the speech samples.

Methodology

The participants were 12 native speakers of English (five male, seven female, mean age 32) teaching English as a foreign language in Barcelona (Spain). They performed the PM, AM and AC tasks described above and a foreign accent rating task containing Spanish/Catalan-accented words. They were familiar with the type of accent in the speech samples they were asked to rate (Spanish/Catalan-accented English).

The foreign accent rating task was the same as that used by Mora *et al.* (2014). It contained 12 English words produced by 23 L1-Spanish/Catalan learners of English ($12 \times 23 = 276$) and a token of each one of the words (12) produced by four native speakers of British English (two words each = eight) and one American English speaker (four words), that is 288 word stimuli in total ($276 + 12$). The words were two-syllable words selected to include the voiceless stops /p, t, k/ at the onset of a word-initial stressed syllable having either /iː/ or /æ/ in the nucleus (*peanut, parrot, peeler, panel, teacher, tablet, teabag, taxi, keeper, cabin, kiwi, candle*). Thus, the deviant (non-English-like) phonetic features listeners could mainly focus on were related to the absence of aspiration or short-lag realization of the initial stops (aspirated in English but non-aspirated in Spanish), the accuracy in the production of the stressed vowel (both /iː/ or /æ/ tend to assimilate to Spanish /i/ and /a/, which differ in quality), and the reduction of the second unstressed syllable (Spanish does not reduce unstressed syllables in either length or quality to the extent that English does).

The 288 English word stimuli were presented to listeners in random order over headphones at a self-adjusted volume for foreign accent assessment on a 9-point Likert scale (1 = Very strong foreign accent versus 9 = No foreign accent). Listeners first labelled the word they heard by clicking on one of 12 buttons identifying the words in standard orthography and then they rated the word on the 9-point scale. Listeners were allowed to listen to each auditory stimulus up to a maximum of three times.

The dependent measure we used as an index of listeners' ability to perceive differences in degree of foreign accent was each listener's standard deviation (SD) of the foreign accent ratings (1–9) given to the 288 word stimuli. We interpreted this SD score as a measure of dispersion providing an average of the differences from the foreign accent scores mean. The higher the SD score, the more spread out scores were for the mean foreign accent score given to the 288 word stimuli and, consequently, the greater the variation in the degree of foreign accent each listener perceived.

Results

The listeners correctly identified all Spanish/Catalan-accented words by selecting the appropriate label, and their judgements were highly consistent, according to the inter-rater reliability analysis (Cronbach's alpha = 0.90). The mean ratings per word ranged from 1.57 to 8.57 and the 276 words produced by L1-Spanish/Catalan learners obtained a mean rating of 5.23 (SD = 1.16). The 12 listeners obtained SDs in the rating of the 288 word stimuli that ranged from 1.13 to 2.57 SDs (mean = 1.88, SD = 0.46).

We first explored the relationship between listeners' cognitive ability and their ability to perceive differences in foreign accent by running Pearson r correlations between PM, AM and AC scores and their SD scores. PM, AM and AC scores appeared to be unrelated to one another (all $r < 0.25$ and non-significant). SD scores correlated strongly and significantly with PM, but not with AM or AC error rate (see Figure 8.8). AC Shift Cost correlated with the SD scores almost moderately but non-significantly. This indicated that listeners with stronger PM perceived more differences in degree of foreign accent than participants with poorer PM.

We explored these results further by assigning listeners to Low and High PM, AM and AC groups by means of a median split (Table 8.4).

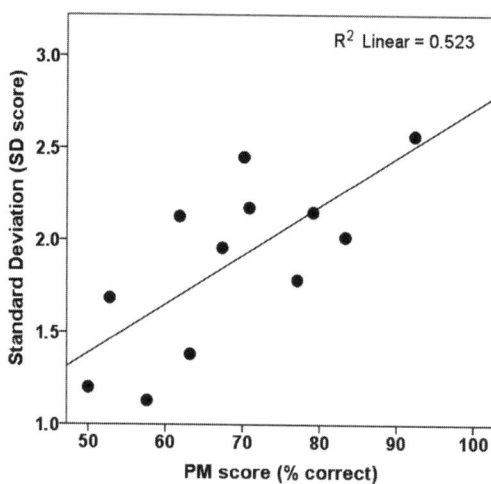

Figure 8.8 Scatterplot illustrating relationship between SD score and PM score

Table 8.4 Group means with standard deviations (SD) and group median scores of the Low and High PM, AM and AC groups

	Low			High			Group
	N	Mean	SD	N	Mean	SD	Median
PM (% correct)	6	58.7	6.5	6	78.8	8.3	68.7
AM (% correct)	6	62.3	3.5	6	80.4	5.7	68.4
AC Shift cost (ms)	6	196.3	36.4	6	29.4	13.4	86.36
AC Error rate (% error)	5	4.7	2.0	7	1.6	0.5	3.12

Table 8.5 SD mean scores, SD and t-test results as a function of Low- and High-ability groups

SD scores	Low			High			t-test	
	N	Mean	SD	N	Mean	SD	$t(10) =$	$p =$
PM	6	1.58	0.4	6	2.19	0.2	−2.99	0.014
AM	6	1.91	0.6	6	1.85	0.3	0.211	0.837
AC Shift cost	6	1.70	0.3	6	2.06	0.5	1.45	0.185
AC Error rate	5	1.97	0.5	7	1.76	0.3	−0.759	0.465

Participants assigned to the High AC groups were those obtaining shorter shift cost RTs and lower error rates. Results show that High-ability groups (except for AM) obtain slightly higher SD scores than Low-ability groups, suggesting that listeners with higher PM and AC in general were better able to perceive differences in foreign accent in the 288 word stimuli.

A series of t-tests comparing the SD mean scores of Low- and High-ability groups for PM, AM and AC revealed a significant difference between means for PM only. This suggests that individual differences in listeners' PM, but not in AM or AC, affected their ability to perceive differences in degree of foreign accent in the speech samples (Table 8.5). Listeners with greater PM capacity therefore showed an advantage over listeners with poorer PM in that they were able to perceive a wider range of degrees of foreign accent in the Spanish/Catalan-accented word stimuli.

Discussion and Conclusion

This chapter has explored the role of individual differences in cognitive ability in the perception of an L2 vowel contrast by L2 learners (Study 1), and in the perception of foreign accent by L1 listeners (Study 3). In these two cases the data support the contribution of cognitive skills to explaining inter-learner differences in the perception of L2 sounds, AM and AC in particular, and inter-listener differences in the judgement of L2 speech, where PM was the only cognitive skill to make a significant contribution. We have also examined the role of listeners' L1 and their degree of experience with non-native accents in the assessment of L2 speech for speaking fluency and foreign accent (Study 2), and we found listeners' L1 to play a more important role than experience in the perception of L2 speech. Overall the findings underscore the importance of individual differences (whether cognitive or experience related) in the processing of L2 speech and suggest that such factors may affect L2 learners and listeners (including their teachers) of L2 speech in similar ways, conditioning phonological development in the former and judgements of L2 speech in the latter.

Investigating the effects of individual variables in L2 speech development provides a deeper understanding of the factors responsible for the large variation typically found in learners' degree of attainment in L2 pronunciation. Such research is useful in improving and adapting the design of perceptual tasks to learners' needs in order to make perceptual training methods more effective (Aliaga-Garcia *et al.*, 2011). Future research is needed to examine these and other cognitive skills involved in L2 speech learning (e.g. musical ability, oral mimicry) and to expand the study of its effects to L2 speech production in order to gain a better understanding of the factors involved in the acquisition of L2 speech.

Listeners' perception of non-native speech has been shown to be consistent across different listener groups for both speaking fluency and foreign accent. However, Study 2 showed that L1-Spanish listeners rated L2-English speech samples as significantly more dysfluent and more strongly accented than L1-English listeners did, and more experienced listeners rated the speech samples for foreign accent more severely, indicating that L1-English listeners (as well as less experienced listeners) were in fact more lenient in their judgements of L2 speech. This has important implications for L2 pronunciation instruction and evaluation as it suggests that listeners' L1 (and experience with L2 accented speech to a lesser extent) may constitute a source of bias in L2 pronunciation assessment.

The listeners' RT data in Study 2 suggest that speed of processing of non-native speech varies as a function of several factors: the level on the rating scale a speech sample is assigned to; the perceptual dimension listeners are asked to rate (speech samples are faster to rate for foreign accent than for fluency); and factors related to listeners' linguistic experience, such as their L1 or their familiarity with the kind of non-native speech they are asked to rate. Just as individual differences in cognitive ability may explain a considerable amount of inter-subject variation in L2 speech perception and ultimate attainment in the acquisition of L2 speech, the findings of Study 3 suggest that inter-rater variation in the perception of non-native speech might also be partly explained by individual differences in speech-processing skills. This constitutes an exciting area of enquiry where much research is needed. Study 3 offers some preliminary findings on the relationship between listeners' perception of non-native speech and speech-related cognitive skills (PM, AM, AC), but much larger listener populations are needed in order to be able to confirm the role of cognitive skills in the judgement of L2 speech.

Overall, the outcome of this research underscores the importance of experiential and cognitive factors as sources of inter-subject variation in speech-processing ability, either in the perception of L2 sounds by L2 learners or in the perception of the speech of L2 learners by native and non-native listeners. These are both largely under-researched areas in the L2 speech acquisition literature, with interesting implications from both the learning/teaching and assessment perspectives of language education. Recent studies on the interaction between learners' aptitudes and instructional methods (see Granena & Long, 2013, for a review) suggest exciting new avenues of research and pedagogical innovation, such as training L2 learners on those language-related cognitive skills that would enhance language acquisition under specific learning conditions. In the domain of L2 pronunciation instruction, for example, training L2 learners on cognitive abilities that improve their speech-processing skills may lead to enhanced L2 speech development.

Acknowledgements

This study was supported by grants FFI2016-80564-R from the Spanish Ministry of Economy and Competitiveness and 2017SGR560 from the Catalan government.

9 A Case of Extreme Phonetic Attrition in the German Rhotic

Esther de Leeuw, Aurela Tusha, Hui Zhao,
Kyle Helke and Alice Greenfield

Introduction

The term 'first language attrition' generally refers to changes in an individual's first language (L1) which occur after a second language (L2) is acquired in adulthood, often in the case of migration. Studies into L1 attrition usually compare a group of bilingual immigrants with a group of monolinguals from the bilinguals' country of origin. The objective of such studies is usually to see whether there is a difference between the two groups in a chosen linguistic variable (e.g. the pronunciation of the language in question, which both the monolinguals and the bilinguals speak). The bilinguals in such studies tend to be late consecutive bilinguals, meaning that they acquired their L2 after adolescence, and therefore after the closing of a proposed critical period (see Li Wei, 2000, for definitions of various types of bilinguals). Often, the objective of such studies is to examine whether, and the extent to which, an L1 can *really* ever structurally change, i.e. undergo L1 attrition, when an L2 is used more frequently and becomes dominant post adolescence such as after immigration.

More recently, the characterization of L1 attrition has been broadened to include studies which have examined changes in the L1 upon acquisition of a new *dialect* in adulthood (see de Leeuw, in press, in *The Oxford Handbook of Language Attrition*). The inclusion of dialects into a definition of L1 attrition is especially relevant when one considers that the terms language and dialect represent a continuum and that their 'edges are extremely ragged and uncertain' (Haugen, 1966: 922). With this wider definition, structural changes induced by a dialect learned post adolescence are also characterized as L1 attrition.

Studies that specifically report phonetic L1 attrition, henceforth phonetic attrition (see de Leeuw, 2014; de Leeuw *et al.*, 2010, 2012, 2013; Evans & Iverson, 2007; Flege, 1987; Hopp & Schmid, 2013; Major, 1992;

Mayr *et al.*, 2012; Mennen, 2004; Munro *et al.*, 1999; Shockey, 1984; Ulbrich & Ordin, 2014) to a certain extent challenge the traditional understanding of how language is represented in the mind, as they reveal that, in an extreme situation such as is the case of immersion after immigration, a native language is more malleable than previously considered.

However, often in such group studies into L1 attrition, bilinguals who go against the overall group trend (i.e. their performance on the experimental tasks is different from that of the bilinguals) are mentioned only in passing, or sometimes even unreported, simply because the objective of such studies is to examine differences between the bilingual and monolingual *groups*. As a result, it is possible for outliers to 'fall through the cracks', although they actually might be quite meaningful in furthering our understanding of how languages are represented in the mind, as they reveal what is *actually possible* rather than what *usually* happens. Moreover, the reasons behind such outliers often remain unexplored (e.g. potentially because of social differences, such as amount of L2 use or level of education; see also Moyer, 2014a), whereas the current investigation attempts to do this (see subsection on methodology used to index language use and mixing).

The purpose of the present study was to focus on one such individual who might otherwise have fallen through the cracks. Our subject, known by the initials of GT, was selected for this case study because he displayed phonetic attrition in all the other group phonetic analyses he previously underwent, whereas the other nine bilingual migrants who had moved from Germany to Canada did not do so as consistently. For example, de Leeuw *et al.* (2012, 2013) found that his realization of his German /l/ in **coda** position adhered to the Canadian English norms and became '**dark**', which is not typical for Standard German. In another phonetic analysis, his realization of the **pre-nuclear rise** in his native German was significantly earlier than is characteristic of German; instead, it fell 'within the English monolingual norm' (de Leeuw *et al.*, 2012: 112). In an additional study which examined the perception of foreign accent in a large group of German native speakers who had moved to either Anglophone Canada or The Netherlands, GT stood out because he was consistently rated to be a non-native speaker of his native German by German monolinguals in Germany (de Leeuw *et al.*, 2010).[1]

The present study builds on these previous studies by investigating the pronunciation of his German rhotic in words like *Reis* 'rice' and *Rat* 'advice'. (The term 'rhotic' is a general term for all r-like sounds.[2]) As will be further explained, we conducted an **impressionistic**, i.e. auditory analysis of potentially foreign accented speech in all of his rhotic realizations. Thereafter, we undertook an **acoustic analysis** of his rhotic realizations to see whether they were more in line with what one would expect from English native speech, rather than German native speech. Finally, an innovative method to analyze language use in bilinguals (see subsection on methodology used to index language use and mixing) is presented in order to interpret the extreme phonetic attrition exhibited by GT.

In brief, the findings from this study revealed phonetic attrition in the rhotic realizations of GT, evidenced in both the impressionistic and acoustic analyses. We suggest that GT may have been particularly susceptible to phonetic attrition due to his prolonged reduced use of German coupled with extended complete immersion in a monolingual English environment. We propose that GT underwent 'extreme' phonetic attrition because he was 'extremely' immersed in the English language – in contrast to the other comparable bilinguals.

Speech Learning Model and Maturational Constraints

Before continuing to examine GT in more detail, we briefly present research from related studies. Flege's (1995, 2003a) Speech Learning Model (SLM) is the focus of this section, which is compared with a maturational constraints perspective. The SLM proposes that the phonetic system(s) of both the L1 and L2 are malleable throughout one's life. In this way, the SLM differs from a maturational constraints perspective, which postulates that the loss of plasticity in the brain (i.e. the brain's ability to develop and change) makes the L1 resistant to change when an L2 is acquired in adulthood (Bylund, 2009). In line with a maturational constraints perspective, since Oyama (1976), studies have suggested that L2 acquisition is moderated by a sensitive period rather than a proposed critical period which 'closes' after a certain age. For example, Long (1990, 2005) suggests a sensitive period, typically between six and 12 years of age, for the development of the L1 phonological system. What unifies such explanatory models, founded within a notion related to the critical period, is that they premise some kind of biological constraint which differentiates language development in adulthood from language development in childhood and, in terms of L1 attrition, they tend to support the notion that an L1, once acquired in full, is relatively resilient to change. Studies which reveal L1 attrition challenge the underlying premise of such models and, should L1 attrition be evidenced by late consecutive bilinguals, indicate that we must look towards other explanations as to how language might be represented in the mind. What is more, some studies indicate that the brain retains some of its plasticity even into old adulthood and is capable of reversing parts of the age-related volume loss, thereby improving cognitive performance (Erickson et al., 2011; Stern, 2012). It is thus all the more important to look into individual differences, as is done in this study.

The SLM is one such model, which is often drawn upon in studies related to phonetics and speech development. According to this model, when the sounds of an L2 are encountered, the L1 phonetic system will either form new categories or modify existing ones to accommodate the new speech sounds. Miscategorization prompts the L2 learner to 'merge' (Flege, 1987: 62) the phonetic properties of L1 and L2 similar

phones into a category that is intermediate to the two respective languages. Accordingly, the interaction between the two languages results in inaccuracies and deviations from monolingual norms in both the L1 and L2. Therefore, the SLM acknowledges accommodation of the L1 speech system upon L2 acquisition *throughout* life, which is not stipulated to the same extent within frameworks based on maturational constraints.

Indeed, some studies have indicated that *both* the L1 and L2 phonetic systems develop and change across the lifespan. For example, in their study of **voice onset time** (VOT)[3] productions of native French speakers living in the United States, Flege and Hillenbrand (1984) found that French native speakers, who were proficient speakers of English and who had moved to the United States at an average age of 26 years, 'produced French /t/ with VOT values that substantially exceeded' the French norm (Flege & Hillenbrand, 1984: 716). According to Flege and Hillenbrand, misclassification led the French speakers of English to merge the phonetic properties of French and English /t/ because they judged these acoustically different phones to be realizations of the same phoneme. This finding was later replicated in Flege (1987), who investigated the VOT of both native American English speakers living in Paris and native French speakers living in Chicago, USA. Again, exposure to the L2 began in late adolescence or adulthood, thus what is generally considered to be past the potential plastic phase for language processing in the brain according to a model aligned with maturational constraints. Results revealed that for both groups the VOT of their native language became more like the VOT of their L2. This meant that the native English speakers immersed in a French environment produced *shorter* English VOT than the English monolinguals and, likewise, the native French speakers living in the United States produced *longer* VOT in French than the monolingual group.

Similar to Flege's studies, Major (1992) examined the VOT of five native American English speakers who had been living in Brazil for between 12 and 35 years. All subjects had moved in adulthood – the youngest age of arrival was 22. This again meant that if maturational constraints determined language learning, the L1 system should not be affected as a result of migration to a country where the L2 is acquired as the dominant language. For the participants in Major's study, using English was an essential part of their daily roles; however, despite 'strong personal and professional reasons to maintain their L1', all of the participants in the study displayed some loss of their native English (Major, 1992: 200). In examining participant GT, our study builds on such research in order to determine whether, as would be predicted from the SLM, his L1 German and L2 English rhotic pronunciations underwent merging, which would be less expected according to a maturational constraints perspective.

Language use

Although the aforementioned studies examined language use indirectly, in the sense that the bilinguals had all moved to a new country in which their L1 was used to a lesser extent than in their country of origin, the studies did not tackle L1 use directly through comparing potential differences in L1 use *between* the bilinguals in the bilingual group. To date, some non-phonetic studies (e.g. Cazzoli-Goeta & Young-Scholten, 2011; Gürel, 2004, 2007; Schmid, 2007) have examined L1 attrition and language use, but there is presently little research examining the relationship between all the different ways a language can be used by migrants and the potential for a native language to undergo attrition. We do not know, for example, whether how often the L1 is used in both absolute and relative terms affects L1 attrition. Nor do we know whether more is always better, or whether it matters with whom one is speaking in the L1. Likewise, does **recency** of L1 use affect any evidenced L1 attrition? Would passive versus active L1 use affect L1 attrition differently? However, in a recent study on German native speakers who migrated to Canada or The Netherlands, in which GT was a bilingual who had moved to Canada, it was found that the German migrants with a high amount of L1 use in which **code-mixing** in the L1 was *not* expected to occur were *less* likely to be rated as non-native speakers of their L1 than those with a high amount of L1 use in which code-mixing between the L1 and L2 *was* expected to occur (de Leeuw *et al.*, 2010).

This study, in which all the migrants were late consecutive bilinguals and had been living abroad for an average of 37 years, also showed that age of L2 acquisition (AOA) and length of residence (LOR) in the L2 country were not significant predictors of their foreign accent ratings. Thus it seemed that those bilinguals who continued to use their native German language in settings in which only German was predicted to be spoken were more likely to maintain their native German pronunciation. Such findings, which differentiate different types of language use in bilingual migrants, call for further investigations examining the relationship between phonetic attrition and language use, as the present study aims to do.

The Present Study

The primary objective of this case study was to investigate whether GT exhibited *any* phonetic attrition of the German rhotic at all. The reason why the rhotic was chosen is that this sound differs greatly in German and English, such that analyzing the rhotic permitted both an impressionistic and acoustic analysis, as will be described in the following sections. Confirmation of phonetic attrition of the German rhotic was interpreted as support for the SLM, rather than for a maturational constraints perspective because, according to a strict interpretation of maturational constraints, one would expect little, if any, phonetic attrition in his German rhotic as he had moved to Canada when he was 21 years old (see Table 9.1).

Table 9.1 Gender, AOA, LOR and AAR of all participants

Participant	Sex	AOA	LOR	AAR
ZD	Male	24	55	79
GT	Male	21	53	73
DI	Female	20	49	69
GB	Male	16	48	72
ZM	Female	32	48	80
WMR	Female	23	40	63
BM	Female	23	38	61
GB	Female	32	29	61
LC	Female	19	22	41
HKI	Female	29	18	47

Furthermore, a secondary objective was to determine whether GT produced two discrete categories for the rhotic, or whether the German and English rhotics were merged into one category. Given that the SLM predicts intermediate merging, i.e. a new **phone** emerges which is intermediate to the two respective language norms, the secondary objective was more specifically to examine whether the predicted new category was indeed merged *between* the German and English norms, or whether it more clearly aligned with *either* the German norm *or* the English norm. Finally, the last objective of this case study was to examine how language use may have impacted the extent of attrition in the speech of GT.

General description of GT

GT was 73 years old and had been living in Anglophone Canada for over 50 years (see Table 9.1) when he was recorded. He moved to Vancouver, Canada at the age of 21 from Diestedde, Nordrhein-Westfalen in northwest Germany. Like the other German native speakers in his group of German L1-English L2 bilinguals (see also de Leeuw *et al.*, 2012, 2013), GT was considered to be a late consecutive bilingual. At the time he was recruited specifically for his late age, which enabled a lengthy time in Canada such that any extreme phonetic attrition was considered to be possible. As such, the purpose was to examine the potential for an outlier, rather than an 'average'. In Canada, he met his Scottish-born wife, with whom he only spoke English and to whom he had been married for 49 years. His biographical data from the questionnaire indicated that, out of all the participants, he was among those who had been with their partner the longest. In addition, he was one of three participants whose partner was a native English speaker and with whom he claimed to speak only English. They had two adult daughters together and three grandchildren, with whom he also claimed to only speak English. GT reported no hearing impairment.

During the interview, GT explained that the reason for his immigration to Canada was primarily economic as he was expecting to find a better job in Canada, although at the time of arrival he claimed to hardly speak any English at all. Regarding education both in Germany and Canada, GT finished the *Realschule* in Germany, taking English, Latin and some French and, after moving to Canada, he completed a four-year BA in English, French, business and economics. GT was retired at the time of recording, but previously he had worked in a relatively high position in the information technology sector of a large company in Vancouver.

The general impression of GT was that he was very outgoing and enjoyed conversing with the interviewers (e.g. after data collection he generously invited the interviewers to dinner). He reported listening to German radio and reading German newspapers only once or twice a month, and he claimed to speak German only once a month, second only to one other participant (WMR), who claimed to never speak German with German contacts (see subsection on methodology used to index language use and mixing).

Finally, GT reported to have no regional accent when speaking German, although he claimed to have learned *Plattdeutsch* before entering school. Similarly, although his wife was Scottish, the interviewers perceived GT to have a standard Canadian accent in his English (the first author of this paper grew up in British Columbia, the province in which Vancouver is located).

German and English rhotic production

In this section we briefly describe German and English rhotic realization such that the reader has a general understanding of both language norms, in order for the rhotic pronunciation of GT to be comprehensible (and see Thomas, 2010, for more details on the specifics of terminology used here). Generally, the IPA symbol /r/ is used to transcribe rhotics when the exact type of rhotic is not specified. In most dialects of Standard American English (AE), /r/ is realized as a **voiced retroflex approximant** (Ladefoged & Maddieson, 1996; Wells, 1982).[4] When there is a need to specify this exact phonetic realization of /r/, the symbol [ɹ] is used for the AE realization. Alternatively, the German rhotic can be articulated either as a **voiced alveolar or uvular trill** (respectively, [r] or [R]), or as a **voiced uvular fricative**, transcribed phonetically as [ʁ]. Today, the voiced uvular fricative is the most common pronunciation of the rhotic in Standard German (Ladefoged & Maddieson, 1996; Wells, 1982). Kohler describes the German rhotic, when it is not vocalized in **post-vocalic** position, as a uvular fricative. More specifically, Kohler (1977: 169) writes: 'In both Schleswig-Holstein and the Alemannic and Bavarian-Austrian German language areas, the apical trill [r] is widely present, or reduced contact; along with the presence of the uvular trill [R]. Otherwise, the uvular fricative and the frication-less sound, which have experienced increased use over time, prevail [...].'[5]

In addition to the different articulatory realizations of rhotics in German and English, and the IPA symbols which represent these various pronunciations, the acoustic manifestations of these R-like sounds differ. Crucial to the current investigation, the Canadian rhotic is characterized by a low third **formant** (F_3)[6] frequency, while the German rhotic is not. For example, Ladefoged and Maddieson (1996: 226) suggest an average F_3 frequency of between 2500 and 3000 Hz for Standard German. The characteristically low F_2 and F_3 frequencies (Ladefoged & Maddieson, 1996; Lawson *et al.*, 2010; Thomas, 2010; Zhou *et al.*, 2007) for the North American retroflex approximant may be associated with a constriction in the lower pharynx, as well as lip rounding (Alwan & Narayanan, 1996: 1085). Indeed, the North American /r/ is reported to have three cavities: 'one between the glottis and the pharyngeal constriction, another between the pharyngeal and dorsal or apical constrictions, and the third in front of the dorsal or apical constrictions, including the space underneath the tongue' (Thomas, 2010: 132). For American English rhotics, Dalston (1975) found average F_2 and F_3 frequencies of 1061 and 1546 Hz. Thomas (2010) provides an F_3 value for English rhotics ranging from 1300 to 1950 Hz, i.e. much lower than Ladefoged and Maddieson's average Standard German F_3 frequency. These differences between the F_2 and F_3 frequencies are relevant to the present investigation, as our aim was to investigate whether GT exhibited any phonetic attrition in the German rhotic through a lowering of his German F_2 and F_3 frequencies into the frequency range characteristic of English.

Methodology

Stage 1 of this study was an impressionistic analysis of /r/ in all 10 of the late consecutive bilinguals (de Leeuw, 2009). Thereafter, an acoustic analysis of specifically /r/ realizations by GT occurred. Note that in the acoustic analysis, only tokens which were impressionistically identified as being within a typical Canadian English pronunciation were measured. This was done in an attempt to obtain clear resonatory **formant frequencies** in the acoustic analysis, which are not evidenced to the same extent in trills and fricatives as they are in vowels and approximants (see, for example, Thomas, 2010, for a detailed explanation as to why this is the case). Finally, language use by GT was compared with the other bilinguals in order to determine whether language use played a role in the process of phonetic attrition.

Data collection

Ten late consecutive bilingual German immigrants to Canada were interviewed at the Interdisciplinary Speech Research Laboratory at the University of British Columbia in Vancouver in December 2006 (see de

Leeuw *et al.*, 2010, 2012, for more information regarding data collection). At the time of interview, all participants completed a questionnaire examining their language backgrounds, conducted to ascertain more information about their language use. They were interviewed in both German and English by native speakers of the respective languages, and languages were strictly separated during data collection to ensure the participants were producing one language with the least influence from the other. Not until the very end of the entire data collection procedure did the participant see both interviewers in the same room. The experimenter responsible for each language read out the questions and took note of the corresponding answers. After answering all questions, participants were asked to read the word list eliciting /r/ in onset position.

A word list was considered more appropriate than spontaneous speech to prevent rhotics occurring in coda position which are vocalized in German (and thus phonetically, strictly speaking, not rhotics). Moreover, syllable complexity was able to be controlled in that all elicited words were monosyllabic. It was thought that if phonetic attrition was revealed in the word list, this would be more convincing evidence that phonetic attrition does indeed occur, as word lists are generally thought to be a formal elicitation method for which participants would monitor their pronunciation more strictly. The word list also contained distracters (see de Leeuw *et al.*, 2012, for more information regarding elicitation of the word lists). Appendix A provides a list of all 26 German /r/ tokens in onset position that were analyzed in this study.

Participants

The bilinguals group was made up of 10 German L1-English L2 migrants, who had moved to Canada in late adolescence or early adulthood and had lived in Canada for 18 years or more (see Table 9.1). Sex, age of arrival to Canada, i.e. age of English acquisition (AOA), length of residence (LOR) in Canada and age at time of recording (AAR) are shown in Table 9.1, which is ordered according to LOR.

As is evident from Table 9.1, GT had lived in Canada for the second longest amount of time, second only to ZD, although ZD was married to a German native speaker with whom he self-reported to always speak German, while GT was married to an English native speaker with whom he reported to always speak English. Likewise, subject DI had lived in Canada for a similar duration to GT, but she was also married to a native German speaker, as was subject ZM. Subject BM was also married to a German native speaker, while subject WMR was not married and had relatively few contacts. Subject BG was also married to a native English speaker. Subjects LC and HKI were similarly in relationships with non-German native speakers with whom they spoke English; however, they had been living in Canada for a much shorter amount of time than GT. Subject GB was the most similar to GT in that he had also been living in

Canada for approximately 50 years and was likewise married to an English native speaker with whom he spoke English. Where the two noticeably differ, though, is that GB reportedly continued to speak German with his children sometimes, while GT ceased speaking German with his family entirely.

Methodology for the impressionistic analysis

Before the impressionistic analysis was conducted, the words with initial /r/ were extracted from each individual participant's interview. For each participant a single sound file was created, containing all of their /r/ tokens, to aid the analysis process. The impressionistic analysis was conducted by two native English speakers, one male and one female, who both had German as an L2 and respectively American English and British English as an L1 (fourth and fifth coauthors of this study). In their assessment, those words which were perceived to be English realizations (i.e. both native English speakers perceived the word to be 'perfectly' English-like in its pronunciation) were marked 1 and those which were perceived to be German-like were marked 0. Note that this task was in a sense skewed in that only those tokens which were perceived to be completely English (with no trace of a German accent) were marked as 1. Both the listeners had to be satisfied that the pronunciation was English-like and, as they came from different regional backgrounds, we considered this task to strictly assess phonetic attrition. We mention this only to emphasize that there was no potential for an over-assessment of phonetic attrition. During this rating task, the listeners were able to listen to the tokens as often as needed and a general judgement was made afterwards. In cases in which neither of the raters could make a judgement with certainty, the token was classified as German-like (0) to ensure the genuineness of all English-like tokens.

Results from the impressionistic analysis

The results from the impressionistic analysis indicated that GT was the most salient of all participants in his English pronunciation of the German rhotic (see Figure 9.1). Thirty-three of 76 tokens produced by GT were perceived to be English-like, and this percentage (43%) was much higher than that of any other participants (ranging from 0% to 17%). Among the other participants, HKI, ZM and WMR had zero English realizations of the German rhotics, while five other participants had some English-like tokens: 1% for GB; 3% for DI and LC; and 5% for BM and GB. Participant ZD came second in the production of English-like realizations of German /r/, having 13 English realizations (17%), which is interesting as he was married to a German native speaker with whom he claimed to always speak German. Where ZD and GT were similar, though, is that they were two of the oldest participants (aside from ZM, who evidenced no phonetic

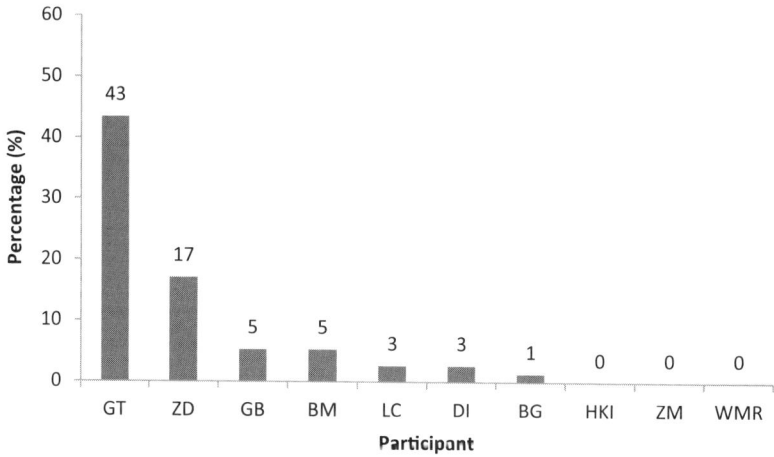

Figure 9.1 Percentage of German tokens pronounced with English realization

attrition in the impressionistic analysis and was also married to a German native speaker). Although the percentage of ZD was also much higher than the other eight speakers, it was nonetheless considerably lower than that of GT. Therefore, in line with the previous phonetic investigations (de Leeuw *et al.*, 2010, 2012), GT again stood out here in what we consider to be extreme attrition in the domain of phonetics.

Discussion of impressionistic analysis

The results of the impressionistic analysis indicated that participant GT consistently performed more English-like than any of the other experimental participants (see Figure 9.2). Accordingly, to a certain extent,

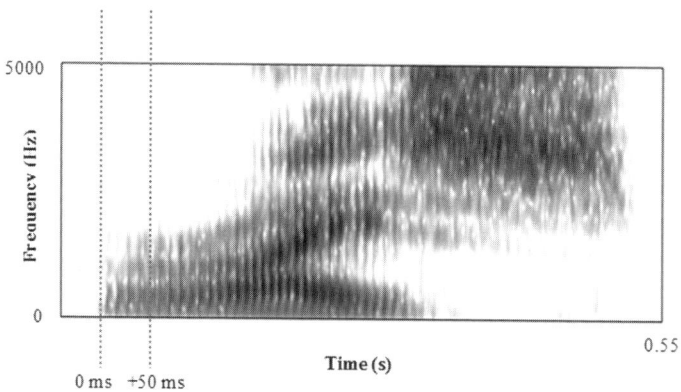

Figure 9.2 The word *Reis* 'rice' as articulated by GT; in this example, F_2 was measured to be 1000 Hz and F_3 was measured to be 1540 Hz, therefore within the English frequency range

these impressionistic results challenge a maturational constraints perspective on L1 speech development, which would not predict an English-like pronunciation in the German words of this late consecutive bilingual. Alternatively, these impressionistic results support the SLM which acknowledges accommodation of the L1 speech system upon L2 acquisition throughout life.

Methodology for the acoustic analysis

The acoustic analysis of word-initial /r/ phonemes in the speech of GT was conducted in order to determine whether the /r/ tokens, impressionistically analyzed as English realizations in his German speech, actually fit within the formant frequency range of English norms. Using Praat (Boersma & Weenink, 2015), which is a widely used software tool for acoustic analysis, F_2 and F_3 frequencies were measured. A number of conventions were followed in order to ensure consistency across the analyses. The start of the articulation of /r/ was carefully measured at the onset of periodicity at the point at which the waveform crossed the 0-axis (i.e. '0 ms' marker in Figure 9.2). A second marker was then automatically inserted 50 ms after the onset of the phoneme and the exact point of measurement was inserted at the point that was visually closest to this 50 ms mark where the waveform crossed the 0-axis (i.e. '+ 50 ms' marker in Figure 9.2). In all cases, it was ensured that this measurement was taken before the increase in amplitude characteristic of the following vowel. Note that alternative points of measurement, e.g. 40 ms and 60 ms after the start of the onset, were trialed, but 50ms most effectively captured formant measurements within a steady state of the /r/ realization.

Using the automatic Praat analysis of formants as a guide, visual measurements of the formant frequencies were taken in Hz for F_2 and F_3. For each formant measurement, the frequency was rounded to the nearest 10 Hz in order to ensure consistency and avoid drawing out major inferences from what may in fact be minor differences in the data (Foulkes *et al.*, 2010).

Results from acoustic analysis

As can be seen from Figure 9.3, F_2 was very similar in German and in English, as was F_3 similar in German and in English; however, for both F_2 and F_3, German had higher frequencies than in English. Tests of normality showed neither F_2 ($p = 0.001$ with $df = 107$) nor F_3 ($p = 0.000$ with $df = 107$) were normally distributed. Therefore, Mann–Whitney U-tests were performed on both F_2 and F_3 frequencies in the English and German speech of GT to examine whether there were significant differences (see Table 9.3).

The F_3 of GT's German rhotic (see Table 9.2) was significantly higher than that of his English rhotic (65.45 versus 48.89 in mean rank, $p < 0.05$).

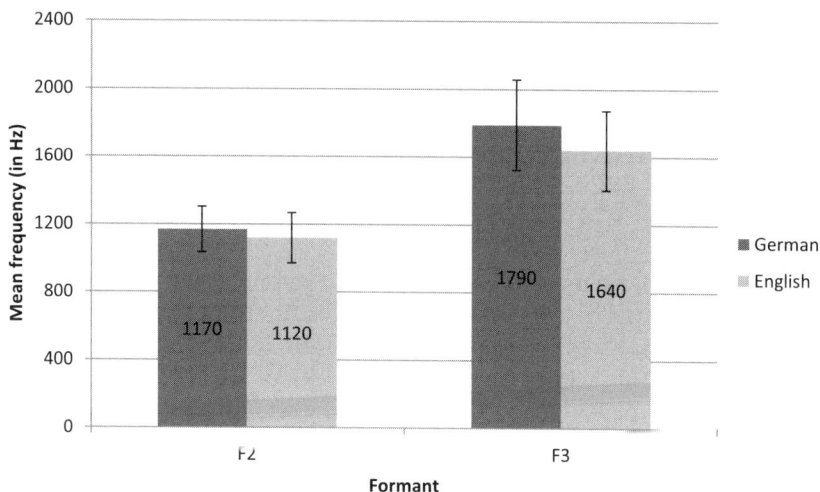

Figure 9.3 Mean F_2 and F_3 frequency (in Hz) for English-like German rhotics and English rhotics for GT

Note: The vertical lines within the bars display standard deviations.

However, this effect size was fairly small ($r = 0.247$). A similar result was obtained regarding his F_2 frequency (63.18 for German versus 49.91 for English in mean rank, $p < 0.05$). Here, however, the effect size was even smaller, $r = 0.189$. However, the formant frequencies for both languages were within the English norm values. Figure 9.4 shows the distribution of F_2 and F_3 frequencies in the rhotics of both his English and German. The larger dark circle in the middle of the cluster represents an approximation of the mean F_2 (1061 Hz) and F_3 (1546 Hz) frequencies in American English, taken from Dalston (1975). It is evident that there is no visual separation of clustering of English and German frequencies, indicating an English-like realization of /r/ in both languages, as already perceived in the impressionistic foreign accent rating.

Table 9.2 Mann–Whitney U-tests on language differences for F_2 and F_3

	Md	Mean rank	N	U	Z	P	r
F_2 (German*English)	1150	**63.18**	33	918	− 2.049	0.040*	0.189
	1110	49.91	74				
F_3 (German*English)	1840	**65.45**	33	843	− 2.552	0.011*	0.247
	1590	48.89	74				

Notes: *$p < 0.05$. Higher ranks shown in bold type.

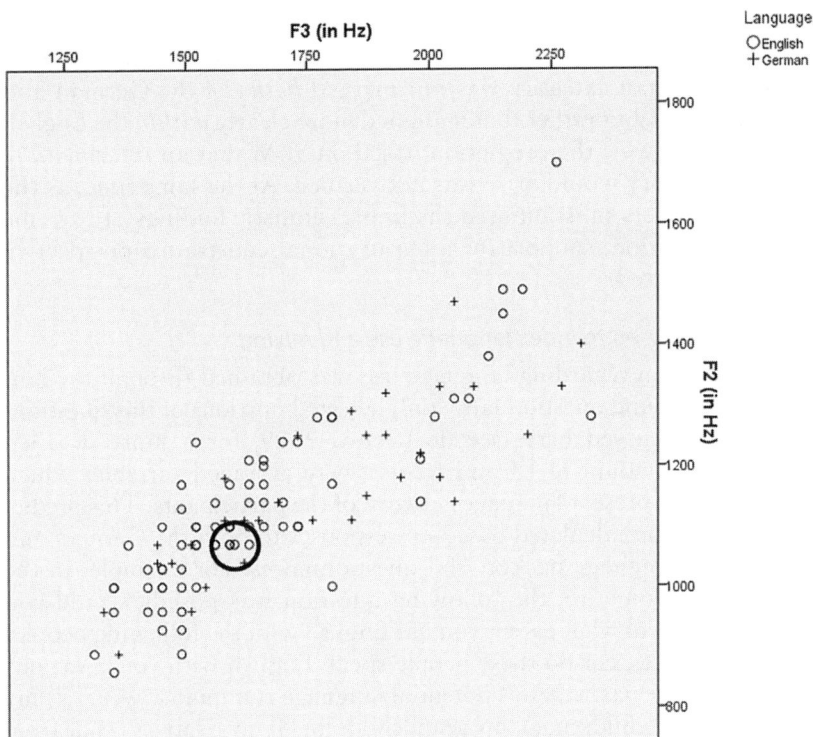

Figure 9.4 Scatterplot of F_2 and F_3 frequencies in American GT English and German rhotics

Note: The bold circle in the middle of the cluster represents an approximation of the mean F_2 (1061 Hz) and F_3 (1546 Hz) frequencies in American English.

Discussion of acoustic analysis

These findings support the earlier acoustic studies indicating extreme L1 phonetic attrition in the speech of GT (de Leeuw *et al.*, 2010, 2012, 2013). To a certain extent, the merging of German and English F_2 and F_3 frequencies is his rhotic are also indicative of the studies which found that high-proficiency bilinguals tended to merge the VOT of their two languages to produce a VOT that was characteristic of neither their L1 nor their L2, but rather formed a new category between those of the L1 and L2 (Flege, 1987; Flege & Hillenbrand, 1984). However, based on the participant's F_2 and F_3 values for both languages, it appears that GT's German rhotic was produced within the monolingual norm of the Canadian English retroflex. For American English rhotics, Dalston (1975) found average F_2 and F_3 frequencies for males of respectively 1061 Hz and 1546 Hz, while Thomas (2010) provided an F_3 value for English rhotics between 1300 Hz and 1950 Hz. Ladefoged and Maddieson's (1996: 226) reported Standard German F_3

frequency is between 2500 Hz and 3000 Hz for male speakers, which is outside the range of Figure 9.4. Consequently, the results indicate that the new German category was *not* merged *between* the German and English norms, but rather that it aligned more clearly *within* the English norm. In this way, the prediction based on SLM that an *intermediate* merged category would arise was not verified. At the same time, as the acoustic analysis substantiated the impressionistic findings of extreme phonetic attrition, support for a maturational constraints perspective was not delivered.

Methodology used to index language use and mixing

Information regarding language use was obtained through the language background questionnaire; only selected portions of this question naire are discussed here (see de Leeuw, 2009, for a more detailed discussion). Amount of L1 and L2 use were averaged variables which focused on the present language network of the participants. This predictor variable was calculated based on responses to both the German and the English language background questionnaires. For example, in the English questionnaire, the following question was posed: 'Could you please indicate to what extent you use English with the following people? Also, to what extent do these people speak English with you?' Various members of the participant's potential language community were: (1) my partner; (2) my children; (3) my grandchildren; (4) my relatives (aside from the above); (5) my partner's relatives (aside from the above); (6) my friends in Canada; (7) my friends in Germany; (8) my colleagues in Canada; and (9) my colleagues in Germany.

For each category, the option of choosing between 'Always', 'Usually', 'Sometimes', 'Rarely' or 'Never' was given. The participant therefore indicated not only the extent to which he or she spoke English, but also the extent to which English was spoken to him or her. When a category was not applicable to the participant, for example because he or she had no children, it was left empty. In the corresponding German questionnaire, which was conducted in the separate German portion of the interview, a translation of the same categories was completed by the participants with the option of choosing between *Immer* 'Always', *Meistens* 'Usually', *Manchmal* 'Sometimes', *Kaum* 'Rarely' or *Nie* 'Never'.

Thereafter, two scales were created from each questionnaire. The first scale (see Table 9.3) represented the amount of language use in either German or English for each category (denoted as, respectively, AmountGUse and AmountEUse). For example, if a participant marked that he or she *always* spoke German to her partner, but that he usually spoke German to her, the average of 0.88 was calculated for this category (1 + 0.75/2 = 0.88). In all but two cases, the amount of German use plus the amount of English use was more than 1.0. This meant that participants tended to over-assess the amount of language use since,

Table 9.3 The scaling used for quantifying the amount of language use for both English and German

Participant's choice	Value on scale of amount of language use
immer 'always'	1
meistens 'usually'	0.75
manchmal 'sometimes'	0.5
kaum 'rarely'	0.25
nie 'never'	0

Table 9.4 The scaling used for quantifying amount of potential language mixing in both English and German

Participant's choice	Value on scale of amount of language use
immer 'always'	0.0
meistens 'usually'	0.25
manchmal 'sometimes'	0.5
kaum 'rarely'	0.25
nie 'never'	0.0

theoretically, AmountEUse + AmountGUse = 1 should hold for each category. In order to solve this discrepancy, the normalized total amount of language use was obtained for each category based on the absolute amount.

The second scale represented the amount of potential mixing the participant had with either English or German (see Table 9.4). If participants noted that they 'Always' or *Immer* spoke either respectively English or German with the specified members of their language community, it was assumed that no mixing occurred with these individuals. The same was true if the participants noted that they 'Never' or *Nie* spoke that language with the specified members. On the other hand, 'Usually' or *Meistens* and 'Rarely' or *Kaum* indicated somewhat more language mixing. 'Sometimes' or *Manchmal* was interpreted as the most language mixing.

Results from language use and mixing analysis

Results from the self-reported language use and mixing analysis can be seen in Table 9.5, which shows that GT used German much less frequently than English, similar to GB, LC and HKI who were also in relationships with English native speakers and at the bottom end of 'Amount of German spoken in network'. According to their self-reports, participants WMR and DI also had more English in their networks than German, but these individuals were not in relationships in which they only spoke English (DI was married to a native German speaker, while subject WMR

Table 9.5 L1 and L2 use and language mixing for all participants

	Amount of German spoken in network	Amount of English spoken in network	German mixing total	English mixing total
ZD	0.657	0.343	0.500	0.500
BG	0.593	0.407	0.286	0.214
ZM	0.539	0.461	0.286	0.281
BM	0.504	0.496	0.250	0.179
WMR	0.426	0.574	0.350	0.200
DI	0.394	0.606	0.194	0.357
LC	0.356	0.644	0.167	0.083
GT	0.354	0.646	0.179	0.028
GB	0.269	0.731	0.250	0.188
HKI	0.250	0.750	0.167	0.250

was not married and had relatively few contacts). In contrast, participants ZD, BG, ZM and BM had an average of more German use than English use according to their self-reports.

In addition to total amount of English and German spoken on a daily basis, Table 9.5 also displays the total amount of language use in which code-mixing was expected to occur. GT displayed a much lower mixing score for English (indeed the lowest of all participants) than in German, suggesting that when he spoke English, which he did predominantly, he was entirely immersed in the English language.

Discussion of language use and mixing analysis

It was observed that GT had one of the lowest rates of German usage and one of the highest rates of English usage. Similarly, he had one of the lowest German mixing indexicals and the lowest English mixing indexical, demonstrating that he rarely, if ever, mixed the two languages. Moreover, it appeared that GT received very little real-world exposure to his native German language: his exposure to German media was limited to radio and newspapers, involving little personal interaction. Having spoken English to a native English partner for 48 years, English – with no mixing from German, i.e. with English monolinguals – was the dominant language in his life. It may have been that this high rate of monolingual English use triggered the extreme phonetic attrition GT appeared to undergo. Recall that de Leeuw *et al.* (2010) found that the bilinguals who were not predicted to code-mix in their L1 were *more* likely to retain their L1. Here similar processes may be at work: although code-mixing in the L1 may prompt phonetic attrition, *no* code-mixing in the L2 may *likewise* trigger attrition.

Arguably, participants LC, HKI and GB had a similar low amount of German spoken in their network (and were likewise in relationships with non-German native speakers), but they did not display such a high amount of English-like rhotics. However, LC and HKI had only lived in Canada for 22 and 18 years, respectively, whereas GT had lived in Canada for 53 years, so it is possible that in future LC and HKI might also undergo phonetic attrition like GT. Participant GB was relatively similar to GT in that he was also married to an English native speaker and had been living in Canada for 48 years; they also had children together, while LC and HKI did not have children. Where GB and GT differ, however, is that GB spoke German more frequently with his own children, whereas GT never reported to speak German with his children. The higher amount of English spoken to his children is similarly reflected in GB's higher amounts of mixing in German and English: GB estimated that he spoke German overall less frequently than GT, but when GB did speak German, it was also with his children, with whom he mixed the two languages sometimes. Alternatively, GT reported that he *never* spoke German with his two daughters. It may be that the complete discontinuation of German with his children contributed to the extreme phonetic attrition observed in GT, whereas GB continued to actively use his German with his children.

General Discussion and Conclusion

As a case study, the present investigation aimed to highlight one particular late bilingual who evidenced extreme phonetic attrition in that all examined phonetic variables in his speech displayed merging towards the English monolingual norm (de Leeuw *et al.*, 2010, 2012, 2013). His exhibiting of phonetic attrition to a certain extent therefore challenges the maturational constraints model which offers no explanation as to why one such late bilingual *would* undergo phonetic attrition to the degree to which he does. What is especially interesting about GT is the fact that his native German category aligned within the English monolingual norm which was reflected in both the impressionistic analysis (in which 43% of his rhotics were considered to be entirely in line with an English-like pronunciation) and the acoustic analysis, which showed that both his F_2 and F_3 frequencies were within the North American English range. As such, the findings in part verified the SLM (Flege, 1995, 2003a), showing that a late-acquired L2 can indeed affect the production of the L1. Alternatively, the results also shed new light on the SLM in that his German rhotic was not merged *between* German and English monolingual norms, but rather, in this extreme case of phonetic attrition, F_2 and F_3 values for both languages were within the monolingual norm of the English retroflex.

In addition to this theoretical contribution towards our understanding of how speech is represented in the bilingual mind, we also propose that GT underwent 'extreme' phonetic attrition because he was 'extremely' immersed in the English language. GT had lived in Canada the second longest of all participants (53 years) and had been married to an English native speaker for 48 years, with whom he had two daughters and with whom he likewise only ever conversed in English. GT reported to use German less than almost all other participants in his network, speaking German only once a month. Moreover, when he spoke English, which he did almost always, he did so with reportedly next to no code-mixing. In view of this general linguistic profile of GT, he differs from the other late bilinguals who all, in one way or another, used German more than GT. We suggest that this complete immersion within an entirely English language setting is what makes GT unique and triggered his extreme attrition in the domain of phonetics. As such, these findings from GT somewhat enhance the results of de Leeuw *et al.* (2010), in which it was found that those bilinguals who code-switched more were more likely to evidence L1 attrition in the domain of phonetics. Alternatively, in conjunction with the current results, it may be that, where overall amount of language use is constant, those who code-mix more evidence more phonetic attrition; however, when the native language is used next to never, code-mixing might actually maintain the L1.

Further research may focus on how language use and phonetic attrition interact through examining larger groups of late consecutive bilinguals, such that language use can be broken down into smaller variables.

Notes

(1)   The foreign accent rating that was implemented in this L1 attrition research was originally developed for L2 acquisition by Alene Moyer (1999).

(2)   See John Wells' blog for an introduction to the term 'rhotic': http://phonetic-blog. blogspot.de/2010/07/rhotic.html (accessed 5 June 2018).

(3)   VOT is probably the most frequently measured acoustic component of any consonant, and for that matter of any sound. VOT is a durational measurement which 'captures the timing relationship between the release of a stop closure and the phonation onset for a following vowel' (Foulkes *et al.*, 2010: 62). Generally, voiced plosives such as /b/ have shorter VOTs than voiceless plosives such as /p/, e.g. the onset of phonation in the vowel following /b/ in *bat* is more closely aligned to the release of /b/ than the onset of phonation in the vowel following /p/ in *pat*. Moreover, VOT can be language specific, e.g. voiceless plosives are often aspirated in English, so they have rather longer VOTs than those of French, which are generally unaspirated.

(4)   It should be noted that the American English retroflex approximant here also includes Canadian English. This is based on studies which show that the consonantal system of American and Canadian English is very similar (Wells, 1982).

(5)   Translated from: '*Im alemannischen und bayrisch-österreichischen Sprachraum, aber auch in Schleswig-Holstein, gilt weithin ein apikaler Vibrant [r] bzw. die*

Reduktion zum Anschlag; auch uvularer Vibrant [R] kommt vor. Sonst sind uvularer Frikativ und friktionsloser Laut vorherrschend, die immer mehr an Vertreitung zunahmen […].'

(6) A formant is a 'resonance of the vocal tract' (Hewlett & Beck, 2006: 329). Formant frequencies can be measured to acoustically characterize vowels and therefore describe the quality of vowels and approximants, and the Canadian rhotic is generally considered to be an approximant.

Appendix A: List of German Words Used in the Experiment

German word	English translation
Reis	rice
Rülps	burp
Rippe	rib
Reh	deer
Rang	rank
Rhein	rhine
riech	smell
Rum	rum
Rost	grate
Riff	reef
rein	clean
rief	called
Reim	rhyme
ran	ran
roch	smelled
Rest	rest
Ruf	call
Rock	skirt
Ross	horse (archaic)
Reiz	charm
Ring	ring
Riet	reed
reit	ride
Riss	rip
reich	rich
reif	mature

Appendix B: English Rhotics at Onset Words Elicited from the Experiment Participants

rights	rust	rang
reap	ripe	read
roast	writes	rice
ride	rock	rum
ring	red	real
rust	ray	ran
reach	rest	roof
rug	rail	reed
rhyme	rich	ribs
reef	rag	

Part 3

Transitions in Acquisition

10 Using Psycholinguistic Techniques in a Second Language Teaching Setting

Theodoros Marinis and Ian Cunnings

Introduction

The curriculum in linguistics, applied linguistics and foreign language teaching programmes includes a large range of subjects, but often it does not include grounding in psycholinguistic techniques that can be used to assess language development in a classroom setting. As a result, when language teachers want to evaluate students' learning, they have to rely on **language assessments/tests** that are part of textbooks or other material developed on the basis of the language syllabus. Many of these tests are in written form and measure the students' explicit knowledge of vocabulary or grammar. The format is often similar to that provided during instruction, and tests the students' explicit knowledge of the material taught rather than the degree to which they have internalized (or have started to internalize) the vocabulary or grammar. Students' performance in these tests is often mixed. For example, some students score highly in written tests but have difficulties in comprehending or using language in real situations. Others are able to use language in real situations but are not particularly successful in these assessments. This can be a puzzle for both teachers and students. What this demonstrates, however, is that these forms of assessment are measuring students' explicit knowledge in the context in which they have learnt it, but not necessarily their ability to use this knowledge for comprehension and/or spontaneous expression. This sort of assessment also demonstrates large individual differences between learners in **learning strategies** but also in the outcomes of these strategies. Some learners focus on learning rules explicitly but do not internalize them; others internalize the rules but they do not have explicit knowledge of them and have difficulties in applying them in the context of a test.

Another important issue is that of **modality**. The aim in learning a language is to develop both comprehension and production skills. However, the two modalities do not develop at the same rate, with comprehension often preceding production at early stages of development. Therefore, it is important to be able to assess comprehension separately from production. This requires careful design of the test material in order to be able to separate the two modalities and measure students' strengths and weaknesses in comprehension separately from their strengths and weaknesses in production.

The field of psycholinguistics has made impressive advances within the last 20 years in terms of developing methods to assess different modalities (comprehension, production) and levels of language representation (phonology, morphology, syntax, semantics, pragmatics) separately from each other, as well as separating **implicit** from **explicit knowledge** of language in assessment. Second language (L2) teachers and research students can use this knowledge and these methods to develop their own assessments and evaluate their students' learning in a classroom setting throughout the year. This can enable them to tailor teaching and learning on the basis of student progress and provide additional activities or to move faster in the syllabus when they see that students have internalized specific rules and properties of the language.

This chapter presents a selection of psycholinguistic techniques together with ideas about how these techniques can be used to assess language abilities in a classroom setting. The chapter focuses on four different psycholinguistic techniques by describing the rationale for each technique, the possible phenomena they can be used for, and the groups they are suitable for, the procedure for each technique, how to analyze the data, and their strengths and limitations. We focus on psycholinguistic techniques that can be implemented using readily available software and hardware (e.g. a standard computer setup), rather than more complex techniques that require specialist equipment and neurological training such as eye-tracking, ERP (event-related potentials measuring brain activity) and fMRI (functional magnetic resonance imaging). The first part of this chapter will focus on production and the second part on comprehension.

Psycholinguistic Techniques Measuring Language Production

A large range of production tasks has been developed within the psycholinguistic tradition which are at the disposal of language teachers and research students, such as elicited imitation, elicited production, narrative tasks and **syntactic priming** tasks, to mention just a few. These tasks have advantages and disadvantages as each one assesses language production in a slightly different way, has specific task demands and may be best suited for specific learner groups depending on the area to be assessed and the age and proficiency level of the learners. Due to space limitations, this chapter will introduce and discuss just two of these tasks, *elicited imitation* and *syntactic priming*. See other chapters in this volume, such as Kahoul *et al.* (Chapter 6), Rogers *et al.* (Chapter 7) and Mora and Safronova (Chapter 8), for illustrations of other tasks which are also used in collecting data for studies of second language acquisition (SLA).

Elicited imitation

Elicited Imitation (EI) or Sentence Repetition has a long tradition in first and second language acquisition research and has often been used by researchers to measure language proficiency in a foreign language teaching setting, although rarely as a formal assessment (for SLA see, for example, Bley-Vroman & Chaudron, 1994; Jessop *et al.*, 2007; Lust *et al.*, 1996). At the heart of EI tasks is the innate human capacity (and spontaneous tendency) to imitate behaviour in our environment, including language, for example sounds, words and sentences. The rationale behind using EI tasks to measure language proficiency is that, although imitating someone else's behaviour is a spontaneous capacity, it is very hard to imitate sentences accurately if the structures in the sentence are not part of one's grammatical system. This is because in order to imitate a sentence participants have to be able to analyze it at all levels of representation (phonological, morphosyntactic, semantic), extract its meaning, store it temporarily in **short-term memory** and then use the production system to repeat it. Accurate verbatim imitation of a sentence depends on all processes and levels of representation related to comprehension and production and the ability to store and retrieve language material from memory using the **episodic buffer**, a temporary storage system with limited capacity that holds integrated chunks (Baddeley, 2000). Hence, verbatim sentence imitation is not possible if someone has not yet acquired the specific structures that are part of the sentence. Exceptions are when the sentences are very short and, as a result, participants can echo the sentence passively without having to use their grammatical system to analyze and reproduce it. Therefore, sentences in EI tasks have to be of a considerable length in order to force the language learner to use their grammatical system to imitate the sentence. Length is relative to a range of factors, such as age, memory capacity and language proficiency. Therefore, it is important to try out sentences of variable length before deciding what length is suitable for specific learners. Very short sentences can lead to passive echoing which cannot inform us about the learner's proficiency, whereas very long sentences can lead to breakdown – the learner may not be able to repeat the sentence at all.

Phenomena

EI tasks can be used to assess a variety of linguistic phenomena with the caveat that sentence length has to be fine-tuned to avoid automatic echoing and still be imitated. For example, previous research has used EI tasks to investigate learners' acquisition of sentence structure, phrase structure, word order and anaphora across a range of languages (for a review, see Lust *et al.*, 1996). Recent work from a multinational network of researchers (COST Action IS0804, *Language Impairment in a Multilingual Society*) has used EI to investigate the morphosyntactic abilities of sequential bilingual children across a range of languages by creating parallel versions of EI tasks in several languages. The EI tasks of the network included a range of different structures grouped around two themes – structures that are syntactically complex across languages, such as relative clauses (*The swan that the deer chased knocked over the plant*), object which-questions (*Which picture did he paint at home yesterday?*) and those involving embedding and/or syntactic movement. A second theme included structures that are challenging in specific languages only, mostly related to the morphological makeup of the language, for example tense and aspect marking in English (*The policeman has been looking at us*) and passives (*She was seen by the doctor in the morning*).

Participant groups

EI tasks can be used with both adults and children, and by both L1 and L2 learners. However, care should be taken that the vocabulary, grammar and sentence length is not only appropriate for the participants' proficiency level but also for their age. If participants do not know specific words the grammatical structure is beyond their proficiency level, or if the sentences are extremely long it will be very difficult for them to imitate the sentence. As a result, the task will not be able to measure the participants' grammatical abilities, but their ability to keep in memory and retrieve novel words, hence their phonological memory. Moreover, hearing loss may affect general listening comprehension in auditory paradigms like the one in EI tasks, so that participants with age- or non-age-related hearing loss may perform worse than those with better hearing, even though there may be no difference between the two groups in their L2 knowledge.

Procedure

The procedure in EI tasks is very straightforward: the sentences are read and learners have to try to repeat each sentence verbatim. To be able to analyze each grammatical structure separately, it is advisable to include four to six different sentences for each sentence type. For experimental purposes, it is useful to pre-record the sentences, so all learners can listen to the sentences in exactly the same way in terms of the speaker's voice, intonation, speed of presentation and loudness. This can be done by playing the pre-recorded sentences from a CD/DVD/MP3 player/tablet or by incorporating the pre-recorded sentence into a PowerPoint presentation. The latter also enables the inclusion of visual support so that participants are aware of the length of the task, as shown in Figure 10.1.

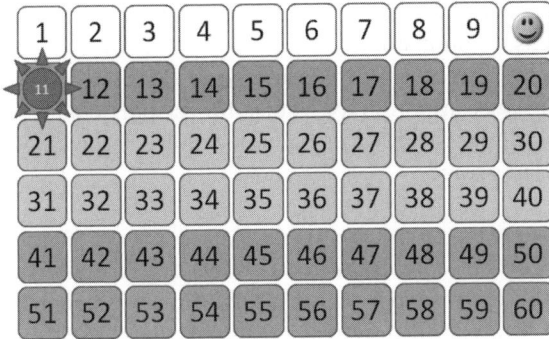

Figure 10.1 PowerPoint for EI in adults

Tasks with children can also have a story supported with pictures, as shown in Figure 10.2, to help ensure engagement with the task. Figure 10.2 comes from a set of EI tasks developed for bilingual children as part of the EU-funded COST Action *Language Impairment in a Multilingual Society* (Marinis & Armon-Lotem, 2015). To make the EI task motivating for children, it was embedded within a treasure hunt game in which a teddy bear was looking for a treasure in several locations.

Figure 10.2 shows the slide in which the teddy bear is moving towards a cave. Each stone corresponded to a sentence. When teddy jumped onto a stone, the children heard a sentence which they had to repeat in order for the teddy bear to jump onto the next stone. This motivated children to repeat all the sentences in order to see where the treasure was and what it

Figure 10.2 PowerPoint for EI in children

was. The sentences they had to repeat were not related in terms of meaning to the treasure hunt story.

Headphones can be used to ensure good-quality listening to the sentences and enhance attention to the task for the participant. The repeated sentences should be recorded using high-quality recording equipment to analyze at a later stage.

Data analysis

EI tasks can be scored in different ways depending on whether they are being used for research or for classroom assessment purposes, the focus of the study, and practical reasons such as the amount of time available. Widely used schemes include giving a score of 1 if the sentence is repeated verbatim and 0 if there are any changes in the sentence. Scaled scoring schemes include scores from 0 to 3, where a score of 3 is given if the sentence is repeated entirely verbatim, a score of 2 if there is one change, a score of 1 if there are two to three changes and a score of 0 if there are four or more changes in the repeated sentence. Structural scoring schemes assign 1 if the learner uses the structure targeted irrespective of whether or not there are changes, e.g. in vocabulary, in other parts of the sentence. Unless pronunciation is the focus of EI assessment, non-target pronunciation is also ignored. A score of 0 is given if the learner makes an error in the sentence structure that was targeted, e.g. omission of an auxiliary in sentences targeting auxiliaries. A score of 0 is also given if the learner does not produce the structure targeted and substitutes it with another structure, e.g. substituting an object relative clause (*The swan that the deer chased knocked over the plant*) with a subject relative clause (*The swan that chased the deer knocked over the plant*).

Strengths and limitations

EI tasks have several advantages compared to other types of tasks, but also limitations. They are quick and easy to administer and they are not very demanding in terms of the procedure. They have clear target sentences, they can include a large range of sentence types and they can be scored in several ways depending on the focus of the analysis. The most important limitation regards the challenge of optimizing the length of the stimulus sentence, that is, the relationship between the developmental stage of the participants and the sentence length. If sentences are too short for the learners' language abilities, they may be able to repeat them passively and the results will not reflect the participants' proficiency. The opposite effect may also occur. If the sentences are too long, they may exceed the participants' memory capacity. Participants may fail to repeat sentences not because they have not acquired a particular structure, such as auxiliaries in the English task, but because of the length of the sentence. This can be partially addressed through structural scoring, which identifies if participants were able to consistently (across similar test items) use the specific structure irrespective of whether or not they repeated the sentence verbatim.

Syntactic priming

Syntactic Priming (SP) tasks, similarly to the EI tasks, make use of the human tendency to imitate behaviour in our environment. However, unlike EI tasks which are designed to produce a verbatim repetition of a sentence uttered by the experimenter, SP tasks measure the participant's unconscious imitation of a specific syntactic structure used by the experimenter while describing a picture. For example, the experimenter describes a picture of a giraffe pushing an elephant, using a sentence in the passive (*the elephant was pushed by the giraffe*). Then the learner has to describe a picture of a similar event, for example a tiger kicking a lion. What is being measured is whether the learner will use the same structure used by the experimenter and produce a sentence in the passive (*the lion was kicked by the tiger*) or an alternative one (*the tiger was kicking the lion*). The sentence produced by the experimenter is called the *prime* whereas the sentence produced by the participant is called the *target*. The rationale behind using SP tasks is similar to the rationale in EI tasks: if a specific structure is part of the learner's grammatical system, the learner will use it to describe a picture. If, on the other hand, a structure is not part of the learner's grammatical system, the learner will not use it to describe a picture even though this structure was used previously by the experimenter. Instead, the learner will use an alternative structure that is part of their grammatical system. This alternative structure is typically less complex than the target structure.

Similar to EI tasks, SP tasks require from the participant the ability to analyze sentences at all levels of representation (phonological, morpho-syntactic, semantic), extract the meaning and use the production system to describe a new picture. Unlike EI tasks, SP tasks do not require storage and retrieval of specific words. Instead, the *prime* is assumed to activate an abstract syntactic representation in the learner's grammatical system and, as a result, the learner is more likely to use the same syntactic representation than an alternative one. If the learner mirrors the experimenter and uses the same syntactic structure to describe a new picture, this provides evidence that the specific structure is part of the learner's repertoire. Sentences do not have to be long in SP tasks because learners do not have to repeat a sentence but to describe a picture that was not already described by the experimenter.

Phenomena

SP tasks can be used with any phenomena that can be expressed using two different sentence structures. Two phenomena that have been studied extensively using SP tasks are transitive constructions that can be expressed using an active (*the tiger was kicking the lion*) or a passive sentence (*the lion was kicked by the tiger*) (e.g. Savage *et al.*, 2003) and double-object constructions that can be expressed either using dative in double-object constructions (*the girl gave the boy the book*) or prepositional-object constructions (*the girl gave the book to the boy*) (e.g. Thothathiri & Snedeker, 2008). For SLA research it is important to take into account how the L1 may influence SP in the L2.

Participant groups

SP tasks can be used both with children (e.g. Bencini & Valian, 2008; Shimpi *et al.*, 2007) and with adults (e.g. Bock, 1986; Branigan, 2007; Branigan *et al.*, 2000; Pickering & Ferreira, 2008), including L2 learners. As with the EI task, the sentences should have appropriate vocabulary for the target group. SP tasks have been successfully used with children as young as three years of age (e.g. Savage *et al.*, 2003) and L2 learners with a range of proficiency levels (e.g. Hartsuiker *et al.*, 2004; McDonough, 2006; McDonough & Mackey, 2008).

Procedure

SP tasks typically involve the experimenter and then the participant describing series of pictures. The experimenter describes a picture first and then the participant describes the next picture. What is being measured is whether or not the participant will be *primed* by the experimenter, that is, whether or not the participant will use the same structure used by the experimenter to describe the picture or an alternative structure (e.g. passive versus active). Therefore, it is crucial that both sentence structures are equally appropriate to describe the event in the picture. Apart from picture description, SP tasks can also involve written or oral sentence completion and dialogue with a confederate (e.g. Branigan *et al.*, 2000). To observe priming effects, it is advisable to use at least 10 different sentences for each of the alternative structures.

Priming between the two alternative structures can be tested in a randomized order or in separate blocks, for example 10 trials priming passives followed by 10 trials priming actives with a break in between the two blocks or the two blocks presented on different days or in two different groups of participants. Depending on the aim of the study, there may be overlap in the words of the prime and the target or the prime and target may have different words. Overlap in the words between the prime and target (e.g. prime: *The elephant was kicked by the giraffe*; target: *the lion was kicked by the tiger*) usually leads to a stronger priming effect because in such cases there is priming not only from the structure (e.g. passive) but also from the specific lexical items used; in this case the same verb (*kicked*) is used in the prime and the target. Therefore, the clearest evidence for priming of the abstract structure is provided when there is no lexical overlap, but only structural overlap between the prime and the target (e.g. prime: *The elephant was kicked by the giraffe*; target: *the lion was pushed by the tiger*).

Unlike EI tasks, sentences in SP tasks are usually not pre-recorded; instead the experimenter and participant describe pictures in turn. As in all production tasks, high-quality recording equipment should be used to record the participants' production in order to be able to conduct analyses after the task has been completed.

Data analysis

In SP tasks the data are not analyzed in terms of accuracy or grammaticality, but in terms of whether the percentage of use of a specific structure, e.g. passives, is higher when it is preceded by primes with the same structure (passives) than when it is preceded by primes with a different structure (actives).

Strengths and limitations

The most important strength of the SP tasks is that, similarly to the EI tasks, they allow us to investigate structures that may not be frequent in naturalistic speech yet are part of a native speaker's linguistic competence. In addition, in the SP task we have specific target sentences that we try to elicit. A second important strength is that SP tasks provide evidence for the availability of a syntactic structure by tapping into the speakers' unconscious knowledge. Practical advantages of SP tasks are that they are easy to administer and score. The prime sentences are also relatively easy to construct, much easier than in EI tasks because the sentence length in SP tasks is not a crucial variable to control for. SP tasks usually involve a small number of sentence types, e.g. passives and actives, rather than a large number of structures, which is often the case with EI tasks.

A challenging issue in SP tasks is the preparation of pictures that go with the sentences. This may require a professional illustrator to ensure that the pairs of pictures of the prime and target sentences are matched on visual features, such as size, picture type and similarity of the event. An important disadvantage of SP tasks is that priming of one structure may be so effective that participants perseverate and use the same structure in consecutive sentences. This can occur when the SP task consists of randomized lists of sentences or blocks. This can be avoided if a large number of filler sentences unrelated to the focus of the investigation/assessment are included in between the experimental sentences that include a range of other structures. These filler sentences can block the effects of perseveration. A further limitation is that it cannot include a large number of structure types within the same task without resulting in a very long test, and crucially it can only address phenomena whose meanings are expressed through two types of structures.

Psycholinguistic Techniques Measuring Second Language Comprehension

As with production tasks, many different types of comprehension tasks have been designed within the psycholinguistics tradition that can also be used by language teachers and research students. Examples of comprehension tasks are picture selection tasks, picture verification tasks, self-paced reading and self-paced listening tasks, eye-tracking while reading and eye-tracking while listening tasks, to mention just a few. Each has specific task demands and measures language comprehension in a slightly different way. Each task also has its advantages and disadvantages and may therefore be best suited for specific groups of learners. This chapter will introduce and discuss two of these tasks, *picture selection* and *self-paced reading*.

Picture selection task

Picture selection (PS) tasks test whether learners are able to comprehend words or sentences accurately. Learners typically listen to or read a word or a sentence and look at a set of pictures, as shown in Figure 10.3.

Figure 10.3 comes from a PS task investigating the comprehension of reflexive pronouns (*himself/herself*) in children with autism (Terzi *et al.*,

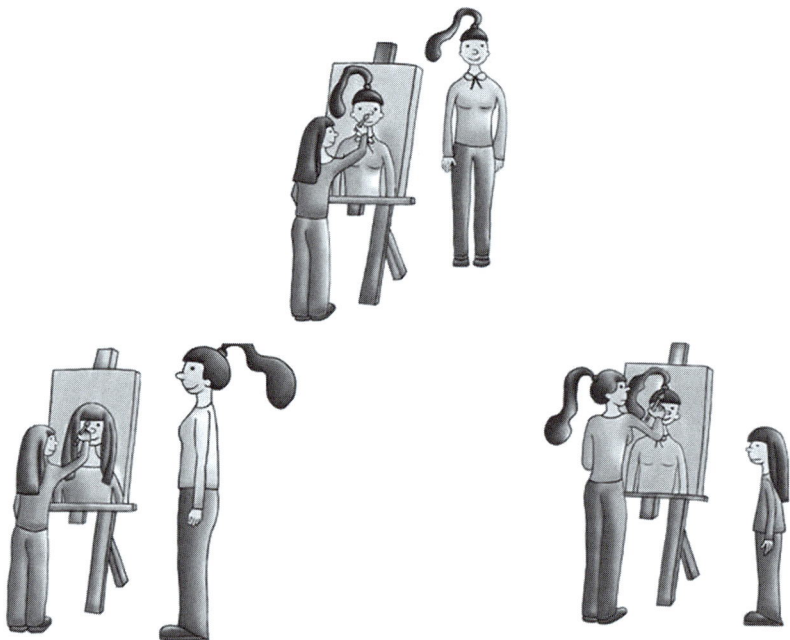

Figure 10.3 Sample picture selection task, comprehension of reflexive pronouns

2014). The target sentence here was *Maria is painting herself* and the pictures show the same two participants in all pictures, Maria (the girl) and her godmother (the adult), taking part in an action of painting. Learners were expected to select the picture on the left-hand side, in which Maria is painting herself while her godmother is standing next to her. Apart from the target picture, PS tasks include at least one more picture that acts as a distractor/foil. Distractors are crucial in PS tasks because they provide an alternative interpretation for the word or sentence. For example, Figure 10.3 has two distractors testing two different interpretations. The picture in the middle tests whether the participants will interpret the reflexive pronoun *herself* as the personal pronoun *her* (*Mary is painting her*). The picture on the right tests whether they will apply the reflexive interpretation to the other person in the picture (*The godmother is painting herself*). This picture is included to ensure participants understand who the intended agent of the 'painting' action is. In this example the key competitor was the picture with the pronoun interpretation because previous research has shown that some children with autism interpret reflexive pronouns, such as herself, as personal pronouns, such as her (Perovic *et al.*, 2013). If participants have not acquired the properties of reflexives and interpret them as personal pronouns, they should select the picture in the middle.

The rationale of PS tasks is that the participants' grammatical system will guide their picture selection. To perform accurately in PS tasks, participants have to be able to analyze the words or sentences at all levels (phonological, morphosyntactic, semantic) and extract the meaning of the word/sentence using their grammatical system. Moreover, they have to scan the pictures, map the meaning of the word/sentence onto the pictures and select the picture that best represents the meaning they have created.

The difficulty of a particular PS task depends on the type and number of distractors. The closer the competitor to the target, the more difficult the task becomes because participants have to compare pictures corresponding to slightly different meanings. For example, in tasks investigating the comprehension of relative clauses (e.g. *The elephant that the giraffe is chasing is pushing the rhino*), it is possible to have several pictures as competitors that have meanings close to the target: Target = giraffe chasing elephant, elephant pushing rhino; Distractor 1: elephant chasing giraffe, giraffe pushing rhino; Distractor 2: elephant chasing giraffe, elephant pushing rhino; Distractor 3: giraffe chasing elephant, elephant pushing rhino. The difficulty also increases with the number of pictures in an array because the more pictures participants have to scan before making a decision, the more interpretations they have to make and the more time it takes to select a picture.

Similar to EI tasks, PS tasks require storage of specific words/sentences and their meaning until participants select a picture. Thus,

PS tasks have memory requirements. The more pictures included, the more the memory demands because it will take longer for participants to scan the pictures and select the right one. Apart from memory, PS tasks place demands on attention, especially when there is a large degree of similarity between the pictures. Participants have to scan the pictures carefully to identify the differences between them, which requires high levels of attention.

Phenomena

PS tasks can be used with any phenomena that can be depicted using words in isolation or sentences. The British Picture Vocabulary Scales III (Dunn *et al.*, 2009), and its American counterpart, the Peabody Picture Vocabulary Test IV (Dunn & Dunn, 2007), is a good example of a PS task at the word level because it includes a range of words belonging to different syntactic categories including nouns and verbs. Similarly, the Test for Reception of Grammar 2 (Bishop, 2003) is a good example of a PS task at the sentence level because it includes sentences of different types.

Participant groups

PS tasks can be used in language acquisition research with both children and adults (e.g. Friedmann & Novogrodsky, 2004; van der Lely, 1996), including L2 learners (e.g. Papadopoulou *et al.*, 2011; Verhagen, 2013). PS tasks have been used with children as young as three years of age (e.g. Johnson *et al.*, 2005).

Procedure

PS tasks involve listening to or reading a word or sentence and selecting the picture that fits best with the word or picture from a set of at least two pictures. It is advisable to include at least six different sentences for each structure in order to have a representative sample of data. If the PS task targets only one structure, for example passives, it is advisable to include a number of filler items targeting other structures to avoid participants guessing the purpose of the task. The ratio between experimental items and fillers should be at least 1:1 for adult participants who are likely to be looking for a pattern in the sentences and for clues to the purpose of the study. For PS tasks with children, the number of filler items may be smaller because they are less likely to be thinking about the purpose of the study. Moreover, the length of tasks should be kept as short as possible with children to avoid fatigue.

It is good practice to pre-record the words/sentences in PS tasks when they are presented orally so all participants listen to the words/sentences in exactly the same way. If the words/sentences are to be presented visually on a computer, they can be presented at the bottom of the screen under the pictures. If the researcher/assessor wants to allow participants time to think about the words/sentences without making high memory demands on the participant, the words/sentences can stay onscreen until a picture is selected. Alternatively, the words/sentences can be presented for a limited, set amount of time. Software such as PowerPoint or E-Prime (Psychology Software Tools) can be used for the presentation of the words/sentences and pictures.

Participants' responses can be recorded by the experimenter or by the participant using paper and pencil. This is the simplest procedure for recording participants' responses. Responses can also be recorded using a keyboard, mouse or button box and computer software. If there is interest in recording the participants' reaction time in selecting the picture, then experimental software, such as E-Prime (Psychology Software Tools), should be used to ensure accurate data logging. Reaction time data can be more sensitive than accuracy data because they show us how quickly people make a response. Robust knowledge of a structure enables the participant to react fast in selecting the right picture, whereas uncertainty about a structure can lead to slower reaction times.

Data analysis

In PS tasks the data are analyzed in terms of accuracy. If reaction times are recorded, the data can also be analyzed in terms of reaction times.

Strengths and limitations

PS tasks have several strengths. They can be used to test structures that learners are not otherwise using in their oral or written production, and thus it is difficult to know if they have been acquired. They can include a range of different words and structures within the same task. At the practical level, PS tasks are relatively easy to set up and quick to administer because the only thing learners have to do is point to pictures or press a button to select a picture. Creating pictures may be challenging and costly if the pictures are created by a professional illustrator. An alternative is to create pictures using photographs. In this case, care should be taken that the photographs are of high quality with a neutral background and the actions and objects are clearly recognisable. An important limitation of the task is that it is not usually timed and learners can thus take their time to choose the correct picture and may develop strategies to complete the task. For example, a participant may select a picture by thinking and rejecting which pictures cannot go with the word/sentence instead of selecting a picture based on their knowledge of the word/picture tested. In other words, they can use their general knowledge of language and metalinguistic awareness to select a picture. Alternatively, it is possible to introduce a time limit, so participants have to make a fast response based on their intuition and implicit knowledge, in order to try and minimize strategic behaviour.

Self-paced reading task

Self-paced reading (SPR) is a task used to measure the time taken to read a text or part thereof. The rationale behind SPR is that difficult portions of text will take longer to read, and the researcher or assessor can draw inferences regarding the cognitive processes underlying language comprehension at any given point in a sentence by recording how long a participant takes to read each portion of text. While tasks such as PS provide an explicit measure of language comprehension, SPR provides an implicit measure of the processes involved in successful comprehension (Marinis, 2010).

In a typical SPR task, participants read a series of texts one segment at a time, pushing a key or button to move through the text segment by segment. The reaction time taken to press the key or button at each segment can then be used to gauge the relative ease or difficulty of processing at different points in time in the stimulus sentence. In the SPR task, participants are first presented with a piece of text covered by a mask, usually a series of Xs, as in Figure 10.4a. The participant then presses a key or button to read the first segment. A segment can be either an individual word, phrase, sentence or paragraph depending on the needs of the researcher or assessor. Figure 10.4 exemplifies word-by-word SPR. When the participant first presses the response key, the first word of the sentence appears, as in Figure 10.4b. Each subsequent key-press reveals the sentence, one word at a time, covering up the previously read word. The reaction time taken to press the response key at each word provides an implicit measure of the cognitive processes underlying language comprehension. Inferences about language processing can be made by comparing reading times at critical portions of text in maximally similar sentences. For example, reaction times at or shortly after the pronoun 'she' in Figure 10.4 will likely be longer in this sentence as compared to a sentence

```
(a)  XXXX XXXXXXXXX XXXX XXX XXX XXXXX.

(b)  John XXXXXXXXX XXXX XXX XXX XXXXX.

(c)  XXXX mentioned XXXX XXX XXX XXXXX.

(d)  XXXX XXXXXXXXX that XXX XXX XXXXX.

(e)  XXXX XXXXXXXXX XXXX she XXX XXXXX.

(f)  XXXX XXXXXXXXX XXXX XXX was XXXXX.

(g)  XXXX XXXXXXXXX XXXX XXX XXX tired.
```

Figure 10.4 Example of word-by-word self-paced reading task studying pronoun-reference resolution

containing a gender-matching antecedent (e.g. *Jane mentioned that she was tired*).

To ensure that participants pay attention to what they read, a comprehension question is typically asked after each trial. This question can require a yes/no or true/false answer, or more complex responses depending on the needs of the researcher/assessor.

Phenomena

Given adequate reading ability, SPR can be used to investigate a wide variety of linguistic phenomena. It has been used to investigate how adult native speakers and L2 learners process and interpret different types of ambiguous sentences (e.g. Felser *et al.*, 2003b; Roberts & Felser, 2011). It has also been used to investigate the acquisition of different morphosyntactic features, such as gender/number agreement (e.g. Sagarra & Herschensohn, 2010). In such cases, the researcher can compare reaction times during the reading of sentences containing grammatical and ungrammatical agreement (e.g. *The boy unsurprisingly was late to school* versus *The boys unsurprisingly was late to school*) as an implicit measure of the acquisition of a particular phenomenon, without the need to require participants to make an explicit sentence judgement. SPR has also been widely used to investigate different linguistic dependencies, such as anaphora resolution and syntactic movement (e.g. Marinis *et al.*, 2005).

Participant groups

SPR can be used to investigate language comprehension in adult native speakers and different groups of adult L2 learners (Marinis, 2003, 2010, 2013). It has also been used with children as young as eight years old (Traxler, 2002).

Procedure

The recording of reaction time data requires specialist software to ensure that reaction times are recorded accurately. SPR tasks are thus usually conducted using experimental software, such as E-Prime (Psychology Software Tools). A free alternative to E-Prime which was developed primarily to run SPR tasks and which is widely used in psycholinguistics is Linger (Rohde, 2005).

SPR tasks involve participants reading sentences or larger pieces of text one segment at a time, pressing a response key to move from one segment to the next. Before beginning a study, the researcher will need to decide how large each segment to be displayed should be, based on their research questions and the populations being studied. Although larger segments may be easier to process, increasingly large segments provide less fine-grained information regarding the time course of language processing compared to smaller segments such as word-by-word presentation.

To ensure that participants do not become explicitly aware of the manipulations being studied, it is important to include a sufficient number of fillers in addition to the experimental items of main interest. In a typical SPR task, the researcher will want to include at least six to eight sentences in each experimental condition. Fillers should include a wide variety of syntactic structures to ensure that participants do not become habituated to the experimental sentences, i.e. that they pay attention to the sentences yet do not figure out which structures are being tested. Usually fillers should be included at a ratio of at least 2:1 for adults, although fewer fillers can be used if the researcher fears the study will become too long.

The post-item comprehension question can differ depending on the needs of the researcher. Often these questions are only included to ensure that participants pay attention to the sentences and the answers may not be of primary interest other than to ensure a certain threshold level of performance (e.g. 75% correct). However, depending on the research question, the researcher may want to also include questions that probe a specific aspect of comprehension. In Figure 10.4, for example, a question could probe interpretation of the pronoun (e.g. *Was John tired?*). Researchers should, however, be wary that the comprehension questions do not afford too much explicit attention to the experimental manipulations.

Data analysis

SPR tasks provide two sources of data. One source of data is the accuracy to the comprehension questions. This provides an 'offline', explicit measure of language comprehension. The second source of data, the reaction times at each segment, provides an 'online' measure of implicit language comprehension. Reaction times are difficult to analyze in absolute terms, and as such relative differences in reaction times need to be compared across experimental conditions. Typically, reaction times will be averaged at each segment, and compared across two or more conditions (e.g. grammatical versus ungrammatical) to see if the conditions differ. This illustrates the need for specialist software when analyzing data from SPR tasks. Extremely short or extremely long reaction times (e.g. 3.5 standard deviations above/below a participant's mean reaction time for a given segment) are sometimes discarded, on the assumption that such 'noisy' data index either a button mis-press or conscious awareness of the experimental manipulation. Reaction times to items in which incorrect responses to the comprehension question are given are also sometimes discarded.

Strengths and limitations

As the task involves reading, it is limited to participant groups who have attained sufficient levels of reading comprehension. It may thus not be appropriate for particularly young children or for those with reading impairments. An alternative to SPR is self-paced listening, where participants press a button to *listen to*, rather than read, a sentence one segment at a time, which might be more appropriate in such cases. Self-paced listening has been used successfully with monolingual and bilingual children as young as six years, including those with language impairment (e.g. Felser *et al.*, 2003a; Marinis & Saddy, 2013). Although the overt button-press in SPR does not exactly mimic normal reading, SPR studies obtain results comparable to methods using more naturalistic reading, such as eye-tracking (Ferreira & Henderson, 1990).

As numerous factors influence reading times (Rayner, 1998), SPR should only be used to investigate sentences that are as maximally similar as possible, and critical regions of comparison (e.g. the pronoun 'she' in Figure 10.4) should ideally be identical across conditions. The researcher also needs to be aware of 'spillover' effects, where effects of experimental manipulations appear in the segments after a critical region of interest (e.g. *was* and *tired* in Figure 10.4). As such, the text immediately after the critical region should ideally be identical across conditions as well.

The length and complexity of the sentences should also be considered, based on factors such as participant age and reading ability. As typical SPR studies use non-cumulative presentation, in which earlier segments of a sentence are masked as the participant reads, it does not allow reread-ing of earlier portions of text, unlike normal reading, which may cause increasing problems if sentences become too long.

Conclusion

Psycholinguistic techniques offer a variety of ways of investigating SLA and have been used in the assessment of language ability in a range of different populations of speakers. The tasks outlined in this chapter provide L2 teachers with alternative ways of investigating and testing dif-ferent linguistic phenomena in both L2 production and comprehension which can complement existing assessment resources. Psycholinguistic techniques are particularly useful in providing implicit measures of lan-guage ability to gauge how well a student or group of students has truly internalized knowledge of the vocabulary and grammar of the language being learnt.

The psycholinguistic tasks outlined in this chapter provide those who are still studying to become teachers with tools that they can use in their research projects when investigating SLA in different learner populations. These can be complemented with existing testing and assessment batter-ies, to examine the extent to which explicit measures of vocabulary and grammatical knowledge correlate with implicit psycholinguistic measures of language production and comprehension.

We have not discussed in detail here best practice in conducting statis-tical analyses of the different types of data obtained in typical psycholin-guistic studies, or how such analyses can be correlated with standardized measures of language assessment. For those interested in going beyond descriptive statistics and using inferential statistics to generalize study findings from a sample of learners to the wider population, we direct the interested reader to Larson-Hall (2015) and Plonsky (2015) for recent introductions to inferential statistical analysis, which both focus on research in SLA. Cunnings (2012) and Linck and Cunnings (2015) also provide an overview of recent advances in the analysis of psycholinguistic data, focusing in particular on its application to research in SLA.

Language teachers and those studying to become language teachers already have a number of assessment tools at their disposal that they can use to gauge learner abilities to help encourage successful language learning. We hope that the psycholinguistic tasks outlined here can complement these existing batteries and provide new insight into internalized, implicit levels of language ability which can provide inspiration in devising new ways of assessing SLA.

11 Research in Memory and Processing in Second Language Acquisition

Clare Wright

Introduction

We know from decades of research on second language acquisition (SLA) that all second language (L2) learners can ultimately develop an internal, systematic grammar (linguistic competence) supporting communicative language use, which operates as far more than a memorized set of rules about language. But we still cannot fully explain why learners show the individual variability they do in developing that grammar, and how memory plays a part in its development. So, for example, it is still unclear why learners can be more target-like in written forms compared to spoken communication, how learners seem to exhibit similar routes of development despite different first languages (L1s) and different educational histories, and why some grammatical constructions remain far from target-like after years of target language exposure. In other words, we need a more integrated understanding of language learning to account for 'what' the properties of the internal grammar are (i.e. a property theory of SLA), alongside 'how' those properties are developed over time and are used in understanding and producing language (i.e. a transition theory of SLA).

This chapter provides insights into what can be established regarding these individual differences from research over the last several decades into memory and processing, and also how findings from research in these areas enrich theories of SLA, in order to create a better understanding of how to connect the 'what' and the 'how' of language development. We begin with an overview of current models of **long-term** and **working memory**, based on distinctions between **declarative** and **procedural memory**, leading to a second section on theories of language learning and how different types of linguistic knowledge are stored in memory and then accessed for using linguistic knowledge in **online** comprehension and production. These theories include generative theories of acquisition, as well as language-processing models which investigate why adult L2 learning results in either similar or variable success. This section concludes with a 'coalition' view of learning, using co-existing relationships between different memory systems. Such an approach can inform future research into language learning which focuses less on a broad-brush distinction of explicit learning versus implicit acquisition, but more precisely investigates different processing interfaces between grammatical properties and memory capacities, including working memory. The chapter then finishes with a third section, briefly examining two empirical studies into the role of memory in the development of L2 *wh*-questions in English. These studies directly address the questions raised by this chapter of how grammatical knowledge is represented and how it develops over time. They use a combination of different methodologies, and illustrate how different language tasks (**offline** versus **online**, written versus spoken) reveal valuable insights into potential interactions between working and long-term memory.

Memory

We start by looking at how knowledge is stored as representations in the mind, and how it is learned (here, we use 'learning' as the general word for developing linguistic knowledge, whether through instruction or naturalistically). Any kind of knowledge, including linguistic knowledge, is stored in long-term memory (LTM). In all standard psychological presentations of memory (e.g. Baddeley *et al.*, 2009; Smith & Kosslyn, 2007; Squire, 1992), there are two types of memory: long-term memory and short-term or working memory (WM). Within LTM, researchers (see, for example, Gazzaniga *et al.*, 2008) propose two further subdivisions: 'knowledge about things' (declarative) and 'knowledge how to do things' (procedural).

The declarative memory store consists of two types of knowledge: semantic knowledge (or encyclopaedic factual knowledge), and episodic knowledge of specific events in time, also known as 'autobiographical memory' or 'experiential memory' (Penfield & Roberts, 1959). The declarative semantic store is where most of our knowledge of language is stored, including vocabulary, prefabricated or chunked phrases (Wray, 2002), and also explicit metalinguistic rules about language, such as 'the verb "to be" is an irregular verb' and 'the "-ed" ending shows past tense on regular verbs'. Episodic knowledge is made up of representations of actual events in which the individual plays a part. Evidence for the separation of semantic and episodic knowledge can be seen from people suffering memory loss in dementia who can remember factual knowledge, but not where they were an hour ago (Baddeley *et al.*, 2009). Episodic knowledge has not yet been widely studied in language-learning terms, but in general learning practice it has been shown that trying to recall where you were or what you were doing the last time you used a certain word or phrase can help in retrieving that phrase (Baddeley *et al.*, 2009).

Episodic and semantic declarative memory systems are flexible, remaining open for continuous updating and storage (i.e. learning) throughout your life. Items are retrieved serially, rather than in parallel, e.g. when you are trying to remember the name of a capital city, and can produce a list of possibilities but not imagine the list all at once. Items can potentially be stored very quickly (hearing a new name once may be sufficient to store it), and retrieved unconsciously and automatically (like when calling your dog's name in the park).

Information is stored in the declarative system when the input is consciously attended to, which, as with non-declarative memory, triggers some kind of text- or sound-meaning connection. Explicitly presented information, such as the definition of a word, feeds into semantic networks (existing connections based on categories of meaning or sensory connections). These networks help make it easier to store new information and to retrieve information (see Rogers *et al.* in this volume). For example, it is easier to learn new words if they are connected in a story or by a theme, or if you can in some way hook them to existing knowledge. Also you will more quickly recall the word for 'fire engine' if you are already prepared by thinking of linked items, e.g. something red or something that signals danger (see Marinis & Cunnings' chapter in this volume for research techniques that exploit this). Connections can be strengthened through conscious rehearsal or repetition, but using existing knowledge when you are presented with new linguistic information, such as letter sounds, word meanings or grammar rules, allows storage to be quick and efficient, and retrieval can even become automatic or non-attended if they are familiar. So this explains why you can immediately name your favourite fruit, but take longer to recall the name of the exotic vegetable your friend told you about once.

Familiar established items can be efficiently recalled, but processing slows down as more items or more complex combinations of items are required, such as thinking of a synonym for a fire engine, or recalling how to create a complex grammatical construction by applying learned rules (Paradis, 1997, 2004). This then justifies the assumption that another system (the procedural system) must control processing for complex tasks like listening to and speaking language, since serial retrieval of individual items from declarative memory would not be fast or efficient enough.

The procedural system for non-declarative or procedural memory is less easily defined and psychology researchers disagree about its precise nature, so unsurprisingly its role for language learning is not yet fully understood. Most researchers (Anderson, 1983; Paradis, 2004; Smith & Kosslyn, 2007) present this system as comprising the different subtypes of implicit knowledge: procedural, priming and conditioning. So-called procedural memory (for habits and motor skills) arises from repeating an activity, such as tying shoelaces, finding our way around a familiar room in the dark, riding a bicycle, learning to ski or playing a musical instrument. Some types of learning rely more specifically on extensive practice (such as learning the spellings of words in English). These are assumed to start as slow explicitly monitored activities but are converted through inferencing into fast, unconscious, automatic 'productions for directly performing the task' (Anderson *et al.*, 2004: 1046). In such cases, the learner may not later have any conscious knowledge of how to perform the skill, e.g. s/he cannot explain how they know complex spellings to someone else.

Another type of procedural knowledge, perceptual priming, is the process in which perceiving an item then influences the processing of a subsequent item, even when you may not be aware of anything special about the first item or are not prompted by any specific information about the subsequent task. An example of this is when we are shown or hear a list of words and then are asked to name as many random words as possible – when we do so, we are more likely to name items from the previous list (Baddeley *et al.*, 2009: 82), even though there is no practice or explicit training in the words on the list. This is connected to the notion of incidental learning, where you can learn what new words mean or a grammatical rule without being told to – e.g. while reading a story or through communicative language tasks. A third type of procedural knowledge is conditioning or associative learning from experience, which was made famous by early experiments on animals by Pavlov and Skinner, training animals in 'stimulus-response' reactions – i.e. a trained dog shows a particular reaction in expectation of a given outcome (such as salivating in expectation of food only when a bell is rung and no food is present; Smith & Kosslyn, 2007). Certain language teaching practices such as **audio-lingual drilling** are based on ideas from stimulus-response training, when long dialogues memorized through drilling are retrieved with a simple stimulus word (Johnson, 2008).

Procedural knowledge is thus knowledge that is incidentally/inductively learned, typically very quickly, using parallel processing. Unlike for declarative knowledge, different elements work in tandem to link up the relevant information required. However, while it is a more efficient system, it is inflexible. For example, it is hard to unlearn touch typing for English spellings when you meet a French keyboard layout with certain letters in different positions, or to adjust a memorized dialogue from the 'you' form to the 'he-she' form.

Researchers currently assume that children use procedural memory before they start to use explicit memory processing. Evidence shows that the neural basis for procedural memory is more developed at birth (Baddeley *et al.*, 2009: 290). Procedural memory does not typically show age-related changes in children, in comparison to declarative memory which develops significantly over time from infancy and throughout the teenage years. Researchers argue that this shift towards declarative memory is facilitated by improvements in WM capacity from the age of around four years, as well as more effective use of memory strategies and actual knowledge based on experience (Baddeley *et al.*, 2009: 274). During adult life, declarative episodic memory of events remains constant from young adulthood (around 20 years old) to around 50 or 60 years old; declarative semantic memory for words is maintained, although speed of access declines around a similar age span (Baddeley *et al.*, 2009: 302). Implicit memory and learning show some age effects, e.g. in testing how successfully people can complete word fragments where letters are missing (Baddeley *et al.*, 2009: 303); motor performance declines with age but researchers debate about whether the rate of motor learning is age affected, e.g. training in how to use a computer mouse to navigate a maze onscreen can be very successful even in the over-50s (Baddeley *et al.*, 2009).

These two LTM systems are supported by the WM system, which is responsible for activating and controlling information to be encoded and retrieved in real time. WM is assumed to act as a kind of mental 'workspace' for the multiple processes involved in order to complete any complex task where the learner must activate information from subconscious or non-activated levels, such as understanding what they are reading, by activating long-term semantic memory to match words with their meaning. There are various theoretical models of WM (Caplan & Waters, 1999; Miyake & Shah, 1999; Wen *et al.*, 2015), but most studies on language development focus on Baddeley's multicomponent model of WM (Baddeley, 2000, 2003, 2007).

This model, first proposed by Baddeley and Hitch in 1974, has separate components for storing and processing: verbal and visual information is stored (limited both temporally and spatially) in the phonological loop and the visuospatial sketchpad; the processing happens via a separate central executive which acts as the mechanism for controlling which items need attention for a specific task. The storage systems operate both to process incoming information and to store retrieved information (such as sounds of new words or recalling a previously learned sound-meaning combination). Recent versions (Baddeley, 2000, 2007) include an additional episodic buffer for a less limited storage system – this supports the central executive in combining different aspects of LTM knowledge which the learner is currently attending to. An example is sitting in an Italian language classroom but imagining the sounds and setting of a real Italian café when practising how to order coffee. The attention and processing role of WM, particularly in classroom language learning, is closely associated with explicit knowledge, operating 'within the context of conscious control' (Erçetin & Alptekin, 2013: 734). This suggests that the LTM system in Baddeley's model refers primarily to declarative memory (Pinker & Ullman, 2002).

However, Baddeley's model does not itself distinguish specifically between the different LTM systems, as distinguished above. Researchers debate how far the notion of activation and control means that the learner is consciously paying attention (Truscott, 2015). Consider when you are reading a long sentence and it becomes difficult to comprehend; then you 'realize' that you have to read some of it again – this realization could be conscious or subconscious. Similarly, both systems require degrees of automaticity in processing speed: the procedural system is inherently automatic since the processes involved are subconscious, but declarative knowledge can also be automatically processed – such as learning word-meaning mappings without conscious attention, as infants do. That implies that there is an element of WM processing that must take place subconsciously, which has not yet been clearly examined, particularly in SLA contexts. Despite ongoing debates between psychology researchers and competing models for WM (Wen *et al.*, 2015), Baddeley's model remains the most widely used model in much SLA research (Juffs & Harrington, 2011) despite its shortcomings, and forms the basis of the two studies referred to at the end of this chapter.

Language Learning and Memory

We turn now to explore in more detail how these memory systems work for language and approaches to teaching and learning. As mentioned briefly above, metalinguistic information such as explanations of grammatical rules, and the lexicon, combining explicit knowledge of word-sound-meaning mappings, form part of the declarative semantic system. Syntax and phonology, by contrast, are procedurally based, using the learner's unconscious knowledge or capacity of how to combine words in the correct order with the relevant verbal and nominal information such as tense marking, agreement and gender. Morphological information which support syntactic and phonological rules is usually seen as part of the declarative system in terms of knowledge of specific affixes and word formation, especially for L2 morphophonology (Herschensohn, 1999), but must be bound to the procedural syntactic system in order for the learner to automatically produce the correct morphological form, even in infant language development (Jackendoff, 2002). The underlying conceptual lexical information is often referred to as the 'lemma', while the morpho-syntactically encoded information is referred to as the 'lexeme', to distinguish the pre- and post-encoding stages of word and phrase creation (Levelt, 1989). However, at what point children learn specific morphological information and the precise nature of how it is bound to the procedural system are not yet clearly known. Children are able to use formulaic phrases before their morphosyntactic system is fully developed, and much adult fluent speech contains formulaic patterns or chunks, suggesting that such phrases are stored as 'whole' lexical chunks (see Rogers *et al.* in this volume; also Pawley & Syder, 1983; Wray, 2009). Current models of SLA tend to assume that early use of L2 formulaic phrases that do require morphosyntax are learned explicitly as prefabricated chunks and later analyzed for relevant procedural syntactic information (see Kessler *et al.* in this volume; Myles, 2004; Wray, 2009). However, the means by which morphological information is stored and retrieved and how explicitly learned **formulaic language** bootstraps procedural syntactic information are not yet well understood, which is partly why SLA researchers have often used morphological accuracy as evidence of language development, given L2 learners' patterns of under- or over-inflection (see Kahoul *et al.* in this volume). Specific accounts of memory processes involved in storing, retrieving chunks or creating online utterances are rarely addressed in SLA-based memory models, and need further study.

Turning now to how we can apply psychological memory constructs to language learning, there are close links between the declarative-procedural distinction and the contrast between explicit and implicit knowledge (N. Ellis, 1994, 2005). R. Ellis (2008a) defines these terms as follows. *Explicit knowledge* is 'conscious, declarative, factual' and may be verbalizable, but may not show any systematicity in its varied forms, being 'anomalous and inconsistent' (Ellis, 2008a: 6). It is accessed through 'controlled processing in planned language use' (Ellis, 2008a: 6); it may well require good knowledge of metalanguage to assist language development, but can be learned at any age. By contrast, *implicit knowledge* is 'intuitive, procedural, systematically variable, automatic and thus available for use in fluent, unplanned language use. It is not verbalizable' (Ellis, 2008a: 7). Hulstijn (2005) elaborates on this, adding that implicit learning is 'input processing without awareness of regularities underlying the input' while explicit learning is 'input processing with the conscious intention to find out whether the input information contains regularities and, if so, to work out the concepts and rules with which these regularities can be captured' (Hulstijn, 2005: 131).

There is some debate about how far the mind or brain have distinct areas for language functions, particularly syntax, in some kind of specific cognitive system or module of the mind (as discussed in several chapters in this volume). This modular view of cognition, in which linguistic competence is separate and not part of general cognition, was first suggested by Fodor in 1983, and is supported, among other evidence, from problems with language in children who have some specific language impairment despite normal cognitive abilities (Pliatsikas & Marinis, 2012; Smith & Tsimpli, 1995). However, there is a good deal of disagreement over this notion of a modular syntactic system. When we look at the brain rather than the mind, there is, for example, increasing evidence of interconnected brain activities from many neural studies (Green, 2003). So it is better to think of specialist areas of the brain supporting different but connected domains of cognitive activity (such as language), rather than arguing for modules that do not directly interact with each other (Jackendoff, 2002).

Some cognitive models of language, processing and memory (e.g. Goldberg, 1994; Tomasello, 2003) and particularly emergentist models (O'Grady, 2005, 2008a, and in this volume) reject any kind of modular or autonomous linguistic system for all language learning, including by children. They suggest that knowledge of words and constructions is learned through the learner's general inductive mechanisms, constrained by WM, which work on input through frequency, salience and ease of processing. Once the input is processed, then it can be stored in memory via construction-specific rules which integrate language within the general memory system, connected by nodes that become stronger with use, in both L1 and L2 (Williams, 1999, 2005). Rule-like behaviour thus emerges as a consequence of 'the way in which individual instances of experience are stored in a single memory system' (Williams, 2005: 4). Simpler constructions emerge first, while longer, complex structures, especially those like passives and relative clauses which depend on greater WM capacity, emerge later. Cognitive accounts, particularly emergentism, therefore see both LTM and WM as central to language learning for either L1 or L2 (Miyake & Friedman, 1998).

Nevertheless, many researchers from a range of paradigms have used a psychological distinction between different aspects of language, particularly distinguishing between lexical and syntactic systems, both in L1 and L2 models of learning. One such model is the 'Words and Rules' or Dual Model System (Pinker, 1999) which applies to the acquisition of English past tense and plural marking (see also Skehan, 1998, more generally for L2). Pinker argues that word knowledge or lexical information, including metalinguistic knowledge about language, is declarative knowledge, stored differently from rule-based abstract generalizations that govern how we automatically put that knowledge together in grammatical sentences. Rule-based abstract generalizations are learned implicitly for children and, typically with naturalistic rather than classroom input, for both younger and older L2 learners; this can be seen as closely parallel to the discussion of procedural learning outlined above, although Pinker himself does not use this term. Lexical and metalinguistic information, by contrast, can be consciously analyzed – we can learn new word meanings out of a dictionary, or explain certain facts about language such as different forms of English plurals.

As well as psycholinguistic evidence of differences between explicit and implicit knowledge and processes, as alluded to above, there is neurolinguistic research supporting the idea of separate systems in the brain. In this line of research (see, for example, Breznitz, 2008; Erçetin & Alptekin, 2013; Sabourin & Stowe, 2008; Wattendorf et al., 2014), language processing can be tracked in different parts of the brain using evidence of electromagnetic activity (measured as Event-related Potentials

(ERPs). ERPs track the brain's response to stimuli as positive or negative shifts in electromagnetic waveforms measured in the left or right hemispheres of the brain and at different times along a processing timeline. Syntactic processing of grammatical violations by native speakers, using automatic, implicit syntactic knowledge, shows up as left-hemisphere positive activity occurring at 600 milliseconds (known as P600). Therefore evidence of similar P600 effects in L2 learners is taken as evidence of implicit or procedural knowledge. By contrast, negative shifts in the ERP waveform, known as an N400 effect, are taken as evidence of explicit or declarative knowledge.

This distinction between declarative and procedural knowledge on a neural basis is taken forward via the Words-Rules Dual System Model used by Ullman in his Declarative-Procedural (DP) model (2001, 2005). His testing in laboratory settings suggests that less proficient L2 learners show significantly more N400 effects compared to monolingual speakers as well as more proficient L2 learners. This is taken as evidence to support a general assumption that declarative knowledge forms the basis of lower proficiency L2 learners' linguistic repertoire. However, there is no discussion of how reliance on declarative knowledge in early stages of proficiency shifts to procedural knowledge over time.

Moving on from different views of LTM, WM also plays a key role in L2 learning (Gilabert & Munoz, 2010; Harrington & Sawyer, 1992; Juffs & Harrington, 2011; Wen et al., 2015; Wright, 2010a). WM is argued to be crucial, particularly for instructed L2 learners, who are shifting between explicit and implicit learning and knowledge retrieval, by providing a 'workspace' for them to bring these together during processing, especially when under pressure of online or real-time speaking and listening. However, evidence from the relatively new and small field of WM studies in SLA is still mixed (see, for example, Wen et al., 2015, and the studies discussed below). Research also does not always closely differentiate how WM and LTM interact, nor address changes in effects through the age span as cognitive processes decline (Wright, 2015).

So how far can we apply these ideas about memory and knowledge systems to SLA? As noted, there are some models which assume language learning is like any other learning. However, other approaches consider that there is something 'special' about language, particularly grammatical knowledge. Generative SLA research in particular has assumed a distinction between acquisition of implicit grammatical knowledge (competence) versus learning explicit knowledge (Krashen, 1985a; Schwartz, 1993). Exploring the implications of how competence is acquired (e.g. White, 2003), researchers suggest that L2 knowledge develops by accessing innate principles as in child language acquisition. The main insight that drives this model of acquisition is the centuries-old logical problem, noted by Plato, that children can generate novel sentences they cannot possibly have heard, and rapidly converge, in normal language acquisition, on a reasonably consistent knowledge of what constitutes their native language, despite the input from the caregiver of highly 'noisy' input (Marcus, 1993) with missing information, half-uttered words and repetitions. In other words, language acquisition is systematically constrained and is not affected by the limited quality of the input and complete absence of information about some aspects of the grammar (known as 'Poverty of the Stimulus', discussed in this volume in Chapter 4 by Gil *et al.*).

Similarly, generative SLA researchers argue that L2 learners of all ages can, without any relevant specific instruction and regardless of their L1 knowledge, detect that phenomena such as certain word orders in, say, English, are not grammatical, due to linguistic representations based around specific features (see, for example, Caink, Kahoul *et al.* and Rogers *et al.* in this volume). One such phenomenon involves word movement in English questions. Children and L2 learners alike grasp the rule that auxiliary and modal verbs in English move to the front in yes-no questions. So, taking the statement in Example 1 below and turning it into a question can produce Example 2. But what makes us move one verb rather than another? Why is Example 3 ungrammatical?

Example 1

Sarah is the girl who is happy.

Example 2

Is Sarah the girl who is happy?

Example 3

*Is Sarah is the girl who happy?

There is argued to be a general Universal Grammar (UG) principle about structure dependency, where embedded clauses, such as the 'who ...' part of Example 1, cannot be split up (known as the Principle of Locality). Teachers do not teach this principle in their L2 classrooms but learners pick it up very quickly (Cook, 2008). Similarly, syntacticians propose universal constraints on forming *wh*-questions from statements such as Example 4, to avoid information crossing structural boundaries of a complex noun-phrase (known as **subjacency**), which make Example 5 grammatical and Example 6 ungrammatical. Again, learners without any relevant instruction seem to grasp the grammatical–ungrammatical distinction consistently (Wright, 2010a).

Example 4

John said that Mary liked the book about Shakespeare.

Example 5

What did John say that Mary liked?

Example 6
    *What did John say that Mary liked the book about?

Most generative SLA researchers argue that L2 learners can, with sufficient input and regardless of their age, use such underlying principles via access to UG (see, for example, Whong *et al.*, 2013). L2 acquisition should then be seen as ensuring sufficient quality and quantity of target-language input to trigger acquisition of relevant L2 features.

Few generative researchers focus much on memory in the learning/development process. Learnability, if defined in terms of triggering acquisition of linguistic features, generally means that memory is involved primarily via procedural or unconscious processes (Carroll, 2001). However, one model that does focus on memory in language learning is Sharwood Smith and Truscott's (2014) Modular Online Growth and Use of Language (MOGUL) framework. MOGUL is based on the assumption that that there is a single processing system for language for both declarative and procedural knowledge/learning and for both comprehension and production, and which combines L1 and L2 use. Linguistic information is stored as representations encoded in LTM, which are assumed to have different **resting levels of activation** derived from frequency of use, either through comprehension or production. There are specific linguistic stores for phonology and syntax which interact with the lexicon (or 'general Conceptual Store'), for semantic interpretation. Monolingual speakers have one set of linguistic representations, all highly activated; L2 speakers have multiple representations for L1 and L2 with differing levels of activation which compete when the two languages are being processed. The more input and output the speaker processes in the L2, the higher the potential for raising the levels of activation of appropriate L2 representations, leading to more target-like use.

Sharwood Smith and Truscott argue that acquisition of novel information is both form/meaning based and usage driven. They claim that active representations are constructed in LTM by matching the input to pre-existing abstract grammatical features (derived from UG), and connected to basic semantic concepts in order to interpret meaning. So for acquisition of a novel functional category, like Tense, they suggest the learnability task is to match features in the Syntactic Store (SS) for Tense (to distinguish past or present, or finiteness) with appropriate items in the Conceptual Store (CS), which would be needed for a correct semantic interpretation, such as when the action happened or for how long. When a learner hears something completely non-active in their L1 and thus requiring a novel functional category, such as an English learner hearing German gender endings [masculine/feminine/neuter], the learner must access the new syntactic item for gender from the innate set of UG-based features, and construct an activated syntactic structure to process the input, while also mapping this new structure to the conceptual system in order to grasp the meaning. Acquisition thus represents long-term or enduring changes in levels of activation as a result of processing. If it is difficult for the learner to change the level of activation to construct the specific item, the item is harder for the learner to acquire and results in their variable success in comprehension or production. Difficulties in changing activation come from the competition from strong levels of activation of L1 SS and CS features. Only sufficient input and output, which together produce very high activation levels, can drive the novel L2 level of activation to win the processing competition.

While the MOGUL model itself needs further empirical investigation, studies have shown that learners can indeed successfully develop implicit linguistic grammatical knowledge of L2 features that they cannot have been taught (see the studies discussed below, and also Kahoul *et al.* in this volume). A generative approach to SLA can thus explain how some learners come to develop such linguistic competence, using UG principles. However, evidence of effective target-like acquisition, particularly for instructed learners in a foreign language setting within the constraints of limited class time, is very mixed (Norris & Ortega, 2000). The generative approach has typically focused on the 'what' of language: how language is represented in the L2 mind. Researchers have not typically explored the 'how' of learning, to explain the variability common across L2 learners, why some learners take longer than others and why some learners completely fail to acquire what they have been taught. The generative account of SLA still lacks an effective transition theory that can apply to both instructed and naturalistic learners (Gregg, 1996; Whong *et al.*, 2013) and also account for individual variability.

An alternative research model proposes that L2 learning by adults (commonly taken as post-puberty) is fundamentally different from L1 acquisition, and from L2 acquisition by children. That is, L2 implicit learning is not through access to innate universal principles, but for adults relies instead on general cognitive learning mechanisms. Therefore, variability in general cognitive capacities and processing explain variability or non-acquisition of the L2 (e.g. Bley-Vroman, 1990; Clahsen & Muysken, 1986; DeKeyser, 1997). Bley-Vroman argues that adult SLA is fundamentally different from L1 acquisition, based on the claim that there is an age limit after which learners can no longer tap UG (i.e. the Critical Period for language acquisition, proposed to end around age 12 by Lenneberg, 1967). Under this view, children acquire language implicitly using generative principles, but adult learners have to rely on general cognitive learning mechanisms, using declarative or explicit knowledge (e.g. as claimed in Johnson & Newport, 1989, but see counter-evidence from Flege *et al.*, 1999).

Evidence that adult L2 learners process language differently from native speakers is proposed in Clahsen and Felser's (2006) Shallow Processing Hypothesis (SPH). They argue that L2 learners' lack of access to UG makes them rely instead on semantic shallow processing, driven by lexical cues (e.g. word order), and surface input such as frequency and salience, rather than on deeper syntactic processing which requires abstract knowledge of syntactic phrase structures. Success or lack of success in acquiring L2 knowledge of structures such as *wh*-questions is therefore seen as due to differences in frequency and salience in the input, which affect the processing load. So, for example, tense marking (using -*s* in English present tense) is non-salient, and therefore carries a higher processing load (DeKeyser, 1997). Similarly, complex constructions such as Examples 7a and 7b are difficult to acquire as they require a learner to do the harder job of inserting an inflected form of *do* ('*do*'-support), whereas Examples 8a and 8b are simpler because they only require moving the unchanged modal verb *can* – also argued by Processability Theory (Pienemann, 1998), and see Kessler *et al.*'s chapter in this volume.

Example 7

(a) John likes the book.
(b) What does John like?

Example 8

(a) John can sing.
(b) Can John sing?

In terms of explaining learning, L2 knowledge, particularly for classroom learners, starts out as explicit learned material, especially in the early stages (Erçetin & Alptekin, 2013; Myles, 2004). This knowledge then becomes procedural/automatized through extensive repetition (Anderson, 1993; Anderson *et al.*, 2004; Segalowitz, 2003; Towell, 2013). DeKeyser (2003) argues that most classroom-based language learning is best explained as increasing automaticity of declarative or explicit knowledge, which can lead to procedural or implicit knowledge, given enough practice. This account of learning underpins the audio-lingual method, drilling and grammar translation methods still prevalent in many foreign language classrooms around the world.

However, critics of these teaching methods highlight the limitations of assuming that faster automatized use of a memorized set of items during classroom teaching can provide a learner with actual linguistic competence (Lightbown, 2000), i.e. acquisition (in the sense used in Krashen, 1985a; Schwartz, 1993). In addition, once beyond the simplest level, language learning, even for L2 adult learners, does not consist of simply repeating and memorizing the input (Myles, 2004). One particular critic of language being skilled memorization is Paradis, a specialist in neurolinguistic bilingual research, who strongly rejects the overlap between the procedural and declarative systems (Paradis, 2004, 2009). He provides ample neurological and theoretical justification for his claim that the two systems of knowledge are separate, supporting the original acquisition/ learning distinction outlined by Krashen (1985a) and Schwartz (1993), among others. Paradis (2009: 16) argues that declarative knowledge cannot be transformed into implicit computational procedures, and that 'nothing outside of implicit linguistic competence can have an influence of any kind on the grammatical system' (Paradis, 2009: 59). While he agrees that both implicit and explicit knowledge can be accessed automatically (non-consciously), he claims that the key difference between the two sources of memory is whether explicit, declarative knowledge can 'be expressed consciously if required' (Paradis, 2004: 43).

The debates about separate systems and a greater or lesser role for memory in language development are far from resolved (see, for example, Hawkins' edited Special Issue of *Lingua*, 2008). However, there is general consensus that language knowledge implicates both explicit and implicit knowledge, and there is a mixture of reliance on both systems, particularly for L2 knowledge and particularly if it has been learned in the classroom (Han & Finneran, 2014). It is clear that L2 learning, especially by classroom learners and by older learners, involves as many cognitive and linguistic resources as possible, combined in a 'coalition' rather than operating as wholly separate systems (Herschensohn, 1999). This coalition supports storage, processing and retrieval in different ways throughout the learning process, and specific targeted research into the LTM and WM mechanisms involved along the way can help teachers understand the ongoing question of why learners do not seem to learn what they are taught. But as Towell (2013: 136) points out, further 'detailed and careful research' is needed to tackle the question of why the rate and ultimate level of learning is so variable in SLA. It is crucial to use findings and tools from psycholinguistic and neurolinguistic research to assess the key characteristics of input (quality and quantity), what noticing really involves and whether comprehension and production use single or multiple processes. Much more research with teachers and learners would help clarify many of the questions discussed in this chapter, and in particular to help crack the methodological challenge of discovering how learners develop linguistic competence over time. In the next section we therefore turn to two examples of longitudinal studies, in order to illustrate some of the questions of memory, input and longitudinal development discussed above.

Empirical Investigations of Memory, Processing and Language

Two small-scale studies of upper-intermediate adult instructed learners of English from China focused on testing knowledge of a range of English question structures to address questions about the role of memory and input (Wright, 2010a, 2012). Accurate knowledge and use of such forms for these learners entails grammatical knowledge of tense and word order rules not present in their L1, since Chinese does not mark tense and leaves *wh*-question words *in situ* like an English echo question ('Zhangsan bought what?'), as in Example 9 below.

Example 9

Zhangsan	yiwei	Lisi	mai-le	shenme
Zhangsan	think	Lisi	buy-ASP	what

'What does Zhangsan think Lisi bought?'

The way to form *wh*-questions in English (as shown in earlier sections) can be described through explicit metalinguistic rules for overt tense morphology and word order rules (e.g. moving a modal or adding 'do' before the subject). Instructed learners can thus potentially demonstrate target-like knowledge of these instructed forms based on explicit taught input alone. However, certain types of more complex questions also require information which learners would not have been taught, such as the ungrammaticality of Example 10, which violates the subjacency constraint demonstrated earlier in Examples 4–6, e.g. in splitting up a complex noun phrase (Radford, 1997):

Example 10

*'What did John ask Mary the question about?'

The studies tested the participants' dependence on explicit or implicit knowledge in judging question forms, where some of the knowledge of ungrammatical structures would have been part of their instruction and other aspects (violating subjacency constraints) would not have been. The hypothesis was that the learners would have no way of consistently judging the untaught structures as ungrammatical without access to some kind of universal constraint as argued by UG theories of SLA.

In the first study (Wright 2010b), 11 learners were presented with paper-and-pencil grammaticality judgement tasks and question formation tasks (based on a previous study on *wh*-movement by White & Juffs, 1998) as offline, untimed tests of their linguistic competence. An additional test of procedural knowledge looked at degree of fluency in an oral task. As suggested earlier, fluent performance in online oral tasks can be evidence of procedural or at least automatized declarative knowledge, while non-fluent oral performance or offline untimed written tasks are seen as more likely to tap declarative knowledge or reveal gaps in procedural implicit knowledge (Ellis *et al.*, 2009). The results showed that learners were more accurate in the offline written tasks than in the online oral task, as is commonly found in comparisons of online and offline tasks (e.g. Murphy, 1997; Temple, 1997; Yuan & Ellis, 2003). The results of the written task also showed that there was no distinction between application of declarative and procedural knowledge, i.e. learned knowledge and linguistic competence, since learners judged equally successfully the grammatical structures that would have been taught in the classroom and ungrammatical subjacency violations that would not have been taught.

The second study built on the results of the first, to test how far the differences between oral and written tasks would still be evident when using an online (timed) grammaticality judgement task and communicative question oral production task, and also how these differences changed over time (Wright, 2012). The study also assessed how memory and processing could interact in L2 learning by looking at the potential role of WM capacity in individual differences in rate of development. This time, a group of 32 Chinese learners were tested before and after a year's immersion in the UK. Using t-tests, at both times the learners were found to show statistically significant better accuracy in the judgement task compared to accurate production of wh-questions in the spoken task ($p < 0.05$), confirming that how we test language knowledge is important. Over time, accuracy did not improve across the group although oral fluency, in terms of fewer repairs and filled pauses, and speed of response on the timed grammaticality judgement task did significantly improve ($p < 0.05$). Tests to associate individual variation in changes over time with WM capacity also showed that WM capacity correlated significantly with improvements in accuracy in the spoken task ($p < 0.05$), supporting the claim that WM facilitates L2 development, at least in some contexts. These studies provide examples of how to combine investigations of L2 representation both in perception and production, how representations may rely on procedural or explicit knowledge, and how memory/processing constraints affect individual development when exposure to input changes. Overall the studies are thus a useful indication of the value of interdisciplinary SLA studies which combine generative linguistic theory with psycholinguistic development.

Conclusion

This chapter has presented a wide-ranging overview of key constructs in memory and has discussed how they are argued to operate in different aspects of L2 learning and processing, especially how the L2 is stored and retrieved and why L2 outcomes seem so variable. We have seen how psychological constructs such as procedural and declarative memory, and WM, cannot always be precisely mapped onto commonly investigated issues in SLA, such as input, implicit and explicit learning or attention and noticing. We have examined how far these constructs may be linked to Krashen's and Schwartz's assumptions about a difference between learning and acquisition. We have compared views that suggest adult L2 knowledge is stored and processed fundamentally differently from L1 knowledge (Ullman's DP model; Clahsen & Felser's SPH). However, we have also seen from two empirical studies of wh-question acquisition by Chinese learners of English, which included the role of WM, that taking a strict separation model of two different systems does not always predict clear outcomes of success in L2 learning. Sharwood Smith and Truscott's (2014) model of 'acquisition by processing' suggests that successful L2 acquisition lies in rich input and output creating increasingly strong levels of activation of L2 representations which can then successfully compete with existing L1 representations. This claim fits well with Herschensohn's (1999) coalitionalist view of SLA and underscores the need for a more holistic attitude to L2 processing, combining research into how linguistic representations may be stored in LTM together with a stronger focus on the longitudinal development of those representations and how they are retrieved at different stages and in different tasks during the learning journey. Such a broad perspective will help lead students and teachers to a more integrated understanding of language learning, bringing together a viable property theory of SLA (the 'what'), but also a viable transition theory of SLA (the 'how').

12 Processability Theory: Architecture and Application

Jörg-U. Keßler, Anke Lenzing and
Anja Plesser

Introduction

In this chapter, a psycholinguistic theory of second language acquisition (SLA) is presented, namely Processability Theory (PT) (Pienemann, 1998; Pienemann & Lenzing, 2015; Pienemann *et al.*, 2005). PT takes a **processing** perspective in order to account for the finding that all learners of a given second language (L2) follow the same path in the acquisition of specific morphosyntactic structures regardless of their first language (L1) (see also Kahoul *et al.* in this volume). As R. Ellis puts it:

> [t]he existence of developmental sequences is one of the most important findings of SLA research to date. There is now general acceptance in the SLA community that the acquisition of an L2 grammar [...] occurs in stages. (R. Ellis, 1994: 21)

The key achievement of PT is a psychologically and typologically plausible explanation for this very developmental path. In this chapter, after introducing PT, we discuss the theoretical cornerstones on which the theory is based: **Lexical-Functional Grammar** (e.g. Bresnan, 2001; Falk, 2001) and Levelt's model of speech processing (e.g. Levelt, 1989; Levelt *et al.*, 1999). We then turn to how PT accounts for the L2 acquisition of specific grammatical structures and we end the chapter with an application of these ideas to the L2 classroom.

Processability Theory: Core Issues

PT takes an **interlanguage** view on SLA in that it aims to 'provide a systematic perspective on some central psychological mechanisms underlying the spontaneous production of interlanguage (IL) speech' (Pienemann, 1998: xv). A core assumption in PT is that the L2 **developmental problem** (or path) is determined by the architecture of the human **language**

processor (Pienemann, 1998: 4; see also O'Grady's chapter in this volume). This means that the learner is only able to produce a linguistic structure if the processor is capable of handling that structure or, in other words, if the necessary **processing procedures** have been acquired by the learner. In PT the existence of specific processing mechanisms is postulated. A core claim of the theory is that these mechanisms are ordered hierarchically, and that they are implicationally related (in an **implicational hierarchy**) in that 'each procedure is a necessary prerequisite for the following procedure' (Pienemann, 1998: 6). What follows from this is that PT can make predictions for L2 development, as the theory can formally predict the morphosyntactic structures an L2 learner can process at a particular point in time in her/his interlanguage development (see Table 12.1).

Table 12.1 provides an overview of the proposed developmental schedule for L2 English. Here the general hierarchy of language processing procedures is applied to the individual developmental sequence of syntactic and morphological structures for English. The hierarchy for L2 English includes six developmental stages. These stages are characterized by a

Table 12.1 Processability hierarchy for English as an L2

Processing procedures	Information exchange	Morphology	Syntax
(6) Subordinate clause-procedure	Main and subordinate clause		Cancel inversion *I wonder what he wants*
(5) S-procedure	Interphrasal information exchange	Interphrasal morph. SV-agreement *The mouse* plays *volleyball*	Neg/Aux-2nd-? *Why **doesn't** he go home?* Aux-2nd *What **do** you collect?*
(4) VP-procedure	Interphrasal information exchange		Wh-copula S (x) *What **is** your number?* Copula S(x) ***Are there** boots?*
(3) Phrasal procedure	Phrasal information exchange	Phrasal morphemes Det + N agreement **Two ears**	Adverb-first ***Today** he stay here.* Wh-SV(O)-? ***What** you like?* Do-SV(O)-? ***Do** you have a sun?*
(2) Category procedure	No information exchange	Lexical morphemes Plural -s (*pets*) Past -ed (*played*)	Canonical word order SVO *The mouse play volleyball*
(1) Word/lemma access	No information exchange	Invariant forms	Formulae *What's your name?*

Source: Adapted and modified from Pienemann (2005: 24); see also Lenzing (2013: 90).

number of morphosyntactic structures which L2 learners are able to process and thus produce once they have acquired the relevant processing procedure, shown in the leftmost column in Table 12.1. The structural options available to L2 learners are constrained by the processing procedures they have acquired at a given developmental stage. Beginning L2 learners of English produce single words or **formulae**, such as 'What's your name?' (Learner C03; Stage 1, examples from Roos, 2007 and Lenzing, 2013).[1] This is followed by declarative sentences and question forms with SVO word order (Stage 2), e.g. 'I like spaghetti' (Learner C08) or 'It's a elephant?' (Learner C06). Early question forms include restricted target-like and non-target-like structures with fronted elements (Do-fronting, *wh*-words), such as 'Do you like milk?' (Learner C12). More complex question forms that require subject-verb inversion occur at Stage 4, as in 'Is there a bee?' (Learner C09), and questions with an auxiliary in second position (e.g. 'What do you collect?') occur at Stage 5 of the hierarchy (see Table 12.1 above). As far as morphology is concerned, L2 learners can produce morphological forms such as the 'past -*ed*' or the 'plural -*s*' at Stage 2 of acquisition (e.g. 'pets'). A feature that is acquired rather late is the '3sg-s', as the processing procedure required for the agreement between subject and verb is acquired at Stage 5 (e.g. 'The mouse plays volleyball') (Table 12.1; see also Kahoul *et al.* in this volume). A detailed explanation of the processes underlying the production of the morphosyntactic structures in Table 12.1 is given below.

Problems in second language acquisition and Processability Theory's point of departure

There are two problems in language acquisition that are generally recognized to be important for a theory of SLA to address: (1) the **logical problem** (see Gil *et al.* in this volume) and (2) the **developmental problem**. The logical problem addresses the question of the origin of linguistic knowledge, and the developmental problem focuses on developmental trajectories in language development (see, for example, Felix, 1984; Clahsen, 1992; Gregg, 1996; Pienemann, 1998).

The original version of PT (Pienemann, 1998) addresses the developmental problem in that it provides an explanation for the universal L2 developmental path for specific morphosyntactic features. The extended version of PT (Pienemann *et al.*, 2005) and recent developments of the theory (Lenzing, 2013) also aim to address aspects of the logical problem. Using specific aspects of Lexical-Functional Grammar (LFG), the initial hypotheses of beginning L2 learners and their mental representations present in the L2 initial state, i.e. when they have just begun to learn the language, are specified.

In order to account for the logical problem and the developmental problem and thus explore the cognitive mechanisms underlying SLA,

Pienemann chose the concept of 'learnability' as his point of departure. From a rationalist perspective, a learnability theory has to specify four components, namely (1) the target grammar, (2) the learner's input, (3) the learning device and (4) the initial state (see Pienemann, 2005: 2). According to Pienemann, this is done in order to 'specify how a learner develops from an initial state to the target grammar with the available input and the given learning device' (Pienemann, 2005: 2). In PT, Pienemann adds the notion of processability to learnability theory by including the human mind's procedural skills for language generation, which are psychologically constrained (see Pienemann, 1998: 1). These psychological restrictions result from the fact that real-time speech production requires rapid online information processing, namely:

- word access: almost instantaneous word retrieval (a matter of milliseconds);
- human memory: carrying out the message generation process without paying particular attention to any of the steps (see Levelt, 1989).

PT is based on two fundamental theoretical components: on the one hand, LFG, mentioned above; and, on the other hand, Levelt's model of speech processing (Levelt, 1989). One key feature that these two components have in common is the underlying principle of 'linearization through unification'. Generally speaking, this principle is achieved by the unification of features and mapping principles. Before Levelt's model and LFG are outlined in more detail, the linearization problem in language production is introduced.

The linearization problem

Linearization in message generation, in essence, refers to the fact that conceptual and linguistic features have to be unified in order for a speaker to produce a both semantically and structurally well-formed sentence. In other words, the conceptual knowledge, i.e. the message to be expressed, is initially 'chaotic' in the individual's mind, in that it comprises unstructured, non-linguistic pieces of information that then have to be given the linguistic shape of the respective target language. It has to be noted here that linguistic systems are rather complex in that they offer different options of expressing one proposition, e.g. declarative sentences or question forms in active or passive voice. For that reason, linearization in speech production constitutes the main cognitive challenge speakers have to overcome with the help of their incomplete mental grammar and the respective processing procedures operating on their mental grammar. This, in turn, is why the linearization problem, i.e. how speakers order the information they intend to express, is so relevant for SLA research.

At first, linearization in language production can occur in a linear as well as in a non-linear way. Non-linearity requires more cognitive effort

linearity	non-linearity
The man mounted his horse, _then_ he rode off. ↓ event 1 ↓ event 2	*Before the man rode off, he mounted his horse.* event 2 ✕ event 1

Figure 12.1 The linearization problem
Source: Adapted from Pienemann (1998: 56).

than linearity. The temporal dimension of linearizing an expression on the sentence level by the speaker refers to the fact that the word order of an utterance can, but does not necessarily have to, mirror the real sequence of events (see Pienemann, 1998: 56; for an illustration see Keßler & Plesser, 2011: 79). In English, a speaker can express a sequence of events by using a temporal adverb as shown in Figure 12.1 in the right-hand box.

This example shows that non-linearity requires additional cognitive effort from the speaker, because s/he has to store one proposition – here 'he mounted his horse' – in memory (Pienemann, 1998: 56). As pointed out by Pienemann (2005: 5), the linearization problem is not limited to propositional content but also applies to the level of morphosyntax. In this case, it is grammatical information that needs to be temporarily stored in memory. In the particular case of the L2 speaker's speech generation, non-linearity poses a further challenge for the learner, as s/he may not have acquired the processing procedures that are necessary to accomplish the task of aligning both semantic and syntactic information.

Having briefly outlined and exemplified the linearization problem in general terms, in what follows we introduce LFG. Once the basics of this linguistic cornerstone of PT are outlined, we will present the linearization problem and the respective unification processes in more detail.

Lexical-Functional Grammar

LFG is a generative theory of grammar, i.e. one of its central aims is to formalize the mental representations underlying linguistic knowledge. LFG successfully accounts for typologically diverse languages such as Warlpiri, Navajo, Greenlandic, Welsh, Irish, German, Dutch, Arabic, Hindi-Urdu, Japanese, English and many more (Falk, 2001: 194). LFG is a unification grammar, as a main focus is on the unification of different features in sentence generation, which results in a semantically and grammatically well-formed final utterance. This process of unification 'ensures that the different parts that constitute a sentence do actually fit together' (Pienemann, 2000: 109). In this respect, the formal design of LFG differs fundamentally from Chomskyan ideas about syntax, which are derivational.

In LFG, three levels of linguistic representation are assumed, at and between which **feature unification** takes place: (1) **functional structure**, (2) **constituent structure** and (3) **argument structure**. At each of these three levels, different types of linguistic knowledge are encoded which are essential for the speaker's production of a potentially infinite number of grammatically well-formed sentences.

(1) *Functional structure (f-structure)*
    In f-structure, universal aspects of grammar are encoded. F-structure contains grammatical functions, such as subject or object. These functions are assumed to be largely universal, i.e. not language specific. That is, every language has subjects and objects.

(2) *Constituent structure (c-structure)*
    C-structure also represents syntactic aspects of language. At this level, the surface syntactic organization of phrases is represented. This means that the relation between words in phrases and sentences is depicted in terms of phrase structure trees. C-structure is language specific, as the surface structure differs across languages.

(3) *Argument structure (a-structure)*
    In a-structure, the core participants in the events being expressed are represented. It contains the verb and its corresponding arguments. Arguments are basically those entities that represent who does what to whom in a sentence. Arguments take specific semantic roles, such as agent or patient. As shown in the following three examples, different verbs require both different numbers and different types of arguments:
    (a) sleep: 1 argument (agent) as in 'John sleeps';
    (b) kick: 2 arguments (agent + patient/theme), as in 'John kicks the ball';
    (c) give: 3 arguments (agent + patient/theme + locative), as in 'John puts the book on the table'.

The number of arguments a verb takes varies cross-linguistically. Therefore, the arguments have to be acquired for each verb of the target language. Apart from the semantic content, a-structure also has a syntactic side. Here, specific syntactic features are encoded which are essential to map the arguments in a-structure onto the grammatical functions in f-structure.

These three levels of linguistic representation are assumed to exist in parallel and are related to each other by specific linking (mapping) principles, which is crucial when it comes to linearization. These principles are the essential prerequisites in order to unify the information that is encoded in each of the three levels as shown in Figure 12.2.

The three levels of representation postulated in LFG are illustrated in Figure 12.2 with example sentences in English and in Warlpiri, an

A-structure chase <agent patient/theme>
⇩ ⇩
F-structure SUBJ OBJ
⇧ ⇧
C-structure The two small children are chasing that dog

```
                        S
         NP
  the two small children    Aux    VP
                             are  V     NP
                                chasing  that dog
```

```
                              S
   NP          Aux        V          NP        NP          NP
 wita-jarra-rlu  ka-pala  wajili-pi-nyi  yalumpu  kurdu-jarra-rlu  maliki
 small-DUAL-ERG  pres-3duSUBJ  chase-NPAST  that.ABS  child-DUAL-ERG  dog.ABS
```

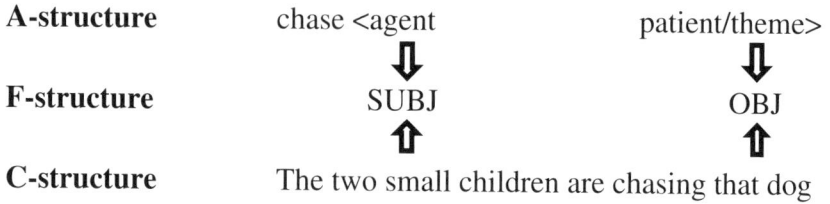

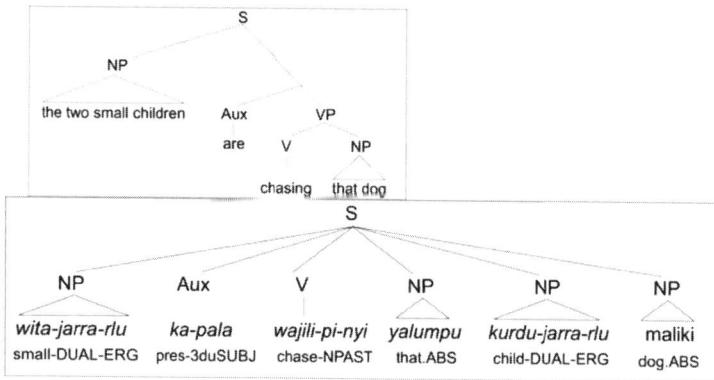

Figure 12.2 Levels of linguistic representation in Lexical-Functional Grammar
Source: Example adapted and modified from Bresnan (2001: 18–20).

Australian Indigenous language. Both sentences express the idea of two children chasing a dog. In this example, a-structure comprises the verb 'chase' and the corresponding arguments with the semantic roles they take (agent and patient). F-structure contains the corresponding grammatical functions SUBJ (subject) and OBJ (object). Finally, c-structure represents the surface structure of the sentence. As can be seen in the example, this surface structure varies across languages. English has a relatively fixed word order, as there is a relation between conceptual units and phrases; i.e. the concept of 'two small children' is structurally represented in one noun phrase (NP). On the other hand, in Warlpiri, which is an agglutinative language, word order is relatively free and the relation between conceptual units is marked by case and number morphology (see Bresnan, 2001).

LFG constitutes a lexicalist approach to syntax in that grammars are assumed to be lexically driven. Therefore, another component that plays a central role in LFG is the (mental) lexicon. That means that there is a substantial amount of grammatical information present in the lexicon, so that 'words, or lexical elements, are as important as syntactic elements in expressing grammatical information' (Bresnan, 2001: 14). In LFG, and thus in PT, the mental lexicon contains lexical entries which provide information about a word's meaning as well as its syntactic category (and

a, D   DEFINITE = -
        NUMBER = SG
        PERSON = 3

boy, N   PRED = 'boy'
          NUMBER = SG
          PERSON = 3

Figure 12.3 Lexical entries

morphophonological form), as illustrated in the example entries for the NP 'a boy' (see Figure 12.3).

As regards the linearization problem introduced above, LFG proposes two major principles: feature unification and mapping principles.

(1) *Feature unification*: transfer of grammatical information within constituent structure;
(2) *Mapping*: transfer of grammatical (and semantic) information between argument and functional structure and between constituent and functional structure.

Feature unification

The term *feature unification* refers to the transfer of grammatical information within constituent structure. This process is illustrated using the example of the NP 'a boy'. In order to generate this NP, the diacritic features of the determiner 'a' and the noun 'boy', which are stored in their respective lexical entries, have to be matched. As illustrated in Figure 12.4 (and Figure 12.3 above), both lexical entries are annotated for 'number' and this value is in both cases 'singular'. This grammatical information is transferred within the phrase, and the unification of this information renders the noun phrase grammatical.

The concept of feature unification is one crucial reason why LFG was chosen as the grammatical formalism in PT (see Pienemann, 1998: 97).

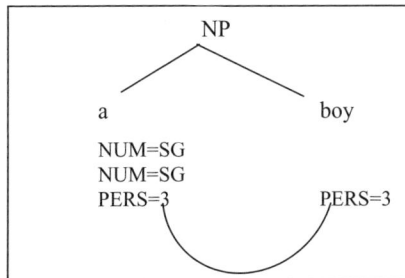

Figure 12.4 Feature unification
Source: Lenzing (2017: 103).

By feature unification the linearization problem can be modelled referring to specific grammatical phenomena (using English in this chapter).

Mapping principles

The term *mapping* refers to the transfer of grammatical (and semantic) information between argument and functional structure and between constituent and functional structure. For the speaker to produce grammatically well-formed sentences, the semantic and syntactic information encoded in a-, f- and c-structure has to be unified. This is achieved by specific 'linking (mapping) principles', which relate: (1) arguments (e.g. agents and patients) in a-structure to grammatical functions (e.g. subjects and objects) in f-structure; and (2) constituents (e.g. noun phrases) in c-structure to grammatical functions. This is exemplified in Figure 12,5.

In order for the speaker to be able to produce the sentence 'John played the guitar', the agent in a-structure needs to be mapped onto the subject in f-structure, and the first NP (John) is also mapped onto the subject function. What is important to note here is that the relationship between the three levels of representation is not necessarily linear. This is what poses a challenge for language learners.

In the following, we present the second conceptual cornerstone of PT, namely the 'Blueprint for the Speaker' as proposed by Levelt (1989).

The Blueprint for the Speaker (Levelt, 1989)

Levelt's model of speech processing (first presented in 1989) covers the range of processes from the initial conceptualization of a message until its final articulation. The model is based on the view of the (adult) monolingual speaker as a complex information processor who transforms propositions into linguistic form. This transformation process happens **incrementally**, i.e. in a stepwise fashion, drawing upon and passing through three modules: the Conceptualizer, the Formulator and the

Mapping process	Structures	Example			These pieces of information have to be unified and linearized by drawing on mapping principles – if acquired.
Linear default mapping	a-structure	*play*	< agent	patient/theme >	
	f-structure		SUBJ	OBJ	
	c-structure		*John* NP$_{subj}$	played *the guitar* NP$_{obj}$	

Figure 12.5 Linear default mapping
Source: Lenzing (2013: 94).

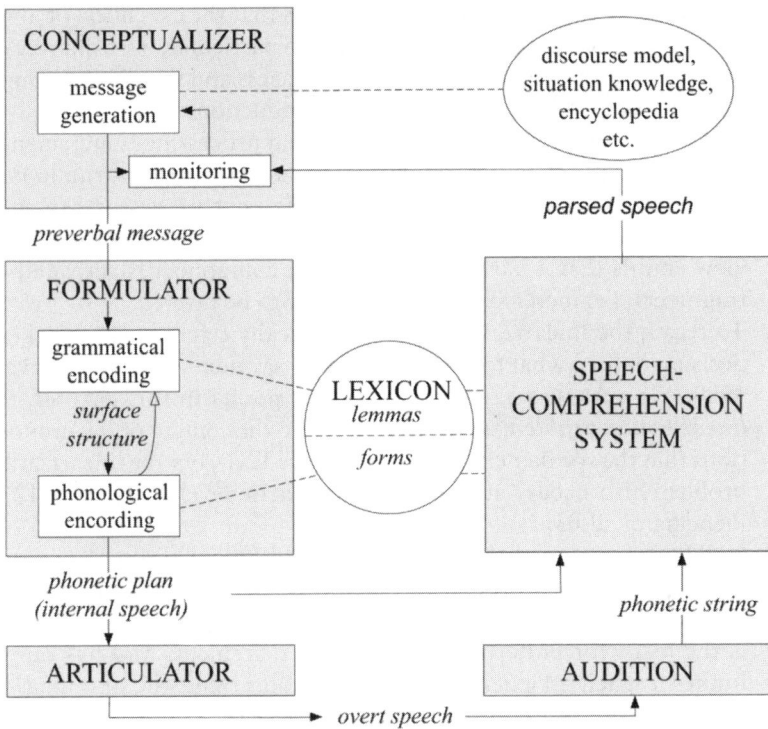

Figure 12.6 A blueprint for the speaker
Source: Levelt (1989: 9).

Articulator. What is important in the context of PT is that the central role Levelt assigns to the mental lexicon (see Figure 12.6), is in line with the key assumption in LFG that grammars are lexically driven.

As PT is mainly concerned with the acquisition of morphology and syntax and with the role of the lexicon in SLA, the theory focuses on the Formulator, where 'the grammatical encoding of the preverbal message' (Pienemann, 1998: 55) takes place. Grammatical encoding is particularly relevant in terms of linearization as is shown at a later point in this chapter. We now summarize the key assumptions of Levelt's model of speech processing, as these constitute part of the theoretical foundations of PT.

(i) Processing components are relatively autonomous specialists which operate largely automatically.
(ii) Processing is incremental.
(iii) The output of the processor is linear, while it may not be mapped onto the underlying meaning in a linear way.
(iv) Grammatical processing has access to a grammatical memory store.
(Pienemann, 2005: 3f.)

(i)   Based on Levelt (1989: 20ff.), PT assumes that the execution of auto-
       matic processes, grammatical encoding in particular, does not rely on
       the speaker's intention or conscious awareness and therefore accounts
       for the observed high speed of speech production.
(ii)   The underlying idea of the assumption that processing is incremental
       is that conceptualizing, formulating and articulating can run in par-
       allel or, as Levelt (1989: 24) puts it, 'the next processor can start
       working on the still-incomplete output of the current processor'. This
       view entails that a particular processing component is activated by
       fragments, i.e. increments of the message to be uttered.
(iii) To recap, the linearization problem basically refers to the speaker's
       decision of '[…] what to say first, what to say next and so on' (Levelt,
       1989: 138). As was explained at earlier points in this chapter, the
       linearization problem is not just limited to the content of the proposi-
       tions that the speaker expresses (see Figure 12.1), but the linearization
       problem also occurs at the morphosyntactic level (see Figure 12.8;
       Pienemann, 2005: 5).
(iv)   In PT, it is assumed that there are two different types of memory
       involved in speech processing. Working memory (Baddeley *et al.*,
       2009; see also de Leeuw *et al.* and Wright's chapters in this volume)
       is the locus for buffering propositional increments and has only a
       limited capacity. Pienemann (2005: 6) notes that: 'the grammatical
       memory store is a requirement that arises from the automatic (i.e.
       inattentive) nature of grammatical processing: grammatical proces-
       sors handle highly specific information which the grammatical
       memory store can hold temporarily.'

Now we turn to how the concepts outlined above in terms of language
generation in general apply to the process of SLA. In particular, we address
the interplay between the assumptions underlying LFG and language production as spelled out by Levelt. We then outline how the application of
these theoretical approaches to interlanguage development is reflected in
the implicational hierarchy in PT (see Table 12.1).

Production constrains second language acquisition

As mentioned at an earlier point in this chapter, the cognitive tasks
underlying the message generation process, in particular the linearization
problem, are accomplished in and by memory. In terms of the acquisition
of an L2, Pienemann (1998 and elsewhere) claims that it is the architecture
of the human **language processor** (see Figure 12.7 below) which in turn
constrains the acquisition process.

In order to give the reader a better understanding of the relationship
between language production and SLA, we first provide a detailed picture
of the stages involved in the production of a sentence. In a next step, we

Conceptualiser

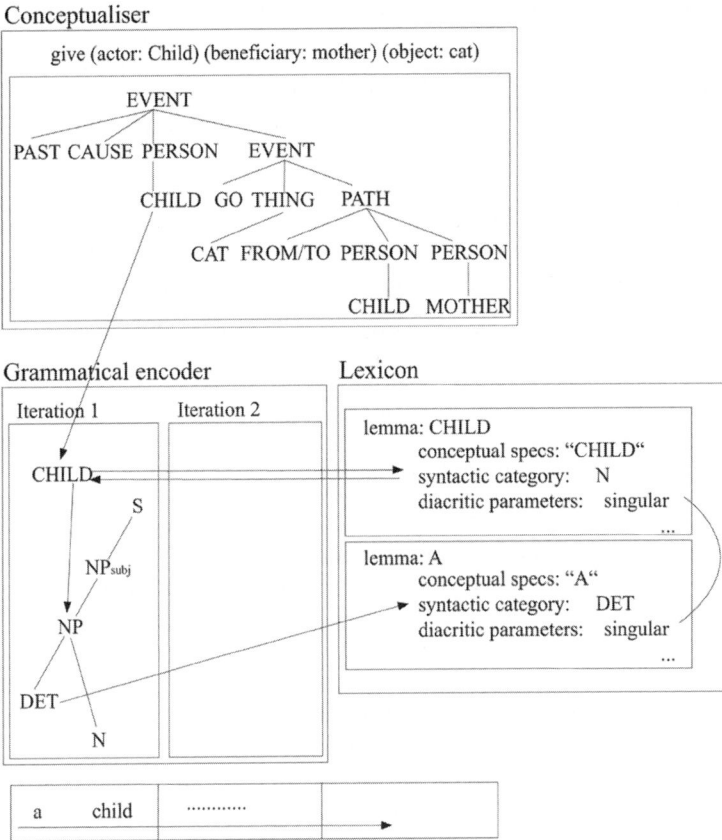

Figure 12.7 Incremental language generation
Source: Pienemann (1998: 68).

discuss the processing procedures applied to English as an L2 as spelled out by Pienemann (1998 and elsewhere).

The particular mechanisms underlying message generation that Pienemann argues to constrain the process of SLA take place predominantly in the Formulator. In line with Levelt (1989), Pienemann assumes that the message generation process is implicationally ordered and follows the sequence of processing procedures outlined below (see Pienemann & Lenzing, 2015: 163).

(1) no procedure
(2) category procedure
(3) noun phrase procedure
(4) verb phrase procedure
(5) sentence procedure
(6) subordinate clause procedure

The English NP 'the boy', for example, is built in a speaker's mind as follows:

(1) The lemma BOY is selected from the mental lexicon.
(2) Since the lemma contains categorical information (BOY = N(oun)), the category procedure N (noun) is triggered.
(3) The particular NP can be built in that 'possible complements and specifiers […] [as well as] diacritic features' (Pienemann, 1998: 67) are identified in order to be linked, as a last step, to the NP. In this case, the specifier 'the' would be selected and linked to 'boy'.

In PT, these processing procedures occur exactly as do those of grammatical encoding as spelled out by Levelt (1989):

> In Processability Theory a set of key grammatical encoding procedures are arranged according to their sequence of activation in the language generation process, and it is demonstrated that this sequence follows an implicational pattern in which each procedure is a necessary prerequisite for the following procedure. The basic thesis in Processability Theory is that in the acquisition of language processing procedures the assembly of the component parts will follow the above implicational sequence. (Pienemann, 1998: 6)

Incremental language generation

The principle of incrementality (Kempen & Hoenkamp, 1987; Levelt, 1989) plays a crucial role in PT's conceptualization of the process of L2 acquisition, and is explained in further detail here. Figure 12.7 shows the process of incremental language generation in some detail with the example sentence 'A child gave the mother a cat' (see Levelt, 1989: 236ff.; Pienemann, 1998: 65ff.).

In a first step, the underlying concepts of the sentence are generated in the Conceptualizer. Following this, the lemma CHILD is selected from the speaker's lexicon. The lemma's syntactic category N (noun) calls the respective categorical procedure NP (noun phrase), and in a next step the corresponding phrasal category NP is constructed with N as head. It is here that phrasal information is stored and the DET (determiner) is linked to the NP. Within the phrasal procedure, any necessary diacritic features of DET and N – in this case number – are unified. Following this, the relationship between the phrase and the rest of the sentence is created, with the sentence procedure containing interphrasal information (see Pienemann, 1998: 67, 2000: 105).

As mentioned before, the processing procedures outlined above are applied to L2 acquisition in PT, in this case to English as an L2. As shown in Figure 12.8, in terms of morphology, PT distinguishes between three types of morphemes: lexical, phrasal and interphrasal morphemes. As for lexical morphemes, such as the '-ed' in 'talked', the lemma contains the relevant diacritic features, in this case the feature 'past'. In addition, the

Stage	Information Exchange		
	Locus of exchange	Example	Illustration
Sentence	within sentence	Peter sees a dog	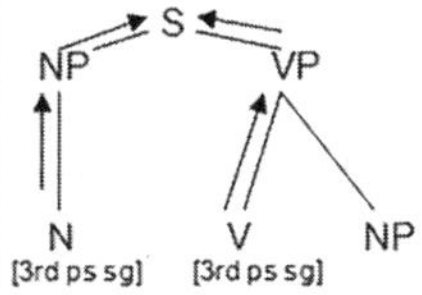 S; NP VP; N [3rd ps sg], V [3rd ps sg], NP
Phrase	within phrase only	two kids	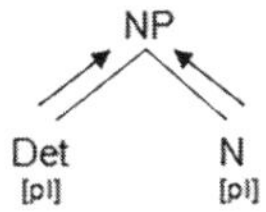 NP; Det [pl], N [pl]
Category	no exchange	talk-ed	V [past]

Figure 12.8 Information exchange
Source: Pienemann & Lenzing (2015: 162).

lexical category (verb) is present in the lemma so that the category procedure can be activated.

At this stage, however, no features have to be unified. Therefore, in the processability hierarchy for English, lexical morphemes occur at Stage 2 in the learner's interlanguage. In the case of phrasal morphemes (e.g. the 'plural -s' as in the NP 'two kids'), grammatical information has to be exchanged between constituents. This process of feature unification requires the phrasal procedure. In the case of the noun phrase 'two kids', feature unification has to occur between the DET 'two' and the N 'kids' (cf. Pienemann, 1998: 171). In line with this, phrasal morphemes occur at Stage 3.

Finally, in the case of interphrasal morphemes, grammatical information has to be exchanged across constituent boundaries, as in the case of Subject-Verb agreement (e.g. the '3sg -s' in the sentence 'Peter sees a dog'). Here, grammatical information is exchanged between the subject and the verb, and thus across constituent boundaries (Pienemann, 1998: 172). This exchange of grammatical information requires the sentence or S-procedure. Thus, the learner cannot process SV-agreement marking ('3sg -s') until s/he reaches Stage 5 (Pienemann, 1998: 172). Once the learner has acquired the relevant procedure required for the processing of a specific structure, s/he is in principle able to produce the respective structure (e.g. the progressive '-ing'). However, this does not mean that the learner is able to produce the structure in all obligatory contexts, and it is not necessarily the case that s/he uses the respective form in a target-like way.

234 Part 3: Transitions in Acquisition

In this context, Pienemann points out that 'the observed sequence of acquisition (lexical before phrasal before interphrasal morphemes) is predicted by the processability of the morphological structures under investigation' (Pienemann, 2000: 112). The issue of predictability is addressed in further detail below in terms of implications for language teaching.

The syntactic structures occurring in the PT hierarchy for English as an L2 (see Table 12.1) can also be accounted for by LFG. This means that the syntactic structures that L2 learners are able to produce at a specific stage of their interlanguage development can be accounted for by language-specific word order rules and in terms of feature unification. As regards sentence formation, L2 learners of English begin with canonical SVO word order (Stage 2), since at this point of the acquisition process, grammatical information exchange is not yet possible. In the course of L2 acquisition, word order rules are modified and annotated in specific ways to allow for the occurrence of words of a particular category (e.g. *wh*-words or adverbs) in a specific position in the sentence. This leads to the learner being able to produce 'Do-SVO-?' question forms at Stage 3 (phrasal procedure), as the specific positions in the sentence need to be processed as phrases (e.g. 'Do you play volleyball?'). The 'Aux 2nd' question form (e.g. 'What do you collect?') is located at Stage 5 of the processability hierarchy, since in this case the exchange of grammatical information occurs between the constituents of the sentence and thus requires the interphrasal procedure.

Extended Processability Theory: Mapping processes

Whereas Pienemann's (1998) version of PT focused on constituent structure and the exchange of grammatical information using feature unification, the extended version (Pienemann *et al.*, 2005) also takes other aspects of language generation into account. In particular, Pienemann *et al.* (2005) focus on the mapping processes between the different levels of linguistic representation outlined above to account for the linguistic non-linearity of a wide range of linguistic phenomena, such as the passive. The linearization problem also applies to the linking of the information encoded in a- (argument), f- (functional) and c- (constituent) structure. As pointed out by Pienemann *et al.* (2005: 201), the relationship between these three levels is not necessarily linear, as there is considerable surface structure variation, such as active and passive forms, or affirmative sentences and questions. These are accounted for by different mapping principles (see Pienemann *et al.*, 2005: 201). This is captured in the **Lexical Mapping Hypothesis** and the **Topic Hypothesis**.

With regard to the developing L2 system, the core hypothesis of PT is the following: at the beginning of the L2 acquisition process, the relationship between the three levels of representation (a-, f- and c-structure) is

Mapping process	Structures	Example
Linear default mapping	a-structure	*play* < agent patient/theme >
	f-structure	SUBJ OBJ
	c-structure	*John* played *the guitar* NP_subj NP_obj

Figure 12.9 Linear mapping
Source: Lenzing (2013: 94).

linear. This is illustrated in Figure 12.9 with the example sentence 'John played the guitar'.

The linear mapping between the different levels of representation results in **Unmarked Alignment**. In terms of PT this is assumed to be the initial state of L2 development (Pienemann & Lenzing, 2015: 168; Pienemann *et al.*, 2005: 145). However, there are structural options to express an intended message other than to use declarative sentences adhering to SVO word order. For instance, the same idea can be expressed using the passive voice. In this case, the focus is on the entity that is being played, i.e. 'the guitar' rather than on the actor 'John', resulting in the sentence 'The guitar was played by John'.

Figure 12.10 shows that in the case of the passive, the relation between arguments and grammatical functions is no longer linear, as the agent is not mapped onto the SUBJ (subject) function. Instead, it is the patient argument that is mapped onto the SUBJ function and that occurs as the initial NP in the sentence. The agent is mapped onto the grammatical function 'oblique' and is realized as a prepositional phrase at the level of c-structure. In terms of processing, this structure is more complex than active sentences adhering to SVO word order due to the non-linearity between a-structure and f-structure mapping, as illustrated by the crossed arrows in Figure 12.10. The increasingly complex relationship between arguments and grammatical functions is accounted for in the Lexical Mapping Hypothesis, which makes predictions concerning the processability of structures involving non-linear a- to f-structure mapping, such as the passive.

A second hypothesis – the Topic Hypothesis – deals with the relationship between c-structure and f-structure, i.e. between constituents and grammatical functions. This hypothesis predicts that initially the first NP in c-structure is mapped onto the SUBJ function, as the learner does not differentiate between SUBJ and TOPIC, a discourse function that entails known information. In English, this results in canonical

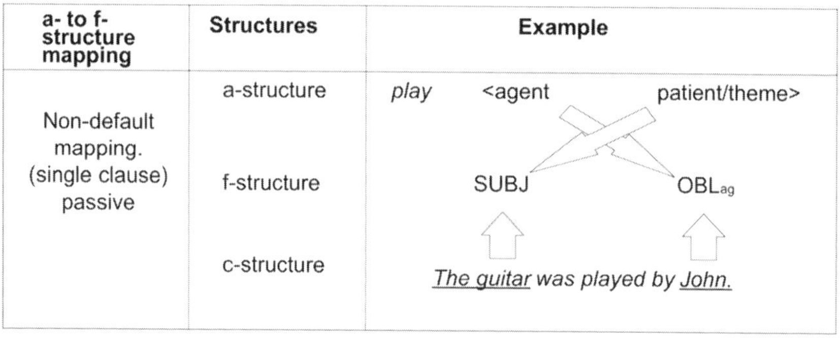

a- to f-structure mapping	Structures	Example
Non-default mapping. (single clause) passive	a-structure	*play* <agent patient/theme>
	f-structure	SUBJ OBL$_{ag}$
	c-structure	*The guitar was played by John.*

Figure 12.10 Non-linear mapping in passive constructions
Source: Lenzing (2013: 103).

SVO sentences. At a later stage, the linear correspondence between constituents and grammatical functions is altered and adjuncts such as adverbs and certain *wh*-words can occur in sentence-initial position. In this case, the relation between c-structure and f-structure is no longer linear, as the initial NP does not bear the subject function. Finally, the TOPIC function is assigned to a core argument that is not the subject (see Pienemann & Lenzing, 2015: 169f.; Pienemann *et al.*, 2005). This applies for instance to the topicalization of objects as exemplified in Figure 12.11.

The initial second language mental grammatical system

As outlined above and as can be seen from Table 12.1, it is assumed in PT that at the very beginning of the L2 acquisition process no L2 processing procedures are available to the learner. This results in the production of single words (e.g. 'Max', 'football') and formulaic utterances (e.g. 'What's your name?'). However, when examining the oral performance

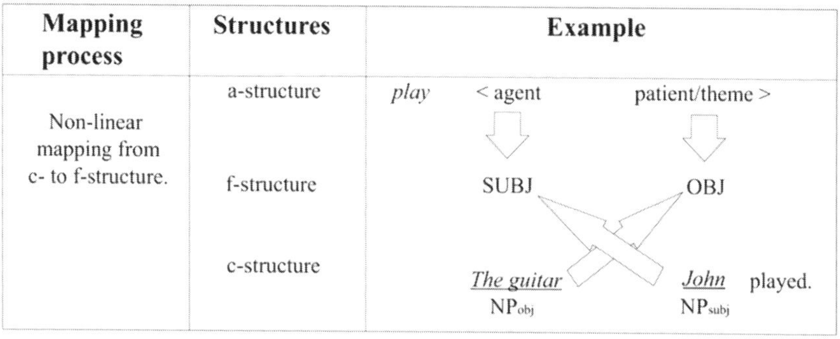

Mapping process	Structures	Example
Non-linear mapping from c- to f-structure.	a-structure	*play* < agent patient/theme >
	f-structure	SUBJ OBJ
	c-structure	*The guitar* *John* played. NP$_{obj}$ NP$_{subj}$

Figure 12.11 Non-linear mapping: Object topicalization
Source: Lenzing (2013: 100).

data of early L2 learners, it can be observed that their interlanguage is much more diverse than it seems at first glance, displaying a range of non-target-like utterances. These utterances do not only deviate syntactically from the target language. In fact, early learners also use idiosyncratic structures which are semantically ill-formed and diverge from the target language as regards the arguments that learners express; i.e. the utterances contain either too many or too few arguments or entirely different arguments from those the learner intends to express. This is illustrated in Table 12.2, which contains utterances produced by early L2 learners of English with German as L1 at primary school level.

To account for these utterances, Lenzing (2013, 2015) proposes a model of the initial L2 mental grammatical system and spells out which linguistic resources the L2 learner can draw on at the initial state of L2 acquisition. The basic premise of this explanatory account of the initial L2 mental grammatical system is the **Multiple Constraints Hypothesis** (MCH), which is based on LFG and PT. The MCH constitutes a conceptual extension of PT, and its core claim is that the initial L2 mental grammatical system is highly constrained in terms of processability. It is hypothesized that the L2 grammatical system is not fully developed at the beginning of L2 acquisition in terms of **mental representations**. The restrictions of this underdeveloped system affect the different levels of linguistic representation as postulated in LFG (a-, f- and c-structure). The restrictions cause problems for the L2 learner in terms of processing and thus shape her/his language production. The **constraints** of the L2 grammatical system also influence the two core processes of feature unification and mapping outlined above which are required to align the semantic and syntactic information encoded at the different levels of linguistic representation. As essential features and functions are underdeveloped or missing at the start of SLA, the two processes cannot be carried out. The explanatory power of the model of the L2 mental grammatical system presented here is that it states exactly which levels of the mental grammar are underdeveloped and in what ways these levels are restricted (see Lenzing, 2013, 2015). The core claims of the MCH are summarized in Figure 12.12.

Table 12.2 Types of deviations in L2 interlanguage

(1) Syntactically	*Ski the mouse* (=The mouse is skiing) (Learner C18)
(2) Semantically	*What's the spaghetti?* (=Do you like spaghetti?) (Learner C02) *What's you {ne}* sister?* (=Do you have a sister?) (Learner C03)
(3) Number of arguments (participants in event)	*sleeping on the {wolk}†*. (=The elephant is sleeping on the cloud) (Learner C09) *She likes you spinach?* (=Do you like spinach?) (Learner C08)

Notes: *ne = a; †wolk = cloud.

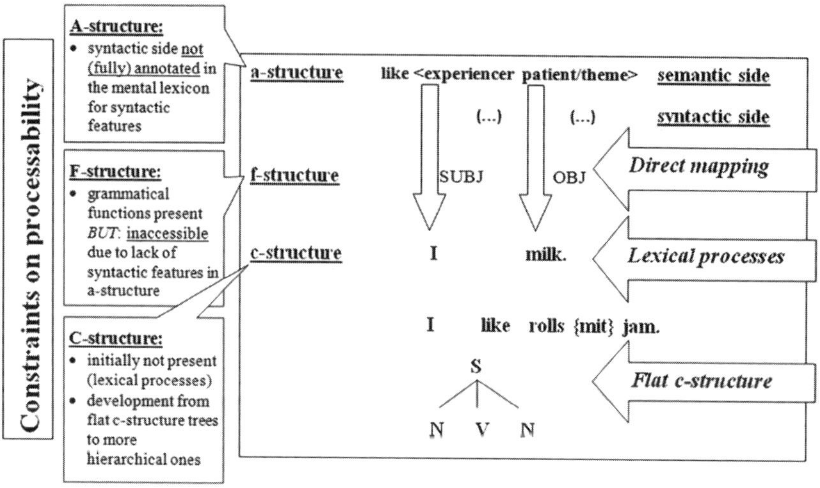

Figure 12.12 The Multiple Constraints Hypothesis
Source: Adapted and modified from Lenzing (2013: 8).

We can now view the constraints proposed in the MCH as they apply to SLA.

Constraints

a-structure: The restrictions at this level primarily affect the syntactic side of a-structure, i.e. the syntactic information which is essential to link arguments to grammatical functions in f-structure. This information is claimed to be underdeveloped or missing. It follows from this that, initially, L2 learners are not able to map arguments onto grammatical functions and instead rely on direct mapping processes from arguments to surface form.

f-structure: The universal grammatical functions (SUBJ, OBJ, etc.) are claimed to be present in the initial L2 mental grammatical system. However, the grammatical functions are assumed to be inaccessible, as the missing features at a-structure level inhibit the mapping process from arguments to grammatical functions. This results in direct mapping processes from a- to f-structure, i.e. from arguments to surface form.

c-structure: C-structure is assumed to develop gradually in the L2 acquisition process following the predictions spelled out in PT. This means that initially no c-structure is present in the L2 learner's mind. Its gradual development is characterized by basic, flat c-structures to more complex, hierarchical ones (see Figure 12.12 above).

Lexicon   The lexicon is being gradually annotated in the L2 learner's mind. This means that initially not all lexical items are annotated for their syntactic category (e.g. noun, verb), resulting in utterances such as * 'It's a pink?' (Learner 06). It is also hypothesized that not all verbs are annotated for both number and type of arguments they take (e.g. agent, patient). This leads to utterances with missing arguments, such as * 'sleeping on the {wolk}' (=The elephant is sleeping on the cloud) (Learner C09), or utterances with too many arguments, such as * 'I'm skiing the mouse' (=The mouse is skiing) (Learner C10).

The MCH and its specific claims about the nature of the L2 initial mental grammatical system and its subsequent development were tested against empirical data in a combined cross-sectional and longitudinal study of 24 beginning German L2 learners of English at primary school level (Lenzing, 2013). Oral speech production data were collected using communicative tasks after one and after two years of classroom instruction. The results of the detailed analysis of both argument and constituent structure support the claims of the MCH. In general, it can be seen that the learners in the study are still at the very beginning of their L2 acquisition process. The analysis of the learner data at the first round of data collection, after one year, reveals that the structures they produced are mainly restricted to single words, formulaic sequences and idiosyncratic utterances. This is exemplified in Table 12.3 with utterances produced by Learner C15.

At the second time of data collection, after two years of instruction, the structures consist of SVO structures and both structurally and lexically restricted question forms. This is illustrated in Table 12.4, which depicts utterances produced by the same learner (C15) after two years of instruction.

Table 12.3 Learner utterances after one year of instruction: Learner C15

C15	Grade 3 (one year of instruction)
	My name is [...].
	I'm fine.
	What's colour?
	Do you I am animal? (=Do you have an animal?)
	Snake?
	Seven teeth

Table 12.4 Learner utterances after two years of instruction: Learner C15

C15	Grade 4 (two years of instruction)
	My mouse ski.
	I have a bird.
	The mouse and the elephant is eat spaghetti.
	Have you a bee?
	Have Max a cap?
	Has Max a red trouser?

The analysis shows that the structures produced by learners after two years of instruction are based on:

(1) *Lexical operations*: this applies to single words, formulaic sequences and idiosyncratic structures. It is assumed that no syntactic sentence generation processes are involved in these structures.
(2) *Simplified constituent structure*: this applies to SVO structures (*'The elephant sleep' (Learner C14)), and restricted question forms ('Do you play football?', 'Do you like milk?' (Learner C12), 'Have you yellow and white boots' (Learner C15)).

The study also demonstrates that the postulated constraints decrease successively as L2 acquisition progresses. This results in a gradual development in early learner language from formulaic speech towards more productive utterances (see Tables 12.3 and 12.4; see also Lenzing & Roos, 2012). This development is in accordance with the predictions made by PT as well as the MCH.

Teaching

As discussed above, PT describes and explains the acquisition of an L2 as a gradual and implicational process. In contrast to Krashen (1982; see also Krashen & Terrell, 1983) and in line with more recent SLA publications (e.g. Ellis, 2008b; Keßler *et al.*, 2011; Mansouri & Duffy, 2005; Pienemann, 1998, 2011), from the psycholinguistic perspective taken in this chapter, no distinction is made between acquisition and learning. For at least 25 years it has been known that learners indeed follow the same universal and predictable developmental path regardless of the setting (i.e. in natural as well as in instructed settings; see, for example, Ellis, 1990; Hawkins, 2001).

The idea that acquiring an L2 is constrained by the architecture of the human language processor is far from new (see Pienemann, 1984, 1985). At an earlier point in this chapter the constraints on learnability were sketched out in detail. Keeping those constraints in mind, it is not surprising to see that L2 learners do not always learn what they are taught and that they sometimes produce structures they have neither been taught nor which have occurred in their input. This led Allwright (1984) to ask 'Why don't learners learn what teachers teach?' This does not mean that learners' production is random; sentences like the following, produced by learners who have not yet acquired a certain structure, illustrate a systematic interlanguage in operation:

(1) I putted the plates on the table. (Lightbown & Spada, 2006)
(2) Where Ø you live? (Pienemann, 2006)
(3) He do his homework every day. (Pienemann, 2006)

Sentence (1) is an example of an **overgeneralization** of a rule the learner has discovered, the 'past -*ed*' rule before s/he has acquired the concept of irregular verbs. Sentences (2) and (3) are examples produced by learners who have not yet reached Stage 5 of the PT hierarchy which provides the learner with the processing prerequisites needed to produce target-like structures.

Taking the PT perspective as explained in detail in this chapter into account, Allwright's question can be revised and reversed by asking: 'Why don't teachers teach what learners are ready for?' (Keßler *et al.*, 2011: 149). It is argued that instruction that follows the predictable sequence of acquisition will be beneficial for instructed SLA.

The Teachability Hypothesis

As discussed above, today it is known and widely accepted in the field of SLA that teaching cannot alter the sequence of acquisition (Pienemann, 1998; see also Norris & Ortega, 2000). In 1984 Pienemann first put forward what has become known as the Teachability Hypothesis, which was then incorporated into the larger concept of PT by Pienemann in 1998:

> ... instruction can only promote language acquisition if the interlanguage is close to the point when the structure to be taught is acquired in the natural setting (so sufficient processing resources are developed). (Pienemann, 1984: 37)

In other words, the Teachability Hypothesis predicts how the constraints on language processing and acquisition apply in instructed settings. In 1988 Long summarized the core concept of this hypothesis by simply stating that 'you can't skip stages'. There have been a number of studies testing the Teachability Hypothesis. Table 12.5 gives a more recent summary and evaluation of these studies, provided in Keßler *et al.* (2011: 151).

Additionally, a number of further studies can be found that clearly confirm that the developmental schedules as defined by PT apply in instructed settings and even are identical to the ones found in natural acquisition independent from the instruction the learners received during their instruction (e.g. Keßler, 2006; Lenzing, 2013; Pienemann, 1985, 1989; Pienemann *et al.*, 2006; Roos, 2007).

Table 12.5 A brief overview of teachability studies

Study	TL	Learners' L1	Design	Findings
Pienemann (1984)	German	Italian	Pre-test, Post-test control group design; whether stages can be skipped	Stages of acquisition cannot be skipped (Formulation of Teachability Hypothesis)
Ellis (1989)	German	English	Pre-test, Post-test control group design; formal versus naturalistic instruction	Support for Teachability Hypothesis
Boss (1996)	German	English/Chinese	Oral language production compared to taught syllabus as opposed to PT sequence	Learners progressed in the predicted order regardless of the taught syllabus
Spada and Lightbown (1999)	ESL	French	Pre-test, Post-test control group design; whether stages can be skipped	Inconclusive; no support for Teachability Hypothesis
Dyson (1996)	ESL	Spanish	Longitudinal study of ESL development based on teachable forms	Overall support for Teachability Hypothesis despite individual learner variation
Mansouri and Duffy (2005)	ESL	Chinese/Korean/Thai	Pre-test, Post-test control group design; developmental versus reversed order group	Support for Teachability Hypothesis

Source: Keßler et al. (2011: 151).

Concerning input in the foreign language classroom, it is vital that this input should cover a wide range of linguistic structures. This is necessary because hardly any foreign language classroom enjoys a homogenous group of learners. Even if at the starting point of instruction all learners are at the same stage of acquisition, due to the fact that the rate of acquisition is individual and can (if at all) be influenced by the teacher peripherally, learners will develop at different rates and their interlanguage will also vary (see Liebner & Pienemann, 2011; Pienemann, 1998, for details). Figure 12.13 illustrates the stages of acquisition and the heterogeneity of a typical EFL classroom at the end of the second year of instructed acquisition.

In Figure 12.13 each square represents one learner in this English as a Foreign Language classroom. As can be seen in this classroom, the range of stages reached is from a more or less standard-oriented Stage 2 up to a full and standard-oriented Stage 5 even though all learners in this classroom had received the same input in both quantity and quality. If a teacher decides to teach a certain exercise from a textbook, as often happens in the classroom, s/he cannot cater for all learners as this one exercise may be too difficult for some of the learners and not challenging at all for others.

In order to cater for all learners in one language classroom, teachers need not only to know the basics of SLA but also to be able to diagnose their learners' current state of interlanguage development. Once they know which stages their learners have attained, they also know what

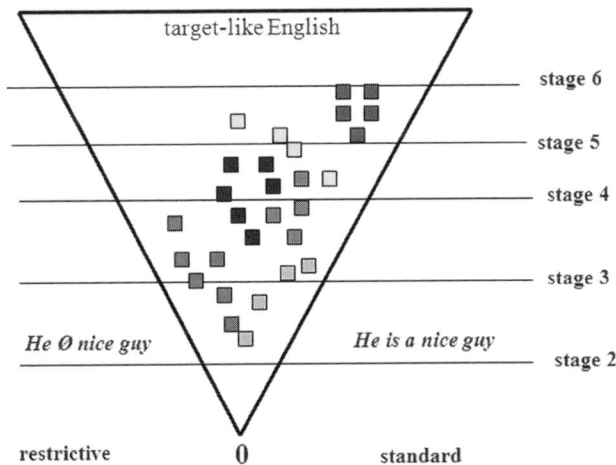

Figure 12.13 A heterogeneous EFL classroom (L1 German)

Notes: The illustration in this figure is based on the concept of Hypothesis Space (Pienemann, 1998), which depicts the range of possible interlanguage structures that can be produced by L2 learners at a given stage of development. For further details see Pienemann (1998, 2011). Source: Keßler (2009: 97).

structures these particular learners are ready to acquire next. What teachers can then do is to provide more open tasks that can be solved by all their learners at the same time but which allow each individual learner to produce structures according to her/his current state of interlanguage. This issue will be dealt with in further detail after introducing and discussing a diagnostic tool based on PT psycholinguistic research.

Diagnosing learner progress

As Pienemann and Keßler (2012) put it:

> the connection between PT and diagnosing language development is obvious. A theory that can account for developmental trajectories and that is based on an abundance of empirical research detailing standard developmental trajectories for a range of L2s […] is in an excellent position to serve as a point of reference for developmental linguistic profiles. (Pienemann & Keßler, 2012: 240)

Rapid Profile (e.g. Keßler, 2006, 2008; Keßler & Liebner, 2011; Pienemann, 1992) is a procedure which is theoretically underpinned by PT and which utilizes the developmental schedules specified by PT for L2 development. It enables a quick, valid and reliable online diagnosis for individual learners. The current version of Rapid Profile offers a refined and well-studied and tested computer-assisted screening procedure. It thus provides a diagnostic tool for online profile analyses of L2 English and also includes a prototype version for L2 German and L2 Turkish.

The use of Rapid Profiling requires training in the use of an inbuilt expert system of software to examine samples of spontaneous speech collected from learners by, for example, the teacher in semi-formal interviews with them. Interviews are conducted along a set of well-designed **diagnostic task**s which provide obligatory contexts for the morphosyntactic structures under scrutiny (see Keßler, 2008; Pienemann, 1998: 280). Basic features of the software comprise a detailed online feedback on the current state of the (inter-)language stage of the learner including background information on verb, noun and pronoun morphology found in that learner's speech sample. Figure 12.14 shows a screenshot of the user interface of the software. The highlighted boxes at the top of this user interface indicate the developmental stages reached by the learner. Figure 12.15 provides more detailed background information on the verb morphology of the same learner. It lists all the verbs found in the speech sample and reveals the verb forms produced by the learner.

While listening to the speech sample (which can either be done directly during the interview or alternatively can be played back at any time as all interviews are recorded), the trained analyst keys in the structures provided by the learner. A ' + ' symbolizes a structure produced by the learner; the ' − ' button is clicked when a structure was not

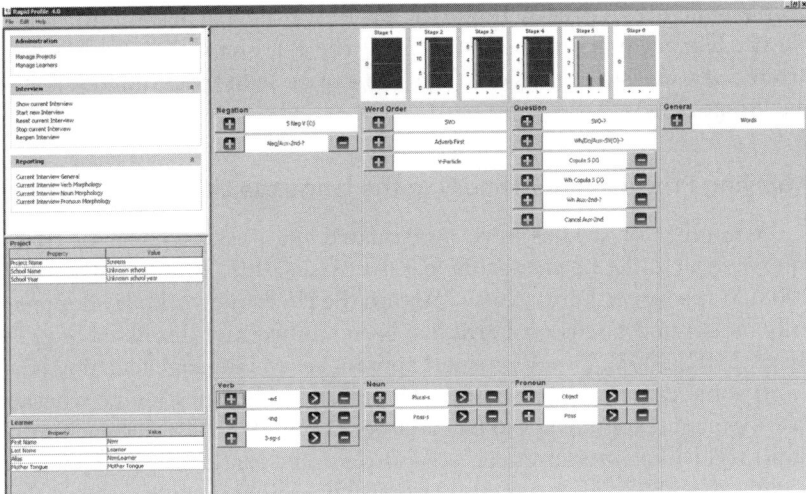

Figure 12.14 User interface of Rapid Profile 4.0

provided by the learner in an obligatory context for the structure. The ' > ' stands for an overproduction of a morphological structure (e.g. 'goed'). In order to calculate the level of target-language development, the software applies the **emergence criterion** of L2 acquisition (i.e. the first productive use – i.e. not a **formulaic use** – of a particular structure); see Pienemann (1998: 144ff.). At the end of the procedure, Rapid

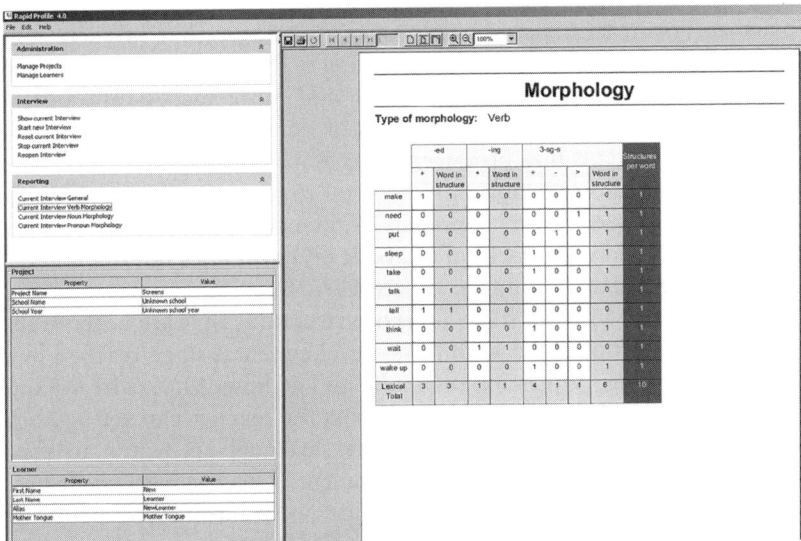

Figure 12.15 Feedback screen on verb morphology (Rapid Profile 4.0)

Profile generates a precise linguistic profile of the learner. In our example the learner has attained Stage 4 of the PT hierarchy and has also produced some structures of Stage 5 as can be seen from the first bar in the 'Stage 5' box.

Applying Processability Theory to the language classroom

A number of studies have investigated the positive effect of timed intervention in the L2 classroom (e.g. Di Biase, 2002, 2008; Keßler, 2007, 2008; Mansouri & Duffy, 2005). Within the PT framework, developmentally moderated **Focus on Form** has been studied and discussed (e.g. Di Biase, 2002, 2008). Developmental approaches to language teaching have faced some criticism, especially with regard to the question of whether developmental approaches to L2 classrooms would include the teaching of non-target-like interlanguage structures (see, for example, Spada & Lightbown, 1999). However, this criticism does not take into account that any teaching of a foreign language from a PT perspective does not at all advocate a strict application of the implicational hierarchy of developmental stages in the input, but rather a well-advised operationalization of the developmental hierarchy with regard to learner output. (For a full discussion of this issue, see Keßler et al., 2011.)

Developmentally moderated Focus on Form?

Focus on Form is a widely accepted approach to L2 teaching (Doughty & Williams, 1998). However, the question remains which form to focus on at a given point in time (Keßler, 2008). This is why Di Biase (2002, 2008) developed the concept of a developmentally moderated approach to Focus on Form. In his study he provides evidence that learners who received form-focused instruction according to their current state of interlanguage development proceeded faster and more successfully up the developmental hierarchy both in terms of development and variation. Current linguistic profiles produced using Rapid Profile (see above) support teachers in choosing appropriate forms to focus on. By doing so, the traditional Focus on Form approach is extended to beneficially timed instruction. Obviously, this kind of Focus on Form does not imply focus on non-target-like interlanguage structures such as a Stage 3 question (e.g. 'What Ø you like?') but a focus on those structures that are both target-like and standard-oriented within the developmental stage reached by a learner (e.g. a Stage 3 question such as 'Can I go home?'). As already suggested above, in heterogeneous classrooms the teacher can set up communicative tasks that can be solved by learners according to their individual stage of interlanguage development. This has been spelled out in detail by Keßler (2008). A short summary of what interfaces between PT and Task-based Language Teaching (TBLT) might look like is provided in the next section.

Interfaces between Task-based Language Teaching and Processability Theory

TBLT (e.g. Ellis, 2003; Willis & Willis, 2007) is a promising approach to foreign language teaching, especially when applied in heterogeneous classrooms. From a PT perspective, TBLT works best when based on a detailed profile analysis (Keßler, 2008; Pienemann & Keßler, 2012). The latest version of Rapid Profile incorporates various databases, one of them providing the teacher with a set of well-researched communicative tasks. These tasks can be used for profile analysis as well as treatment in the foreign language classroom. As Rapid Profile yields linguistic profiles based on individual learners' interlanguage samples, these profiles can be the starting point of an extended approach to TBLT on a valid diagnostic basis. This extended task-based approach can be understood as a diagnostic task cycle: after a range of communicative tasks based on a first Rapid Profile diagnosis have been administered in the L2 classroom, a second round of linguistic profiling evaluates the progress in learners' development and, at the same time, serves as a new diagnosis for further task-based activities (Keßler, 2008). Figure 12.16 provides an outline of this diagnostic task cycle.

The diagnostic task cycle starts with the linguistic profiles from application of Rapid Profile as the diagnostic basis for pedagogical language learning tasks. Once the teacher is familiar with learners' current stages of interlanguage development, the task-as-workplan (Seedhouse, 2005) phase begins with pre-task activities in the classroom. Before the actual language learning task can be set up, the teacher has to provide a setting for successful interactive language learning in the classroom. This is accomplished by pre-task activities. Here, the teacher can, for example,

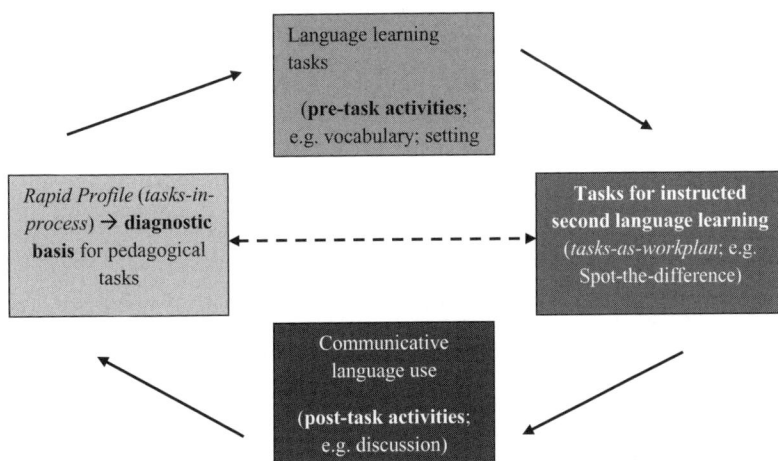

Figure 12.16 Outline of the diagnostic task cycle
Source: Keßler (2008: 301); Keßler and Plesser (2011: 234).

provide the necessary lexical items for learners to be able to work on communicative tasks. Once the setting has been established, the class can proceed to the actual task work. One example is working in pairs on a spot-the-difference task where each learner produces language according to his/her current stage of interlanguage. Thus, TBLT from a PT perspective is output oriented as language production is stipulated by the interaction between individual learners making use of their interlanguage. Whenever the teacher needs to intervene in terms of correcting individual learners within or after the task, this can best be done by providing developmentally moderated Focus on Form as sketched out above.

Conclusion

This chapter has focused on the psycholinguistic theory of SLA called Processability Theory. We have introduced its psycholinguistic basis – Levelt's model of speech processing – as well as its grammatical formalism, Lexical-Functional Grammar. Based on these theoretical premises, PT provides an explanation for the well-attested finding that learners follow the same developmental path in the L2 acquisition of specific morphosyntactic structures. The core of PT is formed by the PT hierarchy, which consists of specific processing procedures. These procedures unfold successively in the L2 learner's mind and their acquisition enables the learner to process target-language specific morphosyntactic features. Recent developments of the theory also address the question of which linguistic resources are available to the learner in the L2 initial state, i.e. at the very beginning of the acquisition process.

In the last third of this chapter, we have shown that PT has a strong connection to teaching practice. It can be fruitfully applied in the L2 classroom, for the diagnosis of learners' stages of development as they reach each stage as well as for pedagogical approaches, methods and techniques in the classroom. We have shown that language teaching which is in line with the stages of acquisition as put forward in PT may be beneficial for the acquisition process both in the pace of acquisition and in the acquisition of a more standard-oriented interlanguage by the learner.

Note

(1) Clearly, the role of formulaic language in SLA is more complex than the early occurrence of formulaic utterances in L2 learner language suggests. The acquisition of formulaic language is not restricted to early SLA, and the development of formulaic language in the course of SLA does not necessarily constitute a linear process. A further issue that we will not address in this chapter relates to the use of formulaic language by native speakers. The point we would like to make concerning formulaic language in early SLA is that from a processing perspective, initially formulaic utterances are stored as holistic units in the mental lexicon and are not the process of syntactic operations.

Glossary

Accentedness: The idea that a speaker's accent is perceived to differ from a listener's target or standard accent, usually measured as a judgement on a scale from more to less similar to the target.

Acoustic analysis: Measurement of sound waves in terms of properties such as duration, frequency and amplitude.

Acoustic memory: Short-term temporary memory storage holding acoustic information (e.g. pitch) for 250–350 milliseconds prior to the phonological encoding of sounds.

Adaptive pressure: See (neo-)Darwinian

Adjective: A word class defined in traditional grammar as a 'describing word' because it expresses an attribute to a noun, either by modifying a noun in the Noun Phrase (*the happy unicorn*) or following a verb like *be* or *seems* and attributing something of the subject (*Andrew seems happy*); they are found in most languages, and are usually open class, in that it is relatively easy to coin new examples. English examples: *pretty, conventional, remarkable, nice*.

Adjective Phrase: A constituent that is headed by an adjective; it appears in any position that an adjective can appear in and includes any words or phrases that modify the head (*he seems remarkably happy about things*; *that is a very nice shirt*).

Adverb: A word class defined in traditional grammar as 'describing the action of a verb' (*he ran quickly*), but may also modify a whole clause in English (*Unfortunately, he died.*); in English, an adverb often ends in *-ly*.

Algorithm: An explicit procedure with consecutive steps that will result in the solution to a specific problem.

Allomorph: Any of the different forms of a bound morpheme. For example, in English for the plural suffix, the *s*-morpheme, e.g. *cats, dogs* and *forces*, the allomorphs are phonetically presented by [s], [z] and [ɪz].

Alveolar: A consonant produced by the front of the tongue touching or nearly touching the gum (alveolar) ridge behind the upper teeth.

Anaphora: The phenomenon of a word or phrase referring back to another word or phrase which was used earlier in a text or conversation. The word or phrase that refers back is an **anaphor**, and the word or phrase that the anaphor refers back to is its **antecedent**. In English, pronouns may be anaphors, e.g. *Tom likes ice cream but Bill can't eat it* (it = ice cream).

Antecedent: See **anaphora**.

Approximant: A consonant where articulators are narrowed (e.g. for English /l/ or /r/) but without as much turbulence as for a **fricative**.

Argument structure/a-structure: The core participants of an event referring to who does what to whom. It contains the verb and its corresponding arguments which take specific thematic roles, such as agent or patient. A-structure is partly language-specific in that the number of arguments a verb takes varies across languages.

Attention control: Cognitive flexibility that allows individuals to regulate their thoughts and behaviours, allowing individuals to switch flexibly between tasks or mental sets such as linguistic functions.

Audio-lingual drilling: A technique used in classroom foreign language teaching to practise sounds or sentence patterns in a language through repetition.

Bark: A psychoacoustic measure of acoustic vowel quality obtained by converting vowel formant frequencies from a linear Hertz (Hz) scale to a band rate scale, more accurately representing acoustic differences in human perception.

British Picture Vocabulary Scales/Peabody Picture Vocabulary Test: Standardized picture selection tasks that test children's vocabulary knowledge in British and American English, respectively.

Call systems: The vocalizations that primates make in response to specific stimuli. Vervet monkeys, for example, have a range of distinct vocal signals that each correspond to different predators, eliciting different reactions in each case from the other monkeys in the group. Animal call systems are generally regarded as being non-compositional. See **compositional**.

Clause: The formal term for a constituent that consists of a subject and a predicate and some element of tense; it may be a *main* clause (*I liked London*) or a *subordinate* clause (embedded clause) inside another constituent, e.g. a sentence (*I knew that you would like London*).

Clitic pronouns: Pronouns that attach themselves to verbs, as in *lo* and *el* in Spanish *No lo tengo* '(I) don't have it.' vs. *No tengo el libro* '(I) don't have the book.'

Coda: The end of a syllable, usually the consonant(s) that follow the nucleus (the peak or centre of the syllable, usually a vowel).

Code-mixing: The transfer of linguistic elements from one language into another, within a sentence, e.g. when a sentence starts in one language and includes a word or phrase from another.

Competence: The passive, subconscious knowledge a speaker has of a language that they have acquired, regardless of how they might use the language in performance.

Complementizer: A word class also termed 'subordinating conjunction' in traditional grammars, introducing a subordinate clause (*I know that you're doing your best; I hope for you to become friends*).

Compositional: Objects which can be freely combined with each other to contribute to the meaning of the overall structure. This contrasts with **non-compositional** units which are meaningful on their own but do not combine with other units to produce novel meanings, for example the **call systems** of primates.

Comprehensibility: The listener's perception of difficulty in understanding a given utterance, usually measured on a scale from less to more difficult.

Comprehension task: An experimental task that aims to examine a specific aspect of language comprehension.

Constituent: A linguistic item or unit such as a word or phrase that forms part of a larger construction (e.g. clause); many syntactic processes apply to constituents rather than individual words.

Constituent structure: In Processability Theory, c(onstituent)-structure is the level at which syntactic aspects of language (features) are connected, representing the surface syntactic organization of utterances (see **Constituent**). C-structure is language specific, as the surface structure differs across languages.

Constraint: In Processability Theory, the restriction on learner grammar deriving from the capacity of the human language processor which means that a learner can only produce linguistic structures which are possible at the current stage of development, e.g. the unification of features at c-structure level.

Critical Period Hypothesis: The view that there is a limited biologically determined age span for language acquisition, generally ending around or before the onset of puberty. Used to argue that L2 achievement is limited if the L2 is learned after puberty. Also expressed as a more gradual 'sensitive' period, in view of evidence that there are individuals who reach native-like levels of an L2 after the presumed cut-off age.

Dark *l*: The velarized /l/ in standard English when /l/ takes on the quality of a back vowel which precedes it, before consonants or in final syllable position.

Darwinian (also **(neo-)Darwinian**): The established theory of evolution that species evolve by means of gradual, incremental genetic changes that bestow a selective advantage on an individual, i.e. one that is better suited to its environment in some way (to a particular adaptive pressure), and thus are more likely to live longer and reproduce more often, passing on more of their genes than other members of the species. Over time the gene that conferred this selective advantage will spread through that particular breeding group of the species.

Declarative knowledge: Knowledge of facts ('knowing that …'). In SLA often used to denote formally learnt language knowledge such as rules teachers use to explain, for example, the conjugation of verbs.

Demonstrative: A member of the word class **determiner** that appears as the first element in a Noun Phrase, signalling a degree of proximity or distance to the speaker and number (*I prefer <u>this</u> book to <u>that</u> book; <u>These</u> books are better than <u>those</u> ones*).

Derivational morphology: Morphology that contributes to the formation of new words from a root by adding an affix, e.g. a prefix to *do* to create *undo* or a suffix to create *doable*). Unlike in **inflectional morphology**, derivational affixes can change the grammatical class of morphemes (e.g. changing a noun such as *nation* to an adjective in English by adding *-al*; similarly, *-ment* derives the noun *establishment* from the verb *establish*).

Determiner: A word class that appears as the first element in a Noun Phrase, signalling the range of applicability (<u>the</u> *book*; <u>a</u> *habit*; <u>some</u> *habits*).

Developmental problem: A key issue in SLA research, which focuses on the question why every L2 learner follows a predictable developmental path in the acquisition of morphosyntax.

Diagnostic task cycle: In Processability Theory, an extended task-based analysis of stage of linguistic development, based on linguistic profile analysis.

Directional entailingness: A feature of determiners, which may be described as either **downward-entailing** (in which the direction is from less specific to more specific) or **upward-entailing** (in which the direction is from more specific to less specific).

Distractor/foil (see also **Filler**): An item in an experimental task that aims to distract the participant from giving a particular response; in picture selection tasks, there may be only one correct answer but multiple distractors (or fillers).

Distributed Morphology: An approach to morphology where morphological processes involve syntactic as well as phonological operations. Derivational Morphology contrasts with models which separate lexical and syntactic operations and assume a distinction between derivational and inflectional morphology.

Domain specific/general: See **Nativism**.

Downward entailment: See **Entailment**.

Elicited Imitation: A data collection procedure which aims to tap the learner's underlying knowledge by asking them to repeat a sentence which they hear. The person may make changes as they repeat the sentence and these changes will reflect their current linguistic knowledge when the sentence uses rules which they have not yet acquired.

Embedded clause: A clause that is inside another syntactic constituent, as opposed to a main clause that can stand alone (*I think <u>that he is a politician</u>; <u>That you didn't bother to call</u> really upset me*).

Emergence criterion: In Processability Theory, used to identify the productive use of a certain structure in the acquisition process of L2 grammatical forms.

Emergentism: The view that the properties of language (including syntactic 'rules') are not innate but emerge as a result of how the human brain perceives and processes input.

Empiricist theory: A view in which experience is seen as the ultimate source of learning; for language acquisition, an empirical approach assumes learners will generalize from experience.

Entailment: A term derived from formal logic and now used as part of the study of semantics; also called **entailingness** to refer to a relation between a pair of propositions such that the truth of the second proposition necessarily follows from (is **entailed** by) the truth of the first, e.g. *I can see a dog – I can see an animal*. One cannot both assert the first and deny the second.

Entrenchment: The strengthening of processing routines to the point where they operate automatically.

Episodic buffer: A limited-capacity memory system that is capable of integrating information from the storage subsystems and from long-term memory into a single episodic representation.

Episodic sentences: Sentences which refer to specific events, for example *The fire was fully extinguished by the use of firefighting foam*. They differ from habitual sentences which refer to general facts, for example *Fires can be extinguished by the use of firefighting foam*.

Epistemology: The study of the nature and values of human knowledge with reference to its limits and validity.

E-Prime: A software tool for designing and running experiments.

Exaptation: An evolutionary process whereby a feature that had evolved under one particular adaptive pressure becomes utilized for an alternative purpose. It has been argued that the human brain grew as large as it is for reasons currently unknown hundreds of thousands of years ago and has only recently been exapted for language.

Existential quantification: A ubiquitous phenomenon in natural language, interpreted as 'there exists', 'there is at least one', 'for some', 'some' or 'at least one'. For example, *Some stores sell bread in town* could be interpreted as *There exists/there is at least one store that sells bread in town*.

Explicit knowledge: Knowledge a person is aware of and can often articulate, whether in specialized terminology or everyday language.

Eye-tracking: An experimental technique in which an individual's eye movements are monitored as they complete a task, e.g. reading a text, or listening to a text while viewing a visual display.

Feature unification: Formalism used in Lexical Functional Grammar (LFG) and in Processability Theory which allows for the matching of features which belong to different parts in an utterance. In language production conceptual and linguistic features have to be unified using **linearization** in order for a speaker to produce a both semantically and structurally well-formed sentence.

Filler: See **Distractor**.

Fluency: Here used in a narrow temporal sense meaning ease or smoothness of spoken language including, for the researcher, measurement of pausing, speech rate and use of repairs.

Focus on Form (FonF): A form focus in a meaning-based setting. In FonF a certain focus on grammatical structures is applied when meaning and use are already evident to the learner but not yet mastered. In a classroom setting both pro-active and re-active FonF can be applied.

Formal feature: A grammatical feature involved in the syntax of a language such as agreement, articles, case, or gender/class on nouns.

Formant frequencies: Acoustic measurement of vocal cord resonances at different frequency levels, particularly used to characterize vowels.

Formant: A resonance of the vocal tract.

Formulaic chunks/formulaic language/formulaic use: Phrases or strings of words that co-occur, such as idioms (*kick the bucket*), collocations (*put on a coat*) or frequent grammatical constructions (*Do you know …?*). These may be learned and used as sets of memorized phrases by language learners before the relevant grammar is fully acquired and used appropriately (*What are you called?* versus **What are he called?*).

Fricative (also **spirant**): A consonant formed when sound passes between two articulators brought close together but not quite closed, making a turbulence, as in the English consonant /f/.

Functional category: Grammatical category (as opposed to lexical category such as Noun and Verb), one which plays a purely grammatical role such as negation, aspect, tense or agreement. See also **X-bar Theory**

Functional magnetic resonance imaging (fMRI) scans: A neuroimaging technique using technology to investigate human brain function by measuring changes in blood flow.

Functional structure: Contains grammatical functions, such as subject or object. These functions are assumed to be largely language universal, e.g. every language has subjects and objects.

Fundamental Difference Hypothesis (FDH): The claim that the processes of first (child) language acquisition are fundamentally different from the acquisition of a second language by adult second language learners. See also **Critical Period Hypothesis**.

Grammaticality judgement task: A task in which speakers are presented with linguistic stimuli (typically sentences) and asked to judge whether or not they are correct in the language. Such tasks have long been widely used in linguistic theory to formulate and refine claims about a native speaker-hearer's internal grammar or competence and are also used in second language acquisition to shed light on a speaker's **interlanguage**.

Guiraud's index: A measure of lexical richness, calculated by dividing the total number of different words (word types) by the square root of the number of tokens.

Hominid/hominin: Hominin refers to members of every species which has descended from the last common ancestor shared with chimpanzees, forming the hominin genus group or clade. The hominid clade consists of hominins plus the great apes: chimpanzees, gorillas and orang-utans.

Identity thesis: The view that language and music are identical in their fundamental building blocks (arbitrary pairings of sound and meaning in the case of language; pitch-classes and pitch-class combinations in the case of music).

I-language: The knowledge a speaker implicitly has of the principles and rules of a language broadly equivalent to competence.

Immersion setting: The typical learning context of immigrant populations who acquire a second language naturalistically, through observation and interaction with target-language speakers while being immersed in the target-language speaking community, compared to instruction in foreign language classroom settings where language is taught for a limited amount of time in an L1-speaking environment. Also refers to certain teaching contexts, where the language to be learned is used as the medium of instruction to teach any subject. Each school subject selected for immersion is taught entirely in the L2, and for several years the L2 is used to teach at least 50% of the school curriculum.

Implicational hierarchy: The view in Processability Theory that the acquisition of a higher stage of language development requires the mental representations of processing procedures and respective particular language-specific linguistic features of all possible prior stages.

Implicit knowledge: Knowledge a person is not aware of and often cannot articulate; i-language and linguistic competence are examples of implicit knowledge.

Impressionistic analysis: Interpreting speech in terms of quality of pitch, resonance, loudness.

Incremental language processing: The view that an utterance is perceived or produced in small steps (increments) in successive stages but rapidly and in parallel, to account for fast comprehension and fluent speech.

Inflectional morphology: Morphology that varies according to the grammar of a sentence, exhibiting, for example, plurality on nouns (*cat, cats*), agreement between the subject of a sentence and the finite verb (*she walks*) or tense (*she walked*). Inflectional affixes do not change the word class of their root (e.g. *cat* remains a noun and *walk* remains a verb in the preceding examples).

Inhibitory control: A cognitive function allowing individuals to suppress a dominant, automatic response or resist interference from information irrelevant to the task. Individuals with stronger inhibitory control may be better able to efficiently avoid cross-language interference.

Intelligibility: The extent to which the form and sounds of an utterance are understood by the listener.

Interlanguage: The internal dynamic learner grammar, based on general cognitive and linguistic constraints. Interlanguage is neither the L1 nor the L2 of an individual learner. The unfolding of specific morphosyntactic structures in a learner's interlanguage follows a predictable path.

Intransitive: Denotes a verb (or clause with such a verb) that does not have a direct object (*Alex snored* in contrast to *Alex ate breakfast*, where *breakfast* is the direct object of the transitive verb *ate*).

Inversion: A process of syntactic change where word order is systematically reversed, e.g. in English to reverse the order of subject and auxiliary for asking questions (*Is he going?*).

Language Acquisition Device (LAD): The hypothesized mechanism with which humans are innately wired for the task of language acquisition. See also **Universal Grammar**

Language assessments/tests: The collection of various types of information to draw conclusions about the proficiency of a student in using a particular language.

Language processor: The set of psycholinguistic mechanisms which work on a learner's interlanguage. Originally proposed in terms of L1 speech production; used and further defined for SLA purposes.

Learning strategies: Ways in which learners consciously attempt to work out the meanings and uses of words, grammatical rules and other aspects of the language they are learning.

Lemma: An abstract representation of a word (or conceptual root), subsuming all its specific morphological variations (e.g. *talk* subsumes *talking, talks* and *talked*).

Lexical density: A measure of the difficulty of a text, using the ratio of the number of different words (the 'word types') to the total number of words (the 'word tokens'): the 'type/token ratio'. See also **Guiraud's Index**.

Lexical-Functional Grammar (LFG): A theory of generative grammar which is characterized by a lexically driven approach to syntax. A core component of the theory is its projection architecture, consisting of three independent levels of linguistic representation that exist in parallel and are related to each other by specific linking or mapping principles. The three levels are argument structure (a-structure), functional structure (f-structure) and constituent structure (c-structure).

Lexical mapping: Formalism used in LFG which denotes the process of linking semantic and syntactic information. In particular, it refers to the process of linking arguments (e.g. agents and patients) represented in argument structure to grammatical functions in functional structure.

Lexical mapping hypothesis: The prediction under Processability Theory that the L2 learner can initially only perform direct mapping operations, such that the most prominent argument – the agent – is mapped onto the subject function. In the course of L2 acquisition, the learner is able to perform non-linear mapping operations, as in the passive where the patient is mapped onto the subject function and the agent is linked to the oblique function.

Linearization (also **linearization problem**): The challenge for a language learner of unifying conceptual and linguistic features in order to produce a semantically and grammatically well-formed utterance. Conceptual knowledge (which is unstructured, non-linguistic information) has to be given linguistic structured shape in the respective target language at surface linear level; the unification of features is an indispensable prerequisite for linearization. See also **feature unification**

Linger: A software tool for designing and running experiments, especially self-paced reading and listening.

Logical problem: How the language learner comes to know what they know if this knowledge is not represented in the input. See also **Universal Grammar.**

Long-term memory: Permanent information (compared to **working memory**), including both consciously retrievable information (**declarative memory**) and information enabling subconscious automatic processing (**procedural memory**).

Maturational constraints perspective: A view that cognitive or biological maturational processes impose constraints on learning required for native-like acquisition of language. See also **Critical Period Hypothesis.**

Mean Length of Utterance (MLU): A measure of the average length of a spoken utterance, calculated in terms of morphemes rather than words, and used to track children's speech. It is a more reliable measure for children's language development than age, since children develop language at different rates.

Median split: A split of a set of scores or participants (usually into two groups) based on the middle score of a set of ordered scores, thereby splitting a population into two groups of approximately equal size.

Mental representation: A theoretical construct used in cognitive science referring to information-bearing structures in the human mind such as phonological, morphological, syntactic and semantic information.

Merge: The only syntactic operation in the **Minimalist Program**, the process whereby two syntactic objects e.g. an adjective (*heavy*) and a noun (*books*) are combined to form a third object, a noun phrase (*heavy books*) which may then be merged with another object and so on.

Minimal Trees Hypothesis: The view that only lexical categories such as VP are projected at the start of language acquisition, while functional categories are not. The learner then projects functional categories and the tree grows – in response to input.

Minimalist Programme (also **Minimalism**): A revised conceptual framework within the general paradigm of the principles and parameters model of **Universal Grammar**. The aim of the programme is to account for the minimal theoretical and computational apparatus necessary to explain characteristics of linguistic phenomena and of acquisition.

Modality: The mode of language transmission, i.e. visual (written, signed), auditory (spoken) or tactile (braille writing), and processing, i.e. comprehension and production.

Modularity: The theory that the mind/brain has discrete, encapsulated modules that process different types of data (e.g. a module for language processing, a separate module for processing visual stimuli).

Multiple Constraints Hypothesis: In Processability Theory, the claim that the initial grammatical system is highly restricted at the semantic level (core participants in the event) and syntactic level (grammatical functions and constituent structure) and that the mental lexicon is only gradually annotated (e.g. for lexical category). These constraints decrease successively as acquisition progresses gradually, from **formulaic speech** towards productive utterances.

Nativism: See **Universal Grammar.**

Negative inversion: When an English clause begins with a negative or limiting adverb like *never, seldom, scarcely, rarely, barely, hardly*, etc. (e.g. *never had I seen such a beautiful sunset*) and the order of the auxiliary verb and the subject is inverted.

Non-compositional: See **compositional.**

Non-finite: Refers to a verb that cannot appear on its own in a main clause, or to a clause without a finite verb. In English, such verbs include participles (*he is sleeping*) and infinitives (*I want him to go*), and do not exhibit inflectional morphology for agreement with the subject (**I want him to goes*), although other languages vary.

Noun Phrase: A constituent that is headed by a noun; it appears in any position that a noun can appear in and, alongside the head noun, may include a determiner and attributive adjectives, and Prepositional Phrases or relative clauses (*that metal box at the back; your new car that I just trashed*).

Offline task: An experimental task that does not monitor the time it takes the participant to complete a particular language task, but instead only records the response given by the participant; it can be used to investigate language comprehension or production.

Online task: An experimental task that measures the time course of language processing, either in terms of production or comprehension (e.g. **eye tracking** during reading); online tasks measure the time it takes to complete a linguistic task or process.

Overgeneralization: Refers to the phenomenon (that language learners) sometimes apply a certain grammar rule to contexts that, in fact, are an exception to that very rule. One example is the overgeneralization of the past *-ed* morpheme to irregular verbs as in *wented.

Phone: The smallest concrete unit of sound. A phone is considered in terms of its articulatory character, without regard to its phonemic status. Phones are enclosed in square brackets [ ].

Phoneme: The smallest abstract unit in phonology, enclosed in slanted brackets / /.

Phonological short-term memory (also called the **phonological loop**): A limited-capacity memory store responsible for temporarily storing verbal-acoustic information, such as sequences of speech sounds, for a few seconds, in Baddeley's (2003) modular model of working memory.

Picture selection task: Assesses language comprehension by presenting participants with a sentence for which they must select an appropriate matching picture from a set of potential pictures.

Polarity items: A term used for those lexical items whose distribution displays sensitivity to whether their grammatical environment is positive or negative. A **negative polarity item** involves negative environments (e.g. *yet*: *I haven't seen that film yet* versus **I have seen that film yet*). A **positive polarity item** involves positive environments (e.g. *somewhat*: *The experiment was somewhat successful* versus **The experiment was not somewhat successful*).

Postdeterminer: A word, often a **quantifier**, which in English occurs after the determiner and before an adjective in a noun phrase (e.g. *the three big chairs*, *the other leading participants*).

Post-vocalic: Sounds occurring in a specific syllabic position (i.e. after a vowel).

Preferential looking task: A technique for evaluating infants' understanding of words and other linguistic structures by assessing infants' visual looking pattern while focusing on two presented stimuli.

Prefix: A morpheme that is attached to the beginning of a word (*kind – unkind*).

Pre-nuclear rising: Rising pitch just before an accented syllable carrying the main prosodic stress (nucleus) in a word or phrase.

Preposition: A word class that combines with a Noun Phrase to form a Prepositional Phrase and, for example, denoting position in space or time (*on the table*, *through the looking glass*, *at nine o'clock*). This class is usually regarded as a closed class in that you cannot coin new examples of prepositions. Some prepositions have no obvious meaning and behave more like closed class functional elements (*the neglect of his children*; *the price of milk*).

Prescriptive grammar: A term used for grammar rules that dictate 'correct' usage according to social convention or the opinion of a self-appointed expert but without any support from theoretical linguistics (e.g. splitting the infinitive: *To go boldly* rather than *To boldly go where no man has gone before*; *It is I!* rather than *It is me!*).

Prime: A stimulus presented to a participant that is expected to influence the participant's subsequent behaviour; in syntactic priming tasks a prime sentence is used in an attempt to elicit a specific subsequent response from the participant.

Priming: An effect in which previous experience of a structure speeds up the time needed to recognize a semantically or syntactically linked target word.

Procedural knowledge: The knowledge of how to perform some task ('knowing how to …').

Processing: In cognitive science and cognitive linguistics, the human mind is seen as an information processor which is constantly retrieving, encoding, decoding or storing information relevant to language production and comprehension. The human language processor responds to stimuli and works creatively on the input received (comprehension) and output to be produced.

Processing procedure: In Processability Theory, mechanisms of the language processor involved in encoding linguistic information during message generation. These procedures are implicationally related, i.e. the acquisition of processing procedures on a higher stage requires the mental representation of all possible previous processing procedures.

Production task: An **offline experimental task** that aims to examine some aspect of language production.

Pro-form: A word or phrase that can replace a constituent, such as a pronoun, which replaces a Noun Phrase (*She painted the ceiling: She painted it*), or the phrase *do so* in English, which replaces a Verb Phrase (*He bought a book and she bought a book too: He bought a book and she did so too*).

Protolanguage: The earliest form of human language to have emerged; a simpler form of language, characterized by a lack of both function words and hierarchical syntax. It is sometimes compared to the language of two-year-old babies and pidgin languages. Use of proto- is used to refer to an earlier form of a language or group of languages; it does not imply linguistic simplicity, but instead refers to a theorized common ancestor, as in Proto-Indo-European.

Psycholinguistics: A field of study that investigates the mental representations and processes, and their acquisition, that underlie language comprehension and production in real time.

Quantifier/quantifying words: See **Postdeterminer**.

Rapid Profile: Computer-assisted screening procedure derived from Processability Theory for the analysis of speech samples collected from L2 learners to identify a learner's current stage of development.

Reaction times or **response latencies**: The time in milliseconds between the onset of a stimulus and the time of the participant's response.

Recency effect: The tendency to remember later items in a sequence of sounds or words; the primacy effect is a listener's recall of the early-presented items within such a sequence. See also **priming**.

Recursive syntax (also **recursion**): Refers to the formal hierarchical constituent structure found, for example, in possessive phrases such as *Karl's brother's friend's uncle*, compared to linearly co-ordinated structures such as *Karl and his brother and his friend and his uncle*. A feature of recursion is that any object of type X can be embedded into another object of the same type, so that an NP may be embedded in an NP, a clause inside a clause and so on.

Register: Denotes a variety of a language that is appropriate for a certain situation, e.g. academic register, formal register.

Relative clause: A clause that qualifies a noun, in English following it in the Noun Phrase (*I just read a novel <u>that won several literary prizes</u>*), often starting with a relative pronoun like *that, who* (*the woman <u>who</u> gave you her novel*) or *which* (*What was the film <u>which</u> bombed at the box office last week?*).

Resting levels of activation: The ease of access to process language or retrieve information such as lexical items stored in long-term memory. Frequent access leads to a higher resting level, making retrieval and processing easier and faster.

Retroflex: A consonant produced with the tip of the tongue curled back to touch or nearly touch the hard palate at the top of the mouth.

Routine: An operation or series of operations involving some aspect of a sentence's form or meaning.

Salience: The ease with which a linguistic item is perceived.

Selective pressure (advantage): See **(neo-)Darwinian evolution**.

Self-paced listening task: An online comprehension task that measures the time course of language processing in which participants listen to a text segment by segment at their own pace.

Self-paced reading task: An online comprehension task in which participants read a text, pressing a button to move through each item one at a time; the time taken to read each item provides a measure of the relative ease or difficulty of implicit language processing at each given point in time.

Semantic/syntactic priming effects: See **Priming**.

Sentence-level processor: The mechanism that analyses the structure of an utterance, including form, meaning and the relationship of the words in the utterance.

Short-term memory: Refers to short-term storage of information within the memory system.

Spillover effects: Effects of experimental manipulations observed in self-paced reading or self-paced listening in which the expected **reaction time** differences appear after a critical region of interest.

Spreading activation: Concepts that are semantically connected are connected in mental networks; when one member of the network is activated, e.g. in a priming experiment, the others are as well (e.g. when the word *doctor* is presented, related words such as *hospital, patient* and *nurse* are also primed. See also **Priming**.

Structure dependence: The view that syntactic structure operates on constituents in a hierarchical relationship, rather than purely in their surface linear order.

Subjacency: A main principle of formal generative syntactic government and binding theory (Chomsky, 1981), identifying boundary limits (bounding node) at certain levels of phrase structure (e.g. NP, CP). Syntactic operations that move constituents are not possible across more than one bounding node. For example, the sentence *What did you hear the claim that John found?* is ungrammatical, because the question word *what* would have to move over two bounding nodes, NP (*the claim*) and CP (*that John found*).

Subordinating conjunction: Traditional grammar term for a **complementizer**, a word that introduces a subordinate clause or embedded clause (*I know that you're in there*).

Suffix: A morpheme that is attached to the end of a word (*kind, kindly* and *go going*).

Syntactic priming: A phenomenon where language users subconsciously repeat a syntactic structure that they have recently been exposed to.

Syntacticon: The parametric variation of the lexicon determined by all lexical information relating to its selection and grammatical features.

Syntax: The branch of grammar that deals with word order in a phrase, clause or sentence.

Teachability Hypothesis: The claim in Processability Theory which predicts that no stage of the PT hierarchy can be skipped or altered by formal instruction. The hypothesis predicts that language instruction is effective when the syllabus follows PT stages, i.e. the current state of a learner's **interlanguage** is close to the point when the structure will be naturally acquired.

Test of Reception of Grammar: A standardized picture selection task that assesses sentence comprehension.

Topic Hypothesis: In **Lexical-Functional Grammar**, the hypothesis that initially the learner maps the initial noun phrase onto the subject function. It is only at a later stage that the learner is able to differentiate between topic and subject and to see that elements such as adverbs or *wh*-words occur in sentence-initial position.

Trill (also **roll**): A consonant in which the tip of the tongue vibrates against the roof of the mouth.

Truth-value judgement tasks: An experimental technique that allows the testing of whether or not participants can access both meanings associated with ambiguous sentences.

Uninterpretable features: Abstract syntactic features of an item that make no contribution to the semantic interpretation of that item (such as Tense); interpretable features make some semantic contribution, such as word class (verb) or number (singular/plural).

Universal Grammar (UG): The innate system of grammatical categories, principles and parameters which defines the nature of language and assists in its acquisition. Characterized in terms of hard-wired syntactic principles, some of which apply invariantly to all languages and some of which include bi- or multi-valued parameters that constrain variation across languages.

Unmarked Alignment: The default mapping principle in Processability Theory that learners rely on at the beginning of the acquisition process where arguments, grammatical functions and surface structure constituents are aligned in a linear way. For instance, in the sentence *Mary played the guitar*, the most prominent argument role – the agent – is linked to the most prominent grammatical function, the subject. At constituent structure level, the subject is realized as the initial noun phrase.

Uvular: A consonant produced by the back of the tongue against the very end of the soft palate (the **uvula**).

Verb Phrase: A constituent that is headed by a main verb and includes any modifying adverbs and complements. It usually forms the predicate in a clause and provides information about the subject (*my car requires a wash*; *I don't believe a word*).

Veridical: Refers to the semantic or grammatical property of an utterance context to imply the truth of its argument; if the context *doesn't* guarantee the truth of its contents, it is **non-veridical**.

Voice onset time (VOT): The time that passes between the release of the closure of a consonant and the moment at which the vocal folds start vibrating.

Voiced: Speech sounds using vibrating vocal cords.

Weak pronouns (see also **clitics**): Phonologically dependent pronouns in that they cannot be isolated, modified or coordinated; they attach to a (verb) host, and they obligatorily move from their base positions.

Wh-word: Question word that begins with *wh-* (except in the case of *how*): *who, what, when, where, why* or its equivalent in another language.

Working memory: The brain's ability to maintain the neural activation needed for temporarily holding and manipulating information required for completing a task. See also **short-term memory**.

X' (X-bar) theory: In generative syntax, the hierarchical principles of constituent structure for any language. The four main lexical categories – verbs, nouns, adjectives and prepositions – identify the head of the phrase in which it is the main constituent, e.g. the noun *dog* is the head of the noun phrase *The dog with black ears*. X'-theory includes functional projections such as AgrP, where the projection is headed by agreement.

References

Aitchison, J. (2003) *Words in the Mind* (3rd edn). Oxford: Blackwell.

Aliaga-Garcia, C., Mora, J.C. and Cerviño-Povedano, E. (2011) Phonological short-term memory and L2 speech learning in adulthood. *Poznań Studies in Contemporary Linguistics* 47 (1), 1–14.

Allen, J. (2009) *The Lives of the Brain: Human Evolution and the Organ of Mind*. Cambridge, MA: Harvard University Press.

Allwright, R. (1984) Why don't learners learn what teachers teach? The interaction hypothesis. In D.M. Singleton and D.G. Little (eds) *Language Learning in Formal and Informal Contexts* (pp. 3–18). Dublin: IRAAL.

Altarriba, J. and Mathis, K. (1997) Conceptual and lexical development in second language acquisition. *Journal of Memory and Language* 36 (4), 550–568.

Alwan, A. and Narayanan, S. (1996) Towards articulatory-acoustic models for liquid approximants based on MRI and EPG data. Part II: The rhotics. *Journal of the Acoustical Society of America* 101 (2), 1078–1989.

Ambridge, B. and Lieven, E. (2011) *Child Language Acquisition: Contrasting Theoretical Approaches*. Cambridge: CUP.

Anderson, J. (1983) *The Architecture of Cognition*. Mahwah, NJ: Lawrence Erlbaum.

Anderson, J. (1993) *Rules of the Mind*. Hillsdale, NJ: Lawrence Erlbaum.

Anderson, J., Bothell, D., Byrne, M., Douglass, S., Lebiere, C. and Qin, Y. (2004) An integrated theory of the mind. *Psychological Review* 111 (4), 1036–1060.

Arbib, M. (ed) (2006) *The Mirror System Hypothesis on the Linkage of Action and Languages*. Cambridge: Cambridge University Press.

Arbib, M. and Bonaiuto, J. (2008) From grasping to complex imitation: Mirror systems on the path to language. *Mind & Society* 7, 43–64.

Arnold, J., Eisenband, J., Brown-Schmidt, S. and Trueswell, J. (2000) The rapid use of gender information: Evidence of the time course of pronoun resolution from eye tracking. *Cognition* 76, 13–26.

Arthur, W. (2011) *Evolution: A Developmental Approach*. Chichester: Wiley-Blackwell.

Baddeley, A. (2000) The episodic buffer: A new component of working memory? *Trends in Cognitive Sciences* 4 (11), 417–423.

Baddeley, A. (2003) Working memory and language: An overview. *Journal of Communication Disorders* 36, 189–208.

Baddeley, A. (2007) *Working Memory, Thought and Action*. Oxford: Oxford University Press.

Baddeley, A. and Hitch, G. (1974) Working memory. In G. Bower (ed.) *The Psychology of Learning and Motivation*. New York, Academic Press.

Baddeley, A., Papagno, C. and Vallar, G. (1988) When long-term learning depends on short-term storage. *Journal of Memory and Language* 27, 586–596.

Baddeley, A., Eysenck, M. and Anderson, M. (2009) *Memory*. Hove: Psychology Press.

Bailey, N., Madden, C. and Krashen, S. (1974) Is there a 'natural sequence' in adult second language learning? *Language Learning* 24, 235–243.

Baker, C. (1978) *Introduction to Generative Transformation Syntax*. Englewood Cliffs, NJ: Prentice Hall.

Balota, D., Cortese, M., Sergent-Marshall, S., Spieler, D. and Yap, M. (2004) Visual word recognition of single-syllable words. *Journal of Experimental Psychology: General* 133 (2), 283–316.

Barfield, A. (2013) Lexical collocations. In C. Chapelle (ed.) *The Encyclopaedia of Applied Linguistics*. London: Blackwell.

Baron-Cohen, S. (1995) *Mindblindness: An Essay on Autism and Theory of Mind*. Cambridge, MA: MIT Press.

Baron-Cohen, S., Leslie, A. and Frith, U. (1985) Does the autistic child have a "theory of mind"? *Cognition* 21, 37–47.

Beck, M. (1998) L2 acquisition and obligatory head movement: English-speaking learners of German and the local impairment hypothesis. *Studies in Second Language Acquisition* 20, 311–348.

Bencini, G. and Valian, V. (2008) Abstract sentence representation in 3-year-olds: Evidence from comprehension and production. *Journal of Memory and Language* 59, 97–113.

Best, C. and Tyler, M. (2007) Non-native and second language speech perception. In O.-S. Bohn and M.J. Munro (eds) *Language Experience in Second Language Speech Learning*. Amsterdam: John Benjamins.

Bickerton, D. (1981) *Roots of Language*. Ann Arbor, MI: Karoma.

Bickerton, D. (2007) Language evolution: A brief guide for linguists. *Lingua* 117, 510–526.

Bishop, D. (2003) *Test for Reception of Grammar, Version 2*. London: Psychological Corporation.

Blesser, B. (1972) Speech perception under conditions of spectral transformation: I. Phonetic characteristics. *Journal of Speech and Hearing Research* 15, 5–41.

Bleyhl, W. (2009) The hidden paradox of foreign language instruction or: Which are the real foreign language learning processes? In T. Piske and M. Young-Scholten (eds) *Input Matters in SLA* (pp. 137–155). Bristol: Multilingual Matters.

Bley-Vroman, R. (1989) What is the logical problem of foreign language learning? In S. Gass and J. Schachter (eds) *Linguistic Perspectives on Second Language Acquisition*. New York: Cambridge University Press.

Bley-Vroman, R. (1990) The logical problem of foreign language learning. *Linguistic Analysis* 20 (1–2), 3–49.

Bley-Vroman, R. (2009) The evolving context of the fundamental difference hypothesis. *Studies in Second Language Acquisition, Special Issue* 31 (2), 175–198.

Bley-Vroman, R. and Chaudron, C. (1994) Elicited imitation as a measure of second-language competence. In E. Tarone, S. Gass and A. Cohen (eds) *Research Methodology in Second-Language Acquisition*. Hillsdale, NJ: Lawrence Erlbaum.

Bock, J.K. (1986) Syntactic persistence in language production. *Cognitive Psychology* 18, 355–387.

Boeckx, C. (2010) A tale of two minimalisms: Reflections on the possibility of crash-proof syntax, and its free merge alternative. In M. Putnam (ed.) *Exploring Crash-Proof Grammars*. Amsterdam: John Benjamins.

Boersma, P. and Weenink, D. (2015) *Praat: Doing phonetics by Computer, Version 5.4.08* [Computer program]. See http://www.praat.org/ (accessed 24 March 2015).

Bohn, O.-S. and Munro, M.J. (eds) (2007) *Language Experience in Second Language Speech Learning*. Amsterdam: John Benjamins.

Boser, K., Lust, B., Santelman, L. and Whitman, J. (1992) The syntax of CP and V-2 in early child German: The strong continuity hypothesis. *NELS Proceedings* 22, 51–65.

Boss, B. (1996). German grammar for Beginners: The Teachability Hypothesis and its relevance to the classroom. In C. Arbonés-Solà, J. Rolin-Iantziti and R. Sussex (eds) *Who's Afraid of Teaching Grammar? University of Queensland Papers in Language and Linguistics* 1. Queensland: University of Queensland Press.

Bradlow, A.R., Akahane-Yamada, R., Pisoni, D.B. and Tohkura, Y. (1999) Training Japanese listeners to identify English /r/ and /l/: Long-term retention of learning in perception and production. *Perception & Psychophysics* 61, 977–985.

Branigan, H. (2007) Syntactic priming. *Language and Linguistics Compass* 1, 1–16.

Branigan, H., Pickering, M. and Cleland, A. (2000) Syntactic co-ordination in dialogue. *Cognition* 75, B13–B25.

Bresnan, J. (2001) *Lexical Functional Syntax*. Malden, MA: Blackwell.

Breznitz, Z. (2008) Special issue on the use of electrophysiological measures in reading research. *Journal of Neurolinguistics* 21 (4), 277–278.

Brown, R. (1973) *A First Language: The Early Stages*. Cambridge, MA: Harvard University Press.

Brysbaert, M., Van Wijnendaele, I. and De Deyne, S. (2000) Age of acquisition effects in semantic tasks. *Acta Psychologica* 104, 215–226.

Burke, D. and Peters, L. (1986) Word associations in old age: Evidence for consistency in semantic encoding during adulthood. *Psychology and Aging* 1, 283–292.

Burling, R. (2005) *The Talking Ape*. Oxford: Oxford University Press.

Bylund, E. (2009) Maturational constraints and first language attrition. *Language Learning* 59 (3), 687–725.

Call, J. and Tomasello, M. (1999) A nonverbal false belief task: The performance of children and great apes. *Child Development* 70, 381–395.

Call, J., Carpenter, M. and Tomasello, M. (2005) Copying results and copying actions in the process of social learning: Chimpanzees (*Pan troglodytes*) and human children (*Homo sapiens*). *Animal Cognition* 8, 151–163.

Cameron, L. (2001) *Teaching Languages to Young Learners*. Cambridge: Cambridge University Press.

Caplan, D. and Waters, G. (1999) Verbal working memory and sentence comprehension. *Behavioral and Brain Sciences* 22 (1), 77–94.

Carpenter, M., Nagell, K. and Tomasello, M. (1998) Social cognition, joint attention, and communicative competence from 9 to 15 months of age. *Monographs of the Society for Research in Child Development* 63, 1–143.

Carroll, S. (2001) *Input and Evidence*. Amsterdam: John Benjamins.

Castro, D. and Gavruseva, E. (2003) Finiteness and aspect in Spanish/English bilingual acquisition. *First Language* 23, 171–192.

Cazzoli-Goeta, M. and Young-Scholten, M. (2011) Expanding choice or syntactic attrition? In K. Potowski and J. Rothman (eds) *Bilingual Youth. Spanish in English-speaking Countries*. Amsterdam: John Benjamins.

Cebrian, J. (2006) Experience and the use of duration in the categorization of L2 vowels. *Journal of Phonetics* 34, 372–387.

Cerviño-Povedano, E. and Mora, J.C. (2011) Investigating Catalan learners of English over-reliance on duration: Vowel cue weighting and phonological short-term memory. In K. Dziubalska-Kołaczyk, M. Wrembel and M. Kul (eds) *Achievements and Perspectives in SLA of Speech: New Sounds 2010. Vol. I*. Frankfurt am Main: Peter Lang.

Cerviño-Povedano, E. and Mora, J.C. (2015) Spanish EFL's identification of /iː–I/ and phonological short-term memory. *Proceedings of the 32nd AESLA Applied Linguistics Conference*, Seville, Spain.

Chater, N., Reali, F. and Christiansen, M. (2009) Restrictions on biological adaptation in language evolution. *Proceedings of the National Academy of Sciences of the United States of America* 106, 1015–1020.

Chen, L., Shu, H., Liu, Y., Zhao, J. and Li, P. (2007) ERP signatures of subject–verb agreement in L2 learning. *Bilingualism: Language and Cognition* 10, 161–174.

Cheung, H. (1996) Nonword span as a unique predictor of second language vocabulary learning. *Developmental Psychology* 32 (5), 867–873.

Chien, Y.-C. and Wexler, K. (1990) Children's knowledge of locality conditions in binding as evidence for the modularity of syntax and pragmatics. *Language Acquisition* 1, 225–295.

Chomsky, N. (1959) A review of B.F. Skinner's *Verbal Behavior. Language* 35, 26–58.

Chomsky, N. (1965) *Aspects of the Theory of Syntax*. Cambridge, MA: MIT Press.

Chomsky, N. (1975) *Reflections on Language*. New York: Pantheon Books.

Chomsky, N. (1980a) On binding. *Linguistic Inquiry* 11, 1–46.

Chomsky, N. (1980b) *Rules and Representations*. Columbia, OH: Columbia University Press.

Chomsky, N. (1981) *Lectures on Government and Binding*. Dordrecht: Foris.

Chomsky, N. (1986) *Knowledge of Language: Its Nature, Origin, and Use*. New York: Praeger.

Chomsky, N. (1987) *Language and Problems of Knowledge: The Managua Lectures*. Cambridge, MA: MIT Press.

Chomsky, N. (1993) A minimalist program for linguistic theory. In K. Hale and S. Keyser (eds) *The View from Building 20: Essays in Linguistics in Honor of Sylvain Bromberger*. Cambridge, MA: MIT Press.

Chomsky, N. (1995) *The Minimalist Program*. Cambridge, MA: MIT Press.

Chomsky, N. (1998) Minimalist inquiries: The framework. MIT Occasional Papers in Linguistics No. 15. Cambridge, MA: MITWPL.

Chomsky, N. (2000) *The Architecture of Language*. New Delhi: Oxford University Press India.

Chomsky, N. (2001) Derivation by phase. In M. Kenstowicz (ed.) *Ken Hale: A Life in Language*. Cambridge, MA: MIT Press.

Chomsky, N. (2002) *On Nature and Language*. Cambridge: Cambridge University Press.

Chomsky, N. (2004) Beyond explanatory adequacy. In A. Belletti (ed.) *The Cartography of Syntactic Structures. Vol. III: Structures and Beyond*. Oxford: Oxford University Press.

Chomsky, N. (2005) Three factors in language design. *Linguistic Inquiry* 36, 1–22.

Chomsky, N. (2006) *Language and Mind* (3rd edn). Cambridge: Cambridge University Press.

Chomsky, N. (2007) Approaching UG from below. In U. Sauerland and H. Gartner (eds) *Interfaces + Recursion = Language?* New York: Mouton de Gruyter.

Chomsky, N.(2008) On Phases. In R. Freidin, C. Peregrín Otero and M. Zubizarreta (eds) *Foundational Issues in Linguistic Theory. Essays in Honor of Jean-Roger Vergnaud*. Cambridge, Massachusetts: MIT Press.

Chomsky, N. (2011) Language and other cognitive systems: What is special about language? *Language Learning and Development* 7, 263–278.

Chomsky, N. (2013) Problems of projection. *Lingua* 130, 33–49.

Chomsky, N. and McGilvray, J. (2012) *The Science of Language*. Cambridge: Cambridge University Press.

Christiansen, M. and Chater, N. (2008) Language as shaped by the brain. *Behavioral and Brain Sciences* 31, 489–558.

Clackson, K., Felser, C. and Clahsen, H. (2011) Children's processing of reflexives and pronouns in English: Evidence from eye-movements during listening. *Journal of Memory and Language* 65, 128–144.

Clahsen, H. (1991) Constraints on parameter setting. A grammatical analysis of some acquisition stages in German child language. *Language Acquisition* 4, 361–391.

Clahsen, H. (1992) Learnability theory and the problem of development in language acquisition. In J. Weissenborn, H. Goodluck and T. Roeper (eds) *Theoretical Issues in Language Acquisition: Continuity and Change* (pp. 53–76). Hillsdale, NJ: Lawrence Erlbaum.

Clahsen, H. (2007) Psycholinguistic perspectives on grammatical representations. In S. Featherston and W. Sternefeld (eds) *Roots: Linguistics in Search of its Evidential Base*. Berlin: Mouton de Gruyter.

Clahsen, H. and Felser, C. (2006) Grammatical processing in language learners. *Applied Psycholinguistics* 27, 3–42.

Clahsen, H. and Muysken, P. (1986) The availability of universal grammar to adult and child learners – a study of the acquisition of German word order. *Second Language Research* 2 (2), 93–119.

Clahsen, H. and Penke, M. (1992) The acquisition of agreement morphology and its syntactic consequences: New evidence on German child language from the Simone-Corpus. In J. Meisel (ed.) *The Acquisition of Verb Placement: Functional Categories and V2 Phenomena in Language Acquisition*. Dordrecht: Kluwer.

Clahsen, H., Eisenbeiss, S. and Vainikka, A. (1994) The seeds of structure: A syntactic analysis of the acquisition of case marking. In T. Hoekstra and B.D. Schwartz (eds) *Language Acquisition Studies in Generative Grammar*. Amsterdam: John Benjamins.

Clahsen, H., Felser, C., Neubauer, K., Sato, M. and Silva, R. (2010) Morphological structure in native and non-native language processing. *Language Learning* 60, 21–43.

Collins, A. and Loftus, E. (1975) A spreading-activation theory of semantic processing. *Psychological Review* 82 (6), 407–428.

Collins, A. and Quillian, M. (1969) Retrieval time from semantic memory. *Journal of Verbal Learning and Verbal Behaviour* 8 (?), 240–248.

Conroy, A., Takahashi, E., Lidz, J. and Phillips, C. (2009) Equal treatment for all antecedents: How children succeed with Principle B. *Linguistic Inquiry* 40, 446–486.

Cook, V. (2008) *Second Language Learning and Language Teaching*. London: Hodder Education.

Cooper, J. (ed.) (1997) *Plato: Complete Works*. Indianapolis, IN and Cambridge: Hackett.

Corballis, M. (2009) The evolution of language. *Annals of the New York Academy of Sciences* 1156, 19–43.

Corballis, M. (2012) The origins of language in manual gestures. In M. Tallerman and K. Gibson (eds) *The Oxford Handbook of Language Evolution*. Oxford: Oxford University Press.

Crain, S. and Nakayama, M. (1987) Structure dependence in grammar formation. *Language* 63, 522–543.

Crain, S. and Thornton, R. (1998) *Investigations in Universal Grammar. A Guide to Experiments on the Acquisition of Syntax and Semantics*. Cambridge, MA: MIT Press.

Crain, S., Gualmini, A. and Meroni, L. (2000) The acquisition of logical words. *LOGOS and Language* 1, 49–59.

Crain, S., Goro, T. and Thornton, R. (2006) Language acquisition is language change. *Journal of Psycholinguistic Research* 35, 31–49.

Crow, T. (2002) ProtocadherinXY: A candidate gene for cerebral asymmetry and language. In A. Wray (ed.) *The Transition to Language*. Oxford: Oxford University Press.

Crowder, R.G. and Morton, J. (1969) Precategorical acoustic storage. *Perception & Psychophysics* 5, 365–373.

Culicover, P. and Jackendoff, R. (2005) *Simpler Syntax*. Oxford University Press.

Cunnings, I. (2012) An overview of mixed-effects statistical models for second language researchers. *Second Language Research* 28, 369–382.

Daller, H., Milton, J. and Treffers-Daller, J. (2007) Editors' introduction: Conventions, terminology and an overview of the book. In M. Daller, J. Milton and J. Treffers-Daller (eds) *Modelling and Assessing Vocabulary Knowledge*. Cambridge: Cambridge University Press.

Dalston, R.M. (1975) Acoustic characteristics of English /w, r, l/ spoken correctly by young children and adults. *Journal of the Acoustical Society of America* 57 (2), 462–469.

Darcy, I., Mora, J.C. and Daidone, D. (2014) Attention control and inhibition influence phonological development in a second language. *Proceedings of the International Symposium on the Acquisition of Second Language Speech. Concordia Working Papers in Applied Linguistics* 5, 115–129.

Darcy, I., Mora, J.C. and Daidone, D. (2016) The role of inhibitory control in second language phonological processing. *Language Learning* 66 (3), 741–773.

Darwin, C. (1871) *The Descent of Man, and Selection in Relation to Sex, Vol. 1*. London: John Murray.

David, A., Myles, F., Rogers, V. and Rule, S. (2009) Lexical development in instructed L2 learners of French: Is there a relationship with morphosyntactic development? In M. Daller, R. Malvern, P. Meara, J. Milton, B. Richards and J. Treffers-Daller (eds) *Vocabulary Studies in First and Second Language Acquisition*. London: Palgrave.

Davidson, L. and Legendre, G. (2003) Defaults and competition in the acquisition of functional categories in Catalan and French. In R. Nuñez-Cedeño, L. López and R. Cameron (eds) *A Romance Perspective on Language Knowledge and Use: Selected Papers from the 2001 Linguistic Symposium on Romance Languages*. Amsterdam: John Benjamins.

Dawkins, R. (1986) *The Blind Watchmaker*. New York: Norton.

de Groot, A. (1989) Representational aspects of word imageability and word frequency as assessed through word association. *Journal of Experimental Psychology: Learning, Memory, and Cognition* 15 (5), 824–845.

de Leeuw, E. (2009) When your native language sounds foreign: A phonetic investigation into first language attrition. PhD thesis, Queen Margaret University, Edinburgh.

de Leeuw, E. (2014) Maturational constraints in bilingual speech. In E. Thomas and I. Mennen (eds) *Advances in the Study of Bilingualism*. Bristol: Multilingual Matters.

de Leeuw, E. (in press) Phonetic attrition. In M.S. Schmid and B. Köpke (eds) *The Oxford Handbook of Language Attrition*. Oxford: Oxford University Press.

de Leeuw, E., Schmid, M.S. and Mennen, I. (2010) The effects of contact on native language pronunciation in an L2 migrant setting. *Bilingualism: Language and Cognition* 13 (Special Issue 1), 33–40.

de Leeuw, E., Mennen, I. and Scobbie, J.M. (2012) Singing a different tune in your native language: First language attrition of prosody. *International Journal of Bilingualism* 16 (1), 101–116.

de Leeuw, E., Mennen, I. and Scobbie, J.M. (2013) Dynamic systems, maturational constraints and L1 phonetic attrition. *International Journal of Bilingualism* 17 (6), 683–700.

DeKeyser, R. (1997) Beyond explicit rule learning: Automatising second language morphosyntax. *Studies in Second Language Acquisition* 19, 195–221.

DeKeyser, R. (2003) Implicit and explicit learning. In C. Doughty and M. Long (eds) *Handbook of Second Language Acquisition*. Oxford: Blackwell.

Dekydtspotter, L., Sprouse, R. and Swanson, K. (2001) Reflexes of the mental architecture in second-language acquisition: The interpretation of *combien* extractions in English-French interlanguage. *Language Acquisition* 9 (9), 175–227.

Demirci, M. (2000) The role of pragmatics in reflexive interpretation by Turkish learners of English. *Second Language Research* 16, 325–353.

Derwing, T.M. and Munro, M.J. (1997) Accent, intelligibility and comprehensibility: Evidence from four L1s. *Studies in Second Language Acquisition* 19, 1–16.

Derwing, T.M., Thomson, R.I. and Munro, M.J. (2006) English pronunciation and fluency development in Mandarin and Slavic speakers. *System* 34, 183–193.

Derwing, T.M., Munro, M.J. and Thomson, R.I. (2008) A longitudinal study of ESL learners' fluency and comprehensibility development. *Applied Linguistics* 29, 359–380.

Dessalles, J. (2008) Why is language well designed for communication? *Behavioral and Brain Sciences* 31, 518–519.

de Villiers, J. and Roeper, T. (eds) (2011) *Handbook of Generative Approaches to Language Acquisition*. New York: Springer.

de Villiers, P. and de Villiers, J. (1973) A crossectional study of the acquisition of grammatical morphemes in child speech. *Journal of Psycholinguistic Research* 2, 267–278.

Di Biase, B. (2002) Focusing strategies in second language development: A classroom-based study of Italian L2 in primary school. In B. Di Biase (ed.) *Developing a Second Language: Acquisition, Processing and Pedagogy Issues in Arabic, Chinese, English, Italian, Japanese, and Swedish* (pp. 95–120). Melbourne: Language Australia.

Di Biase, B. (2008) Focus-on-form and development in L2 learning. In J.-U. Keßler (ed.) *Processability Approaches to Second Language Development and Second Language Learning* (pp. 197–219). Newcastle upon Tyne: Cambridge Scholars.

Diller, K.C. and Cann, R.L. (2012) Genetic influences on language evolution: An evaluation of the evidence. In M. Tallerman and K. Gibson (eds) *The Oxford Handbook of Language Evolution*. Oxford: Oxford University Press.

Dörnyei, Z. (2006) Individual differences in second language acquisition. *AILA Review* 19, 42–68.

Doughty, C. and Williams, J. (eds) (1998) *Focus on Form in Second Language Acquisition*. Cambridge: Cambridge University Press.

Dulay, H. and Burt, M. (1974) Natural sequences in child second language acquisition. *Language Learning* 24, 37–53.

Dunbar, R. (1996) *Grooming, Gossip and the Evolution of Language*. Cambridge, MA: MIT Press.

Dunbar, R. (2012) Gossip and the social origins of language. In M. Tallerman and K. Gibson (eds) *The Oxford Handbook of Language Evolution*. Oxford: Oxford University Press.

Duncan, J.R., Seitz, J., Kolodny, J., Bor, D., Herzog, H., Ahmed, A., Newell, F.N. and Emslie, H. (2000) A neural basis for general intelligence. *Science* 289, 457–460.

Dunn, L.M. and Dunn, D.M. (2007) *Peabody Picture Vocabulary Test IV*. Minneapolis, MN: Pearson Assessments.

Dunn, L.M., Dunn, D.M., Styles, B. and Sewell, J. (2009) *The British Picture Vocabulary Scale III* (3rd edn). London: GL Assessment.

Dyson, B. (1996) The debate on form-focussed instruction: a teacher's perspective. *Australian Review of Applied Linguistics* 19 (2), 59–78.

Eisenbeiss, S. (2009) Generative approaches to language learning. *Linguistics* 47, 273–310.

Ellis, N. (1994) *Implicit and Explicit Learning of Languages*. London: Academic Press.

Ellis, N. (2005) At the interface: Dynamic interactions of explicit and implicit language knowledge. *Studies in Second Language Acquisition* 27, 305–352.

Ellis, R. (1989) Are classroom and naturalistic acquisition the same? A study of the classroom acquisition of German word order rules. *Studies in Second Language Acquisition* 11 (3), 305–328.

Ellis, R. (1990) *Instructed Second Language Acquisition*. Oxford: Blackwell.

Ellis, R. (1994) *The Study of Second Language Acquisition*. Oxford: Oxford University Press.

Ellis, R. (2003) *Task-based Language Learning*. Oxford: Oxford University Press.

Ellis, R. (2008a) Investigating grammatical difficulty in second language learning. *International Journal of Applied Linguistics* 18 (1), 4–22.

Ellis, R. (2008b) *The Study of Second Language Acquisition* (2nd edn). Oxford: Oxford University Press.

Ellis, R., Loewen, S., Elder, C., Erlam, R., Philp, J. and Reinders, H. (2009) *Implicit and Explicit Knowledge in Second Language Learning, Testing and Teaching*. Bristol: Multilingual Matters.

Emonds, J. (2001) *Lexicon and Grammar: The English Syntacticon*. Berlin: De Gruyter Mouton.

Endicott, P., Ho, S. and Stringer, C. (2010) Using genetic evidence to evaluate four palaeo-anthropological hypotheses for the timing of Neanderthal and modern human origins. *Journal of Human Evolution* 59, 87–95.

Entwisle, D., Forsyth, D. and Muuss, R. (1964) The syntagmatic-paradigmatic shift in children's word associations. *Journal of Verbal Learning and Verbal Behaviour* 3, 19–29.

Epstein, S., Flynn, S. and Martohardjono, G. (1998) The strong continuity hypothesis: Some evidence concerning functional categories in adult L2 acquisition. In S. Flynn, G. Martohardjono and W. O'Neil (eds) *The Generative Study of Second Language Acquisition*. Mahwah, NJ: Lawrence Erlbaum.

Erçetin, G. and Alptekin, C. (2013) The explicit/implicit knowledge distinction and working memory: Implications for second-language reading comprehension. *Applied Psycholinguistics* 34, 727–753.

Erickson, K.I., Voss, M.W., Prakash, R.S., Basak, C., Szabo, A., Chaddock, L. and Kramer, A.F. (2011) Exercise training increases size of hippocampus and improves memory. *Proceedings of the National Academy of Sciences* 108 (7), 3017–3022.

Erlam, R. (2006) Elicited imitation as a measure of L2 implicit knowledge: An empirical validation study. *Applied Linguistics* 27, 464–491.

Erlam, R. (2009) Elicited imitation as a measure of L2 implicit knowledge. In R. Ellis, S. Loewen, C. Elder, R. Erlam, J. Philp and H. Reinders (eds) *Implicit and Explicit Knowledge in Second Language Learning, Testing and Teaching*. Bristol: Multilingual Matters.

Ervin, S. (1961) Changes with age in the verbal determinants of word association. *American Journal of Psychology* 74, 361–372.

Escudero, P. and Boersma, P. (2004) Bridging the gap between L2 speech perception research and phonological theory. *Studies in Second Language Acquisition* 26 (4), 551–585.

Evans, B.G. and Iverson, P. (2007) Plasticity in vowel perception and production: A study of accent change in young adults. *Journal of the Acoustical Society of America* 121 (6), 3814–3826.

Fabb, N. (1997) *Language and Literature*. Oxford: Blackwell.

Falk, Y. (2001) *Lexical-functional Grammar: An Introduction to Parallel Constraint-based Syntax*. Stanford, CA: CSLI.

Felix, S.W. (1984) Maturational aspects of universal grammar. In A. Davies, C. Criper and A. Howatt (eds) *Interlanguage* (pp. 133–161). Edinburgh: Edinburgh University Press.

Felser, C. and Cunnings, I. (2012) Processing reflexives in a second language: The timing of structural and discourse-level constraints. *Applied Psycholinguistics* 33, 357–383.

Felser, C., Marinis, T. and Clahsen, H. (2003a) Children's processing of ambiguous sentences: A study of relative clause attachment. *Language Acquisition* 11, 127–163.

Felser, C., Roberts, L., Marinis, T. and Gross, R. (2003b) The processing of ambiguous sentences by first and second language learners of English. *Applied Psycholinguistics* 24, 453–489.

Felser, C., Sato, M. and Bertenshaw, N. (2009) The on-line application of Binding Principle A in English as a second language. *Bilingualism: Language and Cognition* 12, 485–502.

Ferreira, F. and Henderson, J. (1990) Use of verb information in syntactic parsing: Evidence from eye movements and word-by-word self-paced reading. *Journal of Experimental Psychology: Learning, Memory, and Cognition* 16, 555–568.

Fitch, W. (2002) Comparative vocal production and the evolution of speech: Reinterpreting the descent of the larynx. In A. Wray (ed.) *The Transition to Language*. Oxford: Oxford University Press.

Fitch, W. (2010) *The Evolution of Language*. Cambridge: Cambridge University Press.

Fitch, W., Hauser, M.D. and Chomsky, N. (2005) The evolution of the language faculty: Clarifications and implications. *Cognition* 97, 179–210.

Fitzpatrick, T. (2009) Word association profiles in a first and second language: Puzzles and problems. In T. Fitzpatrick and A. Barfield (eds) *Lexical Processing in Second Language Learners*. Bristol: Multilingual Matters.

Fitzpatrick, T., Playfoot, D., Wray, A. and Wright, M. (2013) Establishing the reliability of word association data for investigating individual and group differences. *Applied Linguistics* 36 (1), 23–50.

Flege, J. (1984) The detection of French accent by American listeners. *Journal of the Acoustical Society of America* 76, 692–707.

Flege, J. (1987) The production of 'new' and 'similar' phones in a foreign language: Evidence for the effect of equivalence classification. *Journal of Phonetics* 15, 47–65.

Flege, J. (1995) Second-language speech learning: Theory, findings, and problems. In: W. Strange (ed.) *Speech Perception and Linguistic Experience: Issues in Cross-language Research*. Timonium, MD: York Press.

Flege, J. (2003a) Assessing constraints on second-language segmental production and perception. In A. Meyer and N. Schiller (eds) *Phonetics and Phonology in Language Comprehension and Production: Differences and Similarities*. Berlin: Mouton de Gruyter.

Flege, J. (2003b) Methods for assessing the perception of vowels in a second language. In E. Fava and A. Mioni (eds) *Issues in Clinical Linguistics*. Padova: UniPress.

Flege, J. and Hillenbrand, J. (1984) Limits on phonetic accuracy in foreign language speech production. *Journal of the Acoustical Society of America* 76, 708–721.

Flege, J., Yeni-Komshian, G. and Liu, S. (1999) Age constraints on second language acquisition. *Journal of Memory and Language* 41, 78–104.

Fodor, J. (1983) *The Modularity of Mind: An Essay on Faculty Psychology*. Cambridge, MA: MIT Press.

Fodor, J. (1998) The trouble with psychological Darwinism. *London Review of Books* 20, 11–13.

Foraker, S. and McElree, B. (2007) The role of prominence in pronoun resolution: Active versus passive representations. *Journal of Memory and Language* 56, 357–383.

Forster, K.I. and Forster, J.C. (2003) DMDX: A Windows display program with millisecond accuracy. *Behavior Research Methods, Instruments, & Computers* 35, 116–124.

Foulkes, P., Docherty, G. and Jones, M.J. (2010) *Analysing Stops*. In M. de Paolo and M. Yaeger-Dror (eds) *Sociophonetics: A Student's Guide*. London: Routledge.

French, L. and O'Brien, I. (2008) Phonological memory and children's second language grammar learning. *Applied Psycholinguistics* 29, 463–487.

Friedmann, N. and Novogrodsky, R. (2004) The acquisition of relative clause comprehension in Hebrew: A study of SLI and normal development. *Journal of Child Language* 31, 661–681.

Frith, C. and Frith, U. (2006) The neural basis of mentalizing. *Neuron* 50, 531–534.

Fromkin, V., Rodman, R. and Hyams, N.M. (2013) *An Introduction to Language* (10th edn). Boston, MA: Thomson Wadsworth.

Gagarina, N. and Gülzow, I. (2008) *The Acquisition of Verbs and their Grammar: The Effect of Particular Language*. Berlin: Springer.

Gardner, B. and Gardner, R.A. (1985) Signs of intelligence in cross-fostered chimpanzees. *Philosophical Transactions of the Royal Society of London Series B – Biological Sciences* 308, 159–176.

Gardner, D. (2007) Validating the construct of word in applied corpus-based vocabulary research: A critical survey. *Applied Linguistics* 28 (2), 241–265.

Gardner, R.A. and Gardner, B. (1984) A vocabulary test for chimpanzees (*pan-troglodytes*). *Journal of Comparative Psychology* 98, 381–404.

Gardner, R.C. (2007) Motivation and second language acquisition. *Porta Linguarum* 8, 9–20.

Gathercole, S. and Adams, A. (1994) Children's phonological working memory: Contributions of long-term knowledge and rehearsal. *Journal of Memory and Language* 33, 672–688.

Gathercole, S. and Baddeley, A. (1989) Evaluation of the role of phonological STM in the development of vocabulary in children: A longitudinal study. *Journal of Memory and Language* 28, 200–213.

Gathercole, S., Pickering, S., Hall, M. and Peaker, S.M. (2001) Dissociable lexical and phonological influences on serial recognition and serial recall. *Quarterly Journal of Experimental Psychology* 54 (A), 1–30.

Gazzaniga, M., Ivry, R. and Mangun, G. (2008) *Cognitive Neuroscience: The Biology of the Mind* (3rd edn). New York: Norton.

Giannakidou, A. (1998) *Polarity Sensitivity as (Non)-veridical Dependency*. Amsterdam and Philadelphia, PA: John Benjamins.

Gil, K.-H. and Marsden, H. (2010) Semantics before syntax: L2 knowledge of *anyone* by Korean speaking learners. In M. Iverson, T. Judy, I. Ivanov, J. Rothman, R. Slabakova and M. Tyzna (eds) *Proceedings of the Mind-Context Divide Workshop*. Somerville, MA: Cascadilla Press.

Gil, K.-H., Marsden, H. and Tsoulas, G. (in preparation) On some arguments against the poverty-of-the-stimulus argument. Manuscript, University of Sheffield and University of York.

Gilabert, R. and Muñoz, C. (2010) Differences in attainment and performance in a foreign language: The role of working memory capacity. *International Journal of English Studies* 10 (1). See http://revistas.um.es/ijes/article/view/113961 (accessed 30 May 2013).

Glazko, G., Veeramachaneni, V., Nei, M. and Makayowski, W. (2005) Eighty percent of proteins are different between humans and chimpanzees. *Gene* 346, 215–219.

Goad, H., White, L. and Steele, J. (2003) Missing inflection in L2 acquisition: Defective syntax or L1 constrained prosodic representations? *Canadian Journal of Linguistics* 48, 243–263.

Goldberg, A. (1994) *Constructions*. Chicago, IL: University of Chicago Press.

Golestani, N. and Zatorre, R. (2009) Individual differences in the acquisition of a second language phonology. *Brain and Language* 109, 55–67.

Gollan, T., Salmon, D. and Paxton, J. (2006) Word association in early Alzheimer's disease. *Brain and Language* 99, 289–303.

Goren, C., Sarty, M. and Wu, P. (1975) Visual following and pattern discrimination of face-like stimuli by newborn infants. *Pediatrics* 56, 544–549.

Gould, S. and Eldredge, N. (1993) Punctuated equilibrium comes of age. *Nature* 366, 223–227.

Granena, G. and Long, M. (eds) (2013) *Sensitive Periods, Language Aptitude, and Ultimate L2 Attainment*. Amsterdam: John Benjamins.

Green, D. (2003) Neural basis of lexicon and grammar in L2 acquisition: The convergence hypothesis. In R. van Hout, A. Hulk, F. Kuiken and R. Towell (eds) *The Lexicon-Syntax Interface in Second Language Acquisition*. Amsterdam and Philadelphia, PA: John Benjamins.

Gregg, K. (1996) The logical and developmental problems of second language acquisition. In W. Ritchie and T. Bhatia (eds) *Handbook of Second Language Acquisition* (pp. 50–84). San Diego, CA: Academic Press.

Gualmini, A. (2005) *The Ups and Downs of Child Language: Experimental Studies on Children's Knowledge of Entailment Relationships and Polarity Phenomena*. New York and London: Routledge.

Guasti, M.T. (2002) *Language Acquisition: The Growth of Grammar*. Cambridge, MA: MIT Press.

Gürel, A. (2004) Selectivity in L2 induced L1 attrition. A psycholinguistic account. *Journal of Neurolinguistics* 17, 53–78.

Gürel, A. (2007) (Psycho)linguistic determinants of L1 attrition. In M. Schmid, B. Köpke, M. Keijzer and L. Weilemar (eds) *First Language Attrition: Interdisciplinary Perspectives on Methodological Issues*. Amsterdam: John Benjamins.

Halle, M. and Marantz, A. (1993) Distributed morphology and the pieces of inflection. In K. Hale and S. Keyser (eds) *The View from Building 20: Essays in Linguistics in Honor of Sylvain Bromberger*. Cambridge, MA: MIT Press.

Han, Z. and Finneran, R. (2014) Re-engaging the interface debate: Strong, weak, none, or all? *International Journal of Applied Linguistics* 24 (3), 370–389.

Harley, B. and Wang, W. (1997) The critical period hypothesis: Where are we now? In A. de Groot and J. Kroll (eds) *Tutorials in Bilingualism: Psycholinguistic Perspectives* (pp. 19–51). New York: Psychology Press.

Harrington, M. and Sawyer, M. (1992) L2 working memory and L2 reading skill. *Studies in Second Language Acquisition* 14 (1), 25–38.

Hartsuiker, R., Pickering, M. and Veltkamp, E. (2004) Is syntax shared or separate between languages? Cross-linguistic syntactic priming in Spanish-English bilinguals. *Psychological Science* 15, 409–414.

Haugen, E. (1966) Dialect, language, nation. *American Anthropologist* 68 (4), 922–935.

Hauser, M., Chomsky, N. and Fitch, W. (2002) The faculty of language: What is it, who has it, and how did it evolve? *Science* 298, 1569–1579.

Hawkins, R. (2001) *Second Language Syntax. A Generative Introduction*. Oxford: Blackwell.

Hawkins, R. (2003) 'Representational deficit' theories of adult SLA: Evidence, counter-evidence and implications. Plenary paper presented at the *23rd Annual Conference of the European Second Language Association*, Edinburgh.

Hawkins, R. (ed.) (2008) Current emergentist and nativist perspectives on second language acquisition. *Lingua* 118 (Special Issue 4), 445–642.

Hawkins, R. and Chan, Y.-H.C. (1997) The partial availability of Universal Grammar in second language acquisition: The 'Failed Functional Features Hypothesis'. *Second Language Research* 13, 187–226.

Hawkins, R. and Liszka, S. (2003) Locating the source of defective past tense marking in advanced L2 English speakers. In A. van Hout, A. Hulk, F. Kuiken and R. Towell (eds) *The Lexicon-Syntax Interface in Second Language Acquisition*. Amsterdam: John Benjamins.

Hayhoe, M. and Ballard, D. (2005) Eye movements in natural behavior. *Trends in Cognitive Sciences* 9, 188–194.

Haznedar, B. (1997) L2 acquisition by a Turkish-speaking child: Evidence for L1 influence. In E. Hughes, M. Hughes and A. Greenhill (eds) *Proceedings of the 21st Annual Boston University Conference on Language Acquisition*. Somerville, MA: Cascadilla Press.

Haznedar, B. (2001) The acquisition of the IP system in child L2 English. *Studies in Second Language Acquisition* 23, 1–40.

Haznedar, B. and Schwartz, B.D. (1997) Are there optional infinitives in child L2 acquisition? In E. Hughes, M. Hughes and A. Greenhill (eds) *Proceedings of the 21st Annual Boston University Conference on Language Development*. Somerville, MA: Cascadilla Press.

Heine, B. and Kuteva, T. (2007) *The Genesis of Grammar*. Oxford: Oxford University Press.

Heine, B. and Narrog, H. (2010) Grammaticalization and linguistic analysis. In B. Heine and H. Narrog (eds) *The Oxford Handbook of Linguistic Analysis*. Oxford: Oxford University Press.

Herschensohn, J. (1999) *The Second Time Around: Minimalism and L2 Acquisition*. Amsterdam: John Benjamins.

Hewlett, N. and Beck, J. (2006) *An Introduction to the Science of Phonetics*. London: Lawrence Erlbaum.

Hino, Y. and Lupker, S. (2000) Effects of word frequency and spelling-to-sound regularity in naming with and without preceding lexical decision. *Journal of Experimental Psychology: Human Perception and Performance* 26 (1), 166–183.

Hirakawa, M. (1990) A study on the L2 acquisition of English reflexives. *Second Language Research* 6, 60–85.

Hirsh, K. and Tree, J. (2001) Word association norms for two cohorts of British adults. *Journal of Neurolinguistics* 14, 1–44.

Hopkins, W. and Cantelupo, C. (2003) Does variation in sample size explain individual differences in hand preferences of chimpanzees (*Pan troglodytes*)? An empirical study and reply to Palmer (2002). *American Journal of Physical Anthropology* 121, 378–381.

Hopp, H. and Schmid, M.S. (2013) Perceived foreign accent in first language attrition and second language acquisition: The impact of age of acquisition and bilingualism. *Applied Psycholinguistics* 34 (2), 361–394.

Hornstein, N. (2009) *A Theory of Syntax: Minimal Operations and Universal Grammar*. Cambridge: Cambridge University Press.

Hornstein, N., Nunes, J. and Grohmann, K. (2005) *Understanding Minimalism*. Cambridge: Cambridge University Press.

Hu, X., Ackermann, H., Martin, J., Erb, M., Winkler, S. and Reiterer, S. (2013) Language aptitude for pronunciation in advanced second language (L2) learners: Behavioural predictors and neural substrates. *Brain and Language* 127 (3), 366–376.

Hughes, J., Skaletsky, H., Pyntikova, T., *et al.* (2010) Chimpanzee and human Y chromosomes are remarkably divergent in structure and gene content. *Nature* 463, 536–539.

Hulstijn, J. (2005) Theoretical and empirical issues in the study of implicit and explicit second-language learning. *Studies in Second Language Acquisition* 27, 129–140.

Hurst, J., Baraitser, M., Auger, E., Graham, F. and Norell, S. (1990) An extended family with a dominantly inherited speech disorder. *Developmental Medicine and Child Neurology* 32, 352–355.

Hyams, N. (1992) The genesis of clausal structure. In J. Meisel (ed.) *The Acquisition of Verb Placement*. Dordrecht: Kluwer.

Hyams, N. (2007) Aspectual effects on interpretation in early grammar. *Language Acquisition* 14, 231–268.

Ingham, R. (1998) Tense without agreement in early clause structure. *Language Acquisition* 7, 51–81.

Ionin, T. and Montrul, S. (2010) The role of L1 transfer in the interpretation of articles with definite plurals in L2 English. *Language Learning* 60 (4), 877–925.

Ionin, T. and Wexler, K. (2002) Why is 'is' easier than '-s'?: Acquisition of tense/agreement morphology by child L2-English learners. *Second Language Research* 18, 95–136.

Isaacs, T. and Trofimovich, P. (2011) Phonological memory, attention control, and musical ability: Effects of individual differences on rater judgments of second language speech. *Applied Psycholinguistics* 32, 113–140.

Jackendoff, R. (1977) *X'-Syntax: A Study of Phrase Structure*. Cambridge, MA: Linguistic Inquiry Monographs.

Jackendoff, R. (2002) *Foundations of Language: Brain, Meaning, Grammar, Evolution*. Oxford: Oxford University Press.

Jerison, H. (1974) *Evolution of the Brain and Intelligence*. London: Academic Press.

Jesperson, O. (1933) *Essentials of Grammar*. London: Allen & Unwin.

Jessop, L., Suzuki, W. and Tomita, Y. (2007) Elicited imitation in second language acquisition research. *Canadian Modern Language Review* 64, 215–238.

Jiang, L. (2009) A referential/quantified asymmetry in the second language acquisition of English reflexives by Chinese-speaking learners. *Second Language Research* 25, 469–491.

Johansson, S. (2005) *Origins of Language: Constraints of Hypotheses*. Amsterdam: John Benjamins.

Johnson, J. and Newport, E. (1989) Critical period effects in second language learning: The influence of maturational state on the acquisition of English as a second language. In M. Johnson (ed.) *Brain Development and Cognition*. Oxford: Blackwell.

Johnson, K. (2008) *An Introduction to Foreign Language Learning and Teaching* (2nd edn). Harlow: Longman.

Johnson, V., de Villiers, J. and Seymour, H. (2005) Agreement without understanding? The case of third person singular /s/. *First Language* 25, 317–330.

Juffs, A. and Harrington, M. (2011) Aspects of working memory in L2 learning. *Language Teaching* 44, 137–166.

Kahoul, W. (2014) Arabic and Chinese learners' production, perception and processing of past tense and verbal agreement morphology in L2 English. PhD thesis, Newcastle University.

Kang, B.-M. (1988) Unbounded reflexives. *Linguistics and Philosophy* 11, 415–456.

Kanno, K. (1997) The acquisition of null and overt pronominals in Japanese by English speakers. *Second Language Research* 13 (3), 265–287.

Kanno, K. (1998) The stability of UG principles in second-language acquisition: Evidence from Japanese. *Linguistics* 36 (6), 1125–1146.

Katz, J. and Pesetsky, D. (2011) The identity thesis for language and music. See http://ling.auf.net/lingBuzz/000959 (accessed 5 June 2018).

Kempen, G. and Hoenkamp, E. (1987) An incremental procedural grammar for sentence formulation. *Cognitive Science* 11 (2), 201–258.

Kemper, S. and Sumner, A. (2001) The structure of verbal abilities in young and older adults. *Psychology and Aging* 16, 312–322.

Kennedy, S. and Trofimovich, P. (2008) Intelligibility, comprehensibility, and accentedness of L2 speech: The role of listener experience and semantic context. *Canadian Modern Language Review* 64 (3), 459–489.

Kent, G. and Rosanoff, A. (1910) A study of associations in insanity. *American Journal of Insanity* 67, 317–390.

Keßler, J.-U. (2006) *Englischerwerb im Anfangsunterricht diagnostizieren. Linguistische Profilanalysen am Übergang von der Primar- in die Sekundarstufe I*. Tübingen: Narr.

Keßler, J.-U. (2007) Assessing EFL-development online: A feasibility study of rapid profile. In F. Mansouri (ed.) *Second Language Acquisition Research. Theory-Construction and Testing* (pp. 119–143). Newcastle upon Tyne: Cambridge Scholars.

Keßler, J.-U. (2008) Communicative tasks and second language profiling: Linguistic and pedagogical implications. In J. Eckerth. and S. Siepmann (eds) *Research on Task-based Language Learning and Teaching. Theoretical, Methodological and Pedagogical Perspectives* (pp. 291–310). Frankfurt and New York: Peter Lang.

Keßler, J.-U. (2009) Englischdidaktik in 'Erklärungsnot': Implizites und explizites Wissen und die Rolle der Bewusstmachung im schulischen Englischerwerb. In R. Vogt (ed.) *Erklären: Gesprächsanalytische und fachdidaktische Perspektiven* (pp. 93–107). Tübingen: Stauffenburg.

Keßler, J.-U. and Liebner, M. (2011) Diagnosing L2 development: Rapid profile. In M. Pienemann and J.-U. Keßler (eds) *Studying Processability Theory. An Introductory Textbook* (pp. 133–147). Amsterdam: John Benjamins.

Keßler, J.-U. and Plesser, A. (2011) *Teaching Grammar*. Paderborn: Schöningh/UTB.

Keßler, J.-U., Liebner, M. and Mansouri, F. (2011) Teaching. In M. Pienemann and J.-U. Keßler (eds) *Studying Processability Theory. An Introductory Textbook* (pp. 148–155). Amsterdam: John Benjamins.

Kim, Y. and Hazan, V. (2010) Individual variability in the perceptual learning of L2 speech sounds and its cognitive correlates. In K. Dziubalska-Kołaczyk, M. Wrembel and M. Kul (eds) *New Sounds 2010: Proceedings of the 6th International Symposium on the Acquisition of Second Language Speech*. Frankfurt am Main: Peter Lang.

Kinsella, A. (2009) *Language Evolution and Syntactic Theory*. Cambridge: Cambridge University Press.

Kiss, G., Armstrong, C., Milroy, R. and Piper, J. (1973) An associative thesaurus of English and its computer analysis. In A. Aitken, R. Bailey and N. Hamilton-Smith (eds) *The Computer and Literary Studies*. Edinburgh: Edinburgh University Press.

Klima, E.S. and Bellugi, U. (1966) Syntactic regularities in the speech of children. In J. Lyons and R. Wales (eds) *Psycholinguistic Papers: The Proceedings of the 1966 Edinburgh Conference*. Edinburgh: Edinburgh University Press.

Kohler, K.J. (1977) *Einfuhrung in die Phonetik des Deutschen*. Berlin: Erich Schmidt Verlag.

Kormos, J. and Dénes, M. (2004) Exploring measures and perceptions of fluency in the speech of second language learners. *System* 32, 145–164.

Krashen, S. (1982) *Principles and Practice in Second Language Acquisition*. Upper Saddle River, NJ: Prentice Hall.

Krashen, S. (1985a) *Second Language Acquisition and Second Language Learning*. Oxford: Pergamon.

Krashen, S. (1985b) *The Input Hypothesis*. London: Longman.

Krashen, S. and Terrell, T.D. (1983) *The Natural Approach: Language Acquisition in the Classroom*. San Francisco, CA: Alemany Press.

Kuhl, P., Conboy, B., Coffey-Corina, S., Padden, D., Rivera-Gaxiola, M. and Nelson, T. (2008) Phonetic learning as a pathway to language: New data and native language magnet theory expanded (NLM-e). *Philosophical Transactions of the Royal Society B* 363, 979–1000.

Ladefoged, P. and Maddieson, I. (1996) *The Sounds of the World's Languages*. Oxford: Blackwell.

Lado, R. (1957) *Linguistics Across Cultures*. Ann Arbor, MI: University of Michigan Press.

Lardiere, D. (1998) Case and tense in the 'fossilized' steady state. *Second Language Research* 14, 1–26.

Lardiere, D. (2003) Second language knowledge of [+/− past] vs. [+/− finite]. In J. Liceras, H. Goodluck and H. Zobl (eds) *Proceedings of the 6th Generative Approaches to Second Language Acquisition Conference*. Somerville, MA: Cascadilla Press.

Lardiere, D. (2007) *Ultimate Attainment in Second Language Acquisition: A Case Study*. Mahwah, NJ: Lawrence Erlbaum.

Lardiere, D. (2008) Feature-assembly in second language acquisition. In J. Liceras, H. Zobl and H. Goodluck (eds) *The Role of Features in Second Language Acquisition*. Mahwah, NJ: Lawrence Erlbaum.

Larson-Hall, J. (2015) *A Guide to Doing Statistics in Second Language Research Using SPSS and R* (2nd edn). New York: Routledge.

Laurence, S. and Margolis, E. (2001) The poverty of the stimulus argument. *British Journal for the Philosophy of Science* 52, 217–276.

Lawson, E., Stuart-Smith, J., Scobbie, J., Yaeger-Dror, M. and Maclagan, M. (2010) *Analyzing liquids*. In M. de Paolo and M. Yaeger-Dror (eds) *Sociophonetics*. London: Routledge.

Leech, G. (1969) *A Linguistic Guide to English Poetry*. Harlow: Longman.

Lengeris, A. and Hazan, V. (2010) The effect of native vowel processing ability and frequency discrimination acuity on the phonetic training of English vowels for native speakers of Greek. *Journal of the Acoustical Society of America* 128 (6), 3757–3768.

Lenneberg, E. (1967) *Biological Foundations of Language*. New York: Wiley.

Lenzing, A. (2013) *The Development of the Grammatical System in Early Second Language Acquisition: The Multiple Constraints Hypothesis*. Amsterdam: John Benjamins.

Lenzing, A. (2015) Exploring regularities and dynamic systems in L2 development. *Language Learning, Special Issue* 65 (1), 89–122.

Lenzing, A. (2017) The production-comprehension interface in second language acquisition: An integrated encoding-decoding model. Habilitationsschrift (Post-doctoral thesis), Paderborn University.

Lenzing, A. and Roos, J. (2012) Die sprachliche Entwicklung und die Ausdrucksmöglichkeiten von Grundschülerinnen und Grundschülern im Englischunterricht. In M. Bär, A. Bonnet, H. Decke-Cornill, A. Grünewald and A. Hu (eds) *Globalisierung – Migration – Fremdsprachenunterricht. Dokumentation zum 24. Kongress für Fremdsprachendidaktik der Deutschen Gesellschaft für Fremdsprachenforschung (DGFF) Hamburg* (pp. 207–220). Baltmannsweiler: Schneider Verlag Hohengehren.

Leslie, A. (1988) Some implications of pretence for mechanisms underlying the child's theory of mind. In J. Astington, P. Harris and D. Olson (eds) *Developing Theories of Mind*. Cambridge: Cambridge University Press.

Lev-Ari, S. and Peperkamp, S. (2013) Low inhibitory leads to non-native perception and production in bilinguals' native language. *Journal of Phonetics* 41, 320–331.

Lev-Ari, S. and Peperkamp, S. (2014) The influence of inhibitory skill on phonological representations in production and perception. *Journal of Phonetics* 47, 36–46.

Levelt, W. (1989) *Speaking: From Intention to Articulation*. Cambridge, MA: MIT Press.

Levelt, W., Roelofs, A. and Meyer, A.S. (1999) A theory of lexical access in speech production. *Behavioral and Brain Sciences* 22, 1–75.

Levinson, S. (1987) Pragmatics and the grammar of anaphora: A partial pragmatic reduction of binding and control phenomena. *Journal of Linguistics* 23, 379–434.

Lewis, M. (1993) *The Lexical Approach*. Hove: Language Teaching Publications.

Lidz, J., Waxman, S. and Freedman, J. (2003) What infants know about syntax but couldn't have learned: Experimental evidence for syntactic structure at 18 months. *Cognition* 89, B65–B73.

Lieberman, P. (1975) *On the Origins of Language*. New York: Macmillan.

Liebner, M. and Pienemann, M. (2011) Explaining learner variation. In M. Pienemann and J.-U. Keßler (eds) *Studying Processability Theory* (pp. 64–74). Amsterdam: John Benjamins.

Lightbown, P. (2000) Classroom SLA research and second language teaching. *Applied Linguistics* 21 (4), 431–462.

Lightbown, P. and Spada, N. (2006) *How Languages Are Learned* (8th edn). Oxford: Oxford University Press.

Linck, J. and Cunnings, I. (2015) The utility and application of mixed effects models in second language research. *Language Learning* 65 (S1), 185–207.

Liversedge, S.P. and Findlay, J.M. (2000) Saccadic eye movements and cognition. *Trends in Cognitive Sciences* 4, 6–14.

Long, M. (1988) Instructed interlanguage development. In L. Beebe (ed.) *Issues in Second Language Acquisition: Multiple Perspectives* (pp. 115–141). Cambridge: Newbury House.

Long, M. (1990) Maturational constraints on language development. *Studies in Second Language Acquisition* 12 (3), 251–285.

Long, M. (2005) (ed.) *Second Language Needs Analysis*. Cambridge: Cambridge University Press.

Love, T., Walenski, M. and Swinney, D. (2009) Slowed speech input has a differential impact on on-line and off-line processing in children's comprehension of pronouns. *Journal of Psycholinguistic Research* 38, 285–304.

Lust, B. (2006) *Child Language – Acquisition and Growth*. Cambridge: Cambridge University Press.

Lust, B., Flynn, S. and Foley, C. (1996) What children know about what they say: Elicited imitation as a research method for assessing children's syntax. In D. McDaniel, C. McKee and H. Smith Cairns (eds) *Methods for Assessing Children's Syntax*. Cambridge, MA: MIT Press.

MacDonald, M. and Christiansen, M. (2002) Reassessing working memory: Comment on Just and Carpenter (1992) and Waters and Caplan (1996). *Psychological Review* 109, 35–54.

MacKay, I., Meador, D. and Flege, J. (2001) The identification of English consonants by native speakers of Italian. *Phonetica* 58, 103–125.

MacLarnon, A. (2012) The anatomical and physiological basis of human speech production: Adaptations and exaptations. In M. Tallerman and K. Gibson (eds) *The Oxford Handbook of Language Evolution*. Oxford: Oxford University Press.

MacWhinney, B. (2000) *The CHILDES Project: Tools for Analyzing Talk* (3rd edition). Mahwah, NJ: Lawrence Erlbaum Associates.

Magen, H. (1998) The perception of foreign-accented speech. *Journal of Phonetics* 26, 381–400.

Major, R. (1992) Losing English as a first language. *The Modern Language Journal* 76, 190–208.

Mansouri, F. and Duffy, L. (2005) The pedagogic effectiveness of developmental readiness in ESL grammar instruction. *Australian Review of Applied Linguistics* 28 (1), 81–99.

Marcus, G. (1993) Negative evidence in language acquisition. *Cognition* 46, 53–85.

Marinis, T. (2003) Psycholinguistic techniques in second language acquisition research. *Second Language Research* 19, 144–161.

Marinis, T. (2010) On-line sentence processing methods in typical and atypical populations. In S. Unsworth and E. Blom (eds) *Experimental Methods in Language Acquisition Research*. Amsterdam: John Benjamins.

Marinis, T. (2013) Online psycholinguistic methods in second language acquisition. In C. Chapelle (ed.) *The Encyclopaedia of Applied Linguistics*. Oxford: Wiley-Blackwell.

Marinis, T. and Armon-Lotem, S. (2015) Sentence repetition. In S. Armon-Lotem, J. de Jong and N. Meir (eds) *Assessing Multilingual Children: Disentangling Bilingualism from Language Impairment*. Bristol: Multilingual Matters.

Marinis, T. and Saddy, D. (2013) Parsing the passive: Comparing children with specific language impairment to sequential bilingual children. *Language Acquisition* 20, 155–179.

Marinis, T., Roberts, L., Felser, C. and Clahsen, H. (2005) Gaps in second language sentence processing. *Studies in Second Language Acquisition* 27, 53–78.

Marsden, H. (2008) Pair-list readings in Korean-Japanese, Chinese-Japanese and English-Japanese interlanguage. *Second Language Research* 24, 189–226.

Marsden, H. (2009) Distributive quantifier scope in English-Japanese and Korean-Japanese interlanguage. *Language Acquisition* 16, 135–177.

Mayr, R., Price, S. and Mennen, I. (2012) First language attrition in the speech of Dutch-English bilinguals: The case of monozygotic twin sisters. *Bilingualism: Language and Cognition* 15 (4), 687–700.

McClelland, J. and Elman, J. (1986) The TRACE model of speech perception. *Cognitive Psychology* 18 (1), 1–86.

McClelland, J. and Rumelhart, D. (1981) An interactive activation model of context effects in letter perception: I. An account of basic findings. *Psychological Review* 88 (5), 375–407.

McDonald, J. (2000) Grammaticality judgments in a second language: Influences of age of acquisition and native language. *Applied Psycholinguistics* 21, 395–423.

McDonald, J. (2006) Beyond the critical period: Processing-based explanations for poor grammaticality judgment performance by late second language learners. *Journal of Memory and Language* 55, 381–401.

McDonald, J. and Roussel, C. (2010) Past tense grammaticality judgment and production in non-native and stressed native English speakers. *Bilingualism: Language and Cognition* 13, 429–448.

McDonough, K. (2006) Interaction and syntactic priming: English L2 speakers' production of dative constructions. *Studies in Second Language Acquisition* 28, 179–207.

McDonough, K. and Mackey, A. (2008) Syntactic priming and ESL question development. *Studies in Second Language Acquisition* 30, 31–47.

McMahon, A. and McMahon, R. (2012) *Evolutionary Linguistics.* Cambridge: Cambridge University Press.

McNeill, D. (1992) *Hand and Mind: What Gestures Reveal about Thought.* Chicago, IL: University of Chicago Press.

Meara, P. (1983) Word associations in a foreign language: A report on the Birkbeck Vocabulary Project. *Nottingham Linguistic Circular* 11 (2), 29–38.

Meara, P. (1996) The dimensions of lexical competence. In G. Brown, K. Malmkjaer and J. Williams (eds) *Performance and Competence in Second Language Acquisition.* Cambridge: Cambridge University Press.

Meara, P. (2009) *Connected Words.* Amsterdam: John Benjamins.

Meara, P. and Milton, J. (2003) *X Lex: The Swansea Levels Test.* Newbury: Express.

Meara, P.M. and Miralpeix, I. (2007) *D Tools (Version 2.0; Tools for Vocabulary Researchers· Lognostics)* [Computer software]. Swansea: University of Wales. See http://www.lognostics.co.uk/tools/index.htm (accessed 30 March 2012).

Mennen, I. (2004) Bi-directional interference in the intonation of Dutch speakers of Greek. *Journal of Phonetics* 32 (4), 543–563.

Meyer, D.E. and Schvaneveldt, R.W. (1971) Facilitation in recognizing pairs of words: Evidence of a dependence between retrieval operations. *Journal of Experimental Psychology* 90 (2), 227–234.

Mills, A. (1985) The acquisition of German. In D. Slobin (ed.) *The Cross-linguistic Study of Language Acquisition, Vol. 1: The Data.* London: Lawrence Erlbaum.

Milton, J. (2009) *Measuring Second Language Vocabulary Acquisition.* Bristol: Multilingual Matters.

Milton, J. and Fitzpatrick, T. (2013) Deconstructing vocabulary knowledge. In J. Milton and T. Fitzpatrick (eds) *Dimensions of Vocabulary Knowledge.* Basingstoke: Palgrave.

Miyake, A. and Friedman, N. (1998) Individual differences in second language proficiency: Working memory as language aptitude. In A. Healy and L. Bourne (eds) *Foreign Language Learning.* Mahwah, NJ: Lawrence Erlbaum.

Miyake, A. and Shah, P. (eds) (1999) *Models of Working Memory.* Cambridge: Cambridge University Press.

Mobaraki, M., Vainikka, A. and Young-Scholten, M. (2008) The status of subjects in early child L2 English. In B. Haznedar and E. Gavruseva (eds) *Current Trends in Child Second Language Acquisition.* Amsterdam: John Benjamins.

Monaghan, P. and Ellis, A.W. (2010) Modeling reading development: Cumulative, incremental learning in a computational model of word naming. *Journal of Memory and Language* 63, 506–525.

Monsell, S. (2003) Task switching. *Trends in Cognitive Sciences* 7 (3), 134–140.

Mora, J.C., Rochdi, Y. and Kivistö-de Souza, H. (2014) Mimicking accented speech as L2 phonological awareness. *Language Awareness* 23 (1–2), 57–75.

Morrison, C.M. and Ellis, A.W. (2000) Real age of acquisition effects in word naming and lexical decision. *British Journal of Psychology* 91 (2), 167–180.

Morrison, G.S. (2008) L1-Spanish speakers' acquisition of the English /iː/–/ɪ/ contrast: Duration-based perception is not the initial developmental stage. *Language and Speech* 51, 285–315.

Morrison, G.S. (2009) L1-Spanish speakers' acquisition of the English /iː/–/ɪ/ contrast II: Perception of vowel inherent spectral change. *Language and Speech* 52, 437–462.

Moss, H. and Older, L. (1996) *Birkbeck Word Association Norms.* Hove: Psychology Press.

Moya-Galé, G. and Mora, J.C. (2011) Non-native over-reliance on duration: An interference account of phonetic cue-weighting in vowel perception. Paper presented at the *21st Annual Conference of the European Second Language Association.*

Moyer, A. (1999) Ultimate attainment in L2 phonology: The critical factors of age, motivation, and instruction. *Studies in Second Language Acquisition* 21, 81–108.

Moyer, A. (2014a) What's age got to do with it? Accounting for individual factors in second language accent. *Studies in Second Language Learning and Teaching* 4 (3), 443–464.

Moyer, A. (2014b) Exceptional outcomes in L2 phonology: The critical factors of learner engagement and self-regulation. *Applied Linguistics* 35 (4), 418–440.

Muñoz, C. (2006) (ed.) *Age and the Rate of Foreign Language Learning*. Clevedon: Multilingual Matters.

Munro, M., Derwing, T. and Flege, J. (1999) Canadians in Alabama: A perceptual study of dialect acquisition in adults. *Journal of Phonetics* 27 (4), 385–403.

Munro, M., Derwing, T. and Morton, S. (2006) The mutual intelligibility of L2 speech. *Studies in Second Language Acquisition* 28, 111–131.

Murphy, V. (1997) The effect of modality on a grammaticality judgement task. *Second Language Research* 13 (1), 34–65.

Musolino, J., Crain, S. and Thornton, R. (2000) Navigating negative semantic space. *Linguistics* 38, 1–32.

Myles, F. (2004) From data to theory: The over-representation of linguistic knowledge in SLA. *Transactions of the Philological Society* 102 (2), 139–168.

Myles, F. (2005) The emergence of morpho-syntactic structure in French L2. In J.-M. Dewaele (ed.) *Focus on French as a Foreign Language: Multidisciplinary Approaches*. Clevedon: Multilingual Matters.

Narain, C., Scott, S., Wise, R., Rosen, S., Leff, A., Iversen, S. and Matthews, P. (2003) Defining a left-lateralized response specific to intelligible speech using fMRI. *Cerebral Cortex* 13, 1362–1368.

Nation, I.S.P. (1990) *Teaching and Learning Vocabulary*. Boston, MA: Heinle & Heinle.

Nation, I.S.P. (2001) *Learning Vocabulary in Another Language*. Cambridge: Cambridge University Press.

Nelson, D., McEvoy, C. and Schreiber, T.A. (1998) *The University of South Florida Word Association, Rhyme, and Word Fragment Norms*. See http://w3.usf.edu/FreeAssociation/ (accessed 5 June 2018).

Nissen, H. and Henriksen, B. (2006) Word class influence on word association test results. *International Journal of Applied Linguistics* 16 (3), 389–408.

Norris, J. and Ortega, L. (2000) Effectiveness of L2 instruction. *Language Learning* 50 (3), 417–528.

O'Brien, I., Segalowitz, N., Freed, B. and Collentine, J. (2007) Phonological memory predicts second language oral fluency gains in adults. *Studies in Second Language Acquisition* 29, 577–582.

Odlin, T. (1989) *Language Transfer: Cross-linguistic Influence in Language Learning*. Cambridge: Cambridge University Press.

O'Grady, W. (2005) *Syntactic Carpentry: An Emergentist Approach to Syntax*. Mahwah, NJ: Lawrence Erlbaum.

O'Grady, W. (2006) The problem of verbal inflection in second language acquisition. Invited talk to the *Pan-Pacific Association of Applied Linguistics*.

O'Grady, W. (2008a) The emergentist program. *Lingua* 118 (4), 447–464.

O'Grady, W. (2008b) Innateness, universal grammar, and emergentism. *Lingua* 118 (4), 620–631.

O'Grady, W. (2013a) Reflexive pronouns in second language acquisition. *Second Language* 12, 5–18.

O'Grady, W. (2013b) The illusion of language acquisition. *Linguistic Approaches to Bilingualism* 3, 253–285.

O'Grady, W. (2015a) Anaphor and the case for emergentism. In B. MacWhinney and W. O'Grady (eds) *Handbook of Language Emergence* (pp. 100–122). Boston, MA: Wiley.

O'Grady, W. (2015b) Processing determinism. *Language Learning* 65, 6–32.

Ouhalla, J. (1991) *Functional Categories and Parametric Variation*. Hove: Psychology Press.

Oyama, S. (1976) A sensitive period for the acquisition of a non-native phonological system. *Journal of Psycholinguistic Research* 5, 261–285.

Paivio, A., Clark, J.M. and Lambert, W.E. (1988) Bilingual dual-coding theory and semantic repetition effects on recall. *Journal of Experimental Psychology: Learning, Memory, and Cognition* 14 (1), 163–172.

Palermo, D. and Jenkins, J. (1964) *Word Association Norms: Grade School through College*. Minneapolis, MN: University of Minnesota Press.

Palmer, H.E. (1921) *The Principles of Language Study*. London: Harrap.

Papadopoulou, D., Varlokosta, S., Spyropoulos, V., Kaili, H., Prokou, S. and Revithiadou, A. (2011) Case morphology and word order in L2 Turkish: Evidence from Greek learners. *Second Language Research* 25, 173–204.

Papagno, C. and Vallar, G. (1995) Verbal short-term memory and vocabulary learning in polyglots. *Quarterly Journal of Experimental Psychology* 38 (A), 98 107.

Papagno, C., Valentine, T. and Baddeley, A. (1991) Phonological short-term memory and foreign language vocabulary learning. *Journal of Memory and Language* 30, 331–347.

Paradis, J. and Crago, M. (2000) Tense and temporality: A comparison between children learning a second language and children with SLI. *Journal of Speech, Language, and Hearing Research* 43, 834–848.

Paradis, M. (1997) The cognitive neuropsychology of bilingualism. In A. de Groot and J. Kroll (eds) *Tutorials in Bilingualism: Psycholinguistic Perspectives*. Mahwah, NJ: Lawrence Erlbaum.

Paradis, M. (2004) *A Neurolinguistic Theory of Bilingualism*. Amsterdam and Philadelphia, PA: John Benjamins.

Paradis, M. (2009) *Declarative and Procedural Determinants of Second Languages*. Amsterdam: John Benjamins.

Passingham, R. (2008) *What is Special about the Human Brain?* Oxford: Oxford University Press.

Patel, A. (2008) *Music, Language and the Brain*. Oxford and New York: Oxford University Press.

Pawley, A. and Syder, F. (1983) Two puzzles for linguistic theory: Nativelike selection and nativelike fluency. In J. Richards and R. Schmidt (eds) *Language and Communication* (pp. 191–225). London: Longman.

Penfield, W. and Roberts, L. (1959) *Speech and Brain Mechanisms*. Princeton, NJ: Princeton University Press.

Perovic, A., Modyanova, N. and Wexler, K. (2013) Comprehension of reflexive and personal pronouns in children with autism: A syntactic or pragmatic deficit? *Applied Psycholinguistics* 34, 813–835.

Petrides, M., Cadoret, G. and Mackey, S. (2005) Orofacial somatomotor responses in the macaque monkey homologue of Broca's area. *Nature* 435, 1235–1238.

Pickering, M. and Ferreira, V. (2008) Structural priming: A critical review. *Psychological Bulletin* 134, 427–459.

Pienemann, M. (1984) Psychological constraints on the teachability of languages. *Studies in Second Language Acquisition* 6 (2), 186–214.

Pienemann, M. (1985) Learnability and syllabus construction. In K. Hyltenstam and M. Pienemann (eds) *Modelling and Assessing Second Language Acquisition* (pp. 23–75). Clevedon: Multilingual Matters.

Pienemann, M. (1989) Is language teachable? Psycholinguistic experiments and hypotheses. *Applied Linguistics* 10 (1), 52–79.

Pienemann, M. (1992) Assessing second language acquisition through rapid profile. Unpublished manuscript, Sydney.

Pienemann, M. (1998) *Language Processing and Second Language Development: Processability Theory.* Amsterdam: John Benjamins.

Pienemann, M. (2000) Psycholinguistic mechanisms in the development of English as a second language. In I. Plag and K. Schneider (eds) *Language Use, Language Acquisition and Language History* (pp. 99–118). Trier: WVT Wissenschaftlicher Verlag.

Pienemann, M. (2005) An introduction to processability theory. In M. Pienemann (ed.) *Cross-linguistic Aspects of Processability Theory* (pp. 1–60). Amsterdam: John Benjamins.

Pienemann, M. (2006) Spracherwerb in der Schule: Was in den Köpfen der Kinder vorgeht. In M. Pienemann, J.-U. Keßler and E. Roos (eds) *Englischerwerb in der Grundschule* (pp. 33–63). Paderborn: Schöningh/UTB.

Pienemann, M. (2011) Developmental schedules. In M. Pienemann and J.-U. Keßler (eds) *Studying Processability Theory* (pp. 3–11). Amsterdam: John Benjamins.

Pienemann, M. and Keßler, J.-U. (2012) Processability theory. In S. Gass and A. Mackey (eds) *Handbook of Second Language Acquisition* (pp. 228–247). New York: Routledge/Taylor Francis.

Pienemann, M. and Lenzing, A. (2015) Processability theory. In B. VanPatten and J. Williams (eds) *Theories in Second Language Acquisition: An Introduction* (2nd edn) (pp. 159–179). New York: Routledge.

Pienemann, M., Di Biase, B. and Kawaguchi, S. (2005) Extending processability theory. In M. Pienemann (ed.) *Cross-linguistic Aspects of Processability Theory* (pp. 199–251). Amsterdam: John Benjamins.

Pienemann, M., Keßler, J.-U. and Liebner, M. (2006) Englischerwerb in der Grundschule: Untersuchungsergebnisse im Überblick. In M. Pienemann, J.-U. Keßler and E. Roos (eds) *Englischerwerb in der Grundschule* (pp. 67–88). Paderborn: Schöningh/UTB.

Pinget, A.-F., Bosker, H.R., Quené, H. and De Jong, N.H. (2014) Native speakers' perceptions of fluency and accent in L2 speech. *Language Testing* 31 (3), 349–365.

Pinker, S. (1994) *The Language Instinct.* New York: W. Morrow.

Pinker, S. (1997) *How the Mind Works.* New York: Norton.

Pinker, S. (1999) *Words and Rules: The Ingredients of Language.* New York: HarperCollins.

Pinker, S. and Bloom, P. (1990) Natural language and natural selection. *Behavioral and Brain Sciences* 13, 707–726.

Pinker, S. and Jackendoff, R. (2005) The faculty of language: What's special about it? *Cognition* 95, 201–236.

Pinker, S. and Ullmann, M. (2002) The past and future of the past tense. *Trends in Cognitive Science* 6 (1), 456–463.

Piper, T.H. and Leicester, P.F. (1980) Word association behavior as an indicator of English language proficiency. Educational Resources Information Center (ERIC). See https://eric.ed.gov/?q=ED227651 (accessed 5 June 2018).

Piske, T. and Young-Scholten, M. (eds) (2009) *Input Matters in SLA.* Bristol: Multilingual Matters.

Piske, T., MacKay, I. and Flege, J. (2001) Factors affecting degree of foreign accent in an L2: A review. *Journal of Phonetics* 29, 191–215.

Playfoot, D. and Izura, C. (2013) Imageability, age of acquisition and frequency factors in acronym comprehension. *Quarterly Journal of Experimental Psychology* 66 (6), 1131–1145.

Pliatsikas, C. and Marinis, T. (2012) Processing of regular and irregular past tense morphology in highly proficient second language learners of English: A self-paced reading study. *Applied Psycholinguistics* 34, 943–970.

Plonsky, L. (2015) *Advancing Quantitative Methods in Second Language Research.* New York: Routledge.

Poeppel, D. and Wexler, K. (1993) The full competence hypothesis of clause structure in early German. *Language* 69, 1–33.

Pollock, J.Y. (1989) Verb movement, Universal Grammar, and the structure of IP. *Linguistic Inquiry* 20 (3), 365–424.

Postman, L. and Keppel, G. (1970) *Norms of Word Association.* New York: Academic Press.

Povinelli, D. and Eddy, T. (1996) What young chimpanzees know about seeing. *Monographs of the Society for Research in Child Development* 61, 1–152.

Prévost, P. and White, L. (2000a) Missing surface inflection or impairment in second language acquisition. Evidence from tense and agreement. *Second Language Research* 16, 103–134.

Prévost, P. and White, L. (2000b) Finiteness and variability in SLA: More evidence for missing surface inflection. In A. Greenhill, H. Littlefield and C. Tano (eds) *Proceedings of the 23rd Boston University Conference on Language Development.* Somerville, MA: Cascadilla Press.

Prior, A. and MacWhinney, B. (2010) A bilingual advantage in task switching. *Bilingualism: Language and Cognition* 13 (2), 253–262.

Psychology Software Tools Inc. (2012) *E-Prime 2.0.* See http://www.pstnet.com (accessed 5 June 2018).

Pustejovsky, J., Bouillon, P., Isahara, H., Kanzaki, K. and Lee, C. (2013) *Advances in Generative Lexicon Theory.* Dordrecht: Springer.

Putnam, M. (2010) Exploring crash-proof grammars: An introduction. In M. Putnam (ed.) *Exploring Crash-Proof Grammars.* Amsterdam: John Benjamins.

Putnam, M. and Stroik, T. (2010) Syntactic relations in survive-minimalism. In M. Putnam (ed.) *Exploring Crash-Proof Grammars.* Amsterdam: John Benjamins.

Radford, A. (1988) Small children's small clauses. *Transactions of the Philological Society* 86, 1–43.

Radford, A. (1990) *Syntactic Theory and the Acquisition of English Syntax.* Oxford: Blackwell.

Radford, A. (1995) Children: Architects or brickies? In D. MacLaughlin and S. McEwen (eds) *Proceedings of the 19th Annual Boston University Conference on Language Development.* Somerville, MA: Cascadilla Press.

Radford, A. (1997) *Syntactic Theory and the Structure of English.* Cambridge: Cambridge University Press.

Radford, A. (2016) *Analysing English Sentences* (2nd edn). Cambridge: Cambridge University Press.

Ranta, L. and Lyster, R. (2017) Form-focused instruction. In P. Garrett and J.M. Cots (eds) *The Routledge Handbook of Language Awareness* (pp. 40–56). London: Routledge.

Rayner, K. (1998) Eye-movements in reading and information processing: 20 years of research. *Psychological Bulletin* 124, 372–422.

Reader, J. (2011) *Missing Links: In Search of Human Origins.* Oxford: Oxford University Press.

Reinhart, T. (1983) *Anaphora and Semantic Interpretation.* Chicago, IL: University of Chicago Press.

Reinhart, T. (2006) *Interface Strategies: Reference-set Computation.* Cambridge, MA: MIT Press.

Reiterer, S., Hu, X., Erb, M., Rota, G., Nardo, D., Grodd, W., Winkler, S. and Ackermann, H. (2011) Individual differences in audio-vocal speech imitation aptitude in late bilinguals: Functional neuro-imaging and brain morphology. *Frontiers in Psychology: Language Sciences* 2, 1–12.

Reuland, E. (2011) *Anaphora and Language Design.* Cambridge, MA: MIT Press.

Ridley, M. (2004) *Evolution* (3rd edn). Malden, MA: Blackwell.

Rizzi, L. (1993/1994) Some notes on linguistic theory and language development: The case of root infinitives. *Language Acquisition* 3, 371–393.

Rizzolatti, G., Fadiga, L., Gallese, V. and Fogassi, L. (1996) Premotor cortex and the recognition of motor actions. *Cognitive Brain Research* 3, 131–141.

Roberts, L. and Felser, C. (2011) Plausibility and recovery from garden paths in second language sentence processing. *Applied Psycholinguistics* 32, 299–331.

Robinson, P. (2002) (ed.) *Individual Differences and Instructed Language Learning.* Philadelphia, PA and Amsterdam: John Benjamins.

Rogers, R.D. and Monsell, S. (1995) Costs of a predictable switch between simple cognitive tasks. *Journal of Experimental Psychology: General* 124 (2), 207–231.

Rogers, V. (2009) Syntactic development in the second language acquisition of French by instructed English learners. PhD thesis, University of Newcastle upon Tyne.

Rogers, V. (2010) *Syntactic Development in the L2 Acquisition of French: The Case of Instructed English Learners.* Saarbruecken: VDM Verlag Dr Mueller.

Rohde, D. (2005) Linger: A flexible platform for language processing experiments. Cambridge, MA: MIT. See http://tedlab.mit.edu/~dr/Linger/ (accessed 5 June 2018).

Roos, J. (2007) *Spracherwerb und Sprachproduktion. Lernziele und Lernergebnisse im Englischunterricht der Grundschule.* Tübingen: Narr.

Rumbaugh, D., Gill, T., Glasersfeld, E., Warner, H. and Pisani, P. (1975) Conversations with a chimpanzee in a computer-controlled environment. *Biological Psychiatry* 10, 627–641.

Rumelhart, D. and McClelland, J. (1982) An interactive activation model of context effects in letter perception: II. The contextual enhancement effect and some tests and extensions of the model. *Psychological Review* 89 (1), 60–94.

Sabourin, L. and Stowe, L. (2008) Neurobiology of language learning. In B. Spolsky and F. Hult (eds) *The Handbook of Educational Linguistics.* Oxford: Blackwell.

Safronova, E. and Mora, J.C. (2013) Attention control in L2 phonological acquisition. In A. Llanes Baró, L. Astrid Ciro, L. Gallego Balsà and R.M. Mateus Serra (eds) *Applied Linguistics in the Age of Globalization.* Lleida: Edicions de la Universitat de Lleida.

Sagarra, N. and Herschensohn, J. (2010) The role of proficiency and working memory in gender and number agreement processing in L1 and L2 Spanish. *Lingua* 120, 2022–2039.

Sapir, E. (1921) *Language: An Introduction to the Study of Speech.* New York: Harcourt Brace.

Sato, M. and Felser, C. (2008) Sensitivity to morphosyntactic violations in English as a second language. Unpublished manuscript, University of Essex.

Savage, C., Lieven, E., Theakston, A. and Tomasello, M. (2003) Testing the abstractness of children's linguistic representations: Lexical and structural priming of syntactic constructions in young children. *Developmental Science* 6, 557–567.

Savage-Rumbaugh, E. and Lewin, R. (1994) *Kanzi: The Ape at the Brink of the Human Mind.* New York: Wiley.

Scaife, M. and Bruner, J. (1975) Capacity for joint visual attention in infants. *Nature* 253, 265–266.

Schmid, M. (2007) The role of L1 use for L1 attrition. In M. Schmid, B. Köpke, M. Keijzer and L. Weilemar (eds) *First Language Attrition: Interdisciplinary Perspectives on Methodological Issues.* Amsterdam: John Benjamins.

Schmitt, N. (2010) *Researching Vocabulary: A Vocabulary Research Manual.* Basingstoke: Palgrave MacMillan.

Schmitt, N. and McCarthy, M. (1997) *Vocabulary: Description, Acquisition and Pedagogy.* Cambridge: Cambridge University Press.

Schmitt, N. and Meara, P. (1997) Research vocabulary through a word knowledge framework: Word associations and verbal suffixes. *Studies in Second Language Acquisition* 19, 17–36.

Schwartz, B. (1993) On explicit and negative data effecting and affecting competence and linguistic behaviour. *Studies in Second Language Acquisition* 15, 147–163.

Schwartz, B. and Sprouse, R. (1994) Word order and nominative case in nonnative language acquisition: A longitudinal study of (L1 Turkish) German interlanguage. In

T. Hoekstra and B. Schwartz (eds) *Language Acquisition Studies in Generative Grammar: Papers in Honor of Kenneth Wexler from the 1991 GLOW Workshops.* Amsterdam: John Benjamins.

Schwartz, B. and Sprouse, R. (1996) L2 cognitive states and the full transfer/full access model. *Second Language Research* 12, 40–72.

Schwartz, B. and Sprouse, R. (2000) When syntactic theories evolve: Consequences for L2 acquisition research. In J. Archibald (ed.) *Second Language Acquisition and Linguistic Theory.* Oxford: Wiley-Blackwell.

Scott, S., Blank, C., Rosen, S. and Wise, R. (2000) Identification of a pathway for intelligible speech in the left temporal lobe. *Brain* 123, 2400–2406.

Scott, S., Rosen, S., Lang, H. and Wise, R. (2006) Neural correlates of intelligibility in speech investigated with noise vocoded speech – a positron emission tomography study. *Journal of the Acoustical Society of America* 120 (2), 1075–1083.

Seedhouse, P. (2005) 'Task' as research construct. *Language Learning* 58 (3), 533–570.

Segalowitz, N. (1997) Individual differences in second language acquisition. In A. de Groot and J. Kroll (eds) *Tutorials in Bilingualism.* Mahwah, NJ: Lawrence Erlbaum.

Segalowitz, N. (2003) Automaticity and second languages. In C. Doughty and M. Long (eds) *The Handbook of Second Language Acquisition* (pp. 256–310). Oxford: Blackwell.

Segalowitz, N. (2010) *Cognitive Basis of Second Language Fluency.* New York: Routledge.

Segalowitz, N. and Frenkiel-Fishman, S. (2005) Attention control and ability level in a complex cognitive skill: Attention-shifting and second language proficiency. *Memory and Cognition* 33, 644–653.

Service, E. and Kohonen, V. (1995) Is the relation between phonological memory and foreign-language learning accounted for by vocabulary acquisition? *Applied Psycholinguistics* 16, 155–172.

Seuren, P. (2004) *Chomsky's Minimalism.* Oxford: Oxford University Press.

Sharwood Smith, M. and Truscott, J. (2014) *The Multilingual Mind: A Modular Processing Perspective.* Cambridge: Cambridge University Press.

Shimpi, P., Gamez, P., Huttenlocher, J. and Vasilyeva, M. (2007) Syntactic priming in 3- and 4-year-old children: Evidence for abstract representations of transitive and dative forms. *Developmental Psychology* 43, 1334–1346.

Shockey, L. (1984) All in a flap: Long-term accommodation in phonology. *International Journal of the Sociology of Language* 1984 (46), 87–96.

Singleton, D. and Ryan, L. (2004) *Language Acquisition: The Age Factor.* Clevedon: Multilingual Matters.

Skehan, P. (1998) *A Cognitive Approach to Language Learning.* Oxford: Oxford University Press.

Skrzypek, A. (2009) Phonological short-term memory and L2 collocational development in adult learners. *EUROSLA Yearbook* 9 (1), 160–184.

Slabakova, R. (2000) L1 transfer revisited: The L2 acquisition of telicity marking in English by Spanish and Bulgarian native speakers. *Linguistics* 38, 739–770.

Slater, P. (2012) Bird song and language. In M. Tallerman and K. Gibson (eds) *The Oxford Handbook of Language Evolution.* Oxford: Oxford University Press.

Smith, E. and Kosslyn, S. (2007) *Cognitive Psychology: Mind and Brain.* New York: Prentice Hall.

Smith, K. (2012) Why formal models are useful for evolutionary linguists. In M. Tallerman and K. Gibson (eds) *The Oxford Handbook of Language Evolution.* Oxford: Oxford University Press.

Smith, N. and Tsimpli, I.-M. (1995) *The Mind of a Savant: Language Learning and Modularity.* Oxford: Blackwell.

Snowling, M., Chiat, S. and Hulme, S. (1991) Words, nonwords, and phonological processes: Some comments on Gathercole, Willis, Emslie and Baddeley. *Applied Psycholinguistics* 12, 369–373.

Söderman, T. (1993) Word associations of foreign language learners and native speakers: Different response types and their relevance to lexical development. In B. Hammarberg (ed.) *Problems, Process and Product in Language Learning*. Abo: AFinLA.

Song, H.-J. and Fisher, C. (2007) Discourse prominence effects on 2.5-year-old children's interpretation of pronouns. *Lingua* 117, 1959–1987.

Spada, N. and Lightbown, P. (1999) Instruction, L1 influence and developmental readiness in second language acquisition. *Modern Language Journal* 83, 1–22.

Sperber, D. and Origgi, G. (2004) A pragmatic perspective on the evolution of language and languages. See http://www.summer10.isc.uqam.ca/page/docs/readings/SPERBER_Dan/A%20pragmatic%20perspective%202009%5B1%5D.pdf (accessed 5 June 2018).

Squire, L. (1992) Declarative and non-declarative memory: Multiple brain systems supporting learning and memory. *Journal of Cognitive Neuroscience* 4, 232–243.

Stern, Y. (2012) Cognitive reserve in ageing and Alzheimer's disease. *The Lancet Neurology* 11 (11), 1006–1012.

Steyvers, M. and Tenenbaum, J. (2005) The large-scale structure of semantic networks: Statistical analyses and a model of semantic growth. *Cognitive Science* 29 (1), 41–78.

Stringer, C. (2011) *The Origin of our Species*. London: Allen Lane.

Stromswold, K. (2000) The cognitive neuroscience of language acquisition. In M. Gazzaniga (ed.) *The New Cognitive Neurosciences* (2nd edn). Cambridge, MA: MIT Press.

Számadó, S. and Szathmáry, E. (2012) Evolutionary biological foundations of the origin of language: The coevolution of language and brain. In M. Tallerman and K. Gibson (eds) *The Oxford Handbook of Language Evolution*. Oxford: Oxford University Press.

Tallerman, M. (2007) Did our ancestors speak a holistic protolanguage? *Lingua* 117, 579–604.

Tallerman, M. (2012a) What is syntax? In M. Tallerman and K. Gibson (eds) *The Oxford Handbook of Language Evolution*. Oxford: Oxford University Press.

Tallerman, M. (2012b) Protolanguage. In M. Tallerman and K. Gibson (eds) *The Oxford Handbook of Language Evolution*. Oxford: Oxford University Press.

Tallerman, M. (2014) *Understand Syntax* (4th edn). London: Routledge.

Tallerman, M. and Gibson, K.R. (eds) (2012) *The Oxford Handbook of Language Evolution*. Oxford: Oxford University Press.

Tallerman, M., Newmayer, F., Bickerton, D., Bouchard, D., Kaan, E. and Rizzi, L. (2009) What kinds of syntactic phenomena must biologists, neurobiologists, and computer scientists try to explain and replicate? In D. Bickerton and E. Szathmary (eds) *Biological Foundations and Origins of Syntax*. Cambridge, MA: MIT Press.

Tanenhaus, M. and Trueswell, J. (2006) Eye movements and spoken language comprehension. In M. Traxler and M. Gernsbacher (eds) *The Handbook of Psycholinguistics* (2nd edn). New York: Elsevier.

Temple, L. (1997) Memory and processing modes in language learner speech production. *Communication and Cognition* 30 (1–2), 75–90.

Terrace, H., Petitto, L., Sanders, R. and Bever, T. (1979) Can an ape create a sentence? *Science* 206, 891–902.

Terzi, A., Marinis, T., Kotsopoulou, A. and Francis, K. (2014) Grammatical abilities of Greek-speaking children with autism. *Language Acquisition* 21, 4–44.

Thomas, E. (2010) *Sociophonetics: An Introduction*. Basingstoke: Palgrave Macmillan.

Thomas, M. (1991) Universal Grammar and the interpretation of reflexives in a second language. *Language* 67, 211–339.

Thorn, A. and Gathercole, S. (1999) Language-specific knowledge and short-term memory in bilingual and non-bilingual children. *Quarterly Journal of Experimental Psychology: Section A* 52 (2), 303–324.

Thornton, R. and Wexler, K. (1999) *Principle B, VP Ellipsis, and Interpretation in Child Grammar*. Cambridge, MA: MIT Press.

Thothathiri, M. and Snedeker, J. (2008) Give and take: Syntactic priming during spoken language comprehension. *Cognition* 108, 51–68.

Tomasello, M. (2003) *Constructing a Language: A Usage-based Theory of Language Acquisition*. Cambridge, MA: Harvard University Press.

Tomasello, M. (2008) *Origins of Human Communication*. Cambridge, MA: MIT Press.

Tomasello, M. and Call, J. (1997) *Primate Cognition*. Oxford: Oxford University Press.

Towell, R. (2003) Introduction: Second language acquisition research in search of an interface. In R. van Hout, A. Hulk, F. Kuiken and R. Towell (eds) *The Lexicon-Syntax Interface in Second Language Acquisition*. Amsterdam: John Benjamins.

Towell, R. (2013) Learning mechanisms and automatization. In J. Herschenson and M. Young-Scholten (eds) *Cambridge Handbook of Second Language Acquisition*. Cambridge: Cambridge University Press.

Towell, R., Hawkins, R. and Bazergui, N. (1996) The development of fluency in advanced learners of French. *Applied Linguistics* 17 (1), 84–119.

Traxler, M. (2002) Plausibility and subcategorization preference in children's processing of temporarily ambiguous sentences: Evidence from self paced reading. *Quarterly Journal of Experimental Psychology: Human Experimental Psychology* 55, 75–96.

Truscott, J. (2015) *Consciousness and Second Language Learning*. Bristol: Multilingualism Matters.

Tsimpli, I. and Dimitrakopoulou, M. (2007) The interpretability hypothesis: Evidence from *wh*-interrogatives in second language acquisition. *Second Language Research* 23, 215–242.

Tsoulas, G. (2010) Computations and interfaces: Some notes on the relation between language and the music faculties. *Musica Scientiae* 14 (5), 11–41.

Ulbrich, C. and Ordin, M. (2014) Can L2-English influence L1-German? The case of post-vocalic /r/. *Journal of Phonetics* 45, 26–42.

Ullman, M. (2001) The neural basis of lexicon and grammar in first and second language: The declarative/procedural model. *Bilingualism: Language and Cognition* 4 (2), 105–122.

Ullman, M. (2005) A cognitive neuroscience perspective on second language acquisition: The declarative/procedural model. In C. Sanz (ed.) *Mind and Context in Adult Second Language Acquisition*. Washington, DC: Georgetown University Press.

Unsworth, S. (2005) *Child L2, Adult L2, Child L1: Differences and Similarities. A Study on the Acquisition of Direct Object Scrambling in Dutch*. Utrecht: LOT.

Unsworth, S. (2008) Comparing child L2 development with adult L2 development: How to measure L2 proficiency. In B. Haznedar and E. Gavruseva (eds) *Current Trends in Child Second Language Acquisition*. Amsterdam: John Benjamins.

Vainikka, A. (1993/1994) Case in the development of English syntax. *Language Acquisition* 3, 257–325.

Vainikka, A. and Young-Scholten, M. (1994) Direct access to X'-Theory: Evidence from Korean and Turkish adults learning German. In T. Hoekstra and B.D. Schwartz (eds) *Language Acquisition Studies in Generative Grammar*. Amsterdam: John Benjamins.

Vainikka, A. and Young-Scholten, M. (1998) Morphosyntactic triggers in adult SLA. In M.-L. Beck (ed.) *Morphology and its Interfaces*. Amsterdam: John Benjamins.

Vainikka, A. and Young-Scholten, M. (2005) The roots of syntax and how they grow: Organic grammar, the basic variety and processability theory. *Language Acquisition and Language Disorders* 39, 77–106.

Vainikka, A. and Young-Scholten, M. (2007) Minimalism vs. organic syntax. In S. Karimi, V. Samiian and W. Wilkins (eds) *Clausal and Phrasal Architecture: Syntactic Derivation and Interpretation. Papers in Honor of Joseph Emonds*. Amsterdam: John Benjamins.

Vainikka, A. and Young-Scholten, M. (2011) *The Acquisition of German. Introducing Organic Grammar*. Berlin: de Gruyter.

van de Craats, I. (2003) L1 features in the L2 output. In R. van Hout, A. Hulk, F. Kuiken and R. Towell (eds) *The Lexicon-Syntax Interface in Second Language Acquisition* (pp. 69–96). Amsterdam: John Benjamins.

van der Lely, H. (1996) Specifically language impaired and normally developing children: Verbal passive vs. adjectival passive sentence interpretation. *Lingua* 98, 243–272.

Vargha-Khadem, F., Watkins, K., Alcock, K., Fletcher, P. and Passingham, R. (1995) Praxic and nonverbal cognitive deficits in a large family with a genetically transmitted speech and language disorder. *Proceedings of the National Academy of Sciences of the USA* 92, 930–933.

Verhagen, J. (2013) From dummy auxiliary to auxiliary in Moroccan adult learners' production and comprehension of Dutch. In E. Blom, I. van de Craats and J. Verhagen (eds) *Dummy Auxiliaries in First and Second Language Development*. Berlin and New York: Mouton de Gruyter.

Vermeer, A. (2001) Breadth and depth of vocabulary in relation to L1/L2 acquisition and frequency of input. *Applied Psycholinguistics* 22, 217–234.

Wagner-Gough, J. (1978) Comparative studies in second language learning. In E. Hatch (ed.) *Second Language Acquisition: A Book of Readings*. Rowley, MA: Newbury House.

Wattendorf, E., Festman, J., Westermann, B., Keil, U. and Zappatore, D. (2014) Early bilingualism influences early and subsequently later acquired languages in cortical regions representing control functions. *International Journal of Bilingualism* 18, 48–66.

Wei, L. (2000) Dimensions of bilingualism. In L. Wei (ed.) *The Bilingualism Reader*. London and New York: Routledge.

Wells, J. (1982) *Accents of English, Vol. 1.* Cambridge: Cambridge University Press.

Wen, E., Mota, M. and McNeill, A. (eds) (2015) *Working Memory and SLA*. Bristol: Multilingual Matters.

Wexler, K. (1990) Innateness and maturation in linguistic development. *Developmental Psychobiology* 23 (3), 645–660.

Wexler, K. (1994) Finiteness and head movement in early child grammars. In D. Lightfoot and N. Hornstein (eds) *Verb Movement*. Cambridge: Cambridge University Press.

Wexler, K. (2004) Theory of phrasal development: Perfection in child grammar. In A. Csirmaz, A. Gualmini and A. Nevins (eds) *MIT Working Papers in Linguistics* 48.

Wexler, K., Schütze, C. and Rice, M. (1998) Subject case in children with SLI and unaffected controls: Evidence for the Agr/Tns omission model. *Language Acquisition* 7, 317–344.

White, L. (1989) *Universal Grammar and Second Language Acquisition*. Amsterdam: John Benjamins.

White, L. (2003) *Second Language Acquisition and Universal Grammar*. Cambridge: Cambridge University Press.

White, L. and Juffs, A. (1998) Constraints on *wh*-movement in two different contexts of nonnative language acquisition: Competence and processing. In S. Flynn, G. Martohardjono and W. O'Neil (eds) *The Generative Study of Second Language Acquisition*. Mahwah, NJ: Lawrence Erlbaum.

Whong, M. (2011) *Language Teaching: Linguistic Theory in Practice*. Edinburgh: Edinburgh University Press.

Whong, M., Gil, K.-H. and Marsden, H. (eds) (2013) *Universal Grammar and the Second Language Classroom*. Dordrecht: Springer.

Wilks, C. and Meara, P. (2002) Untangling word webs: Graph theory and the notion of density in second language word association networks. *Second Language Research* 18 (4), 303–324.

Williams, J. (1999) Memory, attention and inductive learning. *Studies in Second Language Acquisition* 21, 1–48.

Williams, J. (2005) Associationism and connectionism. In K. Brown (ed.) *Encyclopedia of Language and Linguistics*. Elsevier: Oxford.

Willis, D. and Willis, J. (2007) *Doing Task-based Teaching*. Oxford: Oxford University Press.

Wolter, B. (2013) Lexis: Overview. In C.A. Chapelle (ed.) *The Encyclopedia of Applied Linguistics*. London: Blackwell.

Wray, A. (1998) Protolanguage as a holistic system for social interaction. *Language and Communication* 18, 47–67.

Wray, A. (2002) *Formulaic Language and the Lexicon*. Cambridge: Cambridge University Press.

Wray, A. (2009) Future directions in formulaic language research. *Journal of Foreign Languages* 32 (6), 2–17.

Wright, C. (2010a) *Working Memory in SLA*. Saarbrucken: VDM Publishing.

Wright, C. (2010b) Variation, asymmetry and working memory in the process of second language acquisition. In K. Franich, K. Iserman and L. Keil (eds) *Proceedings of 34th Annual Boston University Conference on Language Development*. Somerville, MA: Cascadilla Press.

Wright, C. (2012) An investigation of working memory effects on oral grammatical accuracy and fluency in producing questions in English. *TESOL Quarterly* 47 (2), 352–374.

Wright, C. (2015) Working memory and L2 development. In E. Wen, M. Mota and A. McNeill (eds) *Working Memory and SLA*. Bristol: Multilingual Matters.

Wynn, T. (2012) The palaeolithic record. In M. Tallerman and K. Gibson (eds) *The Oxford Handbook of Language Evolution*. Oxford: Oxford University Press.

Yamada-Yamamoto, A. (1993) The acquisition of English syntax by a Japanese-speaking child: With special emphasis on the VO-sequence acquisition. In J. Clibbens and B. Pendleton (eds) *Proceedings of the Child Language Seminar*. Plymouth: University of Plymouth.

Yang, C. (2002) *Knowledge and Learning in Natural Language*. Oxford: Oxford University Press.

Yang, C. (2004) Universal Grammar, statistics or both? *Trends in Cognitive Sciences* 8, 451–456.

Ylinen, S., Uther, M., Latvala, A., Vepsalainen, S., Iverson, P., Akahane-Yamada, R. and Naatanen, R. (2010) Training the brain to weight speech cues differently: A study of Finnish second-language users of English. *Journal of Cognitive Neuroscience* 22 (6), 1319–1332.

Young-Scholten, M. and Ijuin, C. (2006) How can we best measure adult ESL student progress? *TESOL Adult Education Interest Section Newsletter* 4 (2).

Yu, L. and Odlin, T. (2015) *New Perspectives on Transfer in Second Language Learning*. Bristol: Multilingual Matters.

Yuan, F. and Ellis, R. (2003) The effects of pre-task planning and on-line planning on fluency, complexity and accuracy in L2 monologic oral production. *Applied Linguistics* 24 (1), 1–27.

Yusa, N., Koizumi, M., Kim, J., *et al.* (2011) Second-language instinct and instruction effects: Nature and nurture in second-language acquisition. *Journal of Cognitive Neuroscience* 23 (10), 2716–2730.

Zareva, A. (2007) Structure of the L2 mental lexicon: How does it compare to native speakers' lexical organization? *Second Language Research* 23, 123–153.

Zhou, X., Espy-Wilson, C., Boyce, S. and Tiede, M. (2007) An articulatory and acoustic study of 'retroflex' and 'bunched' American English rhotic sound based on MRI. In *Proceedings of INTERSPEECH 2007: 8th Annual Conference of the International Speech Communication Association*. Antwerp: ISCA.

Index

Note: *n* refers to note

Accentedness, 150, 153
Acoustic analysis, 163, 166, 169, 173–176, 179
Acoustic memory, 139, 140–144
Activation, Resting Levels of, 213
Adaptive Pressure, 75, 78, 81, 83, 86 (see also Darwinian)
Adjective, 23–26, 59, 93, 129
Adjective Phrase, 23
Adverb, 12, 23, 66, 68, 132
Algorithm, 17, 71
Allomorph, 106–109, 115
Alveolar, 168
Anaphora, 36–47, 49–50, 60–61, 188, 191
Antecedent (see Anaphora)
Approximant, 168–169, 180n4, 181n6
Arabic, 5, 93, 102–103, 105–106, 108–111, 113–116, 224
Argument Structure, 39, 225
Attention Control, 139–141, 144–146
Audio-lingual drilling, 206
Auditory processing, 142

Bark, 138
Binding, 16, 81
Brain size, 75–77
British Picture Vocabulary Scales/ Peabody Picture Vocabulary Test, 196

Call systems, 89
Cantonese, 49
Chimpanzees, 75–76, 79, 87–89
Clause, 24, 29–30
Clitic pronouns, 131
Coda, 163, 170
Code-mixing, 166, 178, 180
Cognitiveability, 139–141, 150, 158, 160

Competence, 4, 18, 23, 32–34, 97, 101, 109, 114, 137, 141, 146, 148, 193, 203, 209, 211, 215–218
Complementizer, 29, 96, 101
Compositional (also non-compositional), 79
Comprehensibility, 89
Comprehension Task, 1, 49, 194
Computational module, 82
Constituent, 18–21, 23–28, 30, 60, 94, 233, 235
Constituent Structure, 225, 227–228, 234, 239–240
Constraint, 4, 6, 35–37, 64, 66, 81, 87, 106, 109, 118, 164–165, 173, 176, 212, 214, 217, 237–240
Critical Period Hypothesis, 31, 65, 67, 70, 162, 164, 214

Darwinian (also neo-Darwinian), 73–74, 78, 81, 85
Declarative Knowledge, 206, 208, 210–211, 216–217
Determiner, Demonstrative Determiner, 21–22, 29, 59, 85, 93, 129–130, 227, 232
Development (also Developmental Path), 4–8, 14, 46–47, 53–56, 61, 64–65, 68, 71, 76, 79, 81, 85, 88, 90, 100, 103, 109, 114–16, 117, 120, 129, 131–132, 135, 137, 139, 140, 160, 161, 164, 173, 185–186, 203–204, 207–209, 213, 216, 218, 221–222, 230, 234–235, 239–240
Developmental problem, 220, 222
Diagnostic Task, 244, 247
Directional Entailingness (also Entailment), 62–63
Discrete Association Task, 123–124

Discrimination, 142, 146–149
Distractor/Foil (also Filler), 64, 193, 195
Distributed Morphology, 98
Domain Specific, Domain General, 55, 74, 86–87

Elicited Imitation, 103–104, 106, 187
Embedded Clause, 29, 56–57, 96, 101, 131, 212
Emergence Criterion, 245
Emergentism, 4, 7, 35, 210
Empiricism (Empiricist Theory), 55, 87
Entailment, 62–63
Entrenchment, 50
Episodic Buffer, 187, 207
Episodic Memory, 207
Episodic Sentences, 69
Epistemology, 53
E-Prime, 197, 199
Exaptation, 75
Existential Quantification, 62
Explicit Knowledge, 185–186, 207, 209, 214, 218
Eye-Tracking, 186, 194, 201

Faculty of Language (broad, narrow), 4–5, 54, 82–83
Failed Functional Features Hypothesis, 98–99
Feature Reassembly Hypothesis, 99
Feature Unification, 225, 227, 234, 237
Filler, 64, 108, 196, 200
First Language Acquisition, 44–47, 57–62
Fluency, 1, 6, 146, 150, 152–153, 155, 218
Focus On Form (FonF), 246, 248
Formal Features, 93
Formant, 143, 173, 181
Formant Frequencies, 169, 173–174, 181
Formulaic Chunks (also Formulaic Language, Formulaic Use), 79, 118, 209
FoxP2, 77
French, 6, 100, 129–130, 132, 165
Fricative, 145, 168–169
Full Transfer/Full Access Hypothesis, 97, 102, 105–106
Functional Category, 213–214
Functional Magnetic Resonance Imaging (fMRI) Scans, 67, 186

Functional Structure, 99, 225
Fundamental Difference Hypothesis (FDH), 65

Genes, 31, 76–77, 251
Genetic Variation, 74
Gestures, 17–18, 89–90
Grammaticality Judgments, 67, 70, 134–135, 193, 218
Grammaticalization, 80
Grooming, 78
Guiraud's Index, 130

Hominid: See Hominin
Homininm, 74 76, 78, 90
Identity Thesis, 54

I-Language, 17–18
Immersion Settings, 137–138
Implicational Hierarchy, 221, 230, 246
Implicit Knowledge, 197, 205–206, 209, 215, 217–218
Impressionistic Analysis, 169, 171–173, 179
Incremental Language generation, 231, 232–235
Individual Differences, 137–161
Inhibitory Control, 140
Intelligibility, 150
Intentionality, 88, 90
Inter-rater reliability, 152
Interlanguage, 94, 97, 100, 246–248
Interpretability Hypothesis, 99
Interpretation, 35, 39–43, 48, 60–61, 64, 104, 195, 213
Intransitive, 29
Inversion, 55, 66–68

Japanese, 47–48, 50, 67, 93–94, 99–100, 224

Kanzi, 79–80

L2 speech, 6, 139–140, 149, 156, 159–160
Language Acquisition Device (LAD), 32, 54
Language Assessments/Tests, 185
Language Processor, 230, 240
Larynx, 83
Last Common Ancestor, 75

Lateralization, 76
Learnability, 6, 86–87, 213, 223, 240
Learning Context, 137, 139, 151
Learning Strategies, 185
Lemma, 119, 120, 208, 232, 233
Lexical Decision Task, 122, 123
Lexical Density, 131
Lexical Mapping, Lexical Mapping
    Hypothesis, 234, 235
Lexical storage, 118
Lexical-Functional Grammar, 220, 222,
    224–228
Lexicon, 208, 213, 226, 229, 239
Likert Scale, 133, 150, 157
Linearization Problem, 223–224, 228,
    230, 234
Linger, 199
Logical Problem, 87, 222
Long-Term Memory (see also
    Declarative, Procedural)

Marked Structure, 171, 176
Maturational Constraints Perspective,
    164, 165, 166, 173, 176
Mean Length of Utterance (MLU), 130
Mental Representation, 139, 224, 237
Merge, 85, 164, 165
Minimal Pair, 138, 146, 147
Minimal Trees Hypothesis, 99
Minimalist Program (Minimalism), 84,
    85, 129
Modality, 186
Modularity, 33
MOGUL (Modular Online Growth and
    Use of Language), 213, 214
Morphology, Derivational, 13, 80, 120
Morphology, Inflectional, 13, 29, 80, 93,
    97, 120
Multiple Constraints Hypothesis,
    237, 238

Nativism (Nativist), 54, 55, 74, 78, 80, 82
Negative Inversion, 66, 67–68
Non-Finite, 22, 95, 98
Noun Phrase, 16, 19, 85, 212, 226, 228,
    232, 233

Offline/Online Task, 7, 200, 204, 217
Organic Grammar, 99, 100–102, 105,
    106, 113–115
Overgeneralization, 14, 241

Perception, 107–109, 137–161
Phone, 13, 21, 27
Phonetic categories, 148
Phonological categories, 142
Phonological Loop, 141, 207
Phonological Short-Term Memory,
    140, 141
Picture Selection Task, 194–197
Polarity Items, 66, 68
Polarity Sensitivity, 63
Post-Vocalic, 168
Poverty of the Stimulus (POS), 4,
    52–71
Preferential Looking Task, 61
Prefix (also Suffix), 12, 13
Pre-Nuclear Rising, 163
Preposition, 17, 23, 24, 28, 85, 93,
    95, 129
Prescriptive Grammar, 17
Prime, 52, 123, 191, 192, 193
Priming, 192, 193, 205
Procedural Knowledge, 206, 211,
    213, 217
Processing, 38–39, 109–113, 120–123,
    203–218
Processing Cost, 45
Processing Procedure, 221, 222, 224,
    231, 232, 236
Processing Speed, 154, 156, 208
Production Task, 105, 108, 130, 132,
    133, 186, 193, 194, 218
Pro-Form, 27
Propositional Knowledge, 52
Protolanguage, 73, 79–80, 90
Psycholinguistics, 3, 6, 7, 101–102,
    185–201, 210, 216

Quantifier/Quantifying Words (see
    Postdeterminer), 68

Rapid Profile, 244, 245, 246, 247
Reaction Times, 103, 104, 109–110, 113,
    197, 198, 199, 200
Recency Effect, 166
Recursive Syntax, 79, 83, 84
Register, 12, 17, 33
Relative Clause, 22, 55, 66, 67, 96, 130,
    188, 195, 210
Representational Deficit Hypothesis, 99
Retroflex, 168, 169, 175
Routine, 41, 45, 46, 47, 49, 50

Salience, 39, 43, 48, 210, 215
Saltation, 82, 83
Selective Pressure, 73
Self-Paced Listening Task, 194
Sentence-Level Processor, 40, 41, 43, 44,
46, 47, 48, 50
Shift Cost, 146, 148, 158, 159
Short-Term Memory, 87, 140–142,
157, 187
Spectral Cues, 147
Spillover Effects, 201
Spreading Activation, 121, 123
Structure Dependence, 56, 59, 66–68
Subjacency, 212, 217, 218
Subject-Auxiliary Inversion, 57–59, 66
Subordinating Conjunction, 29
Syntacticon, 129, 130, 131, 132, 135
Syntax, 3, 4, 6, 11, 13, 34, 35–51, 59,
79, 80, 83, 96, 98, 99, 117, 126,
129–136

Teachability Hypothesis, 2, 241–244
Temporal Cues, 147
Test of Reception of Grammar, 196
Theory of Mind, 88

Topic Hypothesis, 234, 235
Trill, 169
Truth-Value Judgement Tasks, 63

Uninterpretable Features (see also
Interpretability Hypothesis), 130
Universal Grammar (UG), 4, 11–38, 54,
77, 84, 95, 102, 115, 212
Unmarked Alignment, 235
Uvular, 168

Verb Phrase (VP), 23
Veridicality (Veridical, Non-Veridical),
68, 69
Voice Onset Time (VOT), 165
Voiced, 145, 168
Vowel Quality, 138, 145, 148

Weak Pronoun (see also Clitic), 132
Wh-Word, 14–15, 42, 69, 236
Working Memory (WM), 7, 35, 39, 40,
41, 44, 141, 203, 204

X' (X-Bar) Theory, 102